Comprehensive

Articulatory

Phonetics

Second Edition

ISBN-13: 978-1463683634
ISBN-10: 1463683634

To contact the authors or to obtain an alternative license, send inquiries to info@lrpcenter.org.

Table of Contents

Lesson 13:
Fronting, Retroflexion, and Sibilants...153

Lesson 14:
Back Vowels...163

Lesson 15:
Nasals..175

Preface

Phonetics is the study of sounds. Specifically, it is the study of human speech sounds. A person who only speaks one language may not realize that there are hundreds of different consonants and vowels spoken by humans in different parts of the world. This book will introduce the reader to almost every sound spoken by man.

This book is concerned with articulatory phonetics, meaning that the main purpose of this book is to teach the reader how to recognize, record, and reproduce the sounds of any language. Because this takes verbal instruction and correction, this book is intended to be used in a classroom setting. However, audio recordings are also included to assist readers in self-study.

Since the English alphabet is inadequate to represent every speech sound known to man, the reader will be taught the International Phonetic Alphabet (IPA).[1] This is a special alphabet containing numerous symbols that represent sounds for all languages. IPA symbols are easy to recognize because they are normally written inside of square brackets, such as [ɑ].[2] Charts are included in the back of this book that list many of the symbols used in the IPA. Some IPA symbols will look quite familiar, but others are from foreign languages or were invented specially for the IPA. Learning these symbols and their corresponding sounds is the foundation to accurately learning the sound system of a language.

The reader should also be aware of the fact that not all linguists follow the IPA conventions. Though this book generally follows the standard IPA, alternative symbols and notations will be explained throughout the text.

This book is intended for speakers of American English because many of the sounds are compared to the English language. Speakers of other dialects or languages may need to adjust their pronunciation accordingly.

Though this book is a completely original work, much has been gleaned from William Smalley's *Manual of Articulatory Phonetics*. This book continues in the tradition forged by pioneer linguists who determined to set forth a method for recognizing and recording the sounds of the world's languages.

N. M. Rugg
August 16, 2010

---

1 The International Phonetic Alphabet is standardized by an organization called the International Phonetic Association (also abbreviated IPA).

2 Occasionally, phonemic slashes are used, such as /ɑ/, when words are simplified to their phonemic form.

Acknowledgments

The authors of this book would like to thank all of those who have invested time and effort into this project. This book would not have been possible without them.

This book was produced with the following open source programs: Audacity, GIMP, FontForge, Inkscape, and LibreOffice/OpenOffice.org.

Lesson 1: Introduction to Sounds

Lesson Outline

Glossary Terms

Phonetics is the study of human speech sounds. Most sounds are made by a moving stream of air called the **air stream**. Without the movement of air somewhere in the speech apparatus, no sound is possible. Individual speech sounds are called **phones**. Separate phones are produced when, at some point in the vocal tract, the air stream is modified or obstructed. The study of this modification of the air stream is called **articulatory phonetics**.

In order to identify and classify the sounds that make up human speech, we must first determine the origin and direction of the air stream, the action of the vocal cords during that air movement, the change imposed upon the air stream, and the parts of the speech apparatus that produce that change.

We will begin this study by introducing egressive pulmonic air movement. The term **egressive** refers to outward movement, and **pulmonic** refers to the lungs. Therefore, egressive pulmonic air originates in the lungs and travels outward through the vocal tract. This is the most common type of air movement, and it is found in every language of the world.

The egressive pulmonic air stream, like all air streams, is initiated by complex muscle movements in the vocal tract. As the muscles expand and contract, the shape of the oral and pharyngeal cavities are altered. This in turn alters the quality of the air stream moving through that cavity.

The muscles and cavities used to produce sound are termed **air stream mechanisms**. There are three air stream mechanisms in the human speech apparatus: the lungs, the tongue, and the glottis.

The Speech Apparatus

The **speech apparatus** is made up of the cavities through which the air stream travels, the points of articulation where the air stream is obstructed, and the articulators which create the obstruction. The anatomical configuration of the speech apparatus is the same among all humans, thus making it possible for anyone, with proper training and practice, to produce the same speech sounds as anyone else.

Throughout this course, we will use illustrations, also called facial diagrams, to picture the various parts of the speech apparatus and to demonstrate possible articulations and air stream movements. These diagrams represent a cross section of the human head, showing only those anatomical features relevant to the articulation of speech sounds.

Cavities

To articulate phones, the air stream can travel through three **cavities** in the speech apparatus. These cavities, or chambers, are the **oral cavity** (mouth), the **nasal cavity** (nose), and the **pharyngeal cavity** (the throat just above the larynx), as pictured in Illustration 1.1 below.

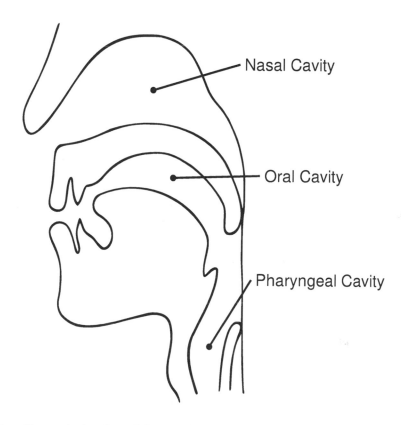

Nasal Cavity

Oral Cavity

Pharyngeal Cavity

Illustration 1.1: Cavities of the Speech Tract

As air passes through these cavities, their size and configuration may be altered, producing a resonance or vibration. If the resonance occurs in the oral cavity, the sound is said to be oral. Likewise, if the resonance occurs in the nasal cavity, it is described as a nasal sound.

Points of Articulation

As we have mentioned, there are certain places throughout the speech tract where the air stream is modified or obstructed during the articulation of a sound. This modification occurs when one part of the speech apparatus approaches another so closely that the air stream is either restricted, redirected, or stopped. If you examine certain portions of the mouth during the articulation of a sound, you will find that some portions are movable while others are relatively stationary. The hinges of the lower jaw, for example, allow the jaw and all of the features attached to it to move up and down freely. This allows the lower lip to move upward to contact the upper lip or teeth. The tongue can also be raised to touch the teeth or the roof of the mouth. The upper surfaces of the mouth, on the other hand, are much less movable. You should be able to feel this difference clearly if you repeat the sound [ɑtɑ] several times. The movable part of your mouth moves upward to contact a stationary portion of the speech tract. We call these stationary points where the air stream is obstructed along the upper part of the oral cavity **points of articulation**.

There are seven major points of articulation: labial, dental, alveolar, alveopalatal, palatal, velar, and uvular. As an infinite number of points exist between the first and last point of articulation, these may be better described as areas of articulation. Many phoneticians prefer to use the term "places" rather than "points," but throughout this manual we will refer to these stationary areas where the air stream is modified as points of articulation. Illustration 1.2 pictures the seven major points of articulation in noun form.

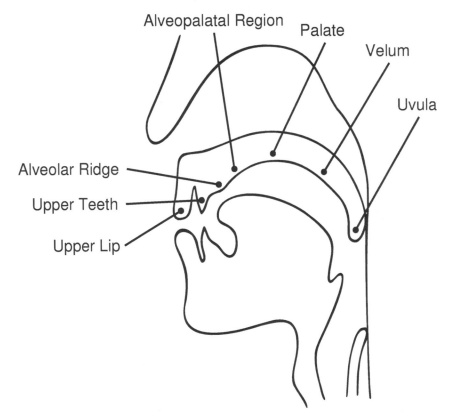

Illustration 1.2: Points of Articulation

Some of these points of articulation will be no trouble for you to learn as you are already familiar with their terminology. The **upper lip** is responsible for all bilabial sounds. Dental sounds are formed using the front **upper teeth**. The **alveolar ridge** is the gum immediately behind the upper teeth. You can feel it by pressing the tip of your tongue firmly against the roof of your mouth and the inside of your upper teeth. This area is the point of articulation used for the English "t." The **alveopalatal region** is the back side of this gum as it slopes upward to the top of the mouth (or the hard palate). It is used in English sounds like "sh." The **palate** is the relatively flat region that you can feel extending from the point where the ridge of gum stops to where the soft palate begins. English speakers do not usually use the palatal point of articulation. The **velum** is what we generally know as the soft palate. The English sound "k" uses this point. Fixed at the lower extremity of the velum is the uvula. The **uvula** is a small, fleshy descender that hangs free in the back of the mouth. There are no English sounds produced at the uvula.

Use the adjective form of the words denoting points of articulation when describing sounds. Thus, when classifying sounds by point of articulation, refer to the points as **Labial, Dental, Alveolar, Alveopalatal,**[1] **Palatal, Velar,** and **Uvular.**

It is important to memorize these points of articulation so that you will be able to use the terminology easily and accurately in describing the sounds involved in this course. The following exercises are formulated to help you gain complete control of the material we have introduced so far. Try to listen to the exercises and give the correct response without following the text. It may be helpful to repeat the utterance after the recording, trying to feel the point of articulation in your own mouth. The first few exercises in this lesson contain only English sounds so you will have no trouble recognizing them.

Listen to the sounds in the following exercise without looking at the text, and respond by telling whether they are labial or not. Do not worry if you do not recognize all of the symbols in the exercises below. At this point, you are only trying to learn the sounds. The symbols will be explained over time.

Exercise 1.1: Recognizing Labial Sounds

1.	[abɑ]	Labial	7.	[atʰɑ]	No	13.	[apʰɑ]	Labial
2.	[asɑ]	No	8.	[apʰɑ]	Labial	14.	[akɑ]	No
3.	[apʰɑ]	Labial	9.	[avɑ]	No	15.	[amɑ]	Labial
4.	[afɑ]	No	10.	[amɑ]	Labial	16.	[alɑ]	No
5.	[abɑ]	Labial	11.	[am]	Labial	17.	[afɑ]	No
6.	[az]	No	12.	[ta]	No	18.	[abɑ]	Labial

Tell whether the sounds in the following exercise are dental or not.

---

1 The alveopalatal region is also commonly referred to as postalveolar.

Exercise 1.2: Recognizing Dental Sounds

1.	[ɑvɑ]	Dental	7.	[ɑdɑ]	No	13.	[ɑθɑ]	Dental
2.	[ɑlɑ]	No	8.	[ðɑ]	Dental	14.	[ɑθɑ]	Dental
3.	[ɑmɑ]	No	9.	[ɑf]	Dental	15.	[ɑb]	No
4.	[ɑsɑ]	No	10.	[ɑfɑ]	Dental	16.	[ɑvɑ]	Dental
5.	[ɑkʰɑ]	No	11.	[ɑgɑ]	No	17.	[ɑkʰɑ]	No
6.	[ɑtɑ]	No	12.	[ɑðɑ]	Dental	18.	[vɑ]	Dental

Tell if the sounds you hear in the following exercise are velar or not.

Exercise 1.3: Recognizing Velar Sounds

1.	[ɑgɑ]	Velar	6.	[ɑŋɑ]	Velar	11.	[ɑsɑ]	No
2.	[ɑkʰɑ]	Velar	7.	[ɑkʰɑ]	Velar	12.	[ɑf]	No
3.	[mɑ]	No	8.	[ɑd]	No	13.	[ɑgɑ]	Velar
4.	[ɑnɑ]	No	9.	[kʰɑ]	Velar	14.	[ɑðɑ]	No
5.	[ɑŋɑ]	Velar	10.	[ɑlɑ]	No	15.	[ɑgɑ]	Velar

In the following exercise, tell whether the consonants are alveolar or not.

Exercise 1.4: Recognizing Alveolar Sounds

1.	[ɑtɑ]	Alveolar	6.	[ɑgɑ]	No	11.	[ɑdɑ]	Alveolar
2.	[ɑvɑ]	No	7.	[ɑbɑ]	No	12.	[lɑ]	Alveolar
3.	[ɑn]	Alveolar	8.	[ɑmɑ]	No	13.	[ɑdɑ]	Alveolar
4.	[ɑsɑ]	Alveolar	9.	[ɑð]	No	14.	[ɑzɑ]	Alveolar
5.	[ɑθ]	No	10.	[ɑkʰɑ]	No	15.	[ɑtɑ]	Alveolar

Listen to the following exercise, and respond by telling whether the consonants are alveopalatal or not.

Exercise 1.5: Recognizing Alveopalatal Sounds

1. [aʃa] Alveopalatal
2. [ana] No
3. [ʒa] Alveopalatal
4. [aʒa] Alveopalatal
5. [aʃa] Alveopalatal
6. [afa] No
7. [apa] No
8. [aza] No
9. [aʒ] Alveopalatal
10. [asa] No
11. [asa] No
12. [aʃa] Alveopalatal
13. [aʒa] Alveopalatal
14. [ala] No
15. [za] No

Tell whether the following sounds are labial or dental.

Exercise 1.6: Recognizing Labial and Dental Sounds

1. [ava] Dental
2. [af] Dental
3. [aða] Dental
4. [aθa] Dental
5. [aba] Labial
6. [ma] Labial
7. [ama] Labial
8. [apʰa] Labial
9. [ava] Dental
10. [afa] Dental
11. [ða] Dental
12. [aba] Labial

Tell whether the following sounds are alveolar or alveopalatal.

Exercise 1.7: Recognizing Alveolar and Alveopalatal Sounds

1. [aza] Alveolar
2. [aʒ] Alveopalatal
3. [asa] Alveolar
4. [ʃa] Alveopalatal
5. [ana] Alveolar
6. [aza] Alveolar
7. [aʒa] Alveopalatal
8. [at] Alveolar
9. [ʒa] Alveopalatal
10. [al] Alveolar
11. [aʃ] Alveopalatal
12. [ad] Alveolar

For the next drill we will combine all of the points of articulation that have been drilled so far. Repeat each sound to yourself to help you feel for the point of articulation before responding.

Exercise 1.8: Recognizing Labial, Dental, Alveolar, Alveopalatal, and Velar Sounds

1. [aba] Labial
2. [ata] Alveolar
3. [ʒa] Alveopalatal
4. [afa] Dental
5. [za] Alveolar
6. [ala] Alveolar

7.	[ɑlɑ]	Alveolar	12. [kʰɑ]	Velar	17. [ɑʃɑ]	Alveopalatal
8.	[ap]	Labial	13. [ɑʒɑ]	Alveopalatal	18. [ab]	Labial
9.	[ɑf]	Dental	14. [gɑ]	Velar	19. [ɑkʰɑ]	Velar
10.	[amɑ]	Labial	15. [ɑzɑ]	Alveolar	20. [ɑdɑ]	Alveolar
11.	[ɑθɑ]	Dental	16. [ɑðɑ]	Dental	21. [nɑ]	Alveolar

Articulators

We have already described points of articulation as the stationary parts along the upper part of the oral cavity. **Articulators** are the movable parts of the speech mechanism which are raised to meet the points of articulation. Many linguists refer to these instruments as active articulators (since they are the ones that actually perform the action) and to the points of articulation as passive articulators (since they perform no action at all). Illustration 1.3 pictures the seven major articulators.

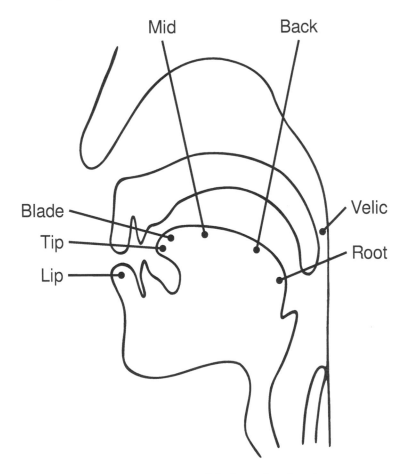

Illustration 1.3: Major Articulators

The lower **lip** is the articulator for labial, bilabial, and labiodental consonants. The adjective form we use for this articulator in sound descriptions is labial. The tongue is divided somewhat arbitrarily because there are no definite lines on it showing where one area ends and another begins. The general areas, however, are not difficult to learn.

The articulator that we refer to as **tip** is the very tip of the tongue. This is the articulator used at the beginning of the English word "tea." Repeat this word, and you should be able to feel the tongue tip touch the alveolar ridge for a brief moment. If you cannot easily feel this, it may be helpful to use a mirror to watch the action of the articulator.

The **blade** of the tongue is the area immediately behind the tip where the tongue begins to flatten out. This area can be felt by placing the tip of the tongue barely through the lips and gently closing your teeth. In this position the teeth should rest on the blade of the tongue. The "sh" sound in English uses the blade of the tongue.

The **mid** part of the tongue is the part that lies directly beneath the palate when the tongue is in a normal, relaxed position. The **back** of the tongue is the part directly below the velum, and the **root** of the tongue is down in the upper part of the throat. English speakers use the back of the tongue as the articulator at the beginning of the word "gap." You may also find it helpful to identify this articulator by watching inside your mouth with a mirror as you say the word "gap."

The velic does not fit precisely with the characteristics of the other articulators because it is not below a point of articulation. It is the flap that separates the oral and nasal cavities. It also contacts the back of the nasal passage when it is closed off. The **velic** may be thought of as the "gate" that opens and closes the passageway to the nasal cavity. This closure between the oral and nasal cavities is an important part of the articulation of many sounds.

The following exercises are based on the same concept as the previous ones, but they drill the articulators rather than the points of articulation. You may notice that some of the articulators have been left out of these exercises, but we will drill them later. Give the correct response for each exercise without following the text.

Respond by telling whether the articulator used in the following sounds is the lip or the back of the tongue.

Exercise 1.9: Recognizing Lip and Back

1.	[abɑ]	Lip	5.	[av]	Lip	9.	[akʰɑ]	Back
2.	[aŋɑ]	Back	6.	[gɑ]	Back	10.	[amɑ]	Lip
3.	[afɑ]	Lip	7.	[apʰɑ]	Lip	11.	[apɑ]	Lip
4.	[akʰɑ]	Back	8.	[gɑ]	Back	12.	[aŋ]	Back

For this next exercise we have combined all of the groupings that have been drilled so far. Practice this set until you can give the correct responses with no hesitation.

Exercise 1.15: Recognizing Bilabial, Labiodental, Tip-Dental, Tip-Alveolar, Tip-Alveopalatal, and Back-Velar Sounds

1. [apʰɑ] Bilabial
2. [af] Labiodental
3. [agɑ] Back-velar
4. [atʰɑ] Tip-alveolar
5. [ʒɑ] Tip-alveopalatal
6. [abɑ] Bilabial
7. [avɑ] Labiodental
8. [amɑ] Bilabial
9. [atʰ] Tip-alveolar
10. [aʃɑ] Tip-alveopalatal
11. [kʰɑ] Back-velar
12. [asɑ] Tip-alveolar
13. [aŋɑ] Back-velar
14. [lɑ] Tip-alveolar
15. [zɑ] Tip-alveolar
16. [aðɑ] Tip-dental
17. [aθɑ] Tip-dental
18. [ðɑ] Tip-dental
19. [agɑ] Back-velar
20. [ʃɑ] Tip-alveopalatal
21. [akʰɑ] Back-velar
22. [anɑ] Tip-alveolar
23. [af] Labiodental
24. [av] Labiodental

Manners of Articulation

So far we have studied the air stream and the basic members of the speech apparatus. Now we must take a look at *how* that air stream is obstructed. Based on the relationship between the articulators and points of articulation, there are several different ways in which the air stream might be modified. They might be pressed tightly against one another, resulting in absolute impedance of the air stream, or they may be positioned a slight distance from each other resulting in lesser degrees of impedance. The air stream modifications which result from this relationship are called **manners of articulation**.

Stops

The manner of articulation which imposes the greatest degree of impedance on the air stream is called **stops**. With stops, the articulator is pressed so firmly against the point of articulation that no air can pass between them. The velic is also closed so that the air stream comes to a complete stop and is then released. Illustrations 1.4–1.6 demonstrate the blocking of the air stream during the articulation of a stop. In normal speech, this blockage may occur so rapidly it is difficult to feel, but for a short period of time, the air stream is entirely stopped. Some common stops in English are P, T, K, B, D, and G. These sounds are represented phonetically in the IPA as the lowercase versions of these letters: [p], [t], [k], [b],

[d], and [g]. These stops are used in the words "pill," "till," "kill," "bill," "dill," and "gill." Many linguists prefer to use the term "plosive" to refer to this type of articulation. Because of inconsistency in the usage of the term, and to keep the terminology simple, we will use the term "stop" throughout this course.

Basic stops are not hard to identify. If you are unsure about a particular consonant, try prolonging the sound to see whether or not air is escaping during the articulation. For example, pronounce the word "Sue," prolonging the initial consonant so that you get "Sssssue." It is evident that no complete stop occurs here. Now say the word "too" prolonging the initial sound. Here we find that the air stream is not able to move at all during the "t." The next exercise should help you to be able to recognize stops quickly and easily. Respond without looking at the transcription.

Exercise 1.16: Recognizing Stops

1.	[akʰɑ]	Stop	5.	[afɑ]	No	9.	[agɑ]	Stop
2.	[zɑ]	No	6.	[tʰɑ]	Stop	10.	[abɑ]	Stop
3.	[av]	No	7.	[alɑ]	No	11.	[axɑ]	No
4.	[adɑ]	Stop	8.	[pʰɑ]	Stop	12.	[aŋɑ]	No

Fricatives

A **fricative** produces slightly less impedance than a stop. In fricatives, the articulator approaches near enough to the point of articulation to restrict the air flow, but not near enough to stop it. The air is forced through a narrow passageway between the articulator and the point of articulation. This creates audible friction, sometimes heard as a hissing or buzzing sound. Illustrations 1.7 and 1.8 depict fricative articulation.

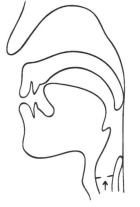

Illustration 1.7: [s]

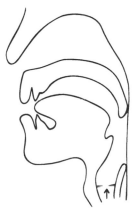

Illustration 1.8: [θ]

Think of using a garden hose and increasing the pressure of the water by covering the end with your finger. Like the water in the hose, the air stream is under higher pressure as the size of its outlet is reduced. The term "fricative" is derived from the friction produced by this restriction.

In the following exercise, listen to the utterances, and tell whether each consonant is a stop or fricative.

Exercise 1.17: Recognizing Stops and Fricatives

1.	[atɑ]	Stop	5.	[zɑ]	Fricative	9.	[aʒ]	Fricative
2.	[axɑ]	Fricative	6.	[aɣɑ]	Fricative	10.	[adɑ]	Stop
3.	[avɑ]	Fricative	7.	[aθɑ]	Fricative	11.	[bɑ]	Stop
4.	[akʰɑ]	Stop	8.	[ag]	Stop	12.	[ʃɑ]	Fricative

Not all consonants that have air escaping during their articulation are fricatives. Remember that for a fricative the velic must be closed, and there must be a definite restriction in the oral cavity that produces audible friction. If there is no definite friction produced as the air passes over the tongue or if the velic is open, the sound is not a fricative. In the next exercise there are sounds that do not fulfill the criteria for either a stop or a fricative. Respond as directed.

Exercise 1.18: Recognizing Sounds as Stops, Fricatives, or Neither

1.	[atɑ]	Stop	6.	[af]	Fricative	11.	[xɑ]	Fricative
2.	[ad]	Stop	7.	[amɑ]	Neither	12.	[pɑ]	Stop
3.	[lɑ]	Neither	8.	[zɑ]	Fricative	13.	[abɑ]	Stop
4.	[asɑ]	Fricative	9.	[anɑ]	Neither	14.	[an]	Neither
5.	[alɑ]	Neither	10.	[avɑ]	Fricative	15.	[amɑ]	Neither

Nasals

You may have noticed in the previous exercise that for some of the sounds, like [m] and [n], the point of articulation and the articulator create a complete blockage to the air stream, but air still escapes through the nasal cavity. We describe this manner of articulation as nasal. In a **nasal** consonant, the air stream must be completely stopped in the oral cavity and the velic must be open, allowing the air to be redirected through the nasal cavity. If you pronounce the utterances [aba] and [ama], you will notice that the articulator and point of articulation are exactly the same for the two consonants. The only difference between these two sounds is that for the [b] the velic is closed, whereas for the [m] it is open. The same is true for the pairs of sounds [d] and [n], and [g] and [ŋ]. Repeat these pairs to yourself several times to get a feel for the difference in the velic. Illustrations 1.9–1.11 below picture nasal articulation.

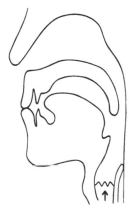 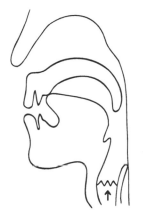 

Illustration 1.9: [m]   **Illustration 1.10: [n]**   **Illustration 1.11: [ŋ]**

To tell whether a consonant is a nasal or not, it may be helpful to prolong the sound and then pinch your nose with your fingers to shut off the air stream. If the consonant is a nasal, the sound will stop when you pinch your nose, since in a nasal the entire air stream is directed through the nasal cavity.

Exercise 1.19: Recognizing Sounds as Stops, Fricatives, or Nasals

1.	[apʰa]	Stop	7.	[axa]	Fricative	13.	[aba]	Stop
2.	[za]	Fricative	8.	[pʰa]	Stop	14.	[aŋ]	Nasal
3.	[da]	Stop	9.	[af]	Fricative	15.	[aða]	Fricative
4.	[aθa]	Fricative	10.	[ama]	Nasal	16.	[aŋa]	Nasal
5.	[av]	Fricative	11.	[ana]	Nasal	17.	[akʰa]	Stop
6.	[ata]	Stop	12.	[ma]	Nasal	18.	[an]	Nasal

Laterals

The lateral manner of articulation involves a lesser degree of impedance to the air stream than fricatives. A **lateral** is a consonant in which the air stream passes around the middle of the tongue as it meets the point of articulation. Lateral consonants usually have an "L-like" quality. If you examine your tongue position during the initial sound of the English word "leaf," you will discover that the tip of the tongue fully contacts the alveolar ridge but does not stop the air stream. It is important to note that the air stream is not restricted enough to produce friction.

Lateral consonants are produced by directing the air stream around one or both sides of the tongue instead of between the articulator and point of articulation. If you repeat the sound [ɑlɑ] and prolong the "l," you should be able to feel how freely the air moves past the sides of the tongue. Some complication may develop here as many speakers of English do not pronounce the "l" in the words "leaf" or "milk" with the tip of their tongue. If you are in the habit of pronouncing "l" without touching the tip of your tongue to the alveolar ridge, you must concentrate on doing so for the purpose of studying these sounds. The "l" sound that feels more natural to you will be studied later on in the course.

Laterals are not portrayed in facial diagrams because diagrams are incapable of portraying the sides of the tongue. In a facial diagram, an alveolar lateral would be indistinguishable from [d].

In the following exercise, try to differentiate between all of the manners of articulation that we have introduced so far. Practice this exercise until you can respond without hesitation. Remember that it may be helpful to repeat the sound to yourself before responding.

Exercise 1.20: Recognizing Sounds as Stops, Fricatives, Nasals, or Laterals

1.	[ɑlɑ]	Lateral	8.	[sɑ]	Fricative	15.	[ɑl]	Lateral
2.	[ɑŋɑ]	Nasal	9.	[ɑðɑ]	Fricative	16.	[ɑmɑ]	Nasal
3.	[ʃɑ]	Fricative	10.	[ɑʒɑ]	Fricative	17.	[bɑ]	Stop
4.	[ɑbɑ]	Stop	11.	[ɑd]	Stop	18.	[ɑŋɑ]	Nasal
5.	[ʒɑ]	Fricative	12.	[ɑʒ]	Fricative	19.	[ɑlɑ]	Lateral
6.	[ɑkʰ]	Stop	13.	[ɑtʰɑ]	Stop	20.	[ɑkʰɑ]	Stop
7.	[ɑxɑ]	Fricative	14.	[lɑ]	Lateral	21.	[zɑ]	Fricative

22. [ɑnɑ]	Nasal	25. [ɑdɑ]	Stop	28. [ɑvɑ]	Fricative
23. [ɑm]	Nasal	26. [ŋɑ]	Nasal	29. [ɑnɑ]	Nasal
24. [ɑnɑ]	Nasal	27. [pʰɑ]	Stop	30. [ɑθɑ]	Fricative

Now, we must learn to combine all of the terminology that has been introduced and use it in the proper order for as full a description of sounds as possible. This skill is foundational to the course and should be mastered with sounds that are familiar to you so that you will have a good point of reference as we begin to discuss sounds with which you are not familiar. The following exercises are formulated to help this terminology become second nature to you.

Exercise 1.21: Recognizing the Articulator and Point of Articulation: Bilabial, Labiodental, Tip-Dental, Tip-Alveolar, Tip-Alveopalatal, or Back-Velar

1. [ɑbɑ]	Bilabial	7. [ɑgɑ]	Back-velar	13. [ɑvɑ]	Labiodental
2. [ʒɑ]	Tip-alveopalatal	8. [ɑk]	Back-velar	14. [ɑvɑ]	Labiodental
3. [ɑgɑ]	Back-velar	9. [ɑfɑ]	Labiodental	15. [ɑŋɑ]	Back-velar
4. [ɑsɑ]	Tip-alveolar	10. [ɑʃɑ]	Tip-alveopalatal	16. [ɑðɑ]	Tip-dental
5. [ɑθ]	Tip-dental	11. [nɑ]	Tip-alveolar	17. [ðɑ]	Tip-dental
6. [lɑ]	Tip-alveolar	12. [ɑʃ]	Tip-alveopalatal	18. [ɑdɑ]	Tip-alveolar

In this exercise, we will combine all of the possibilities that have been introduced. Name the articulator first, the point of articulation next, and the manner of articulation last. You may find this challenging at first, but work at it until you can do it without following the text.

Exercise 1.22: Full Recognition

1. [ɑbɑ]	Bilabial Stop	6. [ɑb]	Bilabial Stop
2. [ɑkʰɑ]	Back-velar Stop	7. [vɑ]	Labiodental Fricative
3. [ɑzɑ]	Tip-Alveolar Fricative	8. [ɑʃɑ]	Tip-alveopalatal Fricative
4. [θɑ]	Tip-dental Fricative	9. [ðɑ]	Tip-dental Fricative
5. [ɑxɑ]	Back-velar Fricative	10. [lɑ]	Tip-alveolar Lateral

11. [ɑkɑ] Back-velar Stop

12. [ɑvɑ] Labiodental Fricative

13. [nɑ] Tip-alveolar Nasal

14. [ɑŋ] Back-velar Nasal

15. [ɑm] Bilabial Nasal

16. [ɑkɑ] Back-velar Stop

17. [ɑðɑ] Tip-dental Fricative

18. [ðɑ] Tip-dental Fricative

19. [ɑlɑ] Tip-alveolar Lateral

20. [ɑl] Tip-alveolar Lateral

21. [ɑdɑ] Tip-alveolar Stop

22. [ɑsɑ] Tip-alveolar Fricative

23. [ɑnɑ] Tip-alveolar Nasal

24. [ɑgɑ] Back-velar Stop

25. [ʒɑ] Tip-alveopalatal Fricative

26. [ʒɑ] Tip-alveopalatal Fricative

27. [ɑŋɑ] Back-velar Nasal

28. [mɑ] Bilabial Nasal

29. [pʰɑ] Bilabial Stop

30. [ɑzɑ] Tip-alveolar Fricative

31. [ɑg] Back-velar Stop

32. [fɑ] Labiodental Fricative

33. [ɑsɑ] Tip-alveolar Fricative

34. [ɑnɑ] Tip-alveolar Nasal

35. [mɑ] Bilabial Nasal

36. [gɑ] Back-velar Stop

37. [ɑn] Tip-alveolar Nasal

38. [ɑθɑ] Tip-dental Fricative

39. [ɑtɑ] Tip-alveolar Stop

40. [ɑʃɑ] Tip-alveopalatal Fricative

Lesson 2:
Fricatives and Voicing

Lesson Outline

Glossary Terms

In Lesson 1 we briefly studied the four manners of articulation. Before a deeper study can be made, there is one more element of speech that must be studied. **Voicing** is the vibration of the vocal chords that creates sound. The **vocal cords** are the mucous membranes that vibrate with the passing of the air stream. Some sounds require the vocal cords to vibrate. These are called voiced sounds. Other consonants involve only the impedance of the air stream and no voicing at all. Those are called voiceless. Every manner of articulation has both voiced and voiceless consonants. Notice in Table 2.1 that every point of articulation has both a voiced and a voiceless fricative. Voicing is the only difference between these vertical pairs.

As each speech sound is represented by a specific phonetic symbol, each sound can also be identified by its technical name (full description) which can describe only that specific sound. Table 2.1 contains the phonetic symbols and descriptions for the fricatives that will be focused on in this lesson. Some of these fricatives are very common in English, while others will require some practice to learn.

Table 2.1: Common Fricatives

	Bilabial	Labiodental	Tip-Dental	Tip-Alveolar	Tip-Alveopalatal	Back-Velar
Voiceless	ɸ	f	θ	s	ʃ	x
Voiced	β	v	ð	z	ʒ	ɣ

Voicing

As we study these fricatives, we will find that some sets of fricatives share the same articulator and point of articulation. For example, [s] and [z] are both tip-alveolar sounds while [f] and [v] are both labiodental. The only distinction between these sets of sounds is voicing. Voicing involves the action of the glottis, or vocal cords, during the articulation of a sound.

Understanding Voicing

Illustration 2.1 below pictures the position of the glottis in the throat. The **glottis**, often referred to as the Adam's Apple, is the organ responsible for voicing. Its location makes it necessary for air traveling outward from the lungs to pass through the vocal cords. The vocal cords are made up of thin layers of membrane which may be either drawn together or spread apart by the muscles of the **larynx**. As the air stream passes between the membrane folds, they either vibrate or remain still based on the measure of tension applied to them. For voiceless sounds, the vocal cords are relaxed and maintain their open position, allowing them to remain still as the air stream moves through unimpeded. During voiced sounds, however, the vocal cords tense and draw closer together. This creates a narrow opening through which the air is forced, making the vocal cords vibrate.

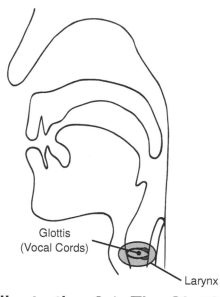

Illustration 2.1: The Glottis

Illustration 2.2 gives a view of the glottis from above, illustrating the position of the vocal cords during voiced and voiceless sounds.

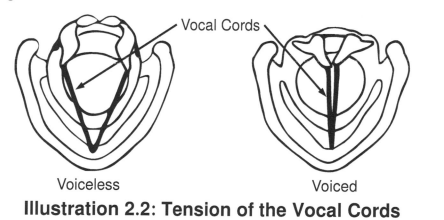

Illustration 2.2: Tension of the Vocal Cords

Recognizing Voicing

The action of the glottis during voicing can be felt by placing your fingertips on your larynx and prolonging the voiced fricative [z] as "zzzzzzzoo." It should be fairly easy to feel the vibration of the vocal cords during this sequence. If you have difficulty sensing the glottal activity with your fingers, try placing the palms of your hands over your ears while pronouncing the same prolonged [z]. The voicing will be perceived as a buzzing sensation inside your head. The following exercise demonstrates pairs of fricatives which contrast voicing and voicelessness. Notice that the articulator and point of articulation are the same for each pair of sounds. The only difference between them is voicing. A pair of sounds with only one phonetic difference is called a **minimal pair**.

Repeat the following sequences of fricatives after the recording while either feeling your larynx or covering your ears with your hands. Try to feel and hear the contrast between the voiced and voiceless sounds.

Exercise 2.1: Demonstrating Voicing

1. [ssssssssszzzzzzzz]

2. [sszzsszzsszzsszzsszzsszz]

3. [ffffffffvvvvvvvv]

4. [ffvvffvvffvvffvvffvv]

Practicing these sequences will help you learn to control your vocal cords. Repeat this exercise until you can switch between voicing and voicelessness easily with no transitional pauses.

Classifying Voicing

Every speech sound can be classified as either voiced or voiceless. Voicing must be included in the technical name (full description) for each sound and is given before the point of articulation. The voicing characteristics may be more difficult to distinguish on some consonants because of their short duration. Learn to distinguish quickly and easily between the voicing and voicelessness of the sounds in the following exercises so that you can apply your knowledge of voicing in more difficult lessons.

The following exercise involves only fricatives. Each fricative will be positioned between two vowels. As you listen for the voicing on the consonants, be careful not to let the voicing of the vowels confuse you. You may find it helpful to repeat the sounds to yourself while feeling your larynx with your fingertips during this exercise. Respond with voiced or voiceless during the pause after each utterance.

Exercise 2.2: Recognizing Voicing

1.	[asɑ]	Voiceless	3.	[afɑ]	Voiceless	5.	[aβɑ]	Voiced
2.	[azɑ]	Voiced	4.	[azɑ]	Voiced	6.	[aʃɑ]	Voiceless

7.	[ɑvɑ]	Voiced	13.	[ɑvɑ]	Voiced	19.	[ɑθɑ]	Voiceless
8.	[ɑfɑ]	Voiceless	14.	[ɑɣɑ]	Voiced	20.	[ɑɸɑ]	Voiceless
9.	[ɑɣɑ]	Voiced	15.	[ɑθɑ]	Voiceless	21.	[ɑðɑ]	Voiced
10.	[ɑzɑ]	Voiced	16.	[ɑfɑ]	Voiceless	22.	[ɑsɑ]	Voiceless
11.	[ɑsɑ]	Voiceless	17.	[ɑðɑ]	Voiced	23.	[ɑvɑ]	Voiced
12.	[ɑβɑ]	Voiced	18.	[ɑʃɑ]	Voiceless	24.	[ɑfɑ]	Voiceless

Voicing must always be included in facial diagrams. Voicelessness is represented by a broken line at the larynx, as demonstrated in Illustration 2.3. Voicing is shown by a wavy line, as shown in Illustration 2.4.

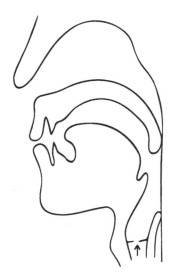

Illustration 2.3: Voicelessness

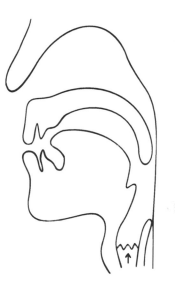

Illustration 2.4: Voicing

Introducing Fricatives

As explained in Lesson 1, manners of articulation deal with the relationship between an articulator and a point of articulation. One manner of articulation we described is fricatives. In a fricative sound, the articulator is held close enough to the point of articulation to restrict the air flow, but not enough to stop it entirely. This relationship produces the audible friction from which the term fricative is derived. Illustrations 2.5 and 2.6 below depict some fricative articulations. Notice that in each diagram, the articulator and point of articulation do not actually touch each other. A small space is left between them through which the air stream is forced.

Many of the fricatives introduced in this lesson are common in normal English speech. These fricatives will be introduced first, followed by those which do not occur in English.

Labiodental Fricatives: F [f] and V [v]

The symbols **F** [f] and **V** [v] represent the same sounds in phonetic transcription as they do in ordinary English. These fricatives are articulated between the lower lip and the upper teeth. The only phonetic difference between this pair of sounds is voicing. The voiceless fricative [f] is found at the beginning of the English word "face," while its voiced counterpart [v] occurs at the beginning of the word "vase."

Tip Alveolar Fricatives: S [s] and Z [z]

The tip-alveolar sounds **S** [s] and **Z** [z] also represent the same sounds phonetically as they represent in English. They are articulated by placing the tip of the tongue near the alveolar ridge. Again, the only phonetic difference between these sounds is voicing. The articulation of the voiceless fricative [s] is demonstrated at the beginning of the word "sap." The voiced fricative [z] occurs in the word "zap."

Tip Dental Fricatives: Theta [θ] and Eth [ð]

The articulation of both voiced and voiceless tip-dental fricatives is shown in Illustrations 2.5 and 2.6. These sounds are articulated by placing the tip of the tongue against the upper teeth. These tip dental fricatives can be described as **interdental** as the tongue actually protrudes slightly between both the upper and lower teeth, even though the involvement of the lower teeth does not affect their sound at all, since the air stream does not pass between the lower teeth and the tongue.

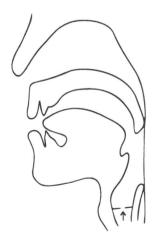
Illustration 2.5: Theta [θ]

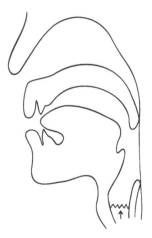
Illustration 2.6: Eth [ð]

The symbols for the tip-dental fricatives, **Theta** [θ] and **Eth** [ð], may be new to you, but the sounds which they represent are very common in English. Theta [θ] represents the voiceless "th" sound as in the English word "thin," and Eth [ð] represents the voiced "th" sound as in the word "then." The English words in the following exercise contain these fricatives in the initial position. Pay close attention to the voicing as you repeat the sounds after the recording. Practice the switch between voicing and voicelessness in utterances 6.a and 6.b until the difference is easily produced and distinguished.

Exercise 2.3: Producing [θ] and [ð]

1. a) θ = **th**igh   b) ð = **th**y

2. a) θ = **th**ick   b) ð = **th**is

3. a) θ = **th**in   b) ð = **th**en

4. a) θ = **th**atch   b) ð = **th**at

5. a) θ = **th**ud   b) ð = **th**us

6. a) θθθθθθθðððððð   b) θθðθθθðθðθðθθðθðθθθðð

Tip-Alveopalatal Fricatives: Esh [ʃ] and Ezh [ʒ]

The fricatives **Esh** [ʃ] and **Ezh** [ʒ] also occur in English, although Ezh [ʒ] is a little less common. For these two fricatives, the tip or blade of the tongue is placed near the alveopalatal point of articulation. Illustrations 2.7 and 2.8 below picture the articulation for Esh [ʃ] and Ezh [ʒ] respectively.

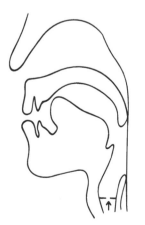

Illustration 2.7: Esh [ʃ]

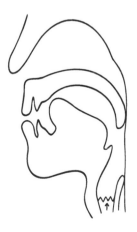

Illustration 2.8: Ezh [ʒ]

Remember that the alveopalatal point is the plane that slants upward just behind the alveolar ridge. Esh [ʃ] represents the what is known as the "sh" sound in English, such as in the word "ship."[1] Ezh [ʒ] is the same as the Esh [ʃ] except that it is voiced. Examples of Ezh [ʒ] in English are the "s" in "vision" and the "g" in "genera."

To produce the Ezh [ʒ], prolong the initial sound in the word "ship" and add voicing. These fricatives are demonstrated in English words in the following exercise. Repeat each word after the recording, paying close attention to the point of articulation and the voicing. In utterances 6.a and 6.b, practice the switch between voicing and voicelessness until the difference is easily produced and distinguished.

Exercise 2.4: Producing [ʃ] and [ʒ]

1. a) ʃ = fi**sh**ing   b) ʒ = vi**s**ion

2. a) ʃ = me**sh**   b) ʒ = mea**s**ure

3. a) ʃ = dilution   b) ʒ = delu**s**ion

4. a) ʃ = racial   b) ʒ = bei**ge**

5. a) ʃ = plu**sh**   b) ʒ = plea**s**ure

6. a) ʃʃʃʃʃʃ333333   b) ʃʃ33ʃʃ33ʃʃ33ʃʃ33ʃʃ33

In the following exercise, practice distinguishing between the tip-alveolar fricatives [s] and [z] from the tip-alveopalatal fricatives [ʃ] and [ʒ]. Respond after each utterance with "alveolar" or "alveopalatal."

Exercise 2.5: Recognizing Alveolar and Alveopalatal Sounds

1. [asɑ]	Alveolar	5. [azɑ]	Alveolar	9. [az]	Alveolar
2. [aʒɑ]	Alveopalatal	6. [aʃ]	Alveopalatal	10. [asɑ]	Alveolar
3. [azɑ]	Alveolar	7. [as]	Alveolar	11. [aʒ]	Alveopalatal
4. [ʒɑ]	Alveopalatal	8. [ʃɑ]	Alveopalatal	12. [zɑ]	Alveolar

Now we must introduce some fricatives which may be altogether new to you. Learn to produce them correctly with the help of the recorded exercises.

---

1   Native English speakers naturally round and protrude their lips when pronouncing alveopalatal sounds and, therefore, distort the pure sound.

Bilabial Fricatives: Phi [ɸ] and Beta [β]

These fricatives, **Phi** [ɸ][2] and **Beta** [β], are bilabial sounds. Fricatives at the labial point of articulation do not occur in English. They are, however, prevalent in many other languages throughout the world. Illustrations 2.9 and 2.10 picture the articulation for these sounds. Notice that primarily the only difference between them is voicing.

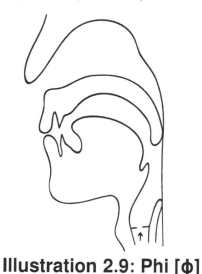
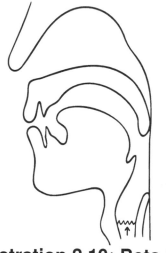

Illustration 2.9: Phi [ɸ]   **Illustration 2.10: Beta [β]**

When learning a new sound, you must often learn entirely new muscle coordination and speech skills. To produce phi [ɸ], the lips must be in about the same position as the sound [p]. They must be near enough to produce friction when the air stream moves between them, but they must not touch each other completely. Place your lips in position for [p] and slowly move them apart until you are able to force air between them. Keep your lips relaxed and flat. Do not let the air escape only from the center of your lips as if you were simply blowing. The air must exit evenly along the entire width of the lips. You may also learn this sound by pretending to blow out a candle while keeping a smile on your face.

The phi must also be kept distinct from [f]. In the articulation of [f], the lower lip approaches the upper teeth and friction is produced between them. The articulation for phi must be kept farther forward so that the friction is produced between both lips. If you have a tendency to produce [f], practice protruding your lower lip past your upper lip. With your lower lip extended, blow air gently upward toward your nose while keeping both lips flat.

Practice the following exercise, mimicking each utterance after the recording. Say the word "pig" keeping your lips relaxed so that they do not close entirely on the [p]. The word will sound more like "fig," but use [ɸ] and not [f].

---

2   The phonetic symbol Phi [ɸ] is slightly different from the Greek lowercase phi (φ).

Exercise 2.6: Producing [ɸ]

1. Pronounce the phi   ɸig

2. Extend the initial consonant   ɸɸɸɸɸɸig

3. Isolate the extended phi   ɸɸɸɸɸɸ

4. Say the phi between vowels   ɑɑɸɸɸɸɸɸɑɑ

5. Say it before the vowel   ɸɸɸɸɸɸɑɑ

6. Say it after the vowel   ɑɑɸɸɸɸɸɸ

Once you have learned to control the action of your vocal cords, you will have no trouble transitioning from [ɸ] to [β]. As was previously mentioned, the only difference between the two sounds is voicing. To produce [β], try humming while prolonging the phi. Another way to learn the sound is to prolong the vowel [ɑ] and, while continuing the voicing, slowly close the lips toward the position for [b]. Do not let the lips touch completely. Keep them relaxed and flat as for the phi. Follow the transcription for the next exercise, and repeat each utterance after the recording.

Exercise 2.7: Producing [β]

1. θθθθθθθθθðððððððð

2. ffffffffvvvvvvvvv

3. ɸɸɸɸɸɸɸɸββββββββ

4. θθððθθððθθððθθððθθðð

5. ffvvffvvffvvffvvffvv

6. ɸɸββɸɸββɸɸββɸɸββɸɸββ

Now say the word "base" without allowing your lips to completely stop the air flow. It may sound like "vase," but use [β] instead of [v].

7. Pronounce the beta   βase

8. Prolong the initial consonant   ββββββase

9. Isolate the extended [β]   ββββββ

10. Say the [β] between vowels   ɑɑββββββɑɑ

11. Say it before a vowel ββββββαα

12. Say it after a vowel ααββββββ

It is just as important to be able to hear and recognize these sounds as it is to produce them. Many people find it much more difficult to hear the difference between labiodental and bilabial fricatives. The following exercise was formulated to help you distinguish between [f] and [ɸ] and between [v] and [β] more easily. Whether or not you encounter these sounds in contrast in any given language, it is important to familiarize yourself with them as much as possible. Listen to the following exercise, and respond by telling whether the sounds you hear are bilabial or labiodental.

Exercise 2.8: Recognizing Bilabial and Labiodental Sounds

1.	[aɸa]	Bilabial	7.	[ɸa]	Bilabial	13.	[aɸa]	Bilabial
2.	[afa]	Labiodental	8.	[afa]	Labiodental	14.	[aɸ]	Bilabial
3.	[afa]	Labiodental	9.	[fa]	Labiodental	15.	[fa]	Labiodental
4.	[aɸa]	Bilabial	10.	[afa]	Labiodental	16.	[aɸa]	Bilabial
5.	[afa]	Labiodental	11.	[ɸa]	Bilabial	17.	[af]	Labiodental
6.	[aɸ]	Bilabial	12.	[af]	Labiodental	18.	[aɸa]	Bilabial

Tell whether the following fricatives are bilabial or labiodental.

Exercise 2.9: Recognizing Bilabial and Labiodental Sounds

1.	[aβa]	Bilabial	7.	[ava]	Labiodental	13.	[aβa]	Bilabial
2.	[ava]	Labiodental	8.	[av]	Labiodental	14.	[va]	Labiodental
3.	[aβa]	Bilabial	9.	[aβa]	Bilabial	15.	[aβ]	Bilabial
4.	[va]	Labiodental	10.	[aβ]	Bilabial	16.	[ava]	Labiodental
5.	[βa]	Bilabial	11.	[ava]	Labiodental	17.	[βa]	Bilabial
6.	[aβ]	Bilabial	12.	[va]	Labiodental	18.	[aβa]	Bilabial

Back-Velar Fricatives: X [x] and Gamma [ɣ]

The Gamma [ɣ] never occurs in English. X [x] occurs in Scottish dialects of English and may occur when an "h" sound precedes a "u" sound, such as in the word "hoop." Both phones are made with the back of the tongue raised toward the velum, very much like the articulation of [g] and [k]. Since they are fricatives, the articulator (tongue) does not quite touch the point of articulation, but allows air to be forced between them. The only difference between the **X** [x] and **gamma** [ɣ] is voicing. Illustrations 2.11 and 2.12 depict these velar fricatives.

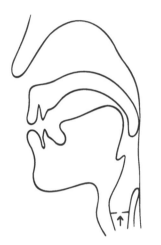

Illustration 2.11: X [x]

Illustration 2.12: Gamma [ɣ]

If you have studied German, you are familiar with the use of the [x] in the word "ach." It is produced by holding the articulation for [k] and slowly lowering the back of the tongue until you are able to force air through. Try saying [ɑɑkxxxxx]. Be sure to keep the vocal cords inactive. It may also help you to think of the sound that a cat makes when hissing at a dog. Try whistling a song with the back of the tongue. You should hear [x] as a prolonged hissing sound during the song.

Repeat the word "cot" after the recording in the following exercise. Notice that the "c" in the word "cot" is pronounced as a [k] phonetically. Next, do not let the back of your tongue stop the air stream, but pronounce it instead as the fricative [x]. The word should sound a little like "hot," but the [x] will have much more friction. "H" is a different sound that will be covered in another lesson.

Exercise 2.10: Producing [x]

1. Pronounce [k]   **c**ot

2. Pronounce the [x]   **x**ot

3. Extend the initial consonant   **xxxxxx**ot

4. Isolate the extended [x]   xxxxxx

5. Say the [x] between vowels   ɑɑxxxxxxxɑɑ

6. Say it before a vowel   xxxxxxɑɑ

7. Say it after a vowel   ɑɑxxxxxx

The gamma [ɣ] is nothing more than a voiced [x]. You can form the articulation of [ɣ] by beginning with a prolonged [ɑ] and slowly closing the gap between the back of your tongue and the velum as for the articulation of [g]. Leave a slight gap between the articulator and point of articulation so room is allowed for the necessary friction. Think "g," but keep it slightly relaxed so that air can flow through, as in the utterance [ɑɑɑɑɣɣɣɣɣ].

Now practice controlling your vocal cords to produce the [ɣ] in the same way that you learned the [β]. Begin with sounds with which you are familiar and move on to unfamiliar ones.

Exercise 2.11: Producing [ɣ]

1. sssssssszzzzzzzz

2. ʃʃʃʃʃʃʃ33333333

3. xxxxxxxxɣɣɣɣɣɣɣɣ

4. sszzsszzsszzsszzsszz

5. ʃʃ33ʃʃ33ʃʃ33ʃʃ33ʃʃ33

6. xxɣɣxxɣɣxxɣɣxxɣɣxxɣɣ

Replace the [g] with [ɣ] in the word "good." Remember not to let it sound like "hood."

7. Pronounce the gamma   ɣood

8. Extend the initial consonant   ɣɣɣɣɣood

9. Isolate the extended [ɣ]   ɣɣɣɣɣ

10. Say the [ɣ] between vowels   ɑɑɣɣɣɣɣɣɣɑɑ

11. Say it before a vowel   ɣɣɣɣɣɣɑɑ

12. Say it after a vowel   ɑɑɣɣɣɣɣɣ

The following exercises will strengthen your recognition of these velar fricatives. You may find it helpful to repeat each sound to yourself before responding so that you can feel each articulation in your own mouth. Determine if each consonant is velar or not.

Exercise 2.12: Recognizing Velar Sounds

1.	[aɣa]	Velar	6.	[aɸa]	No	11.	[ɣa]	Velar
2.	[axa]	Velar	7.	[aβa]	No	12.	[axa]	Velar
3.	[ava]	No	8.	[aɣa]	Velar	13.	[aʒa]	No
4.	[axa]	Velar	9.	[ax]	Velar	14.	[aɣ]	Velar
5.	[asa]	No	10.	[fa]	No	15.	[aʃa]	No

Tell whether the following fricative sounds are voiced or voiceless.

Exercise 2.13: Recognizing Voicing

1.	[axa]	Voiceless	6.	[axa]	Voiceless	11.	[xa]	Voiceless
2.	[aɣa]	Voiced	7.	[aɣa]	Voiced	12.	[axa]	Voiceless
3.	[aɣa]	Voiced	8.	[xa]	Voiceless	13.	[aɣ]	Voiced
4.	[aɣ]	Voiced	9.	[ɣa]	Voiced	14.	[ax]	Voiceless
5.	[ax]	Voiceless	10.	[aɣ]	Voiced	15.	[aɣa]	Voiced

Remember, to produce these new fricatives correctly, you must make sure that the articulator does not contact the point of articulation and form a stop at the beginning of the fricative. These fricatives are often pronounced incorrectly by beginners with an initial stop, as in [kxxx] and [gɣɣɣ]. You must be able to hear this difference and pronounce them without the stop. The following exercise contains some of these incorrect pronunciations. Practice detecting them by responding with "fricative" or "wrong."

Exercise 2.14: Recognizing Fricatives

1.	[axa]	Fricative	4.	[xa]	Fricative	7.	[ax]	Fricative
2.	[akxa]	Wrong	5.	[axa]	Fricative	8.	[akx]	Wrong
3.	[kxa]	Wrong	6.	[akxa]	Wrong	9.	[xa]	Fricative

10. [akɣa]	Wrong	16. [agɣa]	Wrong	22. [gɣa]	Wrong
11. [akx]	Wrong	17. [aɣa]	Fricative	23. [aɣa]	Fricative
12. [axa]	Fricative	18. [gɣa]	Wrong	24. [ɣa]	Fricative
13. [ax]	Fricative	19. [agɣa]	Wrong	25. [aɣa]	Fricative
14. [xa]	Fricative	20. [aɣa]	Fricative	26. [agɣ]	Wrong
15. [akx]	Wrong	21. [agɣa]	Wrong	27. [aɣa]	Fricative

Practice the following sentences, substituting the new fricatives that you have learned for familiar sounds. This will help you to gain control of the use of these new fricatives within utterances. You may find this more difficult than producing them in isolation. Listen to the sentences, and repeat each one after the recording. They will be given slowly at first and then build up to the speed of normal speech.

Exercise 2.15: Producing Sounds in Sentences

1. ɸeter ɸiɸer ɸicked a ɸeck of ɸickled ɸeɸɸers.

2. A βand of βig βad βandits βroke into βill's βank.

3. xween xatherine xan xick a xranxy xing.

4. ɣo ɣet ɣrandmother ɣobs of ɣreat, ɣreen, ɣooey ɣumdrops.

Practice the following mimicry drills by repeating each utterance after the recording. These drills will help you to associate each sound with its symbol. Follow along with the recording.

Exercise 2.16: Producing [ɸ, β, f, v, θ, ð, s, z, ʃ, ʒ, x, and ɣ]

1. [aɸa]		7. [aθa]		13. [aʃa]	
2. [aɸaɸ]		8. [aθaθ]		14. [aʃaʃ]	
3. [ɸaɸaɸ]		9. [θaθaθ]		15. [ʃaʃaʃ]	
4. [aβa]		10. [aða]		16. [aʒa]	
5. [aβaβ]		11. [aðað]		17. [aʒaʒ]	
6. [βaβaβ]		12. [ðaðað]		18. [ʒaʒaʒ]	

| 19. [axa] | 21. [xaxax] | 23. [aɣaɣ] |
| 20. [axax] | 22. [aɣa] | 24. [ɣaɣaɣ] |

Repeat the following sounds after the recording.

Exercise 2.17: Producing Fricatives

1. [saz]	9. [zax]	17. [θax]
2. [ʒas]	10. [βað]	18. [xaβ]
3. [fav]	11. [xax]	19. [ðaɸ]
4. [ʃax]	12. [ʒas]	20. [zaʒ]
5. [xas]	13. [ɣa]	21. [ʃas]
6. [ɸaβ]	14. [xav]	22. [ɣaɸ]
7. [vax]	15. [θaʃ]	23. [sað]
8. [ðaɣ]	16. [ʃaɣ]	24. [βax]

It is important to know the technical name, or full description, of each new sound. To give a full description, give the voicing first, followed by the articulator, point of articulation, and then the manner of articulation. For example, the sound [z] would be described as a voiced tip-alveolar fricative.

The following exercise contains only the fricatives from this lesson which do not occur in English. Respond with the technical name for each sound.

Exercise 2.18: Recognizing [ɸ, β, x, and ɣ]

1. [aɣa]	Vd. Back-velar Fricative	7. [ax]	Vl. Back-velar Fricative
2. [aɸa]	Vl. Bilabial Fricative	8. [aɣa]	Vd. Back-velar Fricative
3. [axa]	Vl. Back-velar Fricative	9. [axa]	Vl. Back-velar Fricative
4. [aβa]	Vd. Bilabial Fricative	10. [aɣa]	Vd. Back-velar Fricative
5. [aɸa]	Vl. Bilabial Fricative	11. [xa]	Vl. Back-velar Fricative
6. [aβa]	Vd. Bilabial Fricative	12. [aβa]	Vd. Bilabial Fricative

13. [βɑ]   Vd. Bilabial Fricative

14. [ɑɸɑ]   Vl. Bilabial Fricative

15. [ɣɑ]   Vd. Back-velar Fricative

16. [ɑxɑ]   Vl. Back-velar Fricative

17. [ɸɑ]   Vl. Bilabial Fricative

18. [ɑx]   Vl. Back-velar Fricative

19. [ɑβ]   Vd. Bilabial Fricative

20. [xɑ]   Vl. Back-velar Fricative

21. [ɑɣ]   Vd. Back-velar Fricative

22. [ɑβɑ]   Vd. Bilabial Fricative

The following exercise contains all of the Fricatives in this lesson. Respond with the full description for each sound.

Exercise 2.19: Recognizing Fricatives [ɸ, β, f, v, θ, ð, s, z, ʃ, ʒ, x, and ɣ]

1.   [ɑɸɑ]   Vl. Bilabial Fricative

2.   [ɑsɑ]   Vl. Tip-alveolar Fricative

3.   [ɑxɑ]   Vl. Back-velar Fricative

4.   [ɑɣɑ]   Vd. Back-velar Fricative

5.   [ɑvɑ]   Vd. Labiodental Fricative

6.   [ɑʒɑ]   Vd. Tip-alveopalatal Fricative

7.   [ɑʃɑ]   Vl. Tip-alveopalatal Fricative

8.   [ɑθɑ]   Vl. Tip-dental Fricative

9.   [ɑðɑ]   Vd. Tip-dental Fricative

10. [ɑfɑ]   Vl. Labiodental Fricative

11. [ɑɣɑ]   Vd. Back-velar Fricative

12. [ɑʃɑ]   Vl. Tip-alveopalatal Fricative

13. [ɑθɑ]   Vl. Tip-dental Fricative

14. [ɑɸɑ]   Vl. Bilabial Fricative

15. [ɑxɑ]   Vl. Back-velar Fricative

16. [ɑβɑ]   Vd. Bilabial Fricative

17. [ɑʒɑ]   Vd. Tip-alveopalatal Fricative

18. [ɑβɑ]   Vd. Bilabial Fricative

19. [ɑðɑ]   Vd. Tip-dental Fricative

20. [ɑʃɑ]   Vl. Tip-alveopalatal Fricative

21. [ɑðɑ]   Vd. Tip-dental Fricative

22. [ɑɣɑ]   Vd. Back-velar Fricative

23. [ɑɸɑ]   Vl. Bilabial Fricative

24. [ɑʒɑ]   Vd. Tip-alveopalatal Fricative

25. [ɑzɑ]   Vd. Tip-alveolar Fricative

26. [ɑθɑ]   Vl. Tip-dental Fricative

27. [ɑxɑ]   Vl. Back-velar Fricative

28. [ɑʃɑ]   Vl. Tip-alveopalatal Fricative

29. [ɑβɑ]   Vd. Bilabial Fricative

30. [ɑɸɑ]   Vl. Bilabial Fricative

Table 2.2 summarizes the fricatives learned in this lesson and gives the alternate symbols used by some linguists for each sound. Familiarize yourself with the Americanist (APA) symbols. Many of the sounds throughout this course will not have English examples.

Table 2.2: Summary of Fricatives

IPA Symbol	Name	Technical Name	English Example	APA Symbol(s)
ɸ	Phi	Voiceless Bilabial Fricative		ᵽ, ɸ
β	Beta	Voiced Bilabial Fricative		ƀ, β
f	F	Voiceless Labiodental Fricative	face	f
v	V	Voiced Labiodental Fricative	vase	v
θ	Theta	Voiceless Tip-dental Fricative	thin	θ
ð	Eth	Voiced Tip-dental Fricative	then	đ, ð
s	S	Voiceless Tip-alveolar Fricative	sap	s
z	Z	Voiced Tip-alveolar Fricative	zap	z
ʃ	Esh	Voiceless Tip-alveopalatal Fricative	fishing	š
ʒ	Ezh	Voiced Tip-alveopalatal Fricative	vision	ž

IPA Symbol	Name	Technical Name	English Example	APA Symbol(s)
X	X	Voiceless Back-velar Fricative	lo**ch** (Scottish)	X
ɣ	Gamma	Voiced Back-velar Fricative		ǥ, ɣ

Lesson 3:
Pitch Variations

Lesson Outline

Glossary Terms

Pitch is the perceived melody that accompanies speech. Pitch is a linguistic feature that is often ignored by beginner language learners, yet it is one of the most important keys to the correct pronunciation of any language. All speech is accompanied by some kind of pitch. As a person speaks, the level of his voice may go up and down or remain steady at some level. In either case, pitch is always present. Pitch can change either the implied meaning or the lexical meaning of a word or phrase. Even in English, the pitch associated with an utterance can determine whether that utterance is interpreted as a statement or a question. In other languages such as Thai, Chinese, and Vietnamese, the lexical meaning of each word changes with differences in pitch. No matter how it affects the meaning of spoken words, pitch should never be overlooked or ignored. It must be practiced and drilled just like any other feature of language. This lesson is designed to help you begin to hear basic changes in pitch. The recorded exercises will build up slowly so that you will have a solid foundation from which you can move on to more challenging lessons. Practice these exercises over again and again until you can distinguish the pitch easily.

Mimicking the pitch patterns of a language is something that must be done from the very first day of exposure to that language. Because language cannot be spoken without some kind of pitch occurring simultaneously, either the correct pitch will be used, or the speaker will carry over the pitch patterns of his native language. Unless the right pitch is practiced while learning the consonants and vowels, wrong pitch habits will be reinforced in the learner's mind.

Linguistic pitch is not absolute, but relative in that it is distinguished by context. When referred to linguistically, pitch does not relate to absolute notes on a musical scale. A speaker of a language may produce a word or utterance with a tone at "middle C" or some other note, but the musical note associated with the utterance is irrelevant. Voice registers will differ between men and women and between children and adults. A person who speaks in a high voice register would find it difficult to produce utterances using exactly the same musical notes as someone with a low voice register. It makes no difference whether a tone is produced higher or lower from one speaker to the next as long as its relationship to the other tones in the utterance remains unchanged. Rather than being related to absolute pitch, levels of linguistic pitch are related to the levels of surrounding pitch. The distinctions that must be focused on in languages are whether a tone is higher than, lower than, or the same as the other tone levels in the same utterance.

Uses of Pitch

There are two key ways in which pitch functions in languages. In some languages the pitch affects the meaning of an utterance on the sentence or phrase level. These are called **intonational languages**. Pitch can also affect the meaning of an utterance on the syllable or word level. Languages in which pitch changes the meanings of words or syllables are called **tonal languages**.

Intonation

Intonation is the relative pitch that affects the implied meaning of a sentence or phrase. In an intonational pitch system, the lexical meaning of individual words is not affected by tone, but the tone changes the implied meaning. The pitch pattern can work to imply different shades of meaning to a specific utterance. It is usually used to distinguish between a statement and a question, to convey various emotional messages, or to indicate the moods or attitudes of the speaker.

In English, an utterance said with a high or rising tone at the end is usually interpreted as a question, while a falling final tone generally means that the utterance is a statement. Intonation can also be used in other ways. In the following English examples, consider how different pitch patterns can affect the implied meaning of the utterance.

Table 3.1: English Intonation Example

Example Sentence	Explanation
I didn't say you stole it.	A high or rising tone on the word "I" implies that someone other than the speaker made the accusation.
I **DIDN'T** say you stole it.	A high tone on the word "didn't" emphatically asserts that the speaker did *not* say who stole the item in question.
I didn't **SAY** you stole it.	A high tone on the word "say" implies that the speaker believes that listener is the thief but did not voice this opinion.
I didn't say **YOU** stole it.	A high tone on the word "you" implies that the speaker said that someone else is the thief.
I didn't say you **STOLE** it.	A high tone on the word "stole" implies that the speaker said that the listener "borrowed without permission" or acquired something through some questionable means.
I didn't say you stole **IT**.	A high tone on the word "it" implies that the speaker made the accusation that one or more other objects were stolen.

In each sentence, the meaning of the individual words is never altered by the change in pitch. The intonation does, however, add a new aspect to the meaning of the sentence as a whole. This is the key difference between an intonational system and a tonal system.

You have already learned that English is a language with an intonational pitch system. Many English speakers are unaware of how important our intonation patterns are for correct understanding of our language. A very common mistake of language learners transitioning from one intonational language to another is to conclude that since tone levels do not make a difference in the meaning of individual words, the intonation patterns are less important and can be ignored. This is definitely a mistake. Incorrect intonation is one of the first things that may point out a speaker as a foreigner, and it can also cause serious confusion. It is very safe to conclude that pitch, or tone, is equally important in every language and should be given a place of top priority in your language study.

Tone

Tone is relative pitch that is used to distinguish the meaning of a single word. In a tonal system, tone levels affect the meaning of an utterance in the same way that a consonant or vowel might. Each word has a specific tone or tone pattern associated with it, and a different tone can change the meaning of the word entirely. This is demonstrated in the following example from Vietnamese.

Table 3.2: Vietnamese Tone Example

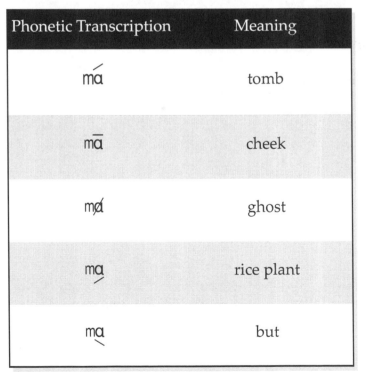

Phonetic Transcription	Meaning
má	tomb
mā	cheek
mọ̃	ghost
mạ	rice plant
mạ̀	but

In each utterance we see that the consonants and vowels remain the same. Here the tone is the only factor that makes the distinction between the meanings of these words. The same is not true of an intonational system such as English. A word may be said with any number of different tone variations and the basic meaning remains the same.

Levels of Pitch

The first step in recognizing pitch is to become aware of the basic changes in pitch levels. **Pitch levels** are the perceived levels of pitch ranging from high to mid to low. In some languages, it will be necessary to recognize up to five different levels of pitch. In this course, however, only three levels of pitch will be drilled.

Representing Pitch Levels

Tone levels will be indicated throughout this manual by lines above or below the utterance. A line above the word represents high tone; a line immediately below the word is mid tone, and a space below that is low tone.

Table 3.3: Simple Pitch Notation

Levels	Short Glides	Long Glides
high _____ mid _____ mopisu low	high _____ mid _____ musopafu low	high _____ mid _____ musø low

Distinguishing Pitch Levels

Regardless of what type of pitch system you may attempt to learn, you must strive to reproduce the tones exactly as the native speaker says them. Many people think that they are incapable of hearing such distinctions, but with the proper training, any person can learn to recognize and reproduce any pitch variation. No matter what language you speak naturally, you have learned subconsciously to produce the correct tone patterns when speaking that language. This learning can be done again for a second language, but it may require more effort.

In the following recorded exercises, listen for a single tone level that is different from the others in the utterance. Each utterance will be the three syllable sequence [mo pi su]. Each example will be given twice. Respond with the syllable which carries a different tone. If all of the tones in the utterance sound the same, respond with "none." The correct answer will be given afterwards on the recording so that you will be able to trace your progress. Complete the exercises without watching the text if you can.

The drills may seem easy for some students at first, but it is important to master these foundational skills before moving on. If you have no trouble with the exercises, try transcribing the tone while you are listening to the recording. If you have trouble hearing the tones, try humming along with the utterances, mimicking the tone pattern, or watch the diagrams of the tone patterns in the text while listening to the recording. Remember that you are not listening for differences in the consonants and vowels. Tune out everything except the tone.

Exercise 3.1: Recognizing Variations in Tone

1. mopisu	pi	8. mopisu	None	15. mopisu	mo
2. mopisu	su	9. mopisu	pi	16. mopisu	None
3. mopisu	None	10. mopisu	mo	17. mopisu	su
4. mopisu	mo	11. mopisu	pi	18. mopisu	pi
5. mopisu	su	12. mopisu	pi	19. mopisu	mo
6. mopisu	mo	13. mopisu	su	20. mopisu	su
7. mopisu	su	14. mopisu	None	21. mopisu	None

The following exercise requires the same response on five-syllable utterances. Remember that you are listening only for differences in tone. Every utterance will again consist of the same consonants and vowels. Name the syllable that carries a different tone.

Exercise 3.2: Recognizing Tone Variations in Longer Words

1. somebikuna	na	5. somebikuna	na
2. somebikuna	so	6. somebikuna	bi
3. somebikuna	me	7. somebikuna	me
4. somebikuna	ku	8. somebikuna	so

9. someb<u>i</u><u>kuna</u> ku   16. someb<u>i</u><u>kuna</u> bi

10. <u>so</u>meb<u>i</u><u>kuna</u> me   17. someb<u>i</u><u>kuna</u> na

11. someb<u>i</u><u>kuna</u> na   18. someb<u>i</u><u>kuna</u> me

12. <u>so</u>meb<u>i</u>kuna me   19. someb<u>i</u><u>kuna</u> ku

13. <u>so</u>meb<u>i</u><u>kuna</u> so   20. <u>so</u>meb<u>i</u><u>kuna</u> so

14. <u>so</u>meb<u>i</u>kuna so   21. someb<u>i</u>kuna bi

15. someb<u>i</u><u>kuna</u> ku   22. someb<u>i</u><u>kuna</u> na

Types of Pitch

So far you have distinguished different levels of pitch. Now you must learn to recognize different types of pitch. The following exercises contrast level pitch with glided pitch.

Level Pitch

Level tone is pitch that does not rise or fall. It occurs when the relative height of the pitch remains constant throughout the duration of a syllable. This condition will be perceived auditorily as an even note with no rise or fall. Whether the pitch is high, mid, or low is irrelevant as long as the level remains unchanged.

Glided Pitch

Up to this point our tones have all been level, remaining at the same height throughout their duration. **Glided pitch** is a tone that begins at some point and then moves either higher or lower. A pitch glide is perceived auditorily as a tone that either falls or rises from one note to another during a single syllable.

In the following exercise each utterance consists of the same one syllable word, while the tones vary. Respond with "level" or "rising" after the utterance is given. The recording will then give the correct response.

Exercise 3.3: Recognizing Level or Rising Tone

1.	look	level	7.	look	rising	13.	look	level
2.	look	rising	8.	look	rising	14.	look	rising
3.	look	level	9.	look	rising	15.	look	level
4.	look	rising	10.	look	level	16.	look	level
5.	look	rising	11.	look	rising	17.	look	rising
6.	look	level	12.	look	level	18.	look	level

Tell whether the tones in the following exercise are level or falling.

Exercise 3.4: Recognizing Level or Falling Tone

1.	where	falling	6.	where	level	11.	where	level
2.	where	level	7.	where	falling	12.	where	falling
3.	where	falling	8.	where	level	13.	where	level
4.	where	falling	9.	where	falling	14.	where	falling
5.	where	level	10.	where	level	15.	where	falling

16. where̲   level   17. w̄h̄ere   level   18. whe̍re   falling

Tell whether the tones in the following exercise are level, rising, or falling.

Exercise 3.5: Recognizing Level, Rising, and Falling Tone

1. sto̍p   rising   7. sto̍p   falling   13. s̄t̄op   level

2. s̲t̲o̲p̲   level   8. sto̍p   rising   14. sto̍p   falling

3. sto̍p   falling   9. sto̍p   rising   15. s̲t̲o̲p̲   level

4. sto̍p   falling   10. s̲t̲o̲p̲   level   16. sto̍p   falling

5. sto̍p   rising   11. sto̍p   rising   17. sto̍p   rising

6. s̲t̲o̲p̲   level   12. sto̍p   falling   18. sto̍p   rising

The next exercises will involve longer sequences of sounds, but your response will remain the same. Each utterance will have a period of level tone at the beginning to help you compare the tone levels. Listen only to the pitch on the last syllable, and tell whether it is rising, falling, or level.

Exercise 3.6: Recognizing Level, Rising, and Falling Tone

1. W̲h̲e̲r̲e̲ ̲h̲a̲v̲e̲ ̲y̲o̲u̲ ̲bee̍n falling   5. w̲h̲e̲r̲e̲ ̲h̲a̲v̲e̲ ̲y̲o̲u̲ ̲b̲e̲e̲n̲ level

2. w̲h̲e̲r̲e̲ ̲h̲a̲v̲e̲ ̲y̲o̲u̲ ̲be̍en rising   6. w̲h̲e̲r̲e̲ ̲h̲a̲v̲e̲ ̲y̲o̲u̲ ̲be̍en rising

3. w̲h̲e̲r̲e̲ ̲h̲a̲v̲e̲ ̲y̲o̲u̲ ̲be̍en rising   7. w̲h̲e̲r̲e̲ ̲h̲a̲v̲e̲ ̲y̲o̲u̲ ̲bee̍n falling

4. w̲h̲e̲r̲e̲ ̲h̲a̲v̲e̲ ̲y̲o̲u̲ ̲b̲e̲e̲n̲ level   8. w̲h̲e̲r̲e̲ ̲h̲a̲v̲e̲ ̲y̲o̲u̲ ̲bee̍n falling

9. <u>where have you been</u> level   15. <u>where have you be∮n</u> rising

10. <u>where have you be∮n</u> falling   16. <u>where have you been</u> level

11. <u>where have you be∮n</u> rising   17. <u>where have you be∮n</u> rising

12. <u>where have you been</u> level   18. <u>where have you be∮n</u> rising

13. <u>where have you be∮n</u> falling   19. <u>where have you been</u> level

14. <u>where have you be∮n</u> falling   20. <u>where have you be∮n</u> falling

Lesson 4:
Stops and Voice Onset Time

Lesson Outline

Glossary

Stops are speech sounds in which the articulator and the point of articulation contact each other and completely obstruct the air stream. The velic is also closed during a stop so that air cannot escape through the nasal cavity. This type of articulation is referred to by many linguists as "**plosive**" rather than "stop." The usage of the term "plosive" is often inconsistent, sometimes referring to a subset of stops, so the term "stop" will be used throughout this course. Table 4.1 gives the phonetic symbols and descriptions for the six common stops presented in this lesson.

Table 4.1: Common Stops

	Bilabial	Tip-Alveolar	Back-Velar
Voiceless	p	t	k
Voiced	b	d	g

Stops

Stops were introduced in Lesson 1 as phones created by stopping the air stream completely. The stops in Table 4.1 are the most common to English speakers. Study the table and familiarize yourself with the articulator and point of articulation for [p], [b], [t], [d], [k], and [g]. If you would like to review stops, you may go back to Exercise 1.16 and Exercise 1.17.

You may have noticed that the stops in the chart above are arranged in pairs that share the same articulator and point of articulation. These stops are not identical, however. The difference between these stops is voicing. Nearly any consonant may be either voiced or voiceless. Table 4.1 above illustrates which stops are voiced and which are voiceless. To fully understand the difference between these stops and the stops in subsequent lessons, you must first understand voice onset time.

Alveolar sounds in English are pronounced using the tip of the tongue; however, they can also be articulated with the blade. Linguists refer to the tip and blade of the tongue as **apical** and **laminal** respectively. Occasionally, it is important to distinguish between apical and laminal phones. To specifically indicate that a sound is articulated with the tip of the tongue, a diacritic called the **Inverted Bridge** [̺] can be placed below or above a symbol, for example [d̺] or [g̺]. A **Square** [̻] diacritic is used to indicate laminal (or blade) articulation, for example [d̻] or [g̻]. Generally, it is not necessary to indicate apical or laminal articulation; therefore, these diacritics will not be used in the exercises.

Voice Onset Time

In the lesson on fricatives you learned to distinguish between voicing and voicelessness. Stops may also be either voiced or voiceless. It may be harder, however, to hear the differences in the voicing of stops because they cannot be prolonged as much as fricatives. This gives less time to hear or feel vocal activity. The stops in the chart above are arranged in pairs that share the same articulators and points of articulation, but they have different voicing characteristics. The sounds [p] and [b], for example, are both bilabial stops, but [p] is voiceless while [b] is voiced.

Since stops cannot be produced without some vowel occurring with them, you may tend to confuse the voicing of the vowels with the voicing of the consonants. The sequences [ɑpɑ] and [ɑbɑ] will sound very much alike as both utterances have voiced vowels at their beginning and end. The only difference between them is a slight break in the vocal activity during the [p]. It may require a little practice for you to be able to distinguish the voicing of the consonants from the voicing of the vowels.

Understanding Voice Onset Time

To thoroughly understand the voicing and voicelessness of stops, we must understand voice onset time (VOT). **Voice onset time** describes the point in time when the vocal cords begin to vibrate in relation to the time of the release of the articulators forming the consonant. In other words, whether a consonant is voiced or not depends on whether the VOT occurs before or after the sound is released. For **voiced** stops, such as [b], the vocal cords begin vibrating before the lips actually open to release the sound. For **voiceless** stops, like [p], voicing doesn't begin until the articulators are released. It may begin precisely at the moment of the release, or a slight moment afterward. This distinction will be explained further in Lesson 6. The voice onset time of consonants can be illustrated in wave forms. The following wave form diagrams will help you to understand VOT in voiced and voiceless stops.

The following diagrams illustrate the voice onset time of voiced and voiceless stops. Illustrations 4.1 and 4.2 represent the same pairs of sounds. The wavy lines represent glottal activity. Notice that for the voiced stop [b], the voicing begins before the release of the articulators. For the voiceless stop [p], however, no glottal activity is present until after the articulators release and the vowel begins. Illustration 4.1 has been simplified slightly to make the glottal activity easier to read. Illustration 4.2 gives a more scientifically accurate version.

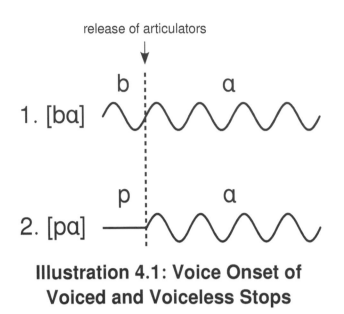

Illustration 4.1: Voice Onset of Voiced and Voiceless Stops

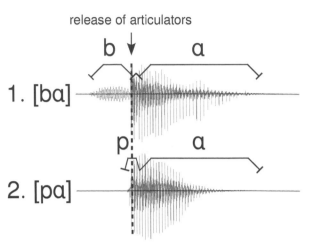

Illustration 4.2: Voice Onset of Voiced and Voiceless Stops

Controlling Voice Onset Time

The symbols for the stops presented in this lesson represent the same sound in phonetic transcription as they do in English orthography. You must make certain, however, that your voicing for the stops [b], [d], and [g] actually begins before the articulators release. Many English speakers tend not to voice these stops fully, especially when speaking rapidly. To gain control of the vocal cords during these sounds, try prolonging the stops and exaggerating their voicing before the release. Remember that a stop can only be prolonged until the oral and pharyngeal cavities fill with air, and then the release must be made. Repeat each utterance after the recording. (The double triangles after the voiced stops indicates lengthening.)

Exercise 4.1: Producing Strong Voicing

1. a) **b**a**b**y   b) **bː**a**bː**y   c) **bː**y

2. a) **b**a**bb**le   b) **bː**a**bbː**le   c) **bː**le

3. a) a**dd**er   b) a**ddː**er   c) **dː**er

4. a) pa**dd**le   b) pa**ddː**le   c) **dː**le

5. a) **g**ro**gg**y   b) **gː**ro**ggː**y   c) **gː**y

6. a) ha**gg**le   b) ha**ggː**le   c) **gː**le

The following exercise contrasts voiced and voiceless stops in common English words. In the first utterance the stop will occur between two vowels. The same stop will then be demonstrated in the initial, medial, and final positions. Repeat each word after the recording, and pay close attention to the differences in vocal activity.

Exercise 4.2: Recognizing Voiced and Voiceless Stops

		Voiceless Stops					Voiced Stops		
1.	[apɑ]	pay	appraise	ape	4.	[abɑ]	boy	obey	ebb
2.	[atɑ]	tea	attack	ate	5.	[adɑ]	die	adorn	Ed
3.	[akɑ]	key	accord	ache	6.	[agɑ]	green	again	egg

The following exercise deals only with stops. You will be asked to tell whether these stops are voiced or voiceless as you did with fricatives in Lesson 2. Do not confuse the voicing of the vowels with that of the consonants. It may help you to repeat the sound and prolong it, feeling your glottis with your fingers to check for voicing.

Exercise 4.3: Recognizing Voiced and Voiceless Stops

1.	[abɑ]	Voiced	6.	[gɑ]	Voiced	11.	[ba]	Voiced
2.	[adɑ]	Voiced	7.	[kʰɑ]	Voiceless	12.	[akʰɑ]	Voiceless
3.	[akʰɑ]	Voiceless	8.	[atʰɑ]	Voiceless	13.	[agɑ]	Voiced
4.	[pʰɑ]	Voiceless	9.	[ad]	Voiced	14.	[da]	Voiced
5.	[atʰɑ]	Voiceless	10.	[apʰɑ]	Voiceless	15.	[apʰɑ]	Voiceless

In the next exercise, give a full description for each sound. Begin by stating whether it is voiced or voiceless. Next name the articulator, the point of articulation, and the manner of articulation. Each sound in this exercise is a stop.

Exercise 4.4: Describing Stops

1.	[abɑ]	Voiced Bilabial Stop	6.	[ad]	Voiced Tip-alveolar Stop
2.	[atʰɑ]	Voiceless Tip-alveolar Stop	7.	[kʰɑ]	Voiceless Back-velar Stop
3.	[gɑ]	Voiced Back-velar Stop	8.	[da]	Voiced Tip-alveolar Stop
4.	[pʰɑ]	Voiceless Bilabial Stop	9.	[apʰɑ]	Voiceless Bilabial Stop
5.	[ba]	Voiced Bilabial Stop	10.	[atʰɑ]	Voiceless Tip-alveolar Stop

11. [ɑdɑ]	Voiced Tip-alveolar Stop	15. [gɑ]	Voiced Back-velar Stop
12. [kʰɑ]	Voiceless Back-velar Stop	16. [dɑ]	Voiced Tip-alveolar Stop
13. [bɑ]	Voiced Bilabial Stop	17. [ɑtʰɑ]	Voiceless Tip-alveolar Stop
14. [ɑtʰɑ]	Voiceless Tip-alveolar Stop	18. [ɑd]	Voiced Tip-alveolar Stop

Now we will combine all of the manners of articulation that we have learned. Respond by telling whether the sound is voiced or voiceless.

Exercise 4.5: Recognizing Voiced and Voiceless Consonants

1. [ʒɑ]	Voiced	7. [kʰɑ]	Voiceless	13. [ɑvɑ]	Voiced
2. [ɑgɑ]	Voiced	8. [ɑfɑ]	Voiceless	14. [ɑŋɑ]	Voiced
3. [ɑbɑ]	Voiced	9. [ɑgɑ]	Voiced	15. [ɑvɑ]	Voiced
4. [ɑθ]	Voiceless	10. [nɑ]	Voiced	16. [ðɑ]	Voiced
5. [lɑ]	Voiced	11. [ɑʃ]	Voiceless	17. [ɑdɑ]	Voiced
6. [ɑsɑ]	Voiceless	12. [ɑpʰɑ]	Voiceless	18. [ɑðɑ]	Voiced

Give a full description of the following sounds. This exercise will include all of the sounds that have been drilled so far in this course.

Exercise 4.6: Describing Consonants

1. [ɑgɑ]	Vd. Back-velar Stop	9. [dɑ]	Vd. Tip-alveolar Stop
2. [ɑbɑ]	Vd. Bilabial Stop	10. [ɑzɑ]	Vd. Tip-alveolar Fricative
3. [ɑxɑ]	Vl. Back-velar Fricative	11. [ɑlɑ]	Vd. Tip-alveolar Lateral
4. [ʒɑ]	Vd. Tip-alveopalatal Fricative	12. [ɑkɑ]	Vl. Back-velar Stop
5. [ɑpʰɑ]	Vl. Bilabial Stop	13. [fɑ]	Vl. Labiodental Fricative
6. [vɑ]	Vd. Labiodental Fricative	14. [ðɑ]	Vd. Tip-dental Fricative
7. [ɑβɑ]	Vd. Bilabial Fricative	15. [ɑɣɑ]	Vd. Back-velar Fricative
8. [ɑxɑ]	Vl. Back-velar Fricative	16. [ɑnɑ]	Vd. Tip-alveolar Nasal

17. [atʰɑ]   Vl. Tip-alveolar Stop

18. [alɑ]   Vd. Tip-alveolar Lateral

19. [gɑ]   Vd. Back-velar Stop

20. [nɑ]   Vd. Tip-alveolar Nasal

21. [θɑ]   Vl. Tip-dental Fricative

22. [ɑθɑ]   Vl. Tip-dental Fricative

23. [ɑm]   Vd. Bilabial Nasal

24. [ɑb]   Vd. Bilabial Stop

25. [ɑɣɑ]   Vd. Back-velar Fricative

26. [ɑpʰɑ]   Vl. Bilabial Stop

27. [ɑʃɑ]   Vl. Tip-alveopalatal Fricative

28. [ɑɸ]   Vl. Bilabial Fricative

29. [lɑ]   Vd. Tip-alveolar Lateral

30. [ɑkʰɑ]   Vl. Back-velar Stop

Lesson 5: Facial Diagrams

Lesson Outline

Glossary

Facial diagrams represent a cross section of the human speech apparatus. These diagrams are simplified for phonetic purposes so that they show only those anatomical features relevant to the articulation of speech sounds. Facial diagrams are helpful tools for visualizing and discussing the articulation of individual phones. They give a better understanding of the interaction of the various parts of the speech mechanism. By drawing the diagrams, you will be forced to pay close attention to the exact details of a given articulation, rather than just having a vague idea of how it works. In this lesson you will learn to produce accurate facial diagrams of basic sounds.

Not all sounds can be depicted by facial diagrams. A few consonants such as laterals and sounds that involve certain actions by the sides of the tongue cannot be shown in a facial diagram due to the side view nature of the diagrams. Because facial diagrams are a static representation of conditions that occur in the speech tract, it is also hard to accurately portray sounds that involve transitions or changes since they would require the diagram to show a series of conditions that occur over a period of time, rather than a single condition as if in a frozen moment. Vowels are also difficult to diagram since they do not involve any definite articulators or points of articulation. Linguists do not usually diagram vowels due to their open, ambiguous nature. Facial diagrams are a very helpful tool for illustrating most sounds, however, and will be used extensively throughout this course to present basic facts about the production of speech sounds.

The Five Variables of Facial Diagrams

There are five important features that must be included in facial diagrams. These organs, which we will call **variable features**, are the lips, the tongue, the velic, the glottis (i.e., vocal cords), and the air stream. It is important to include all of these features when drawing facial diagrams, and not just those which are actively involved in the articulation of a particular sound. For example, in a diagram of the voiced stop [b], only the lips and the velic are actively engaged in the production of the sound, but the tongue and the teeth should still be included in the drawing. The teeth and tongue still affect the acoustical properties of the sound. A diagram is incomplete until all five of the variable features are in the correct position for the sound being represented.

Lips

The **lips** can be actively involved in the articulation of stops, fricatives, and nasals. More detail is given as to how to portray manners of articulation later on in this chapter. Sounds that involve lip rounding can be demonstrated by drawing the lips as protruding outward. When the lips are not being used in the articulation of the phone presented, draw them in an open, relaxed position.

Tongue

The **tongue** is the hardest variable to accurately portray. The rear of the tongue (root) starts as far back as the pharyngeal cavity, while the front of the tongue is anchored at about the midpoint of the floor of the mouth. Since the functions of the tongue are so many, it is divided into five different areas, any of which can act as an articulator. From front to back, these are tip, blade, mid, back, and root.

Velic

The **velic** is the back surface of the uvula. This flap of cartilage separates the nasal cavity from the oral cavity. When closed, it is placed directly against the wall of the pharyngeal cavity. When opened, it hangs freely, allowing the air stream to pass into the nasal cavity.

Glottis

Voicing is just as important to a diagram as the articulators and points of articulation. An even line at the **glottis** with a space or gap in its center, as shown in Illustration 5.1, indicates that the vocal cords are not vibrating during the articulation of the sound. This means that the sound is voiceless. A wavy line that spans the entire width of the glottis represents vibration in the vocal cords, or voicing as illustrated in Illustration 5.2.

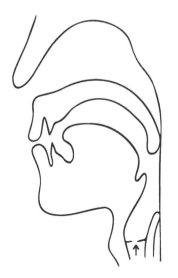

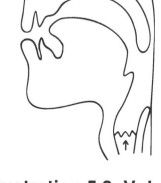

Illustration 5.1: Voiceless   **Illustration 5.2: Voiced**

Air Stream

In addition to voicing, the **air stream** must be indicated in the diagram. So far in this course we have studied only one type of air stream movement. This air stream movement, which we call **egressive pulmonic**, originates in the lungs and moves outwards. Egressive pulmonic air is represented by a small arrow just below the glottis which points upward. Examine the air stream indicators in the previous illustrations. Notice that the arrows do not extend through the vocal cords. This is an important distinction as other air streams are symbolized by arrows that extend through the vocal cords.

Drawing Facial Diagrams

Facial diagrams should always be made facing to your left. The manner of articulation is represented by the relationship drawn between the articulator and the point of articulation.

Stops

For stops, the articulator must be shown as being closed against the point of articulation. The velic must also be completely closed. Illustrations 5.3–5.5 below depict some common stop articulations. Notice the complete closure for the stops in these diagrams.

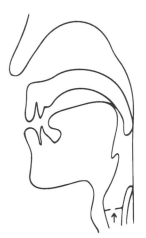

Illustration 5.3: K [k]

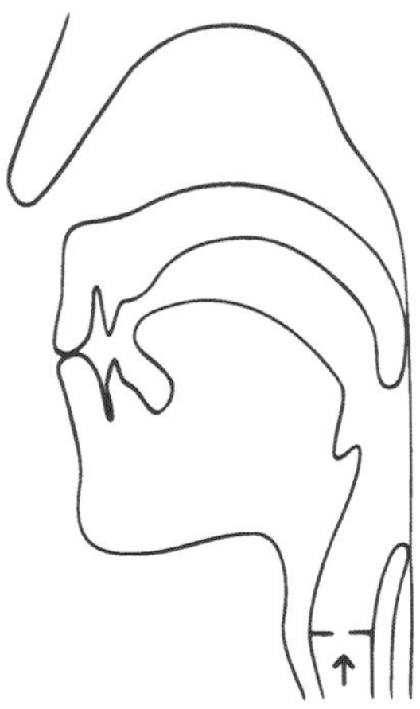

Illustration 5.4: P [p]

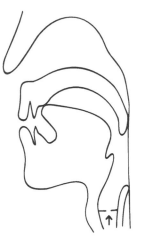

Illustration 5.5: T [t]

Fricatives

To depict fricatives, leave a small space between the articulator and the point of articulation. Illustrations 5.6–5.8 below picture the articulation of the fricatives [ɸ], [s], and [x]. The velic remains closed as for the stops, but a space is left between the tip of the articulator and the point of articulation. This space, or gap, is where the friction is produced. Do not make the space so small that it is confused with a stop, but not so large it seems indefinite.

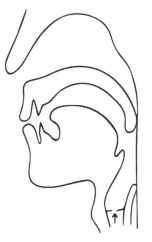
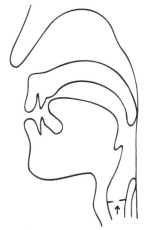
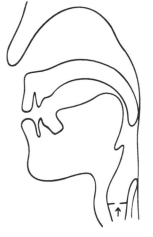

Illustration 5.6: Phi [ɸ] **Illustration 5.7: S [s]** **Illustration 5.8: X [x]**

Nasals

For nasal articulation, the articulator and point of articulation must contact each other completely just as for a stop. The velic, however, must remain open showing that the air stream is allowed to escape through the nasal cavity. This allows the air stream to resonate in both the oral and nasal cavities. The next three illustrations depict nasals at the bilabial, alveolar, and velar points of articulation. Notice that the velic is open for these sounds.

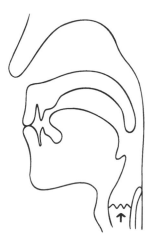
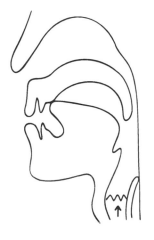
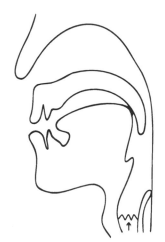

Illustration 5.9: M [m] **Illustration 5.10: N [n]** **Illustration 5.11: Eng [ŋ]**

Incorrectly Drawn Diagrams

It is important to be accurate when creating diagrams of sounds. The following illustrations show some common mistake made when representing sounds.

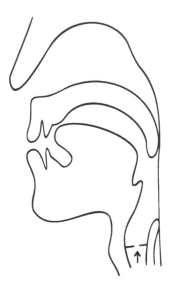

Illustration 5.12: Incorrect [t]. Too much space between the articulator and the point of articulation.

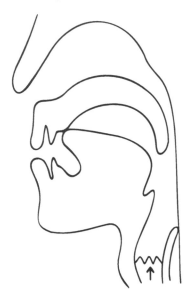

Illustration 5.13: Incorrect [d]. The velic should not be open.

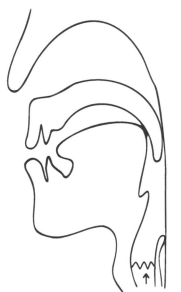

Illustration 5.14: Incorrect [ɣ]. No space between the articulator and point of articulation.

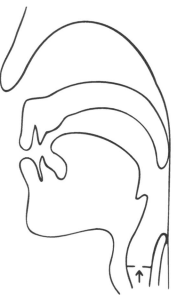

Illustration 5.15: Incorrect [s]. Too much space between articulator and point of articulation.

The illustration below contains the basic framework of the speech apparatus, but the variable features are left blank. You may trace or copy this blank facial diagram and fill in the variable features of any sound. You will be required to diagram the articulation for several sounds during this course.

Illustration 5.16: Blank Facial Diagram

Lesson 6: Progressive Pitch Control

Lesson Outline

Glossary

Lesson 3 introduced the concepts of pitch, tone, and intonation. Individual languages differ in how they are affected by pitch. Pitch affects the implied meaning of a phrase or sentence in an intonational language, while in a tonal language, the meaning of each word or syllable is affected by its pitch. This lesson continues with the study of pitch as it is used in tonal systems. In tonal languages, the pitch belonging to an individual syllable is called a tone.

Types of Tonal Systems

The different types of pitch, level and glided, were introduced in chapter 3. Pitch glides occur when there is a change of pitch, or tone, within a syllable. If the tone remains constant throughout a syllable, it is said to be level. Languages differ as to what types of tones, whether glided or level, may accompany a word or phrase. In many cases, the type of pitch noted on the word and phrase level is also true of the entire language.

Registered Tone Systems

In certain languages, only level tones are utilized. These languages are described as having **registered tone** systems. In a registered system, no pitch glides occur. The only changes in the level of pitch occur between syllables.

Contoured Tone Systems

Some tone systems may contain glided tones as well as level tones. These systems are described as **contoured tone** systems. Thai, for example, has two level tones and three glided tones. In a contoured system, the tone may rise, fall, or both rise and fall within a single syllable.

The following exercise contains multi-syllable utterances with different combinations of level and glided tone. Respond by telling whether each utterance contains registered or contoured tone patterns.

Exercise 6.1: Identifying Tone Systems

1. dakuna   contoured   4. kulige   contoured   7. kozete   contoured

2. nakanu   registered   5. labaru   contoured   8. hakemu   registered

3. fisuwa   registered   6. niwaja   registered   9. numuwa   contoured

10. ʒɑfs\ve   contoured   13. θɑtↄ/gi   contoured   16. ðɛtʰ\sʊ   contoured

11. ʔɑlinhu   registered   14. pʰoɸʊdɛ   registered   17. kɑtɑwe   registered

12. magana   registered   15. buꞮɑga   registered   18. ʔetiga   registered

Advanced Pitch

Languages vary as to how many different levels of pitch can affect the meanings of words. Some tonal languages deal with only two different levels of pitch, while others have been found which contain more than five. Determining how many and what types of tones actually affect the meanings of words will depend upon a phonological analysis of the entire sound system of the language, which is beyond the scope of this book. In your phonetic transcription, however, you must strive to record all the distinctions that you hear in the tone whether they affect the meaning or not.

Multiple Pitch Levels

So far in this course, only two levels of tone have been drilled. However, in actual phonetic transcription, additional tone levels may need to be recognized and transcribed. In this lesson, three different levels of pitch will be introduced and contrasted. These levels will be termed high, mid, and low. Table 6.1 illustrates how the different level and glided tones will be marked.

Table 6.1: Simple Pitch Notation

Levels	Short Glides	Long Glides
high mid .... mopisu low	high mid .... mↄsopafↄ low	high mid .... mↄsø low

When learning to recognize multiple levels of tone, it may be easiest to practice with registered tone before dealing with glides. The following exercise gives examples of three distinct tone levels, first with a meaningless utterance and then with example words common in English. Follow the transcription and mimic the tone levels.

Exercise 6.2: Demonstrating Multiple Tone Levels

1. a) m̄ōp‾i su̲   b) h̄īgh m̲īd l̲ow

2. a) mop̲i s̄ū   b) l̲ow m̲īd h̄īgh

3. a) j̄ōhnn̲y   b) h̄īgh l̲ow

4. a) j̄ōhn‾ny   b) h̄īgh m̲īd

5. a) jo̲hnny̲   b) m̲īd l̲ow

6. a) johnn̄y̲   b) l̲ow h̄īgh

7. a) jo̲hnny   b) l̲ow m̲īd

8. a) jo̲hn‾ny   b) m̲īd h̄īgh

The next exercise contains words with up to three different registered tones. Listen for the different tone levels, and respond by telling how many levels you hear.

Exercise 6.3: Recognizing Multiple Tone Levels

1. mopi‾s̲u	two	5. mopi s̲u	one	9. m̄ōpi s̲u	three
2. m̄ōpi s̲u	three	6. m̄ōpi su	two	10. mop‾i s̲u	three
3. mopi su	one	7. m̄ōpi s̲u	one	11. mopi s̲u	two
4. mopi‾su	three	8. mop‾i s̲u	three	12. mōp‾i su	two

13. mopi̅su   one   15. mopi̲su   two   17. mo̲p̅i̅su   three

14. mopi̲s̅u   three   16. mo̲p̲i̅su   one   18. mopi̲s̲u   two

Multiple Levels in Glides

Learning to recognize the relative length of glides is important when dealing with multiple levels of pitch in contoured pitch systems. Contoured tones can glide between any two pitch levels. Glides are described as long or short depending on what levels they begin and end with. A **short glide**, for example, may glide from the mid level to one of the extremes, either high or low. A **long glide** moves from extreme to extreme, such as from high to low, or vice versa.

It is important to note here that the length of the glide has nothing to do with the duration of time for which it is held. A long glide, for example, may be spoken very quickly, while a shorter glide may be held for a much longer time. The length of the glide is determined by the distance between the pitch levels at the beginning and ending of the glide.

The following exercise gives examples of long and short glides in relation to corresponding registered tones. Follow along in the text, and repeat each utterance.

Exercise 6.4: Demonstrating Long and Short Glides

1. a) J̅o̅h̅n̅ny   b) Jo̔hn   long fall

2. a) J̅o̅h̅nny   b) Jo̔hn   short fall

3. a) Johnny   b) John   short fall

4. a) Johnn̅y   b) Jøhn   long rise

5. a) Johnny   b) John   short rise

6. a) John̅n̅y   b) Jøhn   short rise

In the following exercise you will be asked to distinguish between long and short glides. This exercise will employ the same English word for each utterance. This will allow you to focus on the tones without any distractions. All of the tones will be rising. Respond with "long" or "short."

Exercise 6.5: Recognizing Long and Short Rising Tones

1. nøw	long	6. now	short	11. nøw	short
2. nøw	short	7. nøw	long	12. nøw	long
3. now	short	8. nøw	long	13. now	short
4. nøw	long	9. nøw	short	14. nøw	long
5. nøw	long	10. now	short	15. nøw	long

The next exercise will involve falling tones. Respond with "long" or "short."

Exercise 6.6: Recognizing Long and Short Falling Tones

1. my	short	6. my	short	11. my	short
2. my	long	7. my	long	12. my	long
3. my	short	8. my	short	13. my	long
4. my	long	9. my	long	14. my	short
5. my	long	10. my	short	15. my	short

The following exercise contains both falling and rising tones. Respond by telling whether the glide is a long rise, a short rise, a long fall, or a short fall.

Exercise 6.7: Recognizing Long and Short Glides

1.	go	short rise	8.	gø	long rise	15.	go	short rise
2.	gø	long rise	9.	gø	short fall	16.	go	short fall
3.	gø	long fall	10.	gø	long rise	17.	gø	long rise
4.	go	short fall	11.	gø	long fall	18.	gø	long fall
5.	gø	long rise	12.	go	short fall	19.	go	short rise
6.	go	short fall	13.	gø	long rise	20.	gø	long fall
7.	gø	short rise	14.	go	short rise	21.	gø	short rise

Using Frames to Analyze Multiple Pitch Levels

When analyzing different tones and tone levels, it is often helpful to use a frame. A **frame** is a word or group of words in which the tone does not change. You may use a frame as a reference point with which to compare any individual tone. Placing the frame word adjacent to the tone in question makes it possible to analyze the character of that specific tone in relation to a known, constant tone level.

The following exercise will contain an English sentence as frame words for each utterance. The tone will be level on all but the last syllable of each utterance. Listen to the last syllable and respond by telling whether the tone is a long rise, a short rise, a long fall, a short fall, or a level tone. The frame will provide you with a point of reference for your analysis.

Exercise 6.8: Using Frames

1.	this is my song	level	3.	this is my song	long fall
2.	this is my song	short rise	4.	this is my song	short fall

5. this is my song   long rise   14. this is my song   short rise

6. this is my song   level   15. this is my song   long rise

7. this is my song   short fall   16. this is my song   short fall

8. this is my song   long fall   17. this is my song   level

9. this is my song   long rise   18. this is my song   level

10. this is my song   level   19. this is my song   short fall

11. this is my song   short rise   20. this is my song   long rise

12. this is my song   long fall   21. this is my song   long fall

13. this is my song   long fall   22. this is my song   short rise

Complex Contours

So far all of the tone glides drilled have been unidirectional, moving either up or down during a single syllable. In some systems a **complex contour** exists where the tones can move in both directions, rising and falling or falling and rising within one syllable. In the following exercise, you will be introduced to these complex contours. Listen to each frame word, and respond with "rise" or "rise-fall."

Exercise 6.9: Recognizing Complex Contours

1. sø   rise   3. sø   rise   5. sø   rise-fall

2. so   rise-fall   4. so   rise-fall   6. so   rise

7. sø   rise   10. so   rise-fall   13. so   rise-fall

8. so   rise   11. so   rise   14. sø   rise

9. so   rise-fall   12. so   rise-fall   15. so   rise-fall

In the next exercise, respond with "fall" or "fall-rise."

Exercise 6.10: Recognizing Complex Contours

1. say   fall   6. say   fall   11. say   fall-rise

2. say   fall-rise   7. say   fall-rise   12. say   fall

3. say   fall-rise   8. say   fall   13. say   fall-rise

4. say   fall   9. say   fall   14. say   fall-rise

5. say   fall-rise   10. say   fall   15. say   fall

In the following exercise, respond by telling whether you hear a fall, a rise, a fall-rise, or a rise-fall.

Exercise 6.11: Recognizing Complex Contours

1. how   rise-fall   5. how   fall-rise   9. how   fall

2. how   rise   6. how   rise   10. how   rise-fall

3. how   fall   7. how   fall   11. how   fall-rise

4. how   fall-rise   8. how   rise-fall   12. how   rise

13. how   rise-fall   15. høw   rise   17. how   rise-fall

14. how   fall-rise   16. how   fall-rise   18. høw   rise

Use the following frame words to practice articulating various tone contours. Read each utterance paying particular attention to the pronunciation of the tones.

Exercise 6.12: Reproducing Tone Contours

1. musopɑfu   10. musøpɑfu   19. musøpafu

2. musopɑfu   11. musøpafu   20. musøpɑfu

3. musopɑfu   12. musopɑfu   21. musopafu

4. musopɑfu   13. musøpɑfu   22. musopɑfu

5. musopafu   14. musopɑfu   23. musopafu

6. musopafu   15. musopafu   24. musøpafu

7. musopɑfu   16. musøpɑfu   25. musopɑfu

8. musopafu   17. musøpɑfu   26. musøpɑfu

9. musopɑfu   18. musopafu   27. musøpafu

Methods of Pitch Notation

There are several accepted methods of notation used to represent pitch, each with its advantages and disadvantages. Table 6.2 and Table 6.3 list several pitch transcription methods. Which method you choose to utilize in your future linguistic work is your decision; however, for this course, you should familiarize yourself with each method so that you are able to read and transcribe pitch with each.

Table 6.2: Registered Tone Symbolization

	Contours	Numbers	Diacritics	Tone Letters
Extra High	s͞a	sɑ⁵	sa̋	sɑ˥
High	s͞a	sɑ⁴	sá	sɑ˦
Medium	s̲a	sɑ³	sā	sɑ˧
Low	s̲a̲	sɑ²	sà	sɑ˨
Extra Low	sa	sɑ¹	sȁ	sɑ˩

Table 6.3: Glided Tone Symbolization

	Contours	Numbers	Diacritics	Tone Letters
Long Rise	sɑ͍	sɑ¹⁵	sa̋̌	sɑ˦˥
Long Fall	sɑ͍	sɑ⁵¹	sa̋̂	sɑ˥˩
Rise	sɑ͍	sɑ²⁴	sǎ	sɑ˨˦
Fall	sɑ͍	sɑ⁴²	sâ	sɑ˧˩

High Rise	sá	sa⁴⁵	sa̋	sa꜒
Extra Low Short Rise	sa	sa¹²	sa̎	saꜗ
Short Rise	sa̗	sa³⁴	sa᷄	sa꜓
Low Short Rise	sa̗	sa²³	sa᷅	sa꜔
Rise-Fall	sa	sa²⁴²	sâ	saꜞ
Fall-Rise	sa	sa⁴²⁴	sǎ	saꜟ

Continuous Lines

The most basic tone system is the **continuous line contour system**, used thus far in this course. This system was chosen because of its intuitiveness and simplicity for the education of beginners. This system, however, is rarely encountered in anything beyond personal field transcription. This is because contours are nearly impossible to type on computers and can also cause intelligibility issues when drawn over some phonetic characters or diacritics.

Tone Numbers

When using **tone numbers** to transcribe pitch, a common way is to use [¹] for the lowest level and count upwards for progressively higher pitch levels, ending with [⁵] as the highest tone. Some linguists, especially in Mexico, reverse this number system and use [¹] to indicate the highest tone and [⁵] for the lowest. The numbers are usually superscripted and immediately follow the syllables they describe.

Tone Diacritics

Wherever **tone diacritics** are used, they are placed above the syllable to which they pertain. The current convention is for tone diacritics to point toward the pitch level that they represent. The high tone mark [´], for example, slants upward, representing a high level pitch. A low level pitch is indicated by a downward slant [ˎ]. Glides are represented by combining the diacritics for the beginning and ending levels of the glide.[1] A glide from high to low, for example, is marked by an "up-down" slant [ˆ].

However, the IPA now recommends to interpret tone diacritics as iconic (i.e., picturing the tone). Therefore, [ˆ] represents a rise-fall tone. This method is much more intuitive but lacks the precision of the former method. Because this method is not yet officially accepted, it will not be used in the remainder of this lesson.

Tone Letter

In the **tone letter** system, tone letters can be placed above or following the syllable. If the tone letters are placed following the syllable, care must be taken not to confuse these symbols with the other phonetic segments of the transcription.

Table 6.4 below demonstrates each of the different tone symbolization methods. The phrase used to illustrate the different methods is a phonetic transcription of the title of the famous Chinese poem "施氏食狮史" or, in English, "Lion-Eating Poet in the Stone Den."

Table 6.4: Tone Symbolization Examples

Contours	[s̄i s̀i s̀i s̄i ši]
Superscript Numbers	[si⁵ si⁵¹ si³⁵ si⁵ si²¹⁴]
Diacritics	[si̋ si̖ si̗ si̋ sǐ]
Tone Letters	[si˥ si˥˩ si˧˥ si˥ si˨˩˦]

Identifying Tonal Languages

A definite decision regarding the function of tone in a language must be based upon a complete phonological analysis of that language's tone system. However there are certain conditions that can be noticed in your initial phonetic work that will give you a good indication of whether a language is tonal or intonational. If pairs of words are found whose

---

1 Therefore, with tone diacritics, it is impossible to disambiguate an extra low short rise ([ˎ] + [ˎ] = [ˏ]) from a low fall ([ˎ] + [ˎ] = [ˎ]).

meanings differ, yet the only phonetic difference lies in their tones, you can be fairly certain that the language is tonal. Such pairs of words are called **minimal pairs** since only one phonetic difference exists between them. Minimal pairs are the strongest evidence of a tonal system. Other clues include low tone occurring on stressed syllables, and the absence of length on stressed syllables. In most intonational languages, on the other hand, high tone and length have some correlation to stress in that they usually accompany stressed syllables. Not all pitch systems conform to these patterns, but, in most cases, these tendencies can be regarded as strong indications of the function of tone.

Lesson 7:
Aspiration and Glottal Stops

Lesson Outline

Glossary

In everyday English speech, the voiceless consonants [p], [t], and [k] are not always pronounced as simple voiceless stops. In many situations, these sounds are accompanied by an additional phonetic feature known as aspiration. **Aspiration** is a puff of air accompanying the release of a stop. In American English, all voiceless stops produced in the initial position are aspirated. You can see this condition clearly if you hold a thin piece of paper in front of your lips and pronounce the words "pill," "till," or "kill." Say the words as you normally would in English. You will notice that the paper is blown away from your lips by a puff of air when [p], [t], and [k] are released. The puff of air after each stop is the aspiration. Now contrast these stops with the same stops in the words "spill," "still," and "skill." The slip of paper remains motionless after the release of the stops in these words. These are unaspirated stops. This feature, which may seem insignificant in our English speech, can change the entire meaning of a word in many languages. It will be treated as a distinct phonetic sound in this course. All voiceless stops can be either aspirated or unaspirated. Aspiration is represented by a **Superscript H** [ʰ] immediately after the stop symbol. The phonetic transcription for aspirated stops such as [p] is [pʰ].

The following chart gives the symbols for new sounds introduced in this lesson. Writing aspirated sounds simply involves placing a diacritic near a symbol for the appropriate voiceless stop. The chart also includes the symbol for glottal stop, which will be discussed later in this lesson.

Table 7.1: Voiceless Stops

	Bilabial	Tip-Alveolar	Back-Velar	Glottal
Unaspirated	p	t	k	ʔ
Aspirated	pʰ	tʰ	kʰ	

Aspiration

A wave form diagram of the **voice onset time** of stops can help us better understand aspiration. The VOT of voiceless stops may begin precisely at the moment of the articulator's release or slightly afterwards, as mentioned in Lesson 4. This variance is due to aspiration. The VOT occurs right at the time of the release of an unaspirated stop. In contrast, voicelessness continues briefly after the release of an aspirated stop.

The following wave form illustrations demonstrate the varying voice onset times for an unaspirated stop and an aspirated one. Notice in the diagram how the aspiration of the second utterance occurs in the period of voicelessness after the [p] is released. Two separate diagrams illustrating the same sounds are given so that you may examine both a simplified version and a more scientifically detailed one.

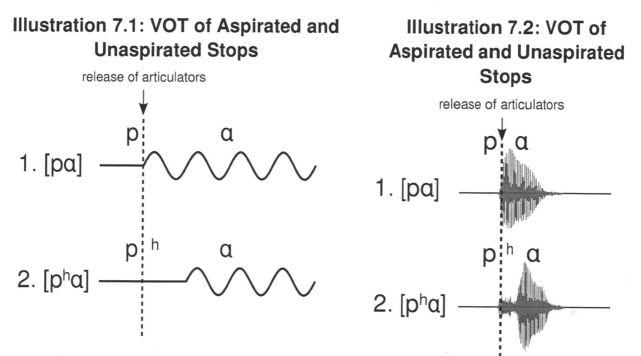

Illustration 7.1: VOT of Aspirated and Unaspirated Stops

Illustration 7.2: VOT of Aspirated and Unaspirated Stops

Aspiration makes no difference in the meaning of English words, so many English speakers find it difficult to hear whether a sound is aspirated or not. Before you can control its use in speech, you must be able to hear aspiration well. The exercises in this lesson are designed to help you recognize aspiration easily.

The following exercise deals only with voiceless stops. Respond by telling whether or not they are aspirated. Listen for the puff of air after the stop.

Exercise 7.1: Recognizing Aspiration

1.	[apʰa]	Aspirated	6.	[apʰa]	Aspirated	11. [apʰa]	Aspirated
2.	[ata]	Unaspirated	7.	[atʰa]	Aspirated	12. [apa]	Unaspirated
3.	[apa]	Unaspirated	8.	[apa]	Unaspirated	13. [atʰa]	Aspirated
4.	[kʰa]	Aspirated	9.	[ta]	Unaspirated	14. [aka]	Unaspirated
5.	[aka]	Unaspirated	10.	[akʰa]	Aspirated	15. [ata]	Unaspirated

The utterances in the next exercise will include other manners of articulation in addition to stops. Remember that aspiration is a condition that applies only to voiceless stops. Try not to let the other consonants in the exercise confuse you. Listen to the voiceless stops, and tell whether they are aspirated or unaspirated.

Exercise 7.2: Recognizing Aspirated Sounds

1.	[zatʰɑ]	Aspirated	7.	[vatɑlɑ]	Unaspirated	13.	[mɑkɑfɑ]	Unaspirated
2.	[ɑkɑmɑ]	Unaspirated	8.	[atʰɑ]	Aspirated	14.	[atʰɑl]	Aspirated
3.	[ʃapʰɑ]	Aspirated	9.	[sɑsɑpɑ]	Unaspirated	15.	[tʰɑx]	Aspirated
4.	[kɑɣɑ]	Unaspirated	10.	[ʒɑkɑl]	Unaspirated	16.	[sɑkɑfɑl]	Unaspirated
5.	[apʰɑ]	Aspirated	11.	[apʰɑlɑvɑ]	Aspirated	17.	[βɑpɑvɑ]	Unaspirated
6.	[ɑkɑsɑ]	Unaspirated	12.	[ʃɑlɑkʰɑ]	Aspirated	18.	[apʰɑsɑzɑ]	Aspirated

Recognizing (Un)Aspirated Stops

All voiceless stops may be either aspirated or un-aspirated. In English, aspiration often helps us distinguish between the voiced and voiceless stops in words like "pit" and "bit," "tick" and "Dick," or "clue" and "glue." Many English speakers find it difficult to hear the difference between unaspirated voiceless stops and voiced stops. One reason is that English speakers do not always fully voice the stops [b], [d], and [g]. Instead they produce unaspirated, voiceless stops. Another reason is that the voice onset time for unaspirated stops can be very close to the voice onset time of some voiced stops. In the following wave form diagram, the voice onset times of voiced stops, unaspirated stops, and aspirated stops are compared.

Notice that the VOT is not the same between all voiced stops or all aspirated stops. In fact, a whole range of voice onset time exists between the first and third examples and the third and fifth examples. There is still, however, much less difference between the VOT of unaspirated stops and voiced stops than between aspirated stops and voiced stops. This is the primary reason that English speakers experience difficulty distinguishing voiced stops from unaspirated voiceless stops.

Follow the recording down the column of diagrammed sounds above. Repeat each sound while

Illustration 7.3: VOT of Voiced and Voiceless Stops

release of articulators

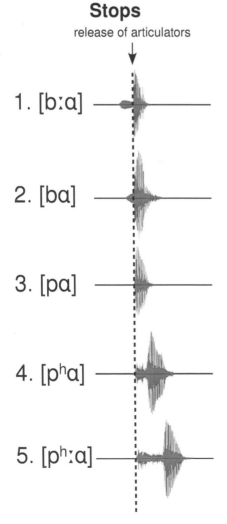

1. [bːɑ]

2. [bɑ]

3. [pɑ]

4. [pʰɑ]

5. [pʰːɑ]

feeling your glottis with your fingertips. Pay close attention to the VOT in relation to the release of your articulators.

The next exercise contains only voiceless, unaspirated stops and voiced stops. Listen for a short period of vocal activity before the release of the voiced consonants. Respond with "voiced" or "voiceless."

Exercise 7.3: Recognizing Voicing with Stops

1.	[abɑ]	Voiced	7.	[dɑ]	Voiced	13.	[atɑ]	Voiceless
2.	[apɑ]	Voiceless	8.	[agɑ]	Voiced	14.	[bɑ]	Voiced
3.	[akɑ]	Voiceless	9.	[tɑ]	Voiceless	15.	[gɑ]	Voiced
4.	[adɑ]	Voiced	10.	[apɑ]	Voiceless	16.	[akɑ]	Voiceless
5.	[atɑ]	Voiceless	11.	[kɑ]	Voiceless	17.	[adɑ]	Voiced
6.	[akɑ]	Voiceless	12.	[adɑ]	Voiced	18.	[pɑ]	Voiceless

This exercise includes aspirated stops as well as other manners of articulation. There will be only one stop in each utterance. Listen for the stop, and respond with "aspirated," "unaspirated," or "voiced."

Exercise 7.4: Recognizing Voiced and Aspirated Stops

1.	[atɑ]	Unaspirated	10.	[apʰɑ]	Aspirated	19.	[kalɑ]	Unaspirated
2.	[apʰɑ]	Aspirated	11.	[bɑ]	Voiced	20.	[ɣapɑ]	Unaspirated
3.	[abɑ]	Voiced	12.	[agɑ]	Voiced	21.	[avatɑ]	Unaspirated
4.	[akʰɑ]	Aspirated	13.	[tɑ]	Unaspirated	22.	[kalasɑ]	Unaspirated
5.	[dɑ]	Voiced	14.	[akɑ]	Unaspirated	23.	[ʃaɸagɑ]	Voiced
6.	[akɑ]	Unaspirated	15.	[akʰɑ]	Aspirated	24.	[bazɑs]	Voiced
7.	[gɑ]	Voiced	16.	[adasɑ]	Voiced	25.	[fadɑx]	Voiced
8.	[apɑ]	Unaspirated	17.	[gɑz]	Voiced	26.	[kaʒafɑ]	Unaspirated
9.	[atʰɑ]	Aspirated	18.	[fabɑ]	Voiced	27.	[apʰaθɑ]	Aspirated

Producing Aspirated and (Un)Aspirated Stops

All English speakers produce both aspirated and unaspirated stops in their natural speech. Because there is no difference in meaning, many speakers will find it difficult to hear or control their aspiration voluntarily. In English aspiration is conditioned by its environment. Stops occurring at the beginning of words or utterances are always aspirated, while those which occur after [s], or word medially, are unaspirated. We pronounce these phonetic differences quite subconsciously. Learning to consciously insert or remove the aspiration may require practice. Begin by developing strong aspiration. Mimic the following exercise, and exaggerate the amount of aspiration more than you normally would in English speech.

Exercise 7.5: Producing Aspiration

1. [hahahaha]

   [pʰapʰapʰapʰa]

   [spʰaspʰaspʰaspʰa]

2. [hahahaha]

   [tʰatʰatʰatʰa]

   [stʰastʰastʰastʰa]

3. [hahahaha]

   [kʰakʰakʰakʰa]

   [skʰaskʰaskʰaskʰa]

4. [hahahaha]

   [hapʰatʰakʰa]

   [haspʰastʰaskʰa]

In the following exercise, the words in column A are naturally aspirated. The words in column B are naturally unaspirated. Repeat the word in column A, and apply the same aspiration to the word in column B. Column B should sound unnatural to you as you exaggerate the aspiration.

Exercise 7.6: Producing Aspirated Stops

1. a) [pʰat]   pot   b) [spʰat]   spot
2. a) [pʰɪt]   pit   b) [spʰɪt]   spit
3. a) [pʰɛk]   peck   b) [spʰɛk]   speck
4. a) [pʰik]   peek   b) [spʰik]   speak
5. a) [pʰoᵘk]   poke   b) [spʰoᵘk]   spoke
6. a) [tʰap]   top   b) [stʰap]   stop
7. a) [tʰu]   two   b) [stʰu]   stew

8. a) [tʰɑ˞]   tar   b) [stʰɑ˞]   star

9. a) [tʰɪk]   tick   b) [stʰɪk]   stick

10. a) [tʰʌf]   tough   b) [stʰʌf]   stuff

11. a) [kʰæt]   cat   b) [skʰæt]   scat

12. a) [kʰɪt]   kit   b) [skʰɪt]   skit

13. a) [kʰɹim]   cream   b) [skʰɹim]   scream

14. a) [kʰɹæm]   cram   b) [skʰɹæm]   scram

15. a) [kʰɑt]   cot   b) [skʰɑt]   Scott

Many English speakers will find it harder to remove the aspiration from sounds where it is not wanted than to insert it intentionally. There are several ways to learn to control aspiration. The best way for English speakers is to take those situations where a stop is naturally unaspirated in English and practice that sound until you can insert it in other environments at will. The following exercises build up from known sounds in familiar English environments to unfamiliar environments. The voiceless stops in the words of the next exercise are preceded by [s], where they are naturally unaspirated. Repeat each sound after the recording until you can produce them as unaspirated stops without the initial [s]. Hold a thin piece of paper in front of your lips to ensure that the aspiration is removed.

Exercise 7.7: Producing Unaspirated Stops

1. spill   sssssssspill   sssssssss pill   pill

2. still   sssssssstill   ssssssss till   till

3. skill   sssssssskill   ssssssss kill   kill

4. spill   still   skill
    sssssssspill   sssssssstill   sssssssskill
    sssssssss pill ssssssss till   ssssssss kill
    pill   till   kill

These utterances contain unaspirated stops in the medial position. Practice them until you can place them in the initial position.

5. [pʰɑpɑ]   [pʰɑpɑpɑpɑpɑ]   [pɑpɑ]

6. [tʰɑtɑ]   [tʰɑtɑtɑtɑtɑ]   [tɑtɑ]

7. [kʰakɑ]   [kʰakakakaka]   [kakɑ]

All voiceless stops may be either aspirated or unaspirated. Once you have learned to control aspiration on these stops, you will be able to pronounce any voiceless stops that you encounter in the future with or without aspiration. Although producing aspirated and unaspirated stops is not a new skill for English speakers, it may require a lot of practice to gain control over your aspiration. Accurate control of aspiration is imperative to the success of learning any foreign language. Incorrect aspiration may be one of the first things that mark your speech with a foreign accent, or even cause you to say something completely unintended. Thai is one example of a language in which aspiration makes a difference in the meaning of words. The following Thai exercise contrasts voiced stops, voiceless aspirated stops, and voiceless unaspirated stops. The words are written phonemically which means that the transcription may vary somewhat from a strictly phonetic transcription. Listen to the exercise once all the way through, and then work through it again mimicking each utterance after the recording. Follow the transcription.

Exercise 7.8: Thai Mimicry

1.	/bit/	twist	15.	/pʰet/	peppery	29.	/pat/	to dust
2.	/pit/	to close	16.	/bai/	leaves	30.	/pʰaat/	to fry
3.	/pʰit/	wrong	17.	/pai/	to go	31.	/dam/	black
4.	/baat/	to wound	18.	/pʰaa/	bamboo	32.	/tam/	to pound
5.	/paak/	mouth	19.	/bok/	dry land	33.	/tʰam/	to do, make
6.	/pʰaak/	forehead	20.	/pok/	book cover	34.	/duaŋ/	particle
7.	/baw/	light weight	21.	/pʰok/	to turn face	35.	/tuaŋ/	measure
8.	/paw/	blow with mouth	22.	/bon/	complain	36.	/tʰuan/	complete
9.	/pʰa/	to burn	23.	/pon/	to mix	37.	/dɔɔŋ/	to pickle
10.	/baa/	crazy	24.	/pʰon/	to be free	38.	/tɔɔŋ/	must
11.	/paa/	older sister	25.	/bɔɔt/	blind	39.	/tʰɔɔŋ/	gold
12.	/pʰaa/	cloth	26.	/pɔɔt/	lungs	40.	/daŋ/	loud
13.	/bet/	fishhook	27.	/pʰɔɔt/	to inhale	41.	/taŋ/	to set or place
14.	/pet/	duck	28.	/bat/	papers or cards	42.	/tʰaŋ/	bucket

43. /dɑɑm/ handle	49. /dom/ to smell	55. /duu/ to look at
44. /tɑɑm/ to follow	50. /tom/ to boil	56. /tuu/ cupboard
45. /tʰɑɑm/ ask	51. /tʰom/ to refill a hole	57. /tʰuu/ to rub
46. /dok/ fertile	52. /dɑk/ to ensnare	58. /dɑɑi/ to be able
47. /tok/ fall	53. /tɑk/ to draw water	59. /tɑi/ torch
48. /tʰok/ flay	54. /tʰɑk/ plait, braid	60. /tʰɑi/ to plow

Glottal Stops [ʔ]

All of the stops that we have studied so far are made in the oral cavity. Now we must examine a special stop produced at the vocal cords. The **Glottal Stop** [ʔ], as its name suggests, is made by a complete closure of the air stream at the glottis. The vocal cords are pressed tightly together so that no air can pass between them. Glottal stops are made quite frequently in English, although we rarely notice them because they do not make a difference in the meaning of English words. In the utterance "Uh-oh!" (an interjection used to indicate that something has or is about to go wrong) the "catch" in the middle of the word is a glottal stop. The catch at the beginning of a deliberate cough is also a glottal stop. Certain dialects of English replace [t] with a glottal stop in some environments, as in the words "kitten" and "mitten." Many speakers say these words without fully articulating the [t]. Instead they cut off the air stream with the vocal cords, producing a glottal stop. In addition, English speakers usually insert a glottal stop before word initial vowels, like in the words "it," "ate," and "ouch." If you say these words naturally, you will probably feel a catch in your throat just as you did in the expression "uh-oh." The symbol for Glottal Stop [ʔ] looks like a question mark without the dot.

The vocal cords must have just the right amount of tension applied to them for voicing to occur. They must be neither completely relaxed or completely tensed. They are directly between the two extremes, in a state of optimum tension for smooth vibration. Air passing through the glottis is required to produce this vibration. It is therefore impossible to voice a glottal stop. During a glottal stop, the tension applied to the vocal cords increases as they are brought together as articulators to form a stop. This increased tension and the fact that air is no longer passing through the vocal cords makes it impossible for the vibrations that produce voicing to occur. Glottal stops do not fit precisely with the definition for voicelessness either, since during voiceless sounds the vocal cords are apart and relaxed. You will learn more about these states of the glottis in a later lesson. However, since there are no vibrations of the vocal cords involved, glottal stops are perceived auditorily as voiceless. You do not need to include voicelessness in a description of glottal stops since there is only one possible voicing state to associate with them.

Aspirated glottal stops do occur in some languages, but are not as common as other aspirated stops and are usually limited to specific environments.

Recognizing Glottal Stops

Glottal stops are very common throughout English speech, but since we are never forced to recognize their existence, you may find it difficult to hear them at first. English speakers insert glottal stops at the beginning of words that start with vowels, for example, "attack" [ʔʌˈtʰæk] and "open" [ˈʔoᵘ.pʰn̩]. Because this sounds so natural for an English speaker, we will find it most difficult to hear glottal stops in the initial position. The following exercise provides examples of occurrences of glottal stops in common English words.[1] They will begin by demonstrating glottal stops in the medial position, which is the easiest for English speakers to distinguish. Follow the transcription, and listen for the catch, or break, in the sounds. Repeat each sound after the recording.

Exercise 7.9: Recognizing Glottal Stops

1.	[ʔʌʔoᵘ]	Uh-oh!	7.	[sɪʔn̩]	sittin'
2.	[hʌʔʌ]	negative grunt	8.	[bɪʔn̩]	bitten
3.	[sɛnʔn̩ts]	sentence	9.	[bɑʔl̩]	bottle
4.	[sæʔɚdei]	Saturday	10.	[kʰæʔl̩]	cattle
5.	[mɪʔn̩]	mitten	11.	[mɛʔl̩]	metal
6.	[kʰɪʔn̩]	kitten	12.	[lɪʔl̩]	little

The following exercise contrasts phrases with and without an utterance-medial glottal stop. The phrases in the left column contain glottal stops, while those in the right column do not.

Exercise 7.10: Producing Glottal Stops

1.	[tʰu ʔæplz]	[tʰu æplz]	two apples
2.	[mɑⁱ ʔiɹz]	[mɑⁱ iɹz]	my ears

---

1   The phonetic transcription of English words in this chapter has been simplified to focus on the purpose of the exercises.

3. [beɪbi ʔænts]   [beɪbi ænts]   baby ants

4. [pʰɑpɑ ʔɪz]   [pʰɑpɑ ɪz]   papa is

5. [kʰliɹ ʔaɪs]   [kʰliɹ aɪs]   clear ice

6. [ænə ʔæsks]   [ænə æsks]   Anna asks

7. [θɹi ʔegz]   [θɹi egz]   three eggs

8. [tʰu ʔoᵘld]   [tʰu oᵘld]   too old

9. [blu ʔaɪz]   [blu aɪz]   blue eyes

10. [seɪ ʔoɪŋk]   [seɪ oɪŋk]   say "oink"

Repeat each word after the recording in the following exercise. Exaggerate the initial glottal stops.

Exercise 7.11: Producing Initial Glottal Stops

1.	[ʔæpl̩z]	apples	6.	[ʔæsks]	asks
2.	[ʔi˞z]	ears	7.	[ʔegz]	eggs
3.	[ʔænts]	ants	8.	[ʔoᵘld]	old
4.	[ʔɪz]	is	9.	[ʔaɪz]	eyes
5.	[ʔʌɪs]	ice	10.	[ʔoɪŋk]	oink

The following exercises will test your ability to hear and recognize glottal stops. Determine if each utterance contains a glottal stop or not. Do not let the other voiceless stops which also occur in the exercise confuse you. Do not follow along with the text.

Exercise 7.12: Recognizing Glottal Stops

1.	[maʔa]	Glottal	6.	[laak]	No	11.	[naʔakata]	Glottal
2.	[maː]	No	7.	[takada]	No	12.	[hapaha]	No
3.	[laʔam]	Glottal	8.	[kaʔaka]	Glottal	13.	[paʔahaʔ]	Glottal
4.	[taʔa]	Glottal	9.	[pata]	No	14.	[anahapap]	No
5.	[kakaka]	No	10.	[tapaʔa]	Glottal	15.	[avdaʔa]	Glottal

| 16. [amaklat] | No | 18. [ʔagaʔmak] | Glottal | 20. [gataʔast] | Glottal |
| 17. [kakatak] | No | 19. [hadatahat] | No | 21. [fakalaʔata] | Glottal |

In the previous exercise, the glottal stops occurred mostly word-medial. It is easiest for English speakers to hear them in this position. In the next exercise, listen for any word-final glottal stops, disregarding any medial ones you may hear. Respond with "glottal" only if it occurs in the final position.

Exercise 7.13: Recognizing Glottal Stops

1. [maː]	No	6. [makala]	No	11. [maʔak]	No
2. [maʔ]	Glottal	7. [maʔaʔ]	Glottal	12. [takakapaʔ]	Glottal
3. [makaʔ]	Glottal	8. [tatamaʔ]	Glottal	13. [takaʔapa]	No
4. [maʔa]	No	9. [ʔaʔaka]	No	14. [lapatataʔ]	Glottal
5. [talaʔ]	Glottal	10. [dataʔa]	No	15. [kakatapaʔ]	Glottal

The next exercise involves glottal stops in the initial position. This is usually the hardest for English speakers to hear. Disregard all medial and final glottal stops, and tell whether glottal stops occur word-initial or not.

Exercise 7.14: Recognizing Glottal Stops

1. [ʔa]	Glottal	6. [ʔaːdaʔ]	Glottal	11. [ʔaʔ]	Glottal
2. [ʔata]	Glottal	7. [aɣdaʔ]	No	12. [alaʔat]	No
3. [aː]	No	8. [ataʔab]	No	13. [ʔakalataʔ]	Glottal
4. [ʔapata]	Glottal	9. [ʔaʔan]	Glottal	14. [akalataʔaʔ]	No
5. [aʔaʔak]	No	10. [ʔaʔanak]	Glottal	15. [ʔaʔapataʔ]	Glottal

Producing Glottal Stops

Once you can recognize glottal stops, it is not hard to produce them. Most English speakers will find it more difficult to remove glottal stops where they are not wanted than to insert them at will. The next exercise will help those who experience difficulty with the production of glottal stops. Repeat each utterance after the recording as it builds up from a single glottal in a normal English environment to a more unnatural sequence of glottal stops.

Exercise 7.15: Producing Glottal Stops

1. [ʔo]	[soʔ]	[ʔosoʔ]	[ʔoʔ]	[ʔoʔoʔ]
2. [ʔɑ]	[sɑʔ]	[ʔɑsɑʔ]	[ʔɑʔ]	[ʔɑʔɑʔ]
3. [ʔi]	[siʔ]	[ʔisiʔ]	[ʔiʔ]	[ʔiʔiʔ]
4. [ʔu]	[suʔ]	[ʔusuʔ]	[ʔuʔ]	[ʔuʔuʔ]
5. [ʔe]	[seʔ]	[ʔeseʔ]	[ʔeʔ]	[ʔeʔeʔ]

Eliminating Glottal Stops

In many languages, glottal stops make a difference in the meaning of words just the same as any other consonant. You must not only be able to insert them at will, but also to keep them from occurring in environments where they would naturally occur in your native speech. Pronouncing utterance-initial vowels without a glottal stop before them can be quite difficult for English speakers. To learn to say a clear vowel without a glottal stop, make a slight [h] just before the vowel. This opens the vocal cords and prevents them from forming the stop. In the next exercise, the first column is pronounced with a glottal stop before the vowel. The second column eliminates the stop by placing [h] before the vowel. In the third column, try to remove the glottal stop without actually saying [h] at the beginning. Repeat each sound after the recording until you can eliminate the glottal stop and the [h].

Exercise 7.16: Eliminating Glottal Stops

1. [ʔo]	[ho]	[oː]
2. [ʔɑ]	[hɑ]	[ɑː]
3. [ʔi]	[hi]	[iː]
4. [ʔu]	[hu]	[uː]
5. [ʔe]	[he]	[eː]

Whether or not the glottal stops differentiate meaning in the language you learn, being able to control their production will significantly improve your pronunciation. The following exercise gives you an example of glottal stops occurring in real language. Kamasau is a language spoken in the East Sepik province of Papua New Guinea. Notice how the glottal stops are used as a meaningful consonant just as [t] or [k]. Follow along in the text, and repeat each utterance after the recording. Each word will be spoken twice.

Exercise 7.17: Kamasau Glottal Stops

1. [ʔi]   ground   13. [hwɑʔ]   We eat.

2. [ˈʔiʔo]   crossways   14. [nɪˈsoʔ]   a little bit

3. [ˈʔounɑmpʰ]   to pull something   15. [nɪˈtʰuʔ]   the calf of the leg

4. [ˈtʰiʔɛ]   village   16. [ʔoruˈmɑi]   a type of frog

5. [ˈtʰuʔowəri]   It smells.   17. [ˈʔwɑʔ ʔwɑʔ]   Thank you.

6. [ˈkʰəʔo]   his/her parents   18. [ˈʔuʔubrɛʔu]   evil spirit

7. [ʔɑm]   my younger siblings   19. [ʔuboˈʔɑtʰ]   crawfish

8. [ˈkʰʌʔɑm]   his/her younger siblings   20. [ˈʔɛʔɛ]   yes

9. [ˈniʔu]   He closes something.   21. [ˈrɑʔɛ]   leaf

10. [ˈwɑpʰiʔu]   chicken   22. [ˈtʰuʔnɑmpʰ]   He blocks something.

11. [ˈkoruniʔu]   He mends a hole.   23. [tʰiʔ]   able

12. [ˈtʰɑʔgɑð]   We tie things.   24. [jɑʔ]   sago leaf

Table 7.2 lists symbols studied in this lesson with additional detail.

Table 7.2: Aspiration and Glottal Stop Summary

IPA Symbol	Name	Technical Name	English Example	APA Symbol
ʰ	Superscript H	Aspirated	Thom	ʰ
ʔ	Glottal Stop	Glottal Stop	uh-oh	ʔ

Lesson 8:
Advanced Intonation

Lesson Outline

In Lesson 3, the concept of intonation was introduced. Intonation involves the use of pitch on the sentence or phrase level. In other words, intonation is the word used to describe pitch that is spread over an entire phrase and does not affect the lexical meaning of individual words. Rather, intonation serves to affect the implied meaning of a sentence or phrase.

Producing Advanced Intonation Patterns

The concepts which govern the modulation of the voice to produce pitch, and subsequently intonation, have already been introduced. This lesson, therefore, will consist mainly of exercises designed to increase your control over the use of intonation in longer sequences of speech.

English is a language which uses an intonational pitch system. English intonations patterns can be very complex, and are used in every utterance by every speaker of the language. These intonational patterns can be used to separate a question from a statement, indicate the mood or intent of the speaker, or lend emphasis to a particular word within a phrase.

When learning a second language, one must learn not only to recognize his native intonation patterns, but learn to control his intonation to fit the pattern of the second language. The exercises in this lesson are designed to take normal English patterns and embellish them so that the speaker must consciously control his intonation to fit the new pattern.

The following exercises begin with simple three-syllable words build in length and complexity. Eventually you will be asked to read an entire story with the intonation of each phrase deliberately controlled. Follow the transcription of the following exercise, and repeat each utterance after the recording.

Exercise 8.1: Controlling Intonation

1. low mid high	5. low low mid	9. low high low
2. low high high	6. low mid low	10. low high mid
3. low high mid	7. low low high	11. low low low
4. low mid mid	8. low low low	12. low high low

13. low high high   14. low mid mid   15. low mid high

Repeat each set of words in the following exercise after the recording.

Exercise 8.2: Controlling Intonation

1. one two three   6. one two two   11. one two three

2. one two one   7. one three three   12. one two one

3. one one two   8. one three one   13. one three one

4. one one three   9. one three two   14. one two two

5. one one one   10. one one three   15. one one two

Repeat each set of words in the following exercise after the recording.

Exercise 8.3: Controlling Intonation

1. three one three   6. one two three   11. two two three

2. two two three   7. two one three   12. three three three

3. three three three   8. three two three   13. three one three

4. one three three   9. two three three   14. three two three

5. one one three   10. two one three   15. two one three

Repeat each of the words in the following exercise after the recording.

Exercise 8.4: Controlling Intonation

1. hakʰemu　　　　　　6. hakʰemu　　　　　　11. hakʰemu

2. hakʰemu　　　　　　7. hakʰemu　　　　　　12. hakʰemu

3. hakʰemu　　　　　　8. hakʰemu　　　　　　13. hakʰemu

4. hakʰemu　　　　　　9. hakʰemu　　　　　　14. hakʰemu

5. hakʰemu　　　　　　10. hakʰemu　　　　　15. hakʰemu

Repeat each sequence of words in the following exercise after the recording.

Exercise 8.5: Controlling Intonation

1. mid low high

2. high mid low high

3. mid high mid low high

4. low mid high mid low high

5. low low mid high mid low high

6. high low low mid high mid low high

7. high mid low mid mid mid high high

8. high low high high mid mid low high

9. mid high low mid high low mid mid

10. mid mid mid high high mid low low

Repeat each of the words in the following exercise after the recording.

Exercise 8.6: Controlling Intonation

1. a) Mansfield   b) Mansfield

2. a) very   b) very

3. a) women   b) women

4. a) husband   b) husband

5. a) he bought   b) he bought

6. a) habit   b) habit

7. a) her hat   b) her hat

8. a) agreed   b) agreed

9. a) I bought   b) I bought

10. a) he did   b) he did

11. a)ā hat   b)ā hat

12. a)t̄h̄e bird   b)t̄h̄e bird

13. a)regularly   b)regularly

14. a)today   b)today

15. a)animal   b)animal

16. a)suppose   b)suppose

Controlling Intonation Across Sentences

Read the following story repeating each sentence after the recording, then practice the story alone until you can produce the intonation patterns as they are written.

Exercise 8.7: Controlling Intonation

1. S̄āl̄ly M̄ān̄sfield, and her h̄ūsband, S̄ām Mansfield,

2. disagreed v̄ēry much about w̄ōmen's hats.

3. S̄ām Mansfield did not l̄īke the hats that S̄āl̄ly bought.

4. He w̄ās t̄ōo c̄ōurteous to his wife to t̄ēll her that he did not like

    them, however.

5. He ūsual̄ly did not say ānything.

6. One day, however, Sally bought a hat with a bird on it.

7. It was not a live bird, but it looked very real.

8. Sally was very happy about the hat with the bird on it.

9. "Have you heard what I bought today?" Sally asked Sam.

10. "You bought a hat I suppose," Sam said.

11. "Women are always buying hats.

12. It's a bad habit."

13. "I don't think you are very nice, Sam," Sally answered.

14. "And it's a very nice hat. It has a bird on it."

15. "Do you have to feed the bird regularly?" Sam asked,

16. but Sally didn't answer him.

17. "The last hat you bought," Sam continued, "had some flowers on it.

18. This hat has a bird on it.

19. The third hat is going to have an animal on it, I suppose.

20. Why don't you buy a hat with a cat on it, for example?"

21. Sally was angry.

22. She was sensitive when Sam talked about hats

23. He always tried to be funny.

24. "That idea is absurd," she said.

25. I have never heard of it before."

26. "I haven't either," said Sam, "but it's an original idea, anyway.

27. I'm going to write a poem about women's hats.

28. It's going to go like this:

29. A bird can sit upon a hat,

30. but a hat can't have a cat upon it.

31. To have a cat would be absurd,

32. but a hat can have a bird upon it.

33. I wonder if it's possible that

34. A bird can have a cat upon it?"

35. Sally went out of the room because her feelings were hurt.

36. She returned quickly and she was crying.

37. "Sam Sam" she said. "Our cat is trying to eat the bird on my hat.

38. The cat thought the bird was alive, and she jumped upon it.

39. What shall I do, Sam?"

40. Sam tried not to laugh, but he could hardly prevent himself.

41. "Where is the cat now," he asked.

42. "It is sitting on my hat in the chair in the living room

43. trying to eat the bird on my hat."

44. Sally began to cry more than before.

45. "I think you are terrible, Sam.

46. I think the cat really heard what you said about hats."

47. Sam did not say anything, but he tried to appear unhappy

48. about the cat, the hat, and the bird.

49. He knew he would laugh if he opened his mouth to say anything.

Repeat each sequence of words in the following exercise after the recording.

Exercise 8.8: Controlling Intonation

1. one three three

2. two one three three

3. two two one three three

4. one two two one three three

5. three one two two one three three

6. two three one two two one three three

7. three one two three one two two three

8. one one three two three three one three one

Repeat each sequence of words in the following exercise after the recording.

Exercise 8.9: Controlling Intonation

1. ha kʰe mu

2. tʰĩ ha kʰe mu

3. so tʰĩ ha kʰe mu

4. ʃe so tʰĩ ha kʰe mu

5. lu ʃe so tʰi ha kʰe mu

6. gi lu ʃe so tʰi ha kʰe mu

7. jo ge ni bu kʰu wa li pʰe

8. tʰu na ʒi ða bo Te hi me

Repeat each sequence of words in the following exercise after the recording.

Exercise 8.10: Controlling Intonation

1. rise fall rise
2. rise rise rise
3. fall rise fall
4. fall fall fall
5. fall rise rise

6. fall fall rise
7. rise fall fall
8. rise rise fall
9. rise fall rise
10. fall fall rise

11. fall rise fall
12. rise fall fall
13. rise fall rise
14. fall fall fall
15. fall rise rise

Repeat each sequence of words in the following exercise after the recording.

Exercise 8.11: Controlling Intonation

1. rise rise fall

2. rise rise fall rise

3. rise rise fall rise fall

4. rise rise fall rise fall fall

5. rise rise fall rise fall fall rise

6. rise rise fall rise fall fall rise rise

7. fall rise rise rise fall rise rise rise

8. rise fall fall fall fall rise rise fall

9. rise fall rise fall rise fall rise fall

10. fall fall rise rise rise fall rise rise

Repeat each sequence of words in the following exercise after the recording.

Exercise 8.12: Controlling Intonation

1. là rè pí

2. là rè pí tʰǫ

3. là rè pí tʰǫ gṵ

4. là rè pí tʰǫ gṵ mṵ

5. là rè pí tʰǫ gṵ mṵ tǿ

6. là rè pí tʰǫ gṵ mṵ tǿ ʃǐ

7. zè nè bí bù jø ɸø mè dɑ̀

8. pʰø θì lø nà tʰè sò xø gò

Repeat each sequence of words in the following exercise after the recording.

Exercise 8.13: Controlling Intonation

1. high high mid
2. rise low mid
3. low fall mid
4. mid rise mid
5. fall mid mid

6. fall high mid
7. mid mid mid
8. low low mid
9. high fall mid
10. rise rise mid

11. fall high mid
12. mid low mid
13. high mid mid
14. low fall mid
15. high rise mid

Repeat each sequence of words in the following exercise after the recording.

Exercise 8.14: Controlling Intonation

1. low fall mid
2. low fall mid mid
3. low fall mid mid rise
4. low fall mid mid rise high
5. low fall mid mid rise high high

6.   low fàll mid mid rise high high rise

7.   fàll fàll rise high mid low fàll fàll

8.   mid high fàll rise low mid high rise

Lesson 9: Affricates

Lesson Outline

Glossary

An **affricate** is a pair of sounds, a stop and a fricative, articulated together in a close sequence. The stop is released into the fricative with no other sounds occurring between them. Affricates can be found in nearly every language. Some view them as being one sound and others as two distinct sounds. The initial sounds in the words "church" and "judge" are two English examples of affricates. In this lesson, you will learn to identify affricates and to accurately describe and reproduce them.

Identifying Affricates

When a stop is formed, the air stream is completely blocked, causing pressure to build up behind the active articulator. There are three ways in which this pressure can be released. When a stop is released directly into a vowel, as in the utterances [bɑ] or [pɑ], we call the sound a stop. When a voiceless stop is released with a puff of air, as in the utterances [pʰɑ], [tʰɑ], or [kʰɑ], we call the sound an aspirated stop. It can also be released into a fricative, as in the sounds [pɸɑ], [tθɑ], or [kxɑ]. Such a sequence is called an affricate. In an affricate, there is no intermediate sound between the stop and the fricative. The stop and fricative in an affricate share the same voicing characteristic; they are either both voiced or both voiceless.

Types of Affricates

The most common type of affricate is **homorganic**. In these affricates the stop and fricative are both produced at the same or very nearly the same point of articulation (for example, [ts]). In homorganic affricates, the stop is released slowly so that as the articulator moves away from the point of articulation, a fricative is produced at that same point of articulation.

The technical names for homorganic affricates specify the point of articulation of the fricative release, rather than that of the stop. For example, the affricate [t͡ʃ] is described as a voiceless, alveopalatal affricate even though the stop is alveolar. Often, the articulation of the preceding stop in such affricates is even modified to coincide more with the point of articulation of the fricative. Most English speakers actually pronounce the affricates [t͡ʃ] and [d͡ʒ] with an alveopalatal "t" and "d." For this reason, the most accurate way to describe these homorganic affricates is by the fricative's point of articulation.

Affricates in which the stop and fricative do not share the same point of articulation are called **heterorganic** (for example, [p͡x]). In heterorganic affricates, the fricative is formed with its own articulator at the same time or before the release of the stop. When the stop is released, the fricative is heard.

For heterorganic affricates, the description should include the point of articulation of both the stop and the fricative. For example, the affricate [p͡x] is described as a voiceless, bilabial stop followed by a voiceless, back-velar fricative or a voiceless, labial-velar affricate.

Symbols for Affricates

For most phonetic transcription purposes, the symbols for the stop and fricative alone are sufficient to represent affricates since a stop and fricative in the same syllable must be an affricate. However, it can be helpful to clearly indicate affricates with special symbols. Usually, a **Tie Bar** [͡] above two symbols is used (for example, [t͡ʃ]). If one or more of the symbols has an ascender, it is recommended to place the tie bar below the symbols (for example, [t͜s]). Another method of representing affricates is to superscript the fricative (for example, [tˢ]). Finally, an affricate can be represented by combining the two symbols together into a single symbol called a **ligature** (for example, [ʧ]). Table 9.1 demonstrates these different methods used by linguists to represent affricates. In this book, a tie bar is used to represent affricates when affricates are the focus of the chapter. However, in generic linguistic material, no special symbols are necessary to represent affricates.

Table 9.1: Affricate Symbolization Methods

Normal	Tie Bar Above	Tie Bar Below	Superscript	Ligature
ts	t͡s	t͜s	tˢ	ʦ

An affricate may function either as a single phonological unit or as two separate units. In English, for example, the [d͡ʒ] affricate is usually considered to be one sound and can be represented by a single letter, the letter "j," as in the word "jeep." The [t͡s] affricate, on the other hand, is heard as two separate sounds and represented by two letters, as in the word "cats." This distinction must be determined by a phonemic analysis, which is beyond the scope of this book. Phonetically, they are both affricates, but the fricative release may tend to be shorter on those affricates which function as a single unit. This difference in the length of the fricative release can be illustrated by comparing the [d͡ʒ] affricate in the word "sledge" with the [d͡z] affricate in the word "sleds."

English contains numerous affricates; however, only two different affricates occur word initial: /t͡ʃ/ and /d͡ʒ/. The following word final affricates frequently occur in English. Follow the text through the exercise paying close attention to the word final stop/fricative combinations. The phonetic transcriptions will vary considerably from the English writing.

Exercise 9.1: Recognizing English Affricates

1. [ʃɪp͡s] ships

2. [snup͡s] snoops

3. [sɑb̂z]   sobs   10. [kʰlʌks̄]   clucks

4. [sʌb̂z]   subs   11. [bɛĝz]   begs

5. [ɹæt͡s]   rats   12. [dɹʌĝz]   drugs

6. [beⁱt͡s]   baits   13. [ʔaᵘt͡ʃ]   ouch

7. [ʔæd͡z]   adze   14. [pʰæt͡ʃ]   patch

8. [bleⁱd͡z]   blades   15. [hɛd͡ʒ]   hedge

9. [pʰɪks̄]   picks   16. [fʌd͡ʒ]   fudge

The next exercise gives several common English words with initial affricates. Follow along in the text.

Exercise 9.2: Recognizing Initial English Affricates

1. [t͡ʃʰuz]   choose   5. [t͡ʃʰʌŋk]   chunk

2. [d͡ʒus]   juice   6. [d͡ʒʌŋk]   junk

3. [t͡ʃʰiˈ]   cheer   7. [t͡ʃʰɚt͡ʃ]   church

4. [d͡ʒiˈ]   jeer   8. [d͡ʒʌd͡ʒ]   judge

There are many other affricates in addition to those used in English. Tables 9.2 and 9.3 list some of the affricates found in languages throughout the world. These charts are by no means exhaustive. Remember that *any* stop and fricative can be combined to make an affricate as long as they share the same voicing characteristics and are in the same syllable.

Table 9.2: Common Homorganic Affricates

	Bilabial	Labiodental	Dental	Alveolar	Alveopalatal	Velar
Voiceless Aspirated	p͡ɸʰ	p͡fʰ	t͡θʰ	t͡sʰ	t͡ʃʰ	k͡xʰ
Voiceless	p͡ɸ	p͡f	t͡θ	t͡s	t͡ʃ	k͡x
Voiced	b͡β	b͡v	d͡ð	d͡z	d͡ʒ	ɡ͡ɣ

Table 9.3: Common Heterorganic Affricates

		Bilabial	Labiodental	Tip-Dental	Tip-Alveolar	Blade-Alveopalatal	Back-Velar
Voiceless Aspirated	Bilabial		p͡fʰ	p͡θʰ	p͡sʰ	p͡ʃʰ	p͡xʰ
	Alveolar	t͡ɸʰ	t͡fʰ				t͡xʰ
	Velar	k͡ɸʰ	k͡fʰ	k͡θʰ	k͡sʰ	k͡ʃʰ	
Voiceless	Bilabial		p͡f	p͡θ	p͡s	p͡ʃ	p͡x
	Alveolar	t͡ɸ	t͡f				t͡x
	Velar	k͡ɸ	k͡f	k͡θ	k͡s	k͡ʃ	
Voiced	Bilabial		b͡v	b͡ð	b͡z	b͡ʒ	b͡ɣ
	Alveolar	d͡β	d͡v				d͡ɣ
	Velar	g͡β	g͡v	g͡ð	g͡z	g͡ʒ	

In some affricates, the sound of the stop is not as prominent as the fricative release, making it difficult to tell whether the sound is an affricate or simply a fricative. The following exercise contains both affricates and fricatives in the initial, medial, and final positions. Respond after each utterance by telling whether the sound is an affricate or a fricative.

Exercise 9.3: Recognizing Affricates

1. [t͡sɑ] Affricate
2. [xɑ] Fricative
3. [p͡sɑ] Affricate
4. [t͡ʃʰɑ] Affricate
5. [d͡zɑ] Affricate
6. [ʒɑ] Fricative
7. [βɑ] Fricative
8. [k͡sɑ] Affricate
9. [k͡zɑ] Affricate
10. [ɑvɑ] Fricative
11. [ɑb͡vɑ] Affricate
12. [ɑɣɑ] Fricative
13. [ɑd͡ʒɑ] Affricate
14. [ɑp͡ɸɑ] Affricate
15. [ɑd͡ðɑ] Affricate
16. [ɑzɑ] Fricative
17. [ɑðɑ] Fricative
18. [ɑt͡ʃʰɑ] Affricate
19. [ɑd͡ð] Affricate
20. [ɑɸ] Fricative
21. [ɑk͡x] Affricate

22. [aʃ]   Fricative   24. [aβ]   Fricative   26. [ag͡ɣ]   Affricate

23. [ag͡z]   Affricate   25. [aɣ]   Fricative   27. [ad͡ʒ]   Affricate

The following exercise contains only affricates. Respond with "voiced" or "voiceless."

Exercise 9.4: Recognizing Voiced and Voiceless Affricates

1. [ak͡xa]   Voiceless   6. [ad͡ʒ]   Voiced   11. [at͡θ]   Voiceless

2. [ab͡va]   Voiced   7. [ad͡ða]   Voiced   12. [ak͡ɸa]   Voiceless

3. [ag͡ɣa]   Voiced   8. [p͡sa]   Voiceless   13. [t͡ʃa]   Voiceless

4. [t͡ʃʰa]   Voiceless   9. [p͡ɸa]   Voiceless   14. [ad͡za]   Voiced

5. [t͡sʰa]   Voiceless   10. [ab͡v]   Voiced   15. [at͡sa]   Voiceless

Aspirated Affricates

Like voiceless stops, voiceless affricates can be released with aspiration. Try saying the word "church," transcribed [t͡ʃʰɚt͡ʃ], while holding a piece of paper in front of your lips. You will notice that the first affricate is aspirated while the second is unaspirated. You may find this distinction difficult to hear at first because the fricative disguises the aspiration. Remember that you are not simply listening for an aspirated stop. It is important to note that the aspiration does not occur between the stop and the fricative, but after the affricate as a whole. Any affricate can be aspirated, but the most common aspirated affricates are alveolar and alveopalatal affricates. The following exercise demonstrates aspirated and unaspirated affricates in English words. Repeat each word after the recording while watching for aspiration with a slip of paper held in front of your lips.

Exercise 9.5: Recognizing Aspirated Affricates

1. [t͡ʃʰ]   **ch**ange   5. [t͡sʰ]   ca**ts h**ere

2. [t͡ʃ]   ex**ch**ange   6. [t͡s]   ca**t's** ear

3. [t͡ʃʰ]   **ch**urn   7. [k͡sʰ]   Ma**c's h**ouse

4. [t͡ʃ]   pas**t**ure   8. [k͡s]   Ma**x**well

The following exercise includes only alveolar and alveopalatal affricates. Respond with "aspirated" or "unaspirated."

Exercise 9.6: Recognizing Aspirated Affricates

1. [at͡ʃʰa]   Aspirated
2. [at͡sʰa]   Aspirated
3. [at͡sa]   Unaspirated
4. [at͡ʃʰa]   Aspirated
5. [at͡ʃa]   Unaspirated
6. [at͡sʰa]   Aspirated

7. [at͡ʃa]   Unaspirated
8. [at͡sa]   Unaspirated
9. [at͡sʰa]   Aspirated
10. [at͡sa]   Unaspirated
11. [at͡ʃʰa]   Aspirated
12. [at͡ʃa]   Unaspirated

13. [at͡ʃa]   Unaspirated
14. [at͡ʃʰa]   Aspirated
15. [at͡sʰa]   Aspirated
16. [at͡ʃa]   Unaspirated
17. [at͡ʃʰa]   Aspirated
18. [at͡sa]   Unaspirated

Practicing Affricates

Now that you are somewhat familiar with affricates, it is important that you be able to identify and reproduce them. Listen to the following recordings, and give the full description of the affricates listed. Remember that the description for homorganic affricates specifies the point of articulation for the fricative release rather than the stop. For heterorganic affricates, the description should include the point of articulation of both the stop and fricative. You may need to practice several times before you are able to give correct answers consistently.

Exercise 9.7: Recognizing Affricates

1. [at͡sʰa]   Vl. Tip-alveolar Affricate
2. [at͡ʃa]   Vl. Tip-alveopalatal Affricate
3. [ak͡xa]   Vl. Back-velar Affricate
4. [ad͡za]   Vd. Tip-alveolar Affricate
5. [at͡θa]   Vl. Tip-dental Affricate
6. [d͡ʒa]   Vd. Tip-alveopalatal Affricate
7. [t͡ʃʰa]   Vl. Tip-alveopalatal Affricate
8. [ap͡ɸa]   Vl. Bilabial Affricate
9. [ag͡ɣa]   Vd. Back-velar Affricate
10. [at͡ʃʰ]   Vl. Tip-alveopalatal Affricate

11. [t͡sa]   Vl. Tip-alveolar Affricate
12. [ad͡ʒ]   Vd. Tip-alveopalatal Affricate
13. [ad͡ða]   Vd. Tip-dental Affricate
14. [b͡βa]   Vd. Bilabial Affricate
15. [ap͡ɸa]   Vl. Bilabial Affricate
16. [k͡xa]   Vl. Back-velar Affricate
17. [ad͡ʒ]   Vd. Tip-alveopalatal Affricate
18. [ad͡ða]   Vd. Tip-dental Affricate
19. [ag͡ɣa]   Vd. Back-velar Affricate
20. [ak͡x]   Vl. Back-velar Affricate

21. [ab͡βɑ]   Vd. Bilabial Affricate   23. [k͡xɑ]   Vl. Back-velar Affricate

22. [at͡ʃ]   Vl. Tip-alveopalatal Affricate   24. [at͡θɑ]   Vl. Tip-dental Affricate

If two consonants occur together in a sequence with no intervening vowels, we call them a **consonant cluster** (CC). Affricates are a type of consonant cluster. However, not all consonant clusters of a stop and a fricative in series are affricates. In some consonant clusters of a stop and a fricative, the stop is released slightly before the fricative actually begins. In some cases, a small amount of aspiration occurs at the transition between the stop and the fricative. These consonant clusters cannot be classified as affricates since in affricates the stop must be released into the fricative with no intervening sounds. In producing affricates, you must make sure that no unwanted transitional sounds occur between the stop and the fricative. The following exercises will help you produce affricates which often give English speakers trouble. Mimic each utterance after the recording, and practice until you can produce the affricates smoothly and easily.

Exercise 9.8: Producing Strongly Aspirated Affricates

1. a) [hɑ]   2. a) [hɑ]   3. a) [hɑ]   4. a) [hɑ]

    b) [pʰɑ]   b) [tʰɑ]   b) [tʰɑ]   b) [kʰɑ]

    c) [p͡sʰɑ]   c) [t͡sʰɑ]   c) [t͡ʃʰɑ]   c) [k͡xʰɑ]

Mimic the sounds in the following exercise.

Exercise 9.9: Producing Unaspirated Affricates

1. a) [ʔɑ]   2. a) [ʔɑ]   3. a) [ʔɑ]   4. a) [ʔɑ]

    b) [pɑ]   b) [tɑ]   b) [tɑ]   b) [kɑ]

    c) [p͡sɑ]   c) [t͡sɑ]   c) [t͡ʃɑ]   c) [k͡xɑ]

As with stops, voiceless affricates can often sound like voiced affricates when they are unaspirated. Exercise 9.10 contrasts voiceless aspirated, unaspirated, and voiced affricates in English words. The unaspirated affricates do not fit English structure, so they will sound foreign. Listen to the exercise twice. The first time just listen; the second time, mimic the recording.

Exercise 9.10: Recognizing Voiceless Aspirated, Unaspirated, and Voiced Affricates

1. [t͡ʃʰ] cheer   [t͡ʃ] cheer   [d͡ʒ] jeer
2. [t͡ʃʰ] chip   [t͡ʃ] chip   [d͡ʒ] jip
3. [t͡ʃʰ] cheap   [t͡ʃ] cheap   [d͡ʒ] jeep
4. [t͡ʃʰ] chunk   [t͡ʃ] chunk   [d͡ʒ] junk
5. [t͡ʃʰ] chew   [t͡ʃ] chew   [d͡ʒ] Jew

Velar affricates can be a particular challenge for English speakers since there are no occurrences of velar fricatives in standard English speech. Listen carefully to the following buildup exercise, and mimic each utterance after the recording.

Exercise 9.11: Producing Velar Affricates

1. a) [kɑ]
   b) [xɑ]
   c) [kɑxɑkɑxɑ]
   d) [k͡xɑk͡xɑk͡xɑk͡xɑ]

2. a) [gɑ]
   b) [ɣɑ]
   c) [gɑɣɑgɑɣɑ]
   d) [g͡ɣɑg͡ɣɑg͡ɣɑg͡ɣɑ]

Practice the affricates in the next exercise until you can produce them smoothly. This exercise will include both homorganic and heterorganic affricates.

Exercise 9.12: Producing Affricates

1. [ɑt͡sʰɑ]
2. [ɑp͡θɑ]
3. [ɑb͡zɑ]
4. [d͡ʒɑ]
5. [ɑk͡xɑ]
6. [g͡ðɑ]
7. [ɑb͡vɑ]
8. [t͡sʰɑ]
9. [ɑk͡x]
10. [p͡xɑ]
11. [ɑt͡θɑ]
12. [ɑp͡fɑ]
13. [g͡zɑ]
14. [ɑb͡z]
15. [ɑg͡ɣɑ]
16. [t͡θɑ]
17. [ɑk͡ɸɑ]
18. [ɑb͡v]
19. [ɑp͡θɑ]
20. [ɑt͡sʰ]
21. [p͡ɸɑ]

22. [ag͡βa]   23. [ag͡z]   24. [ak͡θa]

Mimic the sounds in the following exercise.

Exercise 9.13: Producing Sequences of Affricates

1. [t͡ʃʰa t͡sa]   5. [t͡ʃʰa t͡sa d͡za p͡θa]

2. [k͡sa p͡sa d͡ða]   6. [t͡ʃa b͡βa d͡ʒa t͡sʰa f͡fa]

3. [t͡ʃʰa t͡sa d͡za]   7. [t͡ʃʰa t͡sa d͡za p͡θa g͡za]

4. [g͡ɣa t͡θa t͡sa b͡va]   8. [d͡ða k͡θa g͡za t͡ʃa]

Lesson 10: Introduction to Vowels

Lesson Outline

Glossary

So far we have learned to study consonants by examining their points of articulation, their articulators, and the types of interactivity between the two (manners of articulation). However, we cannot apply this same method to the study of vowels. The articulation of vowels is much less definable than that of consonants. Vowels do not really have any definite point of articulation. Although the tongue is always involved, the main difference between the articulation of vowels and consonants is that vowels are produced with relatively free air flow, with no restriction in the oral cavity or throat. Vowels, therefore, have a more open articulation than consonants. The articulators do not come near enough to the points of articulation to create any impedance.

The Articulation of Vowels

The articulation of different vowel sounds is accomplished primarily by changing the size and shape of the oral and pharyngeal cavities. This is a result of altering the position of the tongue, lips, and velic. Vowels will change in sound, or quality, as the tongue is placed toward the front or the back of the oral cavity. They also change according to the height of the tongue in relation to the roof of the mouth (palate) and the position of the lips. We describe vowels, therefore, by areas of articulation. The position of the tongue determines the area of articulation.

Position

Illustrations 10.1–10.3 show how the placement of the tongue from front to back affects vowel qualities. This is called **vowel position**. The three positions with which vowels are categorized are **front**, **central**, and **back**. The vowel shown in Illustration 10.1, symbolized by [ɛ], corresponds to the vowel sound in the English words "bet" and "pet." In this vowel the highest part of the tongue is more toward the front of the mouth, and so the sound is described as a front vowel.

Illustration 10.2 pictures the position of the tongue for a central vowel. The vowel depicted corresponds with the vowel that you hear when the words "put" and "took" are spoken rapidly. In Illustration 10.3, the vowel [o] corresponds with the vowel sound in the words "soak" and "boat." The highest part of the tongue is toward the back of the oral cavity, therefore the sound is described as a back vowel. Try saying the sequence [oɛoɛoɛoɛoɛoɛoɛ] without any breaks between the vowels and notice your tongue as it transitions from front to back. The position of the tongue is not the only phonetic difference between [ɛ] and [o]. You may also notice a difference in the shape of your lips. This is known as lip rounding and will be discussed later in this chapter.

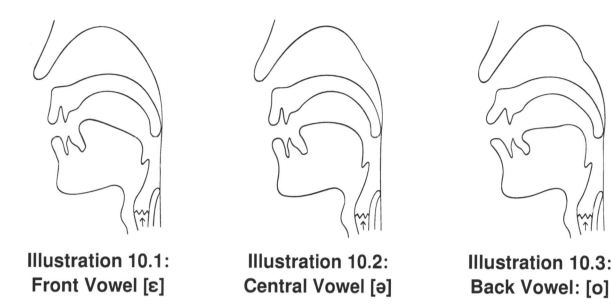

**Illustration 10.1:
Front Vowel [ɛ]**

**Illustration 10.2:
Central Vowel [ə]**

**Illustration 10.3:
Back Vowel: [o]**

Height

Vowels are also described according to the relative **height** of the tongue as they are articulated. The seven vowel height positions from closest to the roof of the mouth to the most open position are **close**, **near-close**, **close-mid**, **mid**, **open-mid**, **near-open**, and **open**. Illustration 10.4 pictures four of these positions. As the mouth opens, the tongue is drawn away from the roof of the mouth. This creates a wider opening in which the vowel sound resonates. As the mouth closes, the tongue moves closer to the palate. This narrows the opening in the oral cavity. Illustration 10.4 shows how the height of the tongue can change the quality of vowels.

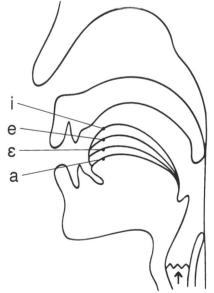

Illustration 10.4: Vowel Height

The vowel sound produced when the tongue is at its highest and front-most position is transcribed as [i]. This vowel is described as a close vowel since the tongue is close to the palate. Its sound corresponds to the vowel sound in the words "bee" and "seat." Vowels produced when the tongue is farthest from the palate are described as open vowels. Say the sequence [iɛiɛiɛiɛiɛiɛiɛiɛ] and try to feel the difference in the height of your tongue between these two vowels.

Rounding

The **rounding**, or shape, of the lips also affects vowel qualities. With some vowels the lips have a rounded shape, while with others they are more or less straight. Watch your lips in a mirror while saying the words "bee" and "boo." Notice that with the word "boo" the lips have a very distinctive rounded shape. Vowels articulated with rounded lips are called **rounded** vowels. On the other hand, the vowel in the word "bee" is described as **unrounded** because the lips remain relatively flat, or straight. In normal English, back vowels are always rounded while the mid and front vowels are unrounded. However, it is possible for any vowel on the chart to be either rounded or unrounded.

Vowel sounds can be charted according to the positions that we have described, which include vowel height, position from front to back, and lip rounding. Illustration 10.5 is the official IPA vowel chart system which plots the position of vowel sounds. The vowel chart corresponds roughly with the position of the vowels in the oral cavity.

Illustration 10.5: Official IPA Vowel Chart

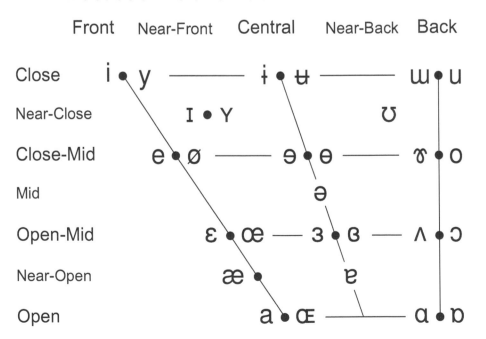

This vowel chart above does not necessarily represent an exact diagram of the vowel system of any particular language. The vowel qualities on the chart are theoretical. It is merely a reference system to which we can compare the vowel sounds of any given language. This provides phoneticians a basic framework with which they can chart the position of any vowel quality.

Additional positions on the chart will be filled in with vowel symbols as our study progresses. The possibilities of vowel qualities are not limited, however, to the symbols on the chart. In fact, there are hundreds of vowel possibilities that may occur anywhere between the ones charted, and some linguists even argue that it is impossible to make two vowel sounds that are exactly alike twice in a row.

Defining Vowels

To clearly define the term "vowel," it is necessary to discuss the classification of sounds in terms of resonance and how the air stream is directed through the mouth. The degree to which a sound resonates is called sonority. Sounds produced with greater restriction to the air stream resonate less and are thus less **sonorant**. Stops and fricatives are classified as **non-sonorant** due to the heavy impedance of the air stream. Sounds produced with relatively free air flow, on the other hand, are more sonorant. Vowels, nasals, laterals, and approximants are classified as sonorants.

Sonorants can be classified as nasal or oral depending on whether the air stream exits the nose or the mouth. Vowels are oral sonorants since the air stream passes through the oral cavity. There are also two types of oral sonorants: lateral and central. For **lateral oral sonorants**, the air stream is directed around the sides of the tongue. This occurs in sounds like L [l]. Vowels are classified as **central oral sonorants** since the air stream passes over the center of the tongue.

The Function of Vowels

Another way in which vowels differ from other phonetic segments is in how they function within syllables. Each syllable contains a nucleus made up of one sound that is more resonant or prominent than the surrounding sounds. The **nucleus**, called the syllabic, carries the main beat of the syllable.

Vowels typically form the syllable nucleus, while consonants normally function as peripheral elements surrounding the vowel. It is important to note, though, that some syllables do not contain a vowel, in which case the most sonorant consonant present functions as the syllabic. Other syllables may contain more than one vowel. In these cases, only one vowel will be **syllabic**, while the other functions more like a consonant. These conditions will be described in detail later in the course.

The Basic Vowel Symbols

Most of the vowels represented in the basic vowel chart correspond roughly with some English word in one dialect or another. In the following list, each vowel's sound is illustrated by English words that match its sound as closely as possible. This list is not intended to become the standard by which these vowel sounds are measured, as the pronunciation of the words will vary depending on the speaker, and some of the illustrations are only approximate to begin with. Also keep in mind that all of the vowels represented here are pure vowels, and English speakers tend to glide the vowels in many of the example words.[1] You should check your pronunciation of the vowels with a qualified person instead of relying on your understanding of the illustrations given.

Table 10.1: English Pure Vowels

Symbol	Name	English Examples
[i]	I	"**ea**t," "b**ea**t," "**e**lite"
[ɪ]	Small Capital I	"**i**t," "l**i**p," "l**i**sten"
[e][2]	E	"**ei**ght," "b**ai**t," "**a**ble"
[ɛ]	Epsilon	"**e**nd," "p**e**t," "**e**dible"
[æ][3]	Ash	"**a**nt," "b**a**t," "**a**pple"
[a][4]	Lowercase A	"**ou**t," "h**ow**," "h**ou**ses"
[ɨ][5]	Barred I	"ros**e**s," "**a**ttic," "**E**nglish"

---

1   Pure vowels are those without glides. For example, the "I" sound in the word "hi" is not a pure vowel because it glides from [ɑ] to [i].

2   Most English speakers often produce [e] with a strong off-glide to [i]. This habit must be overcome in order to produce the pure vowel.

3   English speakers normally add a [ə] off-glide after [æ].

4   The [a] only occurs as a diphthong with a [u] off-glide in normal American English. Some southern U.S. dialects also use [a] in words like "hi," "I," and "pie."

5   The [ɨ] is difficult for English speakers to distinguish from other vowels such as [ɪ]. The [ɨ] occurs in

Symbol	Name	English Examples
[ə][6]	Schwa	"ahead," "degree," "supply"
[u]	U	"boot," "flute," "doable"
[ʊ]	Upsilon	"put," "book," "looking"
[o][7]	O	"own," "boat," "over"
[ʌ]	Turned V	"up," "mud," "under"
[ɔ][8]	Open O	"awl," "saw," "office"
[ɑ]	Script A	"ox," "mom," "father"
[ɒ][9]	Turned Script A	"doll," "Paul," "calling"

Symbolizing Open Vowels

Linguists often use the Lowercase A [a] to represent the Script A [ɑ] for convenience's sake. This should be kept in mind when reading other linguistic material. Also, the Greek letter alpha [α] is occasionally used to instead of Script A [ɑ] because it looks quite similar.

If you examine Illustration 10.5 above, you will notice that there is no symbol in the open central position. The open central unrounded vowel is actually quite common in languages, but no separate symbol is given because linguists use the Script A [ɑ] for both the open central and open back positions. The reason why one symbol is used to represent two vowel positions is because they are not found contrastively in any language. For simplicity, this book will always use the [ɑ] to indicate an open back unrounded vowel.

---

unstressed syllables in normal speech.

6   The [ə] is perhaps the most common vowel in English, but it is difficult for English speakers to distinguish from other vowels, especially [ʌ]. The [ə] occurs in unstressed syllables in American English.

7   The [o] almost always occurs as a diphthong in English with a [u] off-glide. In contrast, Spanish normally has a pure [o].

8   English speakers fluctuate between [ɔ], [ɒ], and (less often) [ɑ].

9   English speakers fluctuate between [ɒ], [ɔ], and (less often) [ɑ].

Lesson 11:
Characteristics of Syllables

Lesson Outline

Glossary Terms

A **syllable** is a sound, or grouping of sounds, that is an uninterrupted unit and carries its own beat. We use syllables as units of organization for sequences of sounds. Every sequence of sounds has a certain rhythm, or beat, associated with it. When this rhythm is divided into its individual beats, the groups of sounds which constitute each beat are called syllables. For example, the word "baby" is composed of two syllables, or beats. The first syllable is formed by the sounds "ba," and the second includes the last two sounds "by." You may clap your hands or tap with your finger to the rhythm of the word to help you determine the number of syllables. Syllables, therefore, are the basis of rhythm and are the phonological building blocks of words.

The division of syllables is marked in this lesson (and in following lessons when necessary) by a **Period** [.], also called a Full Stop. The process of separating words into syllables is called **syllabification**. In the following exercise, use your finger to tap out the rhythm of the following words. Count the number of syllables, and see if your count agrees with the count indicated.

Exercise 11.1: Recognizing Syllable Divisions

1.	[ʔɑ]	1 beat
2.	[ʔɑ.pʰɑ]	2 beats
3.	[ʔɑ.pʰɑ.tʰɑ]	3 beats
4.	[ʔɑ.pʰɑ.tʰɑ.sɑ]	4 beats
5.	[ʔɑ.pʰɑ.tʰɑ.sɑ.lɑ]	5 beats

A syllable may be composed of a variety of sound patterns, or consonant-vowel arrangements. The syllables in exercise 11.1 have a consonant-vowel (or CV) pattern. Exercise 11.2 illustrates several other consonant vowel patterns. Each utterance contains three syllables of the same pattern. Tap out the rhythm of the utterances as you say them, and pay close attention to the consonant-vowel patterns of each syllable.

Exercise 11.2: Syllable Structures

1.	[pʰad.saf.tʰak]	CVC	4.	[tsɑ.glɑ.tsɑ]	CCV
2.	[stam.kʰlad.zbaf]	CCVC	5.	[ɑ.e.i]	V
3.	[mats.laft.dapf]	CVCC	6.	[at.ap.al]	VC

Syllabics

During a sequence of spoken syllables, the articulators are continually transitioning between open and closed positions. Consider the single-syllable word "bat." At the onset of this syllable, the lips are in a closed position for the [b]. This closed position reduces the amount of resonance that can be heard. The audible resonance increases as the articulator opens during the vowel, and then decreases as the articulator closes to form the [t]. The "a" sound therefore is the most prominent sound, or the acoustically resonant peak of the syllable; in other words, it is the nucleus of the syllable.

The nucleus of a syllable is called the **syllabic**. All syllables contain a syllabic and may even consist of a single syllabic sound. The most common syllabic sounds are vowels. Since vowels have a more open position than consonants, they typically occupy the resonant peak of the syllable. Not all syllabics are vowels, however. Some consonants can also be syllabic. Because consonants are not normally syllabic, a diacritic is used to indicate the syllabic quality. A short vertical line is placed either underneath [n̩] or above [ŋ̍] syllabic consonants.

The most common syllabic consonants are voiced sonorants. A **sonorant** is a phone that is produced without a significant restriction to the air stream. The relatively free air flow allows the sound to resonate more strongly than restricted sounds do. Lateral approximants (where the air comes unimpeded around the sides of the tongue), nasals (where the air comes unimpeded through the nose), flaps, and trills are all classified as sonorant because they resonate more strongly due to their lesser degree of restriction. Vowels are classified as central oral sonorants because the air comes unimpeded through the center of the oral cavity. Sonorants contrast with **obstruents**, which involve audible turbulence by obstructing or restricting the air flow. Stops and fricatives are examples of obstruents.

Syllabic consonants are usually similar to vowels in duration, and they can also carry tone. We indicate that a consonant is syllabic by placing a small vertical line, or syllabicity mark (also called a syllabic indicator), beneath the consonant symbol [m̩]. Any unmarked consonant is assumed to be non-syllabic. It is never necessary to use a syllabicity mark beneath a vowel because any time a syllable contains a vowel, the vowel is syllabic. Any unmarked vowel is assumed to be syllabic.

In order to be syllabic, a sound must also be a **continuant**. This is a sound that is produced with incomplete closure of the speech apparatus and can therefore be lengthened, or prolonged, while maintaining its original quality. It is unlikely that stops would be syllabic, since they cannot be significantly prolonged. Fricatives may be syllabic, although they occur much less frequently than sonorants.

The following exercise gives several examples of syllabic consonants in English. Follow along in the text and mimic each word. Each utterance will be given twice.

Exercise 11.3: Recognizing Syllabic Consonants

1. [ˈsmɪ.ʔn̩]   smitten
2. [ˈkʰɑ.ʔn̩]   cotton
3. [ˈbɑ.tl̩]   bottle
4. [ˈæm.pl̩]   ample
5. [ˈkʰɑɹɚ.ʔn̩]   carton
6. [ˈkʰɚ.ʔn̩]   curtain
7. [n̩ˈlɛs]   unless

8. [m̩ˈpʰoᵘz]   impose
9. [ˈtʰɚ.tl̩]   turtle
10. [m̩ˈpʰɑ.sə.bl̩]   impossible
11. [m̩ˈpʰɚt.n̩.ɪnt] impertinent
12. [m̩m̩m̩]   mhm
13. [aⁱ.kn̩ˈsi]   I can see
14. [hi.n̩ˈaⁱ]   he 'n' I

Now identify the syllabic consonants in the following exercise. Remember that if a vowel is present in a syllable, the vowel is the syllabic. Do not watch the text. Respond with "syllabic" if the utterance contains a syllabic consonant and "non-syllabic" if it does not.

Exercise 11.4: Recognizing (Non-)Syllabic Consonants

1. [pɑm]   Non-syllabic
2. [pʰm̩]   Syllabic
3. [sn̩]   Syllabic
4. [sɑn]   Non-syllabic
5. [dɑl]   Non-syllabic
6. [dl̩]   Syllabic

7. [kʰm̩]   Syllabic
8. [m̩]   Syllabic
9. [ɑŋk]   Non-syllabic
10. [spl̩]   Syllabic
11. [spɑn]   Non-syllabic
12. [ɑlt]   Non-syllabic

13. [n̩.tɑt]   Syllabic
14. [ɑ.tn̩t]   Syllabic
15. [ɑ.tɑnt] Non-syllabic
16. [ɑ.n̩.tɑt] Syllabic
17. [ɑn.tɑt] Non-syllabic
18. [mɑ.tʰl̩] Syllabic

In the following exercise, each utterance will be spoken twice. Practice them until you can repeat them smoothly. Be careful not to insert any unwanted vowels.

Exercise 11.5: Reproducing Syllabic Consonants

1. [kl̩ km̩ kn̩ kʃ ks̩ kʃ kx kɹ]
2. [ʔɑ lɑ tʰɹ vɑ tʰl̩ dɑ pʰn̩ ɑ]
3. [l̩ m̩ pʰn̩ stɹ bl̩ dʐ]
4. [xɑ lɑ ɣ ts̩ pʐ kɑ tm̩]
5. [ps̩tʰ pftʰ pʃtʰ pɣtʰ pl̩tʰ pɹtʰ pɣtʰ pn̩tʰ]
6. [tʰl̩ bɹ dɑ z mn̩ kl̩ ŋ̩]

7. [ɑ ʃʐ nm̩ l̩ ad kʰɹ̩ tʰm̩ tʰŋ pʰl̩]   8. [dɑ ml̩ mn̩ stʐ dɣ kʰŋ̍ stʃ pʰx]

Syllable Boundaries

As you learn to identify syllabics, the **syllable boundaries** will also become easier to identify. Sometimes, however, a syllabic belongs as much phonetically to one syllable as to the other. In such cases it may not be possible to determine the exact syllable boundary. (By this we mean phonetic syllable boundaries, and not those boundaries which conform to English grammar rules.) Consider the word "honey" [hʌni]. When diagrammed with a wave form representing the syllable beats, we see that the [n] occurs precisely at the boundary between the two syllables. In this case it is easy to tell which sounds are syllabic, but the syllable boundary is not distinct. The [n] is shared by both syllables. English has many such cases where a consonant belongs to two syllables, but there are other languages in which this phenomenon does not occur at all.

Illustration 11.1: Syllable Peaks and Boundaries

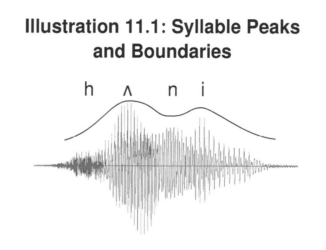

h   ʌ   n   i

Stress

In utterances consisting of multiple syllables, one syllable will usually carry a greater degree of emphasis or prominence than the surrounding syllables. This phenomenon is due to several physiological factors. The muscles of the rib cage, the laryngeal muscles, and in some cases the muscles of the articulatory organs themselves operate with somewhat more force, and/or a broader range of motion than usual. This produces a syllable that stands out from other syllables of the utterance. This prominence which distinguishes one syllable from adjacent syllables is called **stress**. Just like tone, stress is relative to its surroundings. Therefore, we determine whether a syllable is stressed or not based on its relationship with the other syllables in its environment rather than on a fixed scale of stress.

Hearers do not usually perceive the physiological aspects of stress. Stressed syllables nearly always exhibit one or more additional characteristics, such as, being spoken more loudly, having a higher tone, having a longer syllabic, or having a wider range of vowel possibilities than unstressed syllables. Unstressed syllables, on the other hand, are usually spoken more quietly, have a lower tone, a shorter syllabic, or their vowels are reduced. **Vowel reduction** is the phenomenon where a vowel is changed to more closely resemble a central vowel, such as [ə] or [ɨ]. These additional phonetic features help us recognize stressed syllables, but should not be mistaken for stress itself. The characteristics accompanying stress on a syllable will vary from language to language.

Degrees of Stress

Linguistic stress is referred to in terms of degrees. Within an utterance, a syllable may be stressed more than the syllable before it, but not as much as the syllable after it, in which case there exists three different degrees of stress. Theoretically the number of possible degrees of stress is unlimited; however, phoneticians usually do not identify more than four degrees. These degrees of stress are **primary stress**, **secondary stress**, **tertiary stress**, and **weak stress**[1]. Throughout this course, we will usually concern ourselves with only two levels of stress, primary stress and degrees less than primary.

Primary stress is indicated by placing a small **Vertical Line** ['], called a **stress mark**, just before the stressed syllable. The word "paper," for example, in which the first syllable is stressed, is written phonetically as ['pʰeⁱ.pɝ]. Degrees of stress less than primary are left unmarked when recording only two levels of stress. At times, however, it may be helpful to also mark secondary stress. Secondary stress is indicated by a small **Low Vertical Line** [ˌ] preceding the syllable. For example, in the word "diplomatic," the first syllable has second-ary stress while the third syllable has primary stress. Transcribed phonetically, it looks like [ˌdɪp.ləˈmæ.rɨk]. English and many other languages often have words with three and four different degrees of stress, and so in this lesson we will deal with secondary stress. Although you will not be required to recognize secondary stress in subsequent lessons, primary stress should always be indicated when transcribing utterances of more than one syllable.

The following exercise contains some common stress differences in English. Watch the stress mark in the transcription and listen to the difference in stress placement.

Exercise 11.6: Recognizing Stressed Syllables

1. /ˈɔg.mɛnt/   AUGment
2. /ɔgˈmɛnt/   augMENT
3. /ˈɹi.fɚ/   REfer
4. /ɹiˈfɚ/   reFER
5. /ˈtʰoɚ.mɛnt/   TORment
6. /tʰoɚˈmɛnt/   torMENT

---

1 Also known as quaternary stress.

7. /ˈpʰɚ.mɪt/   PERmit   10. /tɹæns.ˈfɚ/   transFER

8. /pʰɚ.ˈmɪt/   perMIT   11. /ˈɪm.pʰoˈt/   IMport

9. /ˈtɹæns.fɚ/   TRANSfer   12. /ɪm.ˈpʰoˈt/   imPORT

The next exercises will help you recognize stressed and unstressed syllables. In the following exercise, pairs of utterances are given. Listen for differences in stress placement between the pairs. If the same syllable is stressed in both utterances, respond with "same." If different syllables are stressed, respond with "different." Do not look at the text.

Exercise 11.7: Recognizing Stress

1.	ˈlɑlɑ	ˈlɑlɑ	Same	6. ˈpɑlɑ	lɑˈpɑ	Different
2.	ˈlɑlɑ	lɑˈlɑ	Different	7. lɑˈlɑlɑ	lɑˈlɑlɑ	Same
3.	lɑˈlɑ	ˈlɑlɑ	Different	8. lɑlɑˈlɑ	ˈlɑlɑlɑ	Different
4.	lɑˈlɑ	lɑˈlɑ	Same	9. lɑpɑˈlɑ	lɑpɑˈlɑ	Same
5.	lɑˈpɑ	ˈlɑpɑ	Different	10. pɑlɑˈpɑ	lɑˈlɑpɑ	Different

In this exercise, tell which syllable is stressed. Respond with "first" or "second."

Exercise 11.8: Recognizing Stressed Syllables

1.	lɑˈlɑ	Second	6. pɑˈlɑ	Second	11. ˈθɑɑz	First
2.	lɑˈlɑ	Second	7. ˈnɑmɑ	First	12. ˈafʃɑ	First
3.	ˈlɑlɑ	First	8. ˈdɑkʰɑ	First	13. dɑlˈkʰaf	Second
4.	pɑˈpɑ	Second	9. ˈkɑtʰɑ	First	14. ðɑsˈgɑ	Second
5.	ˈlɑpɑ	First	10. sɑˈʒɑ	Second	15. ˈaβsɑθ	First

More syllables are included in the utterances of this exercise. Name the syllable that carries the stress. Respond with the stressed syllable.

Exercise 11.9: Recognizing Stressed Syllables

1.	[ˈmopisu]	mo	3. [ˈmopisu]	mo	5. [mopiˈsu]	su
2.	[moˈpisu]	pi	4. [mopiˈsu]	su	6. [moˈpisu]	pi

7.	[mopiˈsu]	su	15.	[mopiˈsu]	su	23. [ˈsomebikunɑ] so
8.	[ˈmopisu]	mo	16.	[soˈmebikunɑ]	me	24. [someˈbikunɑ] bi
9.	[moˈpisu]	pi	17.	[somebikuˈnɑ]	nɑ	25. [soˈmebikunɑ] me
10.	[mopiˈsu]	su	18.	[someˈbikunɑ]	bi	26. [ˈsomebikunɑ] so
11.	[moˈpisu]	pi	19.	[ˈsomebikunɑ]	so	27. [somebiˈkunɑ] ku
12.	[ˈmopisu]	mo	20.	[somebiˈkunɑ]	ku	28. [somebiˈkunɑ] ku
13.	[ˈmopisu]	mo	21.	[soˈmebikunɑ]	me	29. [soˈmebikunɑ] me
14.	[ˈmopisu]	mo	22.	[somebiˈkunɑ]	ku	30. [somebikuˈnɑ] nɑ

Now you must distinguish between three levels of stress. Each utterance of the following exercise will consist of four syllables with varying degrees of stress. Listen only to the third syllable, and tell which degree of stress is present. Respond with "primary," "secondary," or "weak."

Exercise 11.10: Recognizing Three Levels of Stress

1.	[ˌsɑzaˈsɑzɑ]	Pri.	8.	[ˌθaðaˈθaðɑ]	Pri.	15.	[pɑˌtapɑˌta]	Weak
2.	[ˈsɑzaˌsɑzɑ]	Sec.	9.	[θaˌðaˈθaðɑ]	Pri.	16.	[ˈdavagaˌpɑ]	Weak
3.	[ˌsɑzaˈsɑzɑ]	Pri.	10.	[ˌʃazaʃaˈʒɑ]	Weak	17.	[gavaˌtaˈzɑ]	Sec.
4.	[ˌfavafaˈvɑ]	Weak	11.	[ʃaˈʒaˌʃazɑ]	Sec.	18.	[ˌdasaˈfapɑ]	Pri.
5.	[ˈfavaˌfavɑ]	Sec.	12.	[ʃaˌʒaˈʃazɑ]	Pri.	19.	[maˈnaˌlakɑ]	Sec.
6.	[faˈvafaˌvɑ]	Weak	13.	[pataˌpaˈtɑ]	Sec.	20.	[tadabaˈzɑ]	Weak
7.	[ˌθaðaˌθaˈðɑ]	Sec.	14.	[ˈpataˌpatɑ]	Sec.	21.	[laˈʃaˌðasɑ]	Sec.

The stress patterns of the following English words have been reversed from that of normal speech. Practice mimicking each word after the recording, stressing the same syllables as the recording. Be careful that you do not confuse the stress with the tone.

Exercise 11.11: Reproducing Stress in English Words

1.	/ˈɪm.pʰoᵘz/	IMpose	3.	/ɹeɪˈzɪn/	raiSIN
2.	/sɪˈtʰɪŋ/	sitTING	4.	/tʰɚˈki/	turKEY

5. /ˈdi.beⁱt/   DEbate   10. /kʰɑn.tɹeᵊˈɹi/   contraRY

6. /ˈɹi.pʰoᵊt/   REport   11. /sɪlˈʌ.bl̩/   syllABle

7. /pʰɹɑⁱ.meᵊˈɹi/   primaRY   12. /ɛm.fʌˈsɪs/   emphaSIS

8. /ˈɛk.sæm.pl̩/   EXample   13. /ˈkʰɑn.vɚ.seⁱˌʃʌn/   CONversation

9. /sɪˈmɪ.lɚ/   siMIlar   14. /ˌkʰʌ.mⁱuˈnɪ.kʰeⁱt/ commuNIcate

Phrase Stress

Phrases also tend to contain one word with even more emphasis (stress) than the other stressed syllables in that phrase. This is called **phrase stress**. Consider the sentence "I've always suffered terribly from stress." Perhaps the speaker intends to emphasize how long he has suffered from stress. In this case the first syllable of the word "always" will have more stress than the other stressed syllables in the sentence. If he intends to emphasize how much he suffered, the extra stress may be placed on the first syllable of the word "terribly," or on the word "I've" if he wants to clarify who it was that suffered. In English, the word that has phrase stress usually has the highest tone as well.

Phrase stress is symbolized by a small, **Raised Circle** [°] just before the stressed syllable. The primary stress and phrase stress are marked in each of the following sentences. Read the sentences to yourself, and consider the implied meanings of each one.

1. °I've ˈalways ˈsuffered terribly from stress.

2. I've °always ˈsuffered ˈterribly from stress.

3. I've always ˈsuffered °terribly from stress.

Listen to the following sentences, and without looking try to distinguish which syllable carries the phrase stress. Respond by saying the word that contains the stressed syllable.

Exercise 11.12: Recognizing Phrase Stress

1. I °hope this doesn't take long.

2. I hope °this doesn't take long.

3. You can easily get °that right.

4. You can °easily get that right.

5. °I think you're too busy.

6.   I think you're too ᵒbusy.

Juncture

Syllables in a sequence can be separated by an audible break, or pause, which is called **juncture**. Like stress, juncture is relative rather than absolute. The spacing between syllables can vary, ranging from a space too short to be distinguished to fairly long pauses. Juncture is symbolized in phonetic transcription by a space the width of one or two characters. We will not concern ourselves with different degrees of juncture.

In English, junctures usually occur at word or phrase boundaries. In other languages, however, they can occur in the middle of a word. The following utterances contain examples of juncture in actual languages. Listen to the recording and follow along in the text.

Exercise 11.13: Reproducing Juncture

1.   [hɑkɑnɨ ɑnʌ ˈnɨːsəkɑ]
     "I feel good." (Comanche)

2.   [ekʔmɑ tɑtʌ ˈtɨhɨja]
     "That's a good horse." (Comanche)

3.   [enɑh pɨʔ tsɑʔ ˈpɨβɨɑ nɑkɨ̩ kɑtɨ ˈpuʔetu ˈmiʔɑɑɨ̩]
     "The man with big ears is walking in the road." (Comanche)

4.   [toⁱ ʃænɔⁱ ˈlɑɑⁱ ˈʃɑɑᵘ ˈbɑɑ]
     "I shall repeat after you (madam)." (Vietnamese)

5.   [ˈmeᵃ˞ˌɹi ˈdʒeⁱn ˈpʰi.rɝˌsn̩ ˈkʰæn.tʰɑⁱ ˈtʰɹʌs.tju.əˈmɪnɨt̚]
     "Mary Jane Peterson, can't I trust you a minute?" (American English)

Rhythm

The timing of stressed syllables and the time span allotted to each syllable gives a certain **rhythm**, or flow, to phrases. These stress and syllable patterns vary from language to language, giving each language a distinctive rhythm.

There are two major categories in which languages can be grouped according to rhythm: **stress-timed** languages and **syllable-timed** languages. Germanic languages, like English, are stress-timed languages. In stress-timed languages, the stressed syllables are evenly spaced. No matter how many unstressed syllables occur between them, the unstressed syllables are rushed, or squeezed together between the evenly spaced stressed syllables. Examine the rhythm of the following sentence. "Don't 'ever for'get to re'member the 'rhythm." This is a good example of the even spacing of the stressed syllables of a stress-timed language. Notice how the length of time between stressed syllables is more or less the same.

Spanish and French are examples of syllable-timed languages. In these languages, approximately an equal amount of time is allotted for each syllable, whether stressed or unstressed. This can make these languages sound more rapid to English speakers, who are used to having longer syllables periodically on which their minds can "catch up."

Mimicking the rhythm of a language is just as important as a correct pronunciation of the vowels and consonants. Even if you can pronounce each sound of a language perfectly, you cannot sound "natural" without focusing on rhythm. Listen to the following sentences and mimic their rhythm. (The first time they are pronounced, you will hear them with stress-timing, which is the ordinary rhythm for English. The second time they will be with syllable-timing.) Repeat each utterance after the recording.

Exercise 11.14: Reproducing Rhythm

1.	It's 'fun to 'study lin'guistics at 'school.	Stress-timed
2.	It's fun to study linguistics at school.	Syllable-timed
3.	Don't 'ever for'get to re'member the 'rhythm.	Stress-timed
4.	Don't ever forget to remember the rhythm.	Syllable-timed
5.	'You can 'say 'that a'gain.	Stress-timed
6.	You can say that again.	Syllable-timed

Transcribe the following utterances without looking at the text. Listen for primary stress, secondary stress, and juncture. Each utterance will consist of four syllables.

Exercise 11.15: Recording Stress and Juncture

1. ['mopɑ se ˌni]
2. [ˌmo pɑ'seni]
3. [ˌmopɑ'se ni]
4. [mo ˌpɑ se'ni]
5. ['mu ˌsopɑ fu]
6. [muso'pɑ ˌfu]
7. [mu so 'pɑ fu]
8. ['muso ˌpɑfu]
9. [ˌtɑnu lɑ'ki]

Lesson 12: Vowel Glides

Lesson Outline

Glossary Terms

Illustration 12.1: Some Common English Vowels

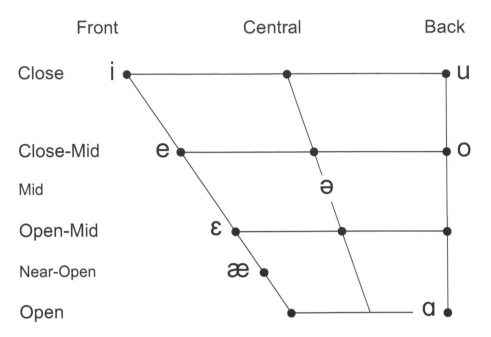

This lesson focuses on the symbols [ɛ], [ɑ], and [o] in the vowel chart above. Epsilon [ɛ], Script A [ɑ], and O [o] were introduced in Lesson 10, but in order to pronounce these vowels correctly, we must first discuss vowel glides.

Sometimes during a vowel sound, the tongue moves from one vowel position toward another. This results in a slur, or glide, between two vowel sounds. Try saying the word "high" while watching your mouth in a mirror. Notice how the jaw moves upward during the vowel, pushing your tongue closer to the palate. Imagine a diagram of your tongue superimposed on the vowel chart. For the word "high," your tongue would start at the [ɑ] position and move up the chart toward the [i] position. This non-syllabic movement of the tongue from one vowel position to another is called a **vowel glide**. A vowel glide is produced any time the tongue moves during the articulation of a vowel sound. In theory, a vowel glide may begin at any point on the vowel chart and end at any other point, but normally the selection is limited to four main vowel glides which we will discuss in this lesson.

A vowel glide may be either an on-glide or an off-glide. In short, this means that the tongue can either glide toward the main vowel position (on-glide) or away from it (off-glide). In a vowel glide, the beginning and ending vowel qualities do not usually carry the same prominence. One or the other will be heard the most. This is the vowel that occupies the nucleus of the syllable (the syllabic). With off-glides, the tongue moves away from the main vowel position. The main vowel sound, or the syllabic, comes first, and then the tongue glides away from that position. In the word "high" [hɑⁱ], the [ɑ] is the syllabic and the [i] is the off-glide. English only has off-glides, so they will be studied first.

Off-Glides

An **off-glide** is the movement of the tongue away from the nucleus of the syllable. Off-glides are symbolized with a superscript character after the main vowel, such as [ɛⁱ], [ɑⁱ], and [ɑᵘ]. In an off-glide, the first vowel is the "main vowel" or the the nucleus of the syllable. This syllabic vowel is followed by a non-syllabic vowel which makes up the glide. The following exercise contains examples of some common English off-glides. There are four common off-glides in English: the [i] off-glide, the [u] off-glide, the [ɚ] off-glide, and the [ə] off-glide.

The following exercise demonstrates the common English off-glides. The fourth will be demonstrated later. Repeat each word after the recording, and pay particular attention to the movements of the tongue and lips. You may find it helpful to watch your mouth in a mirror.

Exercise 12.1: Producing English Off-glides

1.	I	[ʔɑⁱ]	7.	how	[haᵘ]	13.	loud	[laᵘd]
2.	Ow!	[ʔaᵘ]	8.	tar	[tʰɑᵊ˞]	14.	rat	[ɹæᵊt]
3.	are	[ʔɑᵊ˞]	9.	lie	[lɑⁱ]	15.	ark	[ʔɑᵊ˞k]
4.	at	[ʔæᵊt]	10.	cow	[kʰaᵘ]	16.	try	[tʰɹɑⁱ]
5.	hi	[hɑⁱ]	11.	car	[kʰɑᵊ˞]	17.	doubt	[daᵘt]
6.	cab	[kʰæᵊb]	12.	by	[bɑⁱ]	18.	dart	[dɑᵊ˞t]

[i] Off-Glide

For the close front unrounded **I Off-glide** [ⁱ], the tongue begins at any vowel position and moves upward and forward toward the position of the vowel [i]. In reality, the glide consists of the whole continuum of vowel sounds from the nucleus to the [i]. The following diagram uses a vowel chart to illustrate this tongue movement from three different positions.

Illustration 12.2: [i] Off-Glide

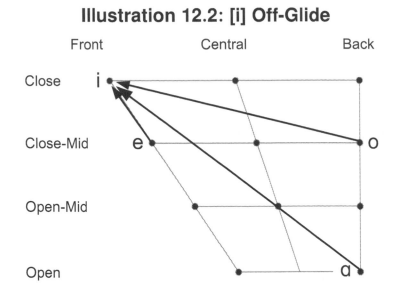

The next exercise demonstrates common English words with [i] off-glides from the vowels [ɛ], [ɑ], and [o] as shown in Illustration 12.2. The glides may not be naturally present in American English. Repeat each utterance, and try to say the words just like the recording so that you can feel the tongue movements during the glides. Do not be distracted by the consonants.

Exercise 12.2: Producing [i] Off-Glides

1.	my	[maⁱ]	8. pain	[pʰeⁱn]	15. noise	[noⁱz]
2.	may	[meⁱ]	9. coin	[kʰoⁱn]	16. liner	[ˈlɑⁱnɚ]
3.	toy	[tʰoⁱ]	10. cry	[kʰɹɑⁱ]	17. labor	[ˈleⁱbɚ]
4.	tie	[tʰaⁱ]	11. crate	[kʰɹeⁱt]	18. annoy	[ʔəˈnoⁱ]
5.	lay	[leⁱ]	12. poise	[pʰoⁱz]	19. grimey	[ˈgɹɑⁱmi]
6.	oink	[ʔoⁱŋk]	13. fried	[fɹɑⁱd]	20. grate	[gɹɛⁱt]
7.	pine	[pʰɑⁱn]	14. frayed	[fɹeⁱd]	21. loiter	[ˈloⁱtɚ]

[u] Off-Glide

When producing the close back rounded **U Off-glide** [ᵘ], the tongue moves upward and back, and the lips become more rounded. Say the word "cow" while watching your lips in a mirror. Watch how they become more rounded as the tongue moves to the [u] position. Illustration 12.3 below pictures three possible tongue movements for the [u] off-glide.

Illustration 12.3: [u] Off-Glide

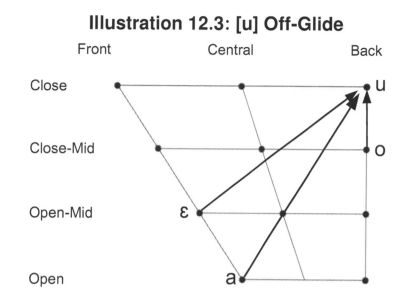

The next exercise includes [u] off-glides from the three positions listed above. Some of the glides will not sound natural because they do not occur in English, but they are important for learning to recognize vowel glides. Repeat each word after the recording.

Exercise 12.3: Producing [u] Off-Glides

1.	Ow!	[aᵘ]	8.	sew	[sɛᵘ]	15.	grow	[gɹoᵘ]
2.	no	[nɛᵘ]	9.	sew	[soᵘ]	16.	drown	[dɹaᵘn]
3.	Oh!	[ʔoᵘ]	10.	allow	[əˈlaᵘ]	17.	go	[gɛᵘ]
4.	how	[haᵘ]	11.	own	[ʔɛᵘn]	18.	go	[goᵘ]
5.	note	[nɛᵘt]	12.	own	[ʔoᵘn]	19.	pound	[pʰaᵘnd]
6.	note	[noᵘt]	13.	loud	[laᵘd]	20.	throne	[θɹɛᵘn]
7.	sow	[saᵘ]	14.	grow	[gɹɛᵘ]	21.	throne	[θɹoᵘn]

[ə] Off-glide

The vowel directly in the center of the vowel chart is called Schwa. The **Schwa [ə]**, symbolized by turned "e," is made with the tongue and other features of the mouth in the most relaxed, neutral position possible. It can also be used as a vowel glide. The chart below illustrates the type of tongue movement involved in the articulation of the mid central unrounded **Schwa Off-glide [ə]**. The tongue may begin at any position on the chart just as all other glides that we have studied, and move toward the mid, central position. Lip rounding is not usually involved with the [ə] off-glide, but keep in mind that it is possible.

Illustration 12.4: [ə] Off-Glide

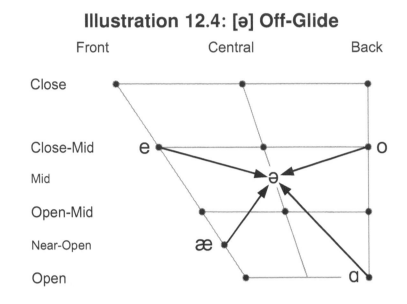

Examples of the schwa off-glide in English are given in the following exercise. These examples are specific to certain dialects or styles of speech. Although you may not normally pronounce these words with the same glide, try imitating the recording as closely as you can.

Exercise 12.4: Producing [ə] Off-Glide

1.	yeah	[jæə]	6.	fine	[fɑən]	11.	boa	[boə]
2.	four	[foə]	7.	fair	[feə]	12.	car	[kʰɑə]
3.	I	[ɑə]	8.	porch	[pʰoətʃ]	13.	mayor	[meə]
4.	there	[ðeə]	9.	mine	[mɑən]	14.	pork	[pʰoək]
5.	sword	[soəd]	10.	prayer	[pɹeə]	15.	far	[fɑə]

[ɚ] Off-Glide

The **Rhotacized Schwa** [ɚ], which corresponds to the American English[1] "r" sound in the words "bird" and "learn," functions as a consonant in English, but is phonetically a vowel.[2] It is exactly the same as the Schwa [ə] except the tongue is retroflexed. It is symbolized by adding a **Right Hook** [˞] to a [ə], and generally, it is rotated slightly. A Right

---

1 British English speakers do not retroflex vowels and, therefore, simply pronounce a schwa [ə].

2 Only syllable final "r" sounds in American English correspond to the rhoticized shwa [ɚ]. Syllable initial "r" sounds are alveolar approximants [ɹ] and will be studied in later lessons.

Hook can be added to any vowel symbol to add the rhotic quality (for example, [ɑ˞]).[3] Sometimes, a **Superscript R** [ʳ] is added after a vowel instead of a Right Hook (for example, [ɑʳ]).

The Rhotacized Schwa [ɚ] is classified as a central oral sonorant. Its articulation is open, allowing free passage of the air stream. Therefore, it does not have any definite articulator or point of articulation. It is a mid central rhoticized (or retroflexed) vowel. It is commonly referred to by linguists as an **R-colored vowel**. Like other retroflexed phones, the tip of the tongue is curled upward slightly, giving the surface of the tongue a cupped shape. This modifies the vowel quality from that of ordinary central vowels.

English speakers pronounce [ɚ] only in stressed syllables. Unstressed syllables are pronounced as a **Rhotacized Reversed Epsilon** [ɝ]. For example, the word "murder" would be transcribed as [ˈmɚ.ɾɝ]. These two phones may sound very similar, but the tongue is slightly lower when pronouncing a [ɝ]. The [ɝ] is not used as a vowel glide in English.

Among English speakers, there are two variations of retroflexion for the [ɚ] sound. Illustrations 12.5 and 12.6 picture these tongue positions. One variation is made by keeping the back of the tongue low and curling the tip and sides upward. The other is made by raising the back of the tongue and curling the tip up slightly. The **Rhotacized Schwa Off-glide** [ᵊ] is produced when the tongue moves away from another position to either retroflexed positions.

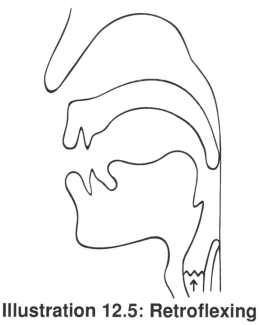

Illustration 12.5: Retroflexing with the back of the tongue

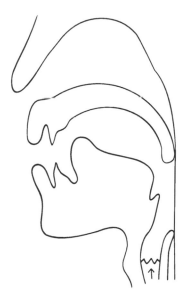

Illustration 12.6: Retroflexing with the tip of the tongue

---

3 Languages may have multiple levels or rhotacity. In such cases, one Right Hook can be used for slight rhotacity [e˞] and two Right Hooks for full rhotacity [e˞˞].

The following exercise demonstrates the [ɚ] off-glide as it is used in American English. However, not all English speakers pronounce each of these words with this off-glide. If you do not normally pronounce the glides like you hear on the recording, practice them until you can produce a clear [ɚ] off-glide.

Exercise 12.5: Producing [ɚ] Off-glide

1. are [ʔɑ˞]		6. door [do˞]		11. scary [ˈske˞.ɹi]	
2. ferry [ˈfe˞.ɹi]		7. mark [mɑ˞k]		12. storm [sto˞m]	
3. oar [ʔo˞]		8. hairy [ˈhe˞.ɹi]		13. pardon [ˈpʰɑ˞.dən]	
4. part [pʰɑ˞t]		9. pork [pʰo˞k]		14. dairy [ˈde˞.i]	
5. merry [ˈme˞.ɹi]		10. startle [ˈstɑ˞.tˌl̩]		15. order [ˈʔo˞.dɚ]	

The next exercise will include all four of the off-glides introduced in this lesson. Name the off-glide used in each utterance. Respond with the name of the glide symbol [i], [u], [ɚ], or [ə].

Exercise 12.6: Recognizing Off-glides

1. [fɛⁱ] i		8. [tʰɛ˞] ɚ		15. [sto˞k] ɚ	
2. [mɛᵘ] u		9. [tʃo˞z] ɚ		16. [ʔaᵘtʃ] u	
3. [mɛᵊ] ə		10. [pʰoⁱnt] i		17. [dʒoᵊ] ə	
4. [mɑ˞] ɚ		11. [ðaᵊ] ə		18. [ɣoⁱt] i	
5. [pʰoᵘz] u		12. [doᵘs] u		19. [ʃuᵊz] ə	
6. [mɛⁱz] i		13. [maⁱt] i		20. [maᵘs] u	
7. [bloᵊ] ə		14. [moᵘt] u		21. [deⁱzd] i	

On-Glides

Just as the tongue moves away from the position of the syllabic vowel to produce off-glides, it also moves toward the position of the syllabic vowel to produce on-glides. You can see a similar type of movement occur by watching your mouth in a mirror while saying the words "watt" or "yacht." The English "w" and "y" sounds in these words are actually consonants called approximants, which are very similar to vowel glides. Approximants will be studied later on, but for now it is enough to know that approximants have a slight fricative sound that vowels do not.

On-glides, are just the opposite of off-glides. In an **on-glide**, the tongue begins at one of the vowel positions and moves to any other position on the chart.

There arc three on-glides that we will study in this less. They correspond with some of the off-glides that we have already introduced. They are the [i] on-glide, the [u] on-glide, and the [ɚ] on-glide. Like off-glides, on-glides are represented by superscript symbols. In the case of on-glides, however, the glide symbol precedes the syllabic vowel.

[i] On-Glide

The close front unrounded **I On-glide** [ⁱ] corresponds with the [i] off-glide in that the tongue glides from the [i] vowel position. This glide sounds similar to the sound at the beginning of the word "yoke." Illustration 12.7 pictures three of the many possible tongue movements for the [i] on-glide.

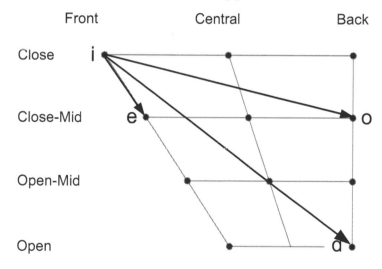

[u] On-Glide

The close back rounded **U On-glide** [ᵘ] corresponds to the [u] off-glide in that the tongue glides from the [u] vowel position. This glide is similar to the initial sound in the word "wax." Illustration 12.8 pictures three tongue movements for the [u] on-glide. Remember that the glide can end at any position on the chart.

Illustration 12.8: [u] On-Glide

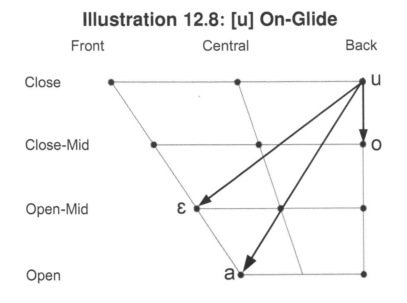

[ɚ] On-Glide

The **Rhotacized Schwa On-glide** [ɚ] corresponds directly to the [ɚ] off-glide. It sounds somewhat similar to the sound at the beginning of the words "red" and "row." In English, the [ɚ] on-glide does not usually occur word initially. Words like "red" and "row" are actually pronounced with the approximant [ɹ], which involves more restriction than the glide [ɚ]. To articulate the [ɚ] on-glide, you can begin with the alveolar approximant [ɹ] as in the example words above and reduce the amount of restriction slightly by making sure your lips remain unrounded.

The next exercise uses English words to illustrate how on-glides are just the reverse of off-glides. The pronunciation of these words must be modified to illustrate on-glides. In normal English pronunciation, the sounds in question are approximant consonants. Also, be careful not to pronounce Glottal Stops [ʔ] before on-glides.

Exercise 12.7: Recognizing On-glides and Off-glides

1.	yes	[ⁱɛs]	7.	wan	[ᵘɑn]
2.	say	[sɛⁱ]	8.	now	[nɑᵘ]
3.	yacht	[ⁱɑt]	9.	woe	[ᵘo̯ᵘ]
4.	tie	[tʰɑⁱ]	10.	woe	[ᵘoᵘ]
5.	Wes	[ᵘɛs]	11.	wreck	[ᵊ˞ɛk]
6.	so	[soᵘ]	12.	care	[kʰe˞]

13. rock   [ˠɑk]   14. car   [kʰɑˠ]

Listen to the following exercise and tell what type of vowel glide you hear. Respond with "on-glide," "off-glide," or "both."

Exercise 12.8: Recognizing Combinations of Glides

1.	[ᵘɑᵘ]	Both	8.	[ˠoᵘ]	Both	15.	[naᵊt]	Off-glide
2.	[ʔoⁱ]	Off-glide	9.	[ⁱɛf]	On-glide	16.	[glɑⁱz]	Off-glide
3.	[nɑᵊ]	Off-glide	10.	[gɛˠ]	Off-glide	17.	[bɛⁱt]	Off-glide
4.	[ⁱok]	On-glide	11.	[tɑⁱ]	Off-glide	18.	[ˠɛˠ]	Both
5.	[doˠ]	Off-glide	12.	[ᵘɛᵊ]	Both	19.	[ⁱaᵘ]	Both
6.	[ˠoⁱ]	Both	13.	[kˠoᵘ]	Both	20.	[mɛᵘt]	Off-glide
7.	[ᵘop]	On-glide	14.	[ⁱost]	On-glide	21.	[ᵘon]	On-glide

Practice controlling the use of on-glides preceded by consonants. Say the following sentences and insert an on-glide after each syllable-initial consonant. Insert the [i] glide after each one first. Next insert the [u] glide and then the [ɚ] glide.

1. Peter Piper picked a peck of pickled peppers.

2. Tiny Tim took ten tin tubs to Toronto.

3. Cream colored cats can conclude careers in car crashes.

4. Many mad men made more mighty missiles Monday morning.

Pure Vowels

A vowel glide is a non-syllabic movement of the tongue from one vowel quality toward another. This results in an uninterrupted sequence of different vowel qualities. Any movement of the tongue during a vowel sound results in a vowel glide. A vowel without a glide is called a **pure vowel**. In order to produce a pure vowel, the tongue and other facial features must remain stationary throughout the articulation of the vowel sound. This is often difficult when it conflicts with natural habits incurred by language or regional accents.

The importance of being able to produce pure vowels and vowel glides cannot be over-emphasized. Speakers have automatic tendencies, dictated by their native language structures, to glide certain vowels in certain ways. Each language has its own patterns of vowel glides which sound natural within that language. Certain vowels may never be glided while others can have several different glides. When we carry the vowel glide tendencies of our mother tongue over into a new language, our speech may be marked by an atrocious foreign accent. It is important, therefore, to be able to consciously control glides and produce pure vowels when necessary.

It is important, while learning the vowel sounds in this course, not to rely too much on English words as examples of the correct vowel sounds. The pronunciation of English words can vary considerably depending on the speaker, and even on the geographical area the speaker is from. It is best to learn the sounds correctly by listening to the instructor and by mimicking the recording.

Producing Pure Vowels

Review the vowel chart in the beginning of this lesson and repeat the vowels Epsilon [ɛ], Script A [ɑ], and O [o] to fix in your mind their positions both in the mouth and on the chart. For each of these vowels there are English habits that keep us from producing them as pure vowels.

Some dialects of English, particularly in the southern United States, glide Epsilon [ɛ] with a Schwa [ə] off-glide, as in the word "well" [wɛᵊl]. This glide movement may be very slight and hard to notice.

Normally, English speakers pronounce an [o] with a [u] off-glide. You should be able to see this glide and the associated lip rounding quite easily in a mirror as you pronounce the word "boat."

The exact position of Script A [ɑ] fluctuates forward and backward from the cardinal position. Occasionally, some English dialects add a Schwa [ə] off-glide or round their lips slightly.

The following exercises are designed to help you overcome these habits and produce pure vowels. Follow along in the text and mimic each utterance after the recordings. Watch your mouth in a mirror to ensure that your articulatory features remain stationary during the vowels.

Exercise 12.9: Producing (Un)Glided [o] and [ɛ]

1. [ʔoᵘ]   [ʔoʔoᵘ]   [ʔoʔo]   [ʔo]

2. [ʔɛⁱ]   [ʔɛʔɛⁱ]   [ʔɛʔɛ]   [ʔɛ]

3. [ʔɛᵊ]   [ʔɛʔɛᵊ]   [ʔɛʔɛ]   [ʔɛ]

The left column in the following exercise pronounces the words with a vowel glide as in normal English. The right column, which eliminates the glides, will sound less natural.

Exercise 12.10: Producing (Un)Glided [o]

1. a) [soᵘ]   b) [so]   so

2. a) [ʔoᵘ]   b) [ʔo]   oh

3. a) [loᵘ]   b) [lo]   low

4. a) [boᵘ]   b) [bo]   bow

5. a) [ˈmoᵘ.tɚ]   b) [ˈmo.tɚ]   motor

6. a) [loᵘf]   b) [lof]   loaf

7. a) [ˈgoᵘ.wiŋ]   b) [ˈgo.iŋ]   going

8. a) [ə.ˈloᵘn]   b) [ə.ˈlon]   alone

The following exercise focuses on the pronunciation of [ɛ]. Follow the transcription, and repeat each sound after the recording.

Exercise 12.11: Producing (Un)Glided [ɛ]

1. a) [jɛᵊp]   b) [jɛp]   yep

2. a) [wɛᵊl]   b) [wɛl]   well

3. a) [lɛᵊt]   b) [lɛt]   let

4. a) [mɛᵊnt]   b) [mɛnt]   meant

5. a) [bɛᵊst]   b) [bɛst]   best

6. a) [fɹɛᵊt]   b) [fɹɛt]   fret

In the next exercise, listen for any vowel glides that may be present, and respond by telling whether the vowels are glided or not. Any of the four glides that we have studied thus far may be included.

Exercise 12.12: Recognizing Glided and Pure Vowels

1. [kɑⁱ]   Glided   2. [pɛt]   No   3. [dɑt]   No

4. [mɛⁱ]	Glided	11. [ⁱɛⁱɛ]	Glided	18. [notog]	No
5. [ᵘɑᵘ]	Glided	12. [fɛᵊfɛᵊ]	Glided	19. [ʔɛ]	No
6. [so]	No	13. [ᵘɑⁱk]	Glided	20. [maᵊsɑᵘ]	Glided
7. [mɑ]	No	14. [xoko]	No	21. [˞okoˠ]	Glided
8. [ɑnk]	No	15. [ⁱoto]	Glided	22. [zɛtɛz]	No
9. [fɛᵊ]	Glided	16. [ɛmɛ]	No	23. [ʔɑ]	No
10. [kɛkɛ]	No	17. [hɛᵊmɛᵊ]	Glided	24. [ʔɑᵊ]	Glided

In the following exercise, mimic each utterance to practice glided and unglided vowels.

Exercise 12.13: Producing (Un)Glided Vowels

1. [soᵘso]	8. [sɛᵊsɛᵊ]	15. [sɑsɑᵊ]
2. [sosoᵘ]	9. [sɛᵘsɛⁱ]	16. [sɑⁱsɑ]
3. [soᵊso]	10. [sɛsɛ]	17. [sɑᵊsɑ]
4. [sosoᵊ]	11. [sɛᵊsɛ]	18. [sɑᵊsɑᵊ]
5. [soso]	12. [sɛⁱsɛᵊ]	19. [soᵘso]
6. [sosoⁱ]	13. [sɑᵊsɑ]	20. [sɛᵊsɛᵊ]
7. [sɛᵊsɛ]	14. [sɑⁱsɑᵘ]	21. [sɑsɑᵊ]

Approximants

Vowel glides are very similar to central approximants. In fact, many phoneticians prefer to use approximant symbols to represent glides. There are slight articulatory differences, however, between approximants and vowel glides. **Approximants** are produced with slightly more restriction to the air stream than vowels. The amount of restriction involved in the articulation of central approximants may be thought of as halfway between that of vowels and fricatives. A glided sound involving an approximant, therefore, will contain a small amount of friction, while a true vowel glide will not. Often glides and approximants are used interchangeably in speech, making transcription difficult if attempting to differentiate between the two. Most linguists prefer to treat them as the same and choose a single symbol to represent both sounds. In this course, we choose to recognize the distinction between the two sounds and represent them accordingly. Central approximants will be studied further in a later lesson.

Methods of Representation

There are several methods of representing vowel glides among linguists today. Some linguists use approximant symbols to represent glides due to the ease of typing that this system affords, despite the ambiguity. Others prefer to use an **Inverted Breve** [̯] either below [i̯] or above [y̑] a symbol to indicate non-syllabic vowels. Many linguists do not use any special symbol to indicate glides, since whenever two vowels are in one syllable, one of them must be a glide, and the phonetic difference between a glide and a vowel is rarely significant.

In this course, superscript symbols are always used to represent glides. This makes it possible to achieve better consistency when dealing with the articulatory differences between glides and approximants. Table 12.1 below lists several different methods for presenting vowel glides. Although some of these methods are more accurate than others, they are all commonly used with no particular method favored strongly by the IPA or linguists in general. In some phonetic material, you may find all four methods implemented; however, this should be avoided as it could generate confusion. The following table lists all of the possible combinations of the different systems to symbolize a triphthong.[4]

Table 12.1: Methods of Vowel Glide Representation

	Initial Approximant	On-Glide (Superscript)	On-Glide (Inverted Breve)	Initial Normal Vowel
Final Approximant	waw	ᵘaw	u̯aw	uaw
Off-Glide (Superscript)	waᵘ	ᵘaᵘ	u̯aᵘ	uaᵘ
Off-Glide (Inverted Breve)	wau̯	ᵘau̯	u̯au̯	uau̯
Final Normal Vowel	wau	ᵘau	u̯au	uau

---

4 A series of three vowel sounds with no intervening consonants

Table 12.2 below lists the vowels introduced in this chapter.

Table 12.2: Vowels and Vowel Glides Summary

IPA symbol	Name	Technical Name	English Example	APA symbol
i	I	Close Front Unrounded Vowel	elite	i
ɛ	Epsilon	Open-mid Front Unrounded Vowel	pet	ɛ
ɑ	Script A	Open Close Unrounded Vowel	father	ɑ
o	O	Close-mid Back Rounded Vowel	vote	o
ɚ	Right-hook Schwa	R-colored Mid Central Vowel	her	r
ɝ	Right-hook Reversed Epsilon	R-colored Open-mid Central Vowel	amber	r
ⁱ	Superscript I	I Glide	say	y
ᵘ	Superscript U	U Glide	cow	w
ᵊ	Superscript Schwa	Schwa Glide	yeah	H
ᵊ˞	Superscript Right-hook Schwa	R-colored Glide	car	r

Lesson 13: Fronting, Retroflexion, and Sibilants

Lesson Outline

Glossary

Thus far in our study of consonants we have discussed labial, dental, alveolar, alveopalatal, palatal, velar, and uvular consonants. The articulation of each of these consonants may be modified, or altered, in a number of ways. Alveolar consonants can be modified by pushing the tongue slightly forward, pulling it farther back, or curling it at the tip. Each of these variations results in a different sound. In this lesson we will discuss the variations of both alveolar and alveopalatal consonants.

Some linguists argue that the sounds presented in this chapter may actually represent separate points of articulation, rather than variations of sounds made at the alveolar and alveopalatal points. However, since the phonetic difference can be slight, and these sounds are not normally found contrastively in languages, these new consonants are not usually given a separate symbol. They are represented with the symbols of the alveolar and alveopalatal consonants, with an added diacritic to denote the modification of the articulation.

Fronted Consonants

Every alveolar sound has a corresponding fronted counterpart. Fronted sounds are symbolized by placing a **Bridge** [̪] (sometimes called a **Tooth**)beneath [t̪] or above [ʒ̄] a symbol. Fronting occurs on alveolar consonants more than any other point of articulation.

Understanding Fronting

Fronted consonants are produced when the tongue is placed slightly forward from its ordinary position. For fronted alveolar sounds, the tip of the tongue is placed firmly against the back of the upper teeth or the roof of the mouth immediately behind the upper teeth. For this reason, fronted sounds are often called **dentalized**. Illustrations 13.1 and 13.2 below contrast the position of the tongue in an alveolar stop to a fronted alveolar stop. The same diagrams could apply to fronted fricatives if a small amount of space is left between the articulator and the point of articulation. Notice, however, that the tip of the tongue is not on the edge of the teeth, or between the teeth as in dental fricatives [θ] and [ð]. We will discuss the distinctions between those sounds later in this chapter.

Affricates can be fronted as well. Although the stop and fricative in an affricate can be made at different points of articulation (heterorganic affricates), you should not worry about practicing affricates with one fronted sound and one alveolar sound. If one element of an affricate is fronted, the other will usually be fronted as well.

Producing Fronted Sounds

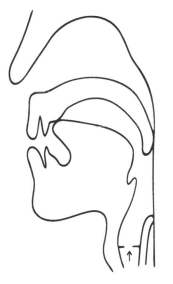

Illustration 13.1: [t]

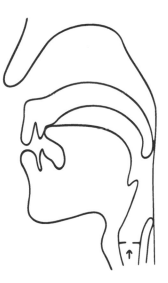

Illustration 13.2: [t̪]

Place the tip of your tongue against the inside of your upper teeth, as shown above in Illustration 13.2. Now say [d̪ɑ], [t̪ɑ], and [t̪ʰɑ]. These are fronted alveolar stops, also described as tip-dental stops. Fronted stops are fairly easy to produce. You can practice them by replacing each alveolar stop with a fronted stop in the following sentences.

1. T̪en t̪an t̪rucks t̪ook T̪erry's t̪rash t̪o t̪own t̪oday.

2. D̪ear D̪ad̪dy d̪on't̪ d̪o that̪.

To produce a fronted alveolar fricative, place the tip of your tongue near the back of your upper teeth and say [sɑ] and [zɑ]. Say the following sentences fronting the alveolar fricatives.

3. S̪ist̪er S̪ue s̪it̪s̪ s̪ewing s̪ock̪s̪ for s̪eas̪ick s̪uffering s̪ailors̪.

4. Z̪any z̪ebras̪ z̪ip and z̪oom.

Fronted stops are easy to articulate and easy to see when watching someone speak, but the acoustic difference is not as easy to detect. Fronted fricatives are much easier to distinguish by ear. The articulation is the same as that of stops, but the air stream is not completely impeded.

Listen to the following exercise, and tell whether the sounds you hear are fronted or not. The exercise begins with fricatives, which are easiest to hear, and builds up to affricates and stops. Respond with "dental" or "alveolar."

Exercise 13.1: Recognizing Fronted Dental and Alveolar Stops

1.	[aṣa]	Dental	11.	[za]	Alveolar	21.	[atsa]	Alveolar
2.	[aẓa]	Dental	12.	[aṣ]	Dental	22.	[atʰa]	Dental
3.	[aza]	Alveolar	13.	[at̪ṣa]	Dental	23.	[at̪a]	Dental
4.	[aṣa]	Dental	14.	[at̪ṣ]	Dental	24.	[ada]	Alveolar
5.	[sa]	Alveolar	15.	[adza]	Alveolar	25.	[ad̪a]	Dental
6.	[aṣa]	Dental	16.	[tsa]	Alveolar	26.	[ata]	Alveolar
7.	[asa]	Alveolar	17.	[ad̪ẓa]	Dental	27.	[ata]	Alveolar
8.	[az]	Alveolar	18.	[t̪ṣa]	Dental	28.	[ad̪a]	Dental
9.	[sa]	Alveolar	19.	[adza]	Alveolar	29.	[at̪ʰa]	Dental
10.	[aẓa]	Dental	20.	[ad̪ẓ]	Dental	30.	[ada]	Alveolar

Retroflexed Consonants

Another variation that can be imposed on alveolar and alveopalatal consonants is retroflexion. The basic concept of retroflexion was introduced with Rhotacized Schwa [ɚ] in Lesson 12. Retroflexion occurs when the tip of the tongue is curled up and/or back slightly during a sound. Retroflexed consonants are found in approximately 20% of the world's languages.

Understanding Retroflexion

As explained for the Rhotacized Schwa [ɚ] in Lesson 12, **retroflexed** sounds are articulated by curling the tongue tip upward and slightly back, creating a cup shape in the surface of the tongue. Study Illustrations 13.3 and 13.4 below to see retroflexed articulation compared with the normal articulation of an alveolar stop.

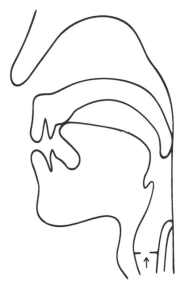

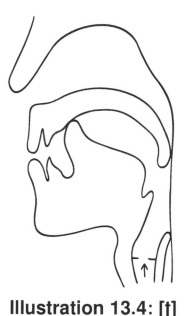

Illustration 13.3: [t]　　　　　　**Illustration 13.4: [ṭ]**

Retroflexion occurs when the front of the tongue touches the hard pallet behind the alveolar ridge. Retroflexed sounds are normally symbolized by adding a **retroflexed hook** diacritic called the **Right Tail** [ˌ] to the base of an alveolar symbol. Therefore a voiced retroflexed stop is symbolized by a **Right-tail D** [ɖ] and a voiceless retroflexed stop is a **Right-tail T** [ʈ]. Illustrations 13.5 and 13.6 below depict the articulation of retroflexed fricatives **Right-tail Esh** [ʂ] and **Right-tail S** [ʂ].

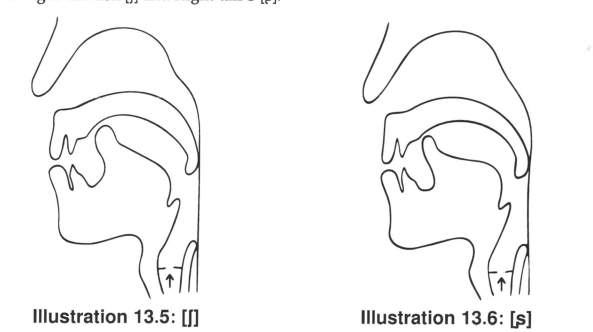

Illustration 13.5: [ʃ]　　　　　　**Illustration 13.6: [ʂ]**

Affricates can also be retroflexed. Just as with fronting, the most common retroflexed affricates are those in which both the stop and fricative are retroflexed.

Producing Retroflexed Sounds

Because the tongue is naturally retroflexed for Rhotacized Schwa [ɚ], you can use this sound to help with the articulation of other retroflexed consonants. Say the word "car" slowly, exaggerating the [ɚ]. Many English speakers curl their tongue in a retroflexed position for this sound. If you can feel that you do not retroflex your tongue automatically during the [ɚ], then you must concentrate on doing so. It will come easier with [ɚ] than with other consonants. Now say "car top" slowly, holding the position of the tongue for the [ɚ], but closing your mouth until a stop is formed. You should produce a Right-tail T[ʈ]. Once you can feel that you have achieved the retroflexed articulation, practice it with sentences one and two of the following exercise. Then repeat the same process with the words "car seat" to learn retroflexed fricatives.

Exercise 13.2: Producing Retroflexed Consonants

1. ʈen ʈan ʈrucks ʈook ʈerry's ʈrash ʈo ʈown ʈoday.

2. ɖear ɖaɖɖy ɖon'ʈ ɖo thaʈ.

3. ʂiʂter ʂue ʂiʈʂ ʂewing ʂockʂ for ʂeaʂick ʂuffering ʂailorʂ.

4. ʐany ʐebraʂ ʐip and ʐoom.

Listen to the following exercises, and determine whether each utterance contains a retroflexed consonant or not. Many retroflexed sounds have a certain "r-like" quality that also affects the surrounding vowels. This is one way to detect whether or not a sound is retroflexed.

Exercise 13.3: Recognizing Retroflexion

1.	[aɖa]	Retroflexed	8.	[ada]	No	15.	[az]	No
2.	[asa]	No	9.	[aʂa]	Retroflexed	16.	[ata]	No
3.	[ata]	No	10.	[da]	No	17.	[aʐ]	Retroflexed
4.	[aʐa]	Retroflexed	11.	[aza]	No	18.	[asa]	No
5.	[aʈa]	Retroflexed	12.	[ʈa]	Retroflexed	19.	[aʐa]	Retroflexed
6.	[aza]	No	13.	[as]	No	20.	[ɖa]	Retroflexed
7.	[ʂa]	Retroflexed	14.	[aʈʂa]	Retroflexed	21.	[sa]	No

In the following exercise, tell whether the sounds that you hear are alveolar or retroflexed.

Exercise 13.4: Recognizing Alveolar or Retroflexed Sounds

1. [atɑ]	Alveolar	6. [aʂɑ]	Retroflexed	11. [aʐɑ]	Retroflexed
2. [aɖɑ]	Retroflexed	7. [azɑ]	Alveolar	12. [atɑ]	Alveolar
3. [aʂɑ]	Retroflexed	8. [sɑ]	Alveolar	13. [as]	Alveolar
4. [aʐɑ]	Retroflexed	9. [aʈʂɑ]	Retroflexed	14. [aɖɑ]	Retroflexed
5. [dɑ]	Alveolar	10. [az]	Alveolar	15. [aɖɑ]	Retroflexed

Tell whether the sounds in the following exercise are alveopalatal or retroflexed.

Exercise 13.5: Recognizing Alveopalatal or Retroflexed Sounds

1. [aʈʂɑ]	Retroflexed	5. [aʃɑ]	Alveopalatal	9. [adʒ]	Alveopalatal
2. [adʒɑ]	Alveopalatal	6. [aʐɑ]	Retroflexed	10. [aʃɑ]	Alveopalatal
3. [aʒɑ]	Alveopalatal	7. [ʂɑ]	Retroflexed	11. [dʐɑ]	Retroflexed
4. [dʐɑ]	Retroflexed	8. [ʈʂɑ]	Retroflexed	12. [atʃɑ]	Alveopalatal

Tell whether the following sounds are velar or retroflexed.

Exercise 13.6: Recognizing Velar or Retroflexed Sounds

1. [axɑ]	Velar	5. [aɣɑ]	Velar	9. [ʂɑ]	Retroflexed
2. [aʐɑ]	Retroflexed	6. [aʐɑ]	Retroflexed	10. [aɡɣ]	Velar
3. [dʐɑ]	Retroflexed	7. [akxɑ]	Velar	11. [aʈʂɑ]	Retroflexed
4. [ʂɑ]	Retroflexed	8. [akx]	Velar	12. [ax]	Velar

Sibilants

As you examine the new fricatives presented in the beginning of this lesson, you may see two different fricatives that can be described as voiceless tip-dental fricatives, [θ] and [ʂ]. We also see two different voiced tip-dental fricatives, [ð] and [ʐ]. These sounds are not identical, though. As you consider these pairs of consonants, you will notice that there are some differences both in their articulation and in their sound.

Understanding Sibilants

One important distinction between these sounds is in the shape of the tongue. For the sounds [θ] and [ð], the surface of the tongue is relatively flat, allowing air to escape evenly along its entire width. These are called **flat fricatives**. The fricatives [s̪] and [z̪], on the other hand, are pronounced with the sides of the tongue cupped slightly upward toward the roof of the mouth. This forces the air to travel through a "channel," or "trough," down the center of the tongue and exit near the tip. Fricatives made with this type of tongue configuration are called **sibilants**. We say that sibilants have **grooved articulation**. Illustration 13.7 and Illustration 13.8 show a head-on view of the tongue illustrating the distinction between flat fricatives and sibilants.

Illustration 13.7: Flat Articulation

Illustration 13.8: Grooved Articulation

Producing Sibilants

Sibilants are usually characterized by a higher frequency hiss than flat fricatives. This is because the air pressure is increased as the size of the exit is reduced. Repeat the fricative pairs [θ] and [s] as well as [ð] and [z] to yourself and feel the difference in the air flow restriction. You should also be able to identify the difference in the shape of the tongue.

You have already been producing the sounds involved in our discussion of sibilants, and there are no new symbols to learn. You simply need to be aware of the different shapes of the tongue and know how to identify fricatives of both types. The tip-dental, or fronted, fricatives [s̪] and [z̪] are classified as sibilants since the tongue is grooved for their articulation. They may be described as voiced/voiceless tip-dental sibilants, or voiced/voiceless tip-dental grooved fricatives. The sounds [θ], [ð], [s̪], and [z̪] are included in the following exercise. Respond with "flat" or "grooved."

Exercise 13.7: Recognizing Flat or Grooved Sounds

1. [aθa]   Flat   3. [as̪a]   Grooved   5. [az̪a]   Grooved

2. [aða]   Flat   4. [aða]   Flat   6. [aθa]   Flat

7.	[ʂɑ]	Grooved	10.	[ɑð]	Flat	13.	[ɑẓ] Grooved
8.	[ɑẓ]	Grooved	11.	[ɑʂɑ]	Grooved	14.	[ɑð] Flat
9.	[ɑẓɑ]	Grooved	12.	[θɑ]	Flat	15.	[ɑθɑ] Flat

In the next exercise you will be required to consider all of the information introduced in this lesson. Respond with "fronted," "alveolar," "alveopalatal," "retroflexed," or "velar."

Exercise 13.8: Recognizing Fronted, Alveolar, Alveopalatal, Retroflexed, and Velar Sounds

1.	[ɑʂɑ]	Fronted	11.	[ɑɣɑ]	Velar	21.	[ɑʂɑ]	Fronted
2.	[ɑʃɑ]	Alveopalatal	12.	[ɑḏẓɑ]	Fronted	22.	[ɑtɑ]	Alveolar
3.	[ɑdɑ]	Alveolar	13.	[ɖʐɑ]	Retroflexed	23.	[ɑʃɑ]	Alveopalatal
4.	[ɑtɑ]	Alveolar	14.	[ɑɖɑ]	Retroflexed	24.	[ɖʐɑ]	Retroflexed
5.	[ɑɖɑ]	Retroflexed	15.	[ɑʈʂɑ]	Retroflexed	25.	[ɑzɑ]	Alveolar
6.	[ɑṭs̱]	Fronted	16.	[ɑdʒɑ]	Alveopalatal	26.	[ɑʐ]	Retroflexed
7.	[ɑʐ]	Retroflexed	17.	[ɑʂɑ]	Fronted	27.	[ɑʃɑ]	Alveopalatal
8.	[ɑdʒɑ]	Alveopalatal	18.	[ɑtɑ]	Alveolar	28.	[ɑḏẓɑ]	Fronted
9.	[ɑkxɑ]	Velar	19.	[ɑṭs̱]	Fronted	29.	[ɑɣɑ]	Velar
10.	[ɑsɑ]	Alveolar	20.	[ɑʐ]	Retroflexed	30.	[ɑʃɑ]	Alveopalatal

Table 13.1: Fronted and Retroflexed Consonants Summary

IPA symbol	Name	Technical Name	English Example	APA symbol
t̪	Fronted T	Voiceless Dental Stop		t̪
d̪	Fronted D	Voiced Dental Stop		d̪
s̪	Fronted S	Voiceless Dental Sibilant		s̪

IPA symbol	Name	Technical Name	English Example	APA symbol
z̪	Fronted Z	Voiced Dental Sibilant		z̪
n̪̊	Fronted Voiceless N	Voiceless Dental Nasal		N̪
n̪	Fronted N	Voiced Dental Nasal		n̪
ʈ	Retroflexed T	Voiceless Retroflexed Stop		ṭ
ɖ	Retroflexed D	Voiced Retroflexed Stop		ḍ
ʂ	Retroflexed S	Voiceless Retroflexed Fricative		ṣ
ʐ	Retroflexed Z	Voiced Retroflexed Fricative		ẓ
ɳ̊	Voiceless Retroflexed N	Voiceless Retroflexed Nasal		N̩
ɳ	Retroflexed N	Voiced Retroflexed Nasal		ṇ

Lesson 14:
Back Vowels

Lesson Outline

Glossary Terms

The vowel chart introduced in Lesson 12 organizes vowel qualities by their position from front to back, by their height from close to open, and by the shape of the lips, either rounded or unrounded. So far you have learned to recognize and reproduce [ɛ], [ɑ], and [o], and some associated glides. This lesson will introduce additional vowel sounds and symbols in the back and central positions.

Study the vowel symbols in the following chart. In English, some back vowels are pronounced with rounded lips, while front and central vowels are pronounced with unrounded lips. This same pattern does not apply to all languages, however. In French, for example, many of the front vowels are rounded, while Vietnamese and Turkish have some back, unrounded vowels. Any vowel may be either rounded or unrounded. In future lessons you will learn to pronounce all of the basic vowels with either rounded or unrounded lips. The bold symbols on the chart are the vowels focused on in this lesson.

Illustration 14.1: Back Vowels

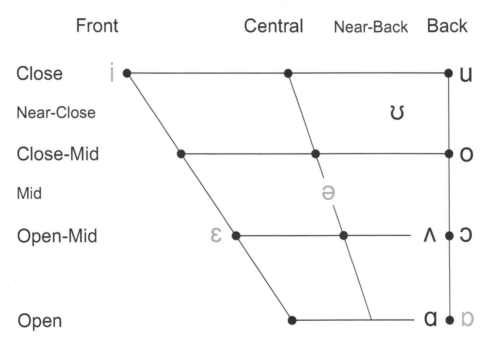

Introduction to [u], [ʊ], [ɔ], and [ʌ]

The new sounds introduced in this lesson are U [u], Upsilon [ʊ], Open O [ɔ], and Turned V [ʌ]. It is important to learn to pronounce these vowels with no glides. You may find it helpful to watch your mouth in a mirror as you practice the sounds.

When pronouncing phonetic vowel sounds, you must remember that they may not match up precisely with similar vowel sounds in your English speech. A vowel may be pronounced differently by different speakers, and there can also be strong tendencies to glide or slur the vowels. When using English words as pronunciation examples, you should always check your pronunciation of the vowel sound in that word with your instructor.

The following facial diagrams illustrate the approximate position of the tongue during the articulation of these new vowel sounds. It is important to note that the articulation of vowels is less definable or clear cut than that of consonants. Facial diagrams may not always be as accurate in portraying them. The following diagrams are included simply to give you a general idea of what makes one vowel quality different from another. Remember that there are hundreds of vowel possibilities. Altering the position of the tongue only slightly can result in a different vowel sound.

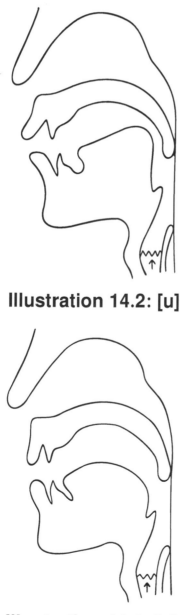

Illustration 14.2: [u]

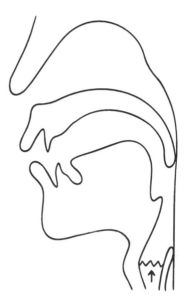

Illustration 14.3: [ʊ]

Illustration 14.4: [ʌ]

Illustration 14.5: [ɔ]

Recognizing [u] and [ʊ]

The symbol at the top right-hand side of the chart, in the close back rounded position, is the **U** [u] corresponds to the vowel sound in the English word "boot" or "tooth." There is often a tendency to precede this vowel with the tongue in a lower or more central position and then glide upward. It is important to keep the lips rounded and watch for glides such as [əᵘ] or [ʊᵘ].

The **Upsilon** [ʊ] is a near-close near-back rounded vowel and corresponds to the vowel in the word "book." Again you must make sure your lips are rounded and your tongue is near the back position. Some English speakers may say "book" with a central vowel [ə]. It may help you to begin with [u] and then open your mouth slightly to get a pure [ʊ].

The following exercises will help you to distinguish between some of the new vowel sounds. Listen to each pair of words, and respond with "same" or "different."

Exercise 14.1: Recognizing [u] and [o]

1.	[guv gov]	Different	5.	[dun dun]	Same	9.	[bunɑ bunɑ]	Same
2.	[gov gov]	Same	6.	[dun dun]	Same	10.	[bɑno bɑno]	Same
3.	[gov guv]	Different	7.	[bunɑ bonɑ]	Different	11.	[bɑnu bɑnu]	Same
4.	[dun don]	Different	8.	[bonɑ bunɑ]	Different	12.	[bɑnu bɑno]	Different

Tell whether the pairs of words in the following exercise are the same or different.

Exercise 14.2: Recognizing [u] and [ʊ]

1.	[fus fus]	Same	5.	[lus lʊs]	Different	9.	[nʊmi numi]	Different
2.	[fʊs fʊs]	Same	6.	[lʊs lus]	Different	10.	[lɑgu lɑgu]	Same
3.	[fus fʊs]	Different	7.	[nʊmi numi]	Different	11.	[lɑgʊ lɑgu]	Different
4.	[lʊm lʊm]	Same	8.	[nʊmi nʊmi]	Same	12.	[lɑgʊ lɑgu]	Different

Tell whether the pairs of words in the following exercise are the same or different.

Exercise 14.3: Recognizing [ʊ] and [o]

1.	[lom lom]	Same	3.	[lʊm lʊm]	Same	5.	[bʊn bon]	Different
2.	[lʊm lom]	Different	4.	[bon bʊn]	Different	6.	[bʊn bʊn]	Same

7. [sʊka sʊkɑ] Same   9. [sʊka soka] Different   11. [dimʊ dimo] Different

8. [soka sʊka] Different   10. [dimʊ dimʊ] Same   12. [dimʊ dimo] Different

Now mimic the vowels that we have just drilled. Be careful not to insert vowel glides. Repeat each utterance after the recording.

Exercise 14.4: Producing [u], [ʊ], and [o]

1. [but]	8. [mʊv]	15. [loztim]
2. [bʊt]	9. [mov]	16. [gudfʊn]
3. [bot]	10. [sumfan]	17. [gʊdfʊn]
4. [suz]	11. [sʊmfan]	18. [godfʊn]
5. [sʊz]	12. [somfan]	19. [lugsof]
6. [soz]	13. [luztim]	20. [lʊgsof]
7. [muv]	14. [lʊztim]	21. [logsof]

In the following sentences, substitute the vowels [u], [ʊ], and [o] for the original vowels of the sentence.

Exercise 14.5: Producing [u], [ʊ], and [o]

1. "Mary had a little lamb."   3. Mʊry hʊd ʊ lʊttle lʊmb.

2. Mury hud u luttle lumb.   4. Mory hod o lottle lomb.

In the next exercise, give the name of the vowel that you hear. Respond with "U," "Upsilon," or "O."

Exercise 14.6: Recognizing Back Vowels

1. [ʔu]	U	6. [ʔʊ]	Upsilon	11. [suʔ]	U
2. [ʔo]	O	7. [bot]	O	12. [kum]	U
3. [ʔʊ]	Upsilon	8. [gʊv]	Upsilon	13. [dok]	O
4. [ʔu]	U	9. [tok]	O	14. [mʊg]	Upsilon
5. [ʔʊ]	Upsilon	10. [bʊd]	Upsilon	15. [ʔuv]	U

Recognizing [ɔ] and [ʌ]

The open-mid back unrounded vowel is called the **Turned V** [ʌ].[1] It corresponds to the vowel in the English words "pup" and "mud." In order to eliminate any lip rounding, try smiling while you say the vowel.

The **Open O** [ɔ] is the rounded counterpart to the Turned V. It is the vowel in the English words "law" and "caught."

The [ɔ] and [ʌ] are often confused with [ɑ] and [o]. Listen to the pairs of sounds in the following series of drills, and respond with "same" or "different." These drills are designed to give you confidence in distinguishing these vowels.

Exercise 14.7: Recognizing [o] and [ɔ]

1.	[gov gɔv]	Different	5.	[don dɔn]	Different	9.	[loga lɔga]	Different
2.	[gov gov]	Same	6.	[dɔn dɔn]	Same	10.	[sɔni sɔni]	Same
3.	[gɔv gɔv]	Same	7.	[lɔga lɔga]	Same	11.	[soni sɔni]	Different
4.	[don dɔn]	Different	8.	[lɔga loga]	Different	12.	[soni sɔni]	Different

Tell whether the pairs of words in the following exercise are the same or different.

Exercise 14.8: Recognizing [ɔ] and [ɑ]

1.	[hɑs hɑs]	Same	5.	[hɔs hɑs]	Different	9.	[lɔgi lɔgi]	Same
2.	[hɔs hɑs]	Different	6.	[hɑs hɑs]	Same	10.	[numɔ numɔ]	Same
3.	[hɑs hɔs]	Different	7.	[lɔgi lɑgi]	Different	11.	[numɑ numɔ]	Different
4.	[hɔs hɔs]	Same	8.	[lɑgi lɑgi]	Same	12.	[numɔ numɑ]	Different

Tell whether the pairs of words in the following exercise are the same or different.

Exercise 14.9: Recognizing [ɑ] and [ʌ]

1.	[sʌf sʌf]	Same	4.	[bʌd bad]	Different	7.	[mʌgɑ mɑgɑ]	Different
2.	[saf saf]	Same	5.	[bʌd bʌd]	Same	8.	[mɑgɑ mɑgɑ]	Same
3.	[sʌf sʌf]	Same	6.	[bʌd bad]	Different	9.	[mɑgɑ mʌgɑ]	Different

---

1 The Turned V [ʌ] has many nicknames, including caret, wedge, hat, and even pup tent.

10. [lisʌ lisɑ]   Different   11. [lisɑ lisɑ]   Same   12. [lisʌ lisɑ]   Different

Mimic the vowels in the following exercise. When pronouncing [ɔ], you must be careful not to finalize it with an off-glide. It is a tendency of many English speakers to conclude the vowel with a glide to the schwa position. Try to keep the tongue in a back position, slightly more open than [o] and a little less rounded.

Exercise 14.10: Producing [o], [ɔ], [ɑ] and [ʌ]

1. [bot]	8. [sʌz]	15. [sɑmfɑn]	22. [gotsɑk]
2. [bɔt]	9. [mov]	16. [sʌmfɑn]	23. [gɑtsɑk]
3. [bɑt]	10. [mɔv]	17. [loztim]	24. [gʌtsɑk]
4. [bʌt]	11. [mɑv]	18. [lɔztim]	25. [logsof]
5. [soz]	12. [mʌv]	19. [lɑztim]	26. [lɔgsof]
6. [sɔz]	13. [somfɑn]	20. [lʌztim]	27. [lɑgsof]
7. [sɑz]	14. [sɔmfɑn]	21. [gotsɑk]	28. [lʌgsof]

Now try the sentence "Mary had a little lamb" replacing each vowel with one of the four vowels [o], [ɔ], [ɑ], and [ʌ].

Exercise 14.11: Producing [o], [ɔ], [ɑ], and [ʌ]

1. Mory hod o lottle lomb.   3. Mɑry hɑd ɑ lɑttle lɑmb.

2. Mɔry hɔd ɔ lɔttle lɔmb.   4. Mʌry hʌd ʌ lʌttle lʌmb.

Give the name of the vowels you hear. Respond with "O," "Open O," "Script A," or "Turned V."

Exercise 14.12: Recognizing Back Vowels

1. [bɑt]	Script A	5. [dok]	O	9. [pʰɔnt]	Open O
2. [tʰɔk]	Open O	6. [lʌf]	Turned V	10. [dɔg]	Open O
3. [mʌt]	Turned V	7. [wɑs]	Script ɑ	11. [lʌpt]	Turned V
4. [sɔz]	Open O	8. [kop]	O	12. [gʌdz]	Turned V

13. [tʰɑf]	Script ɑ	16. [doʊ]	O	19. [fʌs]	Turned V
14. [spʌn]	Turned V	17. [mɔld]	Open O	20. [mɑdz]	Script ɑ
15. [nɔm]	Open O	18. [pod]	O	21. [ɔm]	Open O

Producing [u], [ʊ], [ɔ], and [ʌ] with Glides

Now that you are familiar with the sounds of the new vowels, focus on controlling the on-glides and off-glides that may be associated with them. Listen for the off-glides in the following exercise, and determine if each syllable contains a vowel glide or not.

Exercise 14.13: Recognizing Glided and Pure Vowels

1.	[sʌᵘ]	Glided	6.	[sʊᵊt]	Glided	11. [zɔᵊk]	Glided
2.	[sʌ]	No	7.	[sʊm]	No	12. [ʃʊz]	No
3.	[sɔᵊ]	Glided	8.	[suk]	No	13. [mʌⁱt]	Glided
4.	[sut]	No	9.	[sɔl]	No	14. [nuf]	No
5.	[sɔt]	No	10.	[ʊᵘm]	Glided	15. [bʊᵘs]	Glided

Follow the text in the next exercise, and repeat each sound after the recording.

Exercise 14.14: Producing Glided and Pure Vowels

1. [sʊᵘsʊ]	7. [sɔᵘsɔ]	13. [sʌᵘsʌ]
2. [sʊsʊᵘ]	8. [sɔsɔᵘ]	14. [sʌsʌᵘ]
3. [sʊsʊ]	9. [sɔsɔ]	15. [sʌsʌ]
4. [sʊᵊsʊ]	10. [sɔᵊsɔ]	16. [sʌⁱsʌ]
5. [sʊsʊᵊ]	11. [sɔsɔᵊ]	17. [sʌsʌⁱ]
6. [sʊᵊsʊⁱ]	12. [sɔᵊsɔⁱ]	18. [sʌᵊsʌⁱ]

Describing Back Vowels

Just like consonants, vowel qualities may also be described in terms of their articulatory characteristics and conditions. A vowel's technical name gives its position from front to back, the height of the tongue, and the shape of the lips. The vowel [u], for instance, is described as a close back rounded vowel. The vowel [ɑ] is an open back unrounded vowel. Notice that the term for height is given first, followed by the vowel's position and finally lip rounding.

The following exercises will help you learn to describe vowels by giving their technical names. Begin by telling whether the vowel you hear is rounded or unrounded. You may look at the vowel chart at first if necessary. These exercises will include all of the vowels introduced so far.

Exercise 14.15: Recognizing Rounded and Unrounded Vowels

1. [ʔɔ] Rounded	7. [ʔʊ] Rounded	13. [tʊp] Rounded
2. [ʔu] Rounded	8. [pɛm] Unrounded	14. [suf] Rounded
3. [ʔɑ] Unrounded	9. [dɑs] Unrounded	15. [lɑd] Unrounded
4. [ʔɛ] Unrounded	10. [gʌv] Unrounded	16. [gʊm] Rounded
5. [ʔo] Rounded	11. [bɔf] Rounded	17. [bɛg] Unrounded
6. [ʔʌ] Unrounded	12. [lɛz] Unrounded	18. [mɔk] Rounded

In the following exercise, give the vowel's position from front to back, as well as the rounding of the vowel. Respond with "front unrounded," "central unrounded," or "back rounded."

Exercise 14.16: Recognizing Vowel Position and Rounding

1. [sʊ] Back Rounded	7. [mu] Back Rounded	13. [sɛv] Front Unrounded
2. [sʌ] Back Unrounded	8. [su] Back Rounded	14. [ɔg] Back Rouned
3. [sɔ] Back Rounded	9. [no] Back Rounded	15. [fɑnz] Back Unrounded
4. [lɛ] Front Unrounded	10. [lom] Back Rounded	16. [ʌm] Back Unrounded
5. [lʊ] Back Rounded	11. [tʌk] Back Unrounded	17. [lʊgz] Back Rounded
6. [lɛ] Front Unrounded	12. [bʊf] Back Rounded	18. [gɑm] Back Unrounded

Now give the height of the vowel in each utterance. Respond with "close," "near-close," "close-mid," "open-mid," or "open." It may be necessary to look at the vowel chart at first.

Exercise 14.17: Recognizing Vowel Height

1. [nɔ]   Open-mid
2. [nɛ]   Open-mid
3. [nʊ]   Near-Close
4. [ʃo]   Close-Mid
5. [ʃɔ]   Open-mid
6. [ʃʌ]   Open-mid

7. [uʒ]   Close
8. [fo]   Close-Mid
9. [ʒɑʒ]   Open
10. [ɛm]   Open-mid
11. [tʌʃ]   Open-mid
12. [mʊf]   Near-Close

13. [ðɑt]   Open
14. [tʰɔg]   Open-mid
15. [kʰup]   Close
16. [sodz]   Close-Mid
17. [ɛd]   Open-mid
18. [ʃʊð]   Near-Close

Now combine all of the terms that we have practiced to give the full technical name of each vowel. First give the term for the vowel's height, and then its position from front to back and finally, its lip rounding. You may need to look at the chart to begin with.

Exercise 14.18: Full Technical Names of Vowels

1. [ʔɛ]   Open-mid Front Unrounded
2. [ʔʊ]   Near-close Back Rounded
3. [ʔɔ]   Open-mid Back Rounded
4. [ʔʌ]   Open-mid Back Unrounded
5. [gʌŋ]   Open-mid Back Unrounded
6. [tʰuʒ]   Closelose Back Rounded
7. [mɑt]   Open Back Unrounded
8. [lɛʃ]   Open-mid Front Unrounded
9. [ʊv]   Near-close Back Rounded
10. [pʰɑk]   Open Back Unrounded
11. [nʌlz]   Open-mid Back Unrounded

12. [ŋom]   Close-mid Back Rounded
13. [u]   Close Back Rounded
14. [xɔv]   Open-mid Back Rounded
15. [ʃɑʃ]   Open Back Unrounded
16. [doʒ]   Close-mid Back Rounded
17. [ʒʊ]   Near-close Back Rounded
18. [ɛs]   Open-mid Front Unrounded
19. [tu]   Close Back Rounded
20. [o]   Close-mid Back Rounded
21. [ʔɔf]   Open-mid Back Rounded
22. [zɑŋ]   Open Back Unrounded

23. [ʊ]	Near-close Back Rounded		27. [lɔg]	Open-mid Back Rounded
24. [kʰʊʔ]	Near-close Back Rounded		28. [ʃɛl]	Open-mid Front Unrounded
25. [fɛs]	Open-mid Front Unrounded		29. [ʃuvz]	Close Back Rounded
26. [pʰok]	Close-mid Back Rounded		30. [ʔʌʔ]	Open-mid Back Unrounded

The following table summarizes the vowel sounds and symbols introduced in this lesson and gives the corresponding APA symbol for each. Many of the basic vowel symbols are the same in both IPA and APA. The technical names, however, may differ considerably.

Table 14.1: Back and Central Vowels

IPA Symbol	Name	Technical Name	English Example	APA Symbol
u	U	Close Back Rounded Vowel	flute	u
ʊ	Upsilon	Near-close Near-back Rounded Vowel	put	ʊ
o	O	Close-mid Back Rounded Vowel	vote	o
ɔ	Open O	Open-mid Back Rounded Vowel	office	ɔ
ʌ	Turned V	Open-mid Back Unrounded Vowel	mud	ʌ
ɑ	Script A	Open Back Unrounded Vowel	father	ɑ

Lesson 15: Nasals

Lesson Outline

Glossary

In Lesson 1, we introduced the nasal manner of articulation. Nasal sounds are produced when the articulator and point of articulation create a complete closure in the oral cavity and the velic is open, allowing the air stream to pass through the nose. This results in a sound that resonates more in the nasal cavity than the oral cavity. If the velic were to be closed, the resulting consonant would be a stop. Nasal consonants usually involve very little restriction of the air stream.

There are many different possibilities for nasal articulation. Any stop formed in the oral cavity can be changed into a nasal by simply opening the velic. The following chart of nasal consonants gives the new sounds that will be introduced in this lesson.

Table 15.1: Introducing Nasals

	Bilabial	Labiodental	Tip-Dental	Tip-Alveolar	Tip/Blade-Alveopalatal	Tip-Retroflexed	Blade-Palatal	Back-Velar
Voiceless	m̥	ɱ̥	n̪̥	n̥	ñ̥	ɳ̥	ɲ̥	ŋ̊
Voiced	m	ɱ	n̪	n	ñ	ɳ	ɲ	ŋ

Introduction to Common Nasals

You are already familiar with the nasal consonants M [m], N [n], and to a lesser extent, Eng [ŋ], all of which occur in English. **M** [m] is simply a bilabial nasal, and **N** [n] is an alveolar nasal.

We will focus on some nasals with which you may not be so familiar. Remember that good control over the velic is paramount when dealing with nasals. You must be able to open and close your velic at will during any articulation. Try repeating the following sequences to help gain control of your velic. During the following transitions between stops and nasals, the position of the articulators and points of articulation do not change; only the velic opens and closes.

Exercise 15.1: Controlling the Velic

1. [bmbmbmbmbm]

2. [dndndndndn]

3. [gŋgŋgŋgŋgŋ]

Producing Initial Eng [ŋ]

The **Eng** [ŋ] is articulated by the back of the tongue contacting the velar point of articulation. If you are a native English speaker, you have used this sound extensively in the medial and final positions. However, its production in the initial position may be new to you, since this sound never occurs at the beginning of an utterance in English. English speakers trying to produce an initial [ŋ] have a tendency to put their tongue tip against the alveolar ridge, resulting in [n]. Placing the tip of your tongue down behind your lower teeth while pronouncing the [ŋ] can help you avoid this tendency.

To produce initial [ŋ], start by saying the word "singing," and repeat the "ing" several times. Then say the same sequence changing the stress placement to stress the [ŋ] rather than the "i." Now try to isolate the syllables to arrive at [ŋi]. This procedure is demonstrated in the following exercise. Follow along in the text, and repeat each utterance after the recording.

Exercise 15.2: Producing Initial [ŋ]

1. [ˈsiŋ ˈiŋ ˈiŋ ˈiŋ ˈiŋ]

2. [ˈsi ˈŋi ˈŋi ˈŋi ˈŋi]

3. [ˈŋi ˈŋi ˈŋi ˈŋi ˈŋi]

4. [ˈŋi ˈŋi ˈŋi ˈŋi ˈŋi]

Repeat each of the following utterances after the recording.

Exercise 15.3: Producing Initial [ŋ]

1. a) [ŋɛ] b) [ɛŋɛ] c) [ŋɛŋɛ] d) [ŋɛŋɛŋ]

2. a) [ŋɑ] b) [ɑŋɑ] c) [ŋɑŋɑ] d) [ŋɑŋɑŋ]

3. a) [ŋo] b) [oŋo] c) [ŋoŋo] d) [ŋoŋoŋ]

When pronouncing the [ŋ], many English speakers tend to close the velic before actually releasing the nasal. This results in a nasal/stop sequence such as [ɑŋgɑ]. Listen to the following exercise, and try to detect the nasal/stop sequences. Respond with "nasal," "stop," or "both." Do not look at the text.

Exercise 15.4: Recognizing Nasals and Stops

1.	[ɑgɑ]	Stop	4.	[ɛŋgɛ]	Both	7.	[ogo]	Stop
2.	[ɑŋgɑ]	Both	5.	[ɛŋgɛ]	Both	8.	[oŋo]	Nasal
3.	[ɑŋɑ]	Nasal	6.	[ɛŋɛ]	Nasal	9.	[oŋo]	Nasal

| 10. [aŋg] | Both | 12. [ɛn] | Nasal | 14. [ɛgɛ] | Stop |
| 11. [ŋɛ] | Nasal | 13. [oɲ] | Nasal | 15. [ŋgo] | Both |

Producing [ñ]

The **Enye** [ñ] is produced when the blade of the tongue contacts the alveopalatal area. This sound does not normally occur in English, but is quite prevalent in Spanish and many other languages. It is used in the Spanish word "año" (year).

The symbol presented in this course, [ñ], is an APA symbol, which is used widely for this sound.[1] The diacritic above the consonant is called a **Tilde** [~].

The position of the tongue for [ñ] corresponds roughly with its position for [i]. Its position is the same from front to back, but the tongue is higher for the nasal than it is for a the vowel. If you begin with the vowel [i] and gradually close your mouth while keeping the tongue in the same position from front to back, you should arrive at [ñ] once the articulator and point of articulation meet. For this reason, the [ñ] is often accompanied by a palatal approximant [j],[2] which is similar in sound to an [i] glide, as the articulator moves either toward or away from the articulation of [ñ]. Although this glided quality occurs quite naturally, it is technically not a part of [ñ] articulation. It is safe to say, however, that in most cases, the [ñ] will have a slight [i] sound associated with it. In this course, when the glided quality is present, you will not be required to transcribe it.

Alveopalatal nasals are demonstrated in the following exercise both with and without glides. Listen to the recording, and mimic each utterance paying specific attention to the glides.

Exercise 15.5: Producing [ñ] With and Without Glides

1. [aña]	4. [ɛñɛ]	7. [oño]
2. [añⁱa]	5. [ɛñⁱɛ]	8. [oñⁱo]
3. [aⁱña]	6. [ɛⁱñɛ]	9. [oⁱño]

Use Illustrations 15.1–15.3 below to compare the articulations of [n], [ñ], and [ŋ]. You may also use them as a reference point for the articulation of the new nasal. Notice how the tip of the tongue is slightly lowered for [ñ] as the blade contacts the alveopalatal area.

---

1   Officially, the IPA interprets the Spanish enye as a palatal nasal and symbolizes it as [ɲ]. An alveopalatal nasal is officially symbolized in the IPA as a retracted alveolar nasal [n̠].

2   The J [j], and other approximants, will be studied in detail in later chapters.

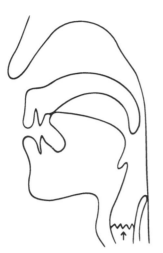
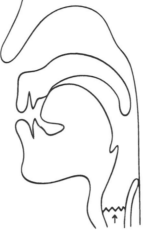
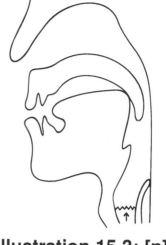

Illustration 15.1: [n] **Illustration 15.2: [ñ]** **Illustration 15.3: [ŋ]**

To produce [ñ], use the blade of your tongue to touch the alveopalatal area. Make sure the tip of your tongue is down behind your lower teeth to prevent it from touching the alveolar ridge. Follow the text and mimic the nasals in the following recording.

Exercise 15.6: Producing [ñ]

1. a) [ña]   b) [aña]   c) [ñaña]   d) [ñañañ]

2. a) [ñɛ]   b) [ɛñɛ]   c) [ñɛñɛ]   d) [ñɛñɛñ]

3. a) [ño]   b) [oño]   c) [ñoño]   d) [ñoñoñ]

Fronted and Retroflexed Nasals

In Lesson 11 you learned that alveolar consonants are fronted by placing the tip of the tongue firmly against the back of the upper teeth, and retroflexed consonants are articulated by curling the tongue upward and slightly back. In this lesson, you will apply these principles to the nasal manner of articulation to produce the sounds [n̪], and [ɳ].

Producing Fronted N [n̪]

The articulation of **fronted N** [n̪] corresponds to [d̪] presented in Lesson 11. The only difference in articulation is that, for the nasal, the velic is open. Illustration 15.4 below depicts the articulation of [n̪]. Try saying the words "ten things" ['tʰɛn̪.θiŋz]. Many English speakers replace the alveolar [n] with a fronted nasal as they prepare for the dental fricative. When producing fronted sounds, make sure that the tip of your tongue does not protrude past your teeth.

Producing Right-Tail N [ɳ]

A retroflexed nasal is represented by a symbol called **Right-tail N** [ɳ]. Notice that its articulation is the same as [ɖ] except that the velic is open. Some English speakers might retroflex the "n" in "doorknob" [ˈdo˞.ɳɑb]. If you do not feel retroflexed articulation in this sequence, start with [ɖ] and then open the velic while holding the same articulation. Be careful that you do not go too far and place the tip of the tongue at the palatal area.

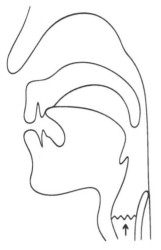
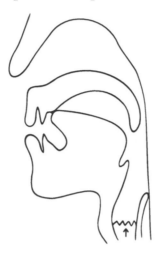

Illustration 15.4: [n̪]   **Illustration 15.5: [n]**   **Illustration 15.6: [ɳ]**

The difference between fronted and alveolar nasals can be hard to hear, but the distinction is important. The following recording demonstrates and contrasts [n̪], [n], and [ɳ] in a sequence. The exercise will be given twice. Listen to the recording the first time, and mimic the second time.

Exercise 15.7: Producing [n̪], [n],and [ɳ]

1. a) [aɳa ana an̪a]   b) [n̪anana]

2. a) [ɛɳɛ ɛnɛ ɛn̪ɛ]   b) [n̪ɛnɛnɛ]

3. a) [oɳo ono on̪o]   b) [n̪onono]

Follow the text, and repeat each utterance with the articulation indicated.

Exercise 15.8: Producing [n̪] and [ɳ]

1. a) [n̪a]   b) [an̪a]   c) [n̪an̪a]   d) [n̪an̪an̪]

2. a) [ɳa]   b) [aɳa]   c) [ɳaɳa]   d) [ɳaɳaɳ]

3. a) [n̪ɛ]   b) [ɛn̪ɛ]   c) [n̪ɛn̪ɛ]   d) [n̪ɛn̪ɛn̪]

4.   a) [ɳɛ]   b) [ɛɳɛ]   c) [ɳɛɳɛ]   d) [ɳɛɳɛɳ]

5.   a) [n̪o]   b) [on̪o]   c) [n̪on̪o]   d) [n̪on̪on̪]

6.   a) [ɳo]   b) [oɳo]   c) [ɳoɳo]   d) [ɳoɳoɳ]

Repeat the following sentences, and replace the [n] in each word with each of the new nasal sounds. Follow the transcriptions.

Exercise 15.9: Producing [n̪], [ñ], [ɳ], and [ŋ]

1.   "Næ næ næ said the little fox."

    a) ŋæ ŋæ ŋæ said the little fox

    b) ñæ ñæ ñæ said the little fox

    c) ɳæ ɳæ ɳæ said the little fox

    d) n̪æ n̪æ n̪æ said the little fox

2.   "Ned never knew Nancy's new number."

    a) n̪ed n̪ever n̪ew n̪an̪cy's n̪ew n̪umber

    b) ñed ñever ñew ñañcy's ñew ñumber

    c) ɳed ɳever ɳew ɳaɳcy's ɳew ɳumber

    d) ŋed ŋever ŋew ŋaŋcy's ŋew ŋumber

3.   "Ten thin men man one gun."

    a) ten̪ thin̪ men̪ man̪ on̪e gun̪

    b) teñ thiñ meñ mañ oñe guñ

    c) teɳ thiɳ meɳ maɳ oɳe guɳ

    d) teŋ thiŋ meŋ maŋ oŋe guŋ

The following exercise contains [ñ], [ɳ], and [ŋ]. Respond with "alveopalatal," "retroflexed," or "velar." Do not look at the text.

Exercise 15.10: Recognizing Alveopalatal, Retroflexed, and Velar Nasals

1.	[aŋa]	Velar	7.	[oŋo]	Velar	13.	[ɛñɛ]	Alveopalatal
2.	[aña]	Alveopalatal	8.	[oɳo]	Retroflexed	14.	[aŋo]	Retroflexed
3.	[aɳa]	Retroflexed	9.	[oño]	Alveopalatal	15.	[oɳ]	Retroflexed
4.	[ɛñɛ]	Alveopalatal	10.	[oñ]	Alveopalatal	16.	[aŋ]	Velar
5.	[ɛɳɛ]	Retroflexed	11.	[ɛɳo]	Retroflexed	17.	[oñɛ]	Alveopalatal
6.	[ɛŋɛ]	Velar	12.	[ŋɛ]	Velar	18.	[ɛña]	Alveopalatal

Producing [ɱ]

The symbol for labiodental nasals is a lowercase "M" with a left tail on its right leg. Some linguists call it **Meng** [ɱ] (pronounced [miɳ]). Labiodental nasals are less common than most other nasals. When they do occur, they usually precede a labiodental fricative like [f] or [v]. In such cases, the articulation of the nasal is being modified to conform to the articulation of the fricative. English speakers often say the words "comfort" and "circumvent" with [ɱ] rather than [m].

To produce the voiced labiodental nasal [ɱ], put your lower lip and upper teeth in position for [v] and say "mama." Make sure that your velic is open and the air stream does not exit through your mouth. You may also prolong [ɱ] while gradually moving your lower lip backward to the dental position. Repeat the following utterances after the recording.

Exercise 15.11: Producing [ɱ]

1. [vavavavava]

2. [vaɱavaɱavaɱavaɱavaɱa]

3. [ɱaɱaɱaɱaɱa]

Although the voiceless labiodental nasal appears on the nasal chart, it rarely, if ever, regularly occurs in any actual language. Some English speakers could pronounce the [ɱ̊] in rapid speech instead of [m] when followed by a voiceless labiodental fricative [f], for example, "comfort" [ˈkʌɱ̊.fɚt].

Voiceless Nasals

For every voiced nasal, it is possible to articulate a voiceless counterpart. **Voiceless nasals** are found in many languages throughout the world. They often occur immediately before or after voiced nasals of the same point of articulation. However, in some languages they can occur alone just as any other consonant.

An **Under-ring** [ˌ] beneath a nasal symbol indicates that the nasal is voiceless. If the symbol has a descender, like [ŋ], an Over-ring [˚] is placed above it, such as [ŋ̊].

Voiceless nasals are produced by simply controlling the glottis, or vocal cords. It involves nothing more than blowing air through the nose during the articulation of a given nasal consonant. Consider the English interjection "Hmmm." The [h] sound at the beginning of this utterance is actually a voiceless bilabial nasal if the lips are closed and the air escapes through the nose. Repeat this interjection to yourself several times and notice that the only thing that changes between the so-called "h" and the "mmm" is the voicing. You must not confuse voiceless nasals with [h], however. In a nasal the entire air stream exits through the nasal cavity, while with [h] it exits through the oral cavity. If you have trouble telling whether a voiceless sound is a nasal or not, try holding your nose while saying the sound. If the air stream is entirely stopped, the sound is a nasal.

Say the following English interjections several times and then replace the [m] with other nasals. Repeat each utterance after the recording.

Exercise 15.12: Producing Voiceless Nasals

1. a) [m̥m]   b) [n̥n]   c) [ɲ̊ɲ]   d) [ŋ̊ŋ]

2. a) [m̥mʔm]   b) [n̥nʔn]   c) [ɲ̊ɲʔɲ]   d) [ŋ̊ŋʔŋ]

3. a) [ʔmm̥m]   b) [ʔnn̥n]   c) [ʔɲɲ̊ɲ]   d) [ʔŋŋ̊ŋ]

You must be able to pronounce voiceless nasals without their voiced counterparts. Some speakers may find this difficult at first. The following exercise will help you to hear the difference between voiceless nasals and voiced/voiceless combinations. Respond with "voiced," "voiceless," or "both."

Exercise 15.13: Recognizing Voiced and Voiceless Nasals

1. [am̥ma] Both   4. [on̥o] Voiceless   7. [aŋ̊] Voiceless

2. [ama] Voiced   5. [ɛŋɛ] Voiced   8. [m̥ma] Both

3. [am̥a] Voiceless   6. [aɲ̊ɲa] Both   9. [ɛnn̥] Both

10. [ɑñ̥]   Voiced   12. [ɛñɛ]   Voiced   14. [ɛn̥ɛ]   Voiceless

11. [om̥mo] Both   13. [ɛm̥ɛ]   Voiceless   15. [ŋ̥ŋo]   Both

Now try saying the same sentences as before, substituting voiceless nasals for voiced ones. Be careful not to insert unwanted voiced nasals along with the voiceless ones. Follow the transcription.

Exercise 15.14: Producing Voiceless Nasals

1. "Næ næ næ said the little fox."

   a) m̥æ m̥æ m̥æ said the little fox

   b) n̥æ n̥æ n̥æ said the little fox

   c) ñ̥æ ñ̥æ ñ̥æ said the little fox

   d) ŋ̥æ ŋ̥æ ŋ̥æ said the little fox

2. "Ned never knew Nancy's new number."

   a) m̥ed m̥ever m̥ew m̥am̥cy's m̥ew m̥umber

   b) n̥ed n̥ever n̥ew n̥an̥cy's n̥ew n̥umber

   c) ñ̥ed ñ̥ever ñ̥ew ñ̥añ̥cy's ñ̥ew ñ̥umber

   d) ŋ̥ed ŋ̥ever ŋ̥ew ŋ̥añ̥cy's ŋ̥ew ŋ̥umber

3. "Ten thin men man one gun."

   a) tem̥ thim̥ mem̥ mam̥ om̥e gum̥

   b) ten̥ thin̥ men̥ man̥ on̥e gun̥

   c) teñ̥ thiñ̥ meñ̥ mañ̥ oñ̥e guñ̥

   d) teŋ̥ thiŋ̥ meŋ̥ maŋ̥ oŋ̥e guŋ̥

Table 15.2: Nasals Summary

IPA Symbol	Name	Technical Name	English Example	APA Symbol(s)
m̥	Voiceless M	Voiceless Bilabial Nasal	hmmm	M
m	M	Voiced Bilabial Nasal	mom	m
ɱ̊	Voiceless Meng	Voiceless Labiodental Nasal		Ṃ
ɱ	Meng	Voiced Labiodental Nasal	comfort	ṃ
n̪̊	Voiceless Fronted N	Voiceless Tip-Dental Nasal		N̪
n̪	Fronted N	Voiced Tip-Dental Nasal		n̪
n̥	Voiceless N	Voiceless Tip-Alveolar Nasal		N
n	N	Voiced Tip-Alveolar Nasal	nun	n
ñ̥,[3] n̥̲	Voiceless Enye, Voiceless Retracted N	Voiceless Blade-Alveopalatal Nasal		Ñ
ñ,[4] n̲	Enye, Voiced Retracted Nasal	Voiced Blade-Alveopalatal Nasal		ñ

---

3   This symbol is adopted from APA.

4   This symbol is adopted from APA.

IPA Symbol	Name	Technical Name	English Example	APA Symbol(s)
ɳ̥	Voiceless Right-Tail N	Voiceless Tip-Retroflexed Nasal		Ṇ
ɳ	Right-Tail N	Voiced Tip-Retroflexed Nasal	doorknob	ṇ
ɲ̥	Voiceless Left-Hook N	Voiceless Blade-Palatal Nasal		ŋ̂, Ñ
ɲ	Left-Hook N	Voiced Blade-Palatal Nasal		ɲ, ŋ̂, ñ
ŋ̊	Voiceless Eng	Voiceless Back-Velar Nasal		ŋ
ŋ	Eng	Voiced Back-Velar Nasal	si**ng**	ŋ

Lesson 16:
Front Vowels

Lesson Outline

Glossary

All of the vowels in this lesson are unrounded. You will not be required to learn much new terminology since you are already familiar with the terms for vowel height and position. We will simply add a few new symbols and sounds to fill in the empty positions on the chart.

As we work with more vowel sounds, remember that we cannot claim absolute precision in the articulation and position of a given vowel since there is always a small amount of variation in their pronunciation. With the vowel chart we are dealing more with how vowel sounds are perceived than exactly how they are produced.

Illustration 16.1: Front and Near-Front Vowels

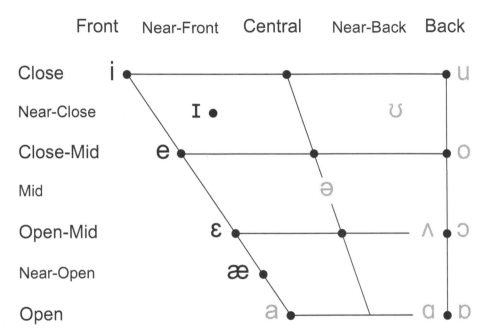

The bold symbols [i], [ɪ], [e], and [æ] in Illustration 16.1 are the front/near-front vowel sounds introduced in this lesson. They are quite similar to many English sounds, but you must produce them without the glides and modifications that are native to most dialects of English. English front vowels are often produced slightly farther back than the true front position, and [i] is usually produced slightly more open than a true [i] vowel as well. You must be aware of these habits before you can begin to produce phonetically pure vowel sounds. The emphasis throughout the remainder of this course is the production of unglided vowels unless a glide is specifically indicated in the transcription.

Illustration 16.2 below indicates the approximate tongue position for the four vowels [i], [ɪ], [e], and [æ]. Notice that the tip is not the highest part of the tongue for front vowels. The tip is usually just behind or against the lower teeth. This diagram shows only the different positions of the tongue and not that of the other facial features. In reality the entire lower jaw moves with the tongue for each different vowel.

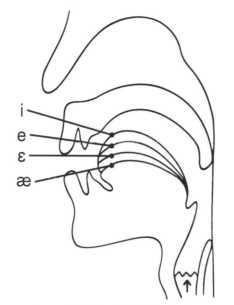

Illustration 16.2: [i], [ɪ], [e], and [æ]

Producing [i]

The close front unrounded vowel **I** [i] corresponds to the vowel sound in the words "bee" and "tea." As we have already mentioned, many English speakers do not pronounce [i] as high or as far forward as it should be. With [i], we are striving for articulation as high and as front as possible for a vowel sound. You must also make sure that you do not pronounce this vowel as [ɪⁱ], as is often the tendency. Practice saying [i] with no vowel glide and as far forward as possible.

The following exercise will help you learn to recognize [i]. Listen to the recording and respond with "same" or "different."

Exercise 16.1: Recognizing [i] and [ɪ]

1.	[pʰɹik pʰɹik]	Same	5.	[pʰɹɪk pʰɹɪk]	Same	9.	[lɪfɑ lifɑ]	Different
2.	[pʰɹik pʰɹɪk]	Different	6.	[pʰɹik pʰɹik]	Same	10.	[soni soni]	Same
3.	[pʰɹɪk pʰɹik]	Different	7.	[lifɑ lɪfɑ]	Different	11.	[sonɪ sonɪ]	Same
4.	[pʰɹɪk pʰɹik]	Different	8.	[lɪfɑ lɪfɑ]	Same	12.	[soni sonɪ]	Different

Listen for on-glides and off-glides in the following exercise. Determine if each syllable contains a vowel glide or not.

Exercise 16.2: Recognizing Glided and Pure Vowels

1.	[briᵗ]	Glide	4.	[tʊrⁱ]	Glide	7.	[tʰiks]	No
2.	[tʰiᵊm]	Glide	5.	[pʰiz]	No	8.	[pʰrⁱz]	Glide
3.	[mit]	No	6.	[xif]	No	9.	[fist]	No

Producing [ɪ]

The near-close near-front unrounded vowel is represented by a **Small Capital I** [ɪ] and corresponds to the vowel sound in the words "bit" and "stick." Note that when pronouncing [ɪ], the tongue's position is slightly farther back in the mouth. Be careful not to produce the [ɪ] with a [ə] off-glide, such as many English speakers do in the word "bit" [bɪᵊt].

To practice recognizing the Small Capital I, listen to the next exercise, and respond with "same" or "different." Do not follow along with the text.

Exercise 16.3: Recognizing [ɪ] and [e]

1.	[ʔɪ ʔe]	Different	5.	[ʔɪt ʔet]	Different	9.	[bɪte bɪte]	Same
2.	[gɪf gɪf]	Same	6.	[sef sɪf]	Different	10.	[nɑke nɑkɪ]	Different
3.	[mɪd mɪd]	Same	7.	[dɪkɑ dɪkɑ]	Same	11.	[sofɪ sofɪ]	Same
4.	[nek nɪk]	Different	8.	[mɛsɑ mɪsɑ]	Different	12.	[tikɪ tiki]	Different

A Small Capital I [ɪ] pronounced with a [ə] off-glide can often be difficult to distinguish from a pure [ɪ] sound. This next exercise will contrast glided [ɪ] with pure [ɪ]. Each word will be given twice. The first time the word will contain a pure vowel. The second word will include a [ə] off-glide. Follow the transcription.

Exercise 16.4: Recognizing [ɪ] and [ɪᵊ]

1.	[bɪt bɪᵊt]	4.	[mɪt mɪᵊt]	7.	[wɪl wɪᵊl]
2.	[pʰɪt pʰɪᵊt]	5.	[pʰɪg pʰɪᵊg]	8.	[skɪt skɪᵊt]
3.	[tʰɪk tʰɪᵊk]	6.	[tʰɹɪk tʰɹɪᵊk]	9.	[bɹɪdʒ bɹɪᵊdʒ]

Listen to the vowels in the following exercise, and determine if there is a vowel glide or not.

Exercise 16.5: Recognizing Glided [ɪ]

1.	[bɪt]	No	5.	[xɪᵉf]	Glide	9.	[tɪd]	No
2.	[bɪᵉt]	Glide	6.	[θɪm]	No	10.	[zɪᵉb]	Glide
3.	[sɪf]	No	7.	[sɪᵉt]	Glide	11.	[ðɪᵉm]	Glide
4.	[ðɪᵉθ]	Glide	8.	[θɪp]	No	12.	[hɪn]	No

Producing [e]

The close-mid front unrounded vowel **E** [e] is similar to the sound in the words "bait" and "mate." This vowel is one of the hardest for English speakers to produce as a pure vowel because it virtually never occurs as such in English. It is usually accompanied by a strong [i] off-glide. To produce this vowel correctly, say "bay," and make sure that your mouth does not close to the [i] position. Your tongue must remain stationary throughout the articulation of the vowel to eliminate the glide. Practice saying [e] without gliding to another vowel.

Listen to the difference between glided [eⁱ] and pure [e] in the following exercise. Each word will be given twice. The English pronunciation will be given first and then be followed by a pure vowel. Watch your mouth in a mirror.

Exercise 16.6: Recognizing [eⁱ] and [e]

1.	[weⁱt wet]	5.	[geⁱm gem]	9.	[ʃeⁱm ʃem]
2.	[tʰeⁱl tʰel]	6.	[beⁱl bel]	10.	[tʃʰeⁱn tʃʰen]
3.	[seⁱ se]	7.	[bleⁱm blem]	11.	[bleⁱd bled]
4.	[tʰeⁱk tʰek]	8.	[weⁱd wed]	12.	[meⁱbi mebi]

Now practice distinguishing [e] from other similar vowels. Respond with "same" or "different."

Exercise 16.7: Recognizing [e] and [ɛ]

1.	[bet bet]	Same	2.	[tef tɪf]	Different	3.	[gem gem]	Same

4.	[nev nɪv]	Different	8.	[ʒem ʒem]	Same	12.	[ben bɛn]	Different
5.	[fen fɪn]	Different	9.	[bez bez]	Same	13.	[veʒ veʒ]	Same
6.	[kel kel]	Same	10.	[ʔɛk ʔɛk]	Same	14.	[tɛð teð]	Different
7.	[gen gɛn]	Different	11.	[tɛk tek]	Different	15.	[fed fed]	Same

Listen to the vowels in the following exercise, and determine if there is a vowel glide or not.

Exercise 16.8: Recognizing Glided [e]

1.	[fet]	No	6.	[den]	No	11.	[tʰʲeⁱl]	Glide
2.	[deⁱs]	Glide	7.	[ʃeⁱk]	Glide	12.	[ʃel]	No
3.	[ʃeⁱf]	Glide	8.	[ʔem]	No	13.	[tʰʲeⁱs]	Glide
4.	[ʔen]	No	9.	[vex]	No	14.	[ʃeⁱdʒ]	Glide
5.	[dʒeⁱt]	Glide	10.	[mep]	No	15.	[gedʒ]	No

Producing [æ]

Ash [æ][1] is a near-open front unrounded vowel. It corresponds to the vowel sound in the words "bat" and "sad." English speakers normally produce this vowel with a [ə] off-glide. Although this is not a characteristic of all dialects, you should still be aware of this tendency and strive to produce a pure Ash.

The next exercise compares [æ] with other similar vowels. Respond with "same" or "different."

Exercise 16.9: Recognizing [ɛ] and [æ]

1.	[fæʃ fæʃ]	Same	5.	[jæf jæf]	Same	9.	[bæʃ bɑʃ]	Different
2.	[sæv sɛv]	Different	6.	[tædʒ tɛdʒ]	Different	10.	[ʃæk ʃɑk]	Different
3.	[dæk dɛk]	Different	7.	[dʒæz dʒɑz]	Different	11.	[tæp tɑp]	Different
4.	[ʔæm ʔɛm]	Different	8.	[ʔæʔ ʔæʔ]	Same	12.	[mæg mæg]	Same

---

1 Ash [æ] has also been called Digraph; however, technically, a digraph is a combination of two unconnected symbols. The Ash [æ] therefore is not a digraph but a ligature of an "a" and an "e."

To produce a pure [æ], you must learn to produce it without a [ə] off-glide. The following exercise demonstrates this glide in English words. The first time a word is given it will contain a pure vowel. The second time it will be glided. Follow along in the text.

Exercise 16.10: Recognizing [æ] and [æᵊ]

1. [bæd bæᵊd]
2. [læf læᵊf]
3. [sæt sæᵊt]
4. [kʰɹæb kʰɹæᵊb]

5. [gæs gæᵊs]
6. [pʰæd pʰæᵊd]
7. [mætʃ mæᵊtʃ]
8. [tʰæd tʰæᵊd]

9. [ʌ'tʰæk ʌ'tʰæᵊk]
10. [ʃæft ʃæᵊft]
11. [stæk stæᵊk]
12. [skɹætʃ skɹæᵊtʃ]

It is important to distinguish a glided Ash from a pure one. Listen to the next exercise, and determine if there is a vowel glide or not.

Exercise 16.11: Recognizing Glided [æ]

1. [pʰæᵊd] Glide
2. [læᵊf] Glide
3. [mætʃ] No
4. [bæᵊt] Glide
5. [sæᵊf] Glide

6. [zæf] No
7. [ʒæᵊm] Glide
8. [læp] No
9. [tæʒ] No
10. [spæl] No

11. [mæᵊg] Glide
12. [skæf] No
13. [væᵊʃ] Glide
14. [ʃæʃ] No
15. [mæᵊks] Glide

The following exercise uses frame words to drill each of the new vowels that have been introduced in this lesson. Repeat each utterance after the recording. Focus on producing them as pure vowels. Begin each row with [i] and work your way down the chart.

Exercise 16.12: Producing [i], [ɪ], [e], and [æ]

1. [bit]
2. [bɪt]
3. [bet]
4. [bæt]
5. [dif]

6. [dɪf]
7. [def]
8. [dæf]
9. [ʃip]
10. [ʃɪp]

11. [ʃep]
12. [ʃæp]
13. [nis]
14. [nɪs]
15. [nes]

16. [næs]
17. [tið]
18. [tɪð]
19. [teð]
20. [tæð]

21. [θiŋ]   24. [θæŋ]   27. [ŋed]   30. [dɪx]

22. [θɪŋ]   25. [ŋid]   28. [ŋæd]   31. [dex]

23. [θeŋ]   26. [ŋɪd]   29. [dix]   32. [dæx]

Give the full technical names of the vowels you have just learned. Remember to give the vowel's height first, followed by its position from front to back, and finally its rounding. This exercise contains the vowels [i], [ɪ], [e], and [æ].

Exercise 16.13: Technical Names of Vowels

1. [ʔi]   Close Front Unrounded   11. [ʃeθ]   Close-mid Front Unrounded

2. [ʔe]   Close-mid Front Unrounded   12. [ŋiʒ]   Close Front Unrounded

3. [ʔæ]   Near-open Front Unrounded   13. [dɪf]   Near-close Front Unrounded

4. [ʔɪ]   Near-close Front Unrounded   14. [θæt]   Near-open Front Unrounded

5. [ðɪŋ]   Near-close Front Unrounded   15. [ʔɪʔ]   Near-close Front Unrounded

6. [læʒ]   Near-open Front Unrounded   16. [tek]   Close-mid Front Unrounded

7. [θim]   Close Front Unrounded   17. [ðið]   Close Front Unrounded

8. [ðek]   Close-mid Front Unrounded   18. [ʃæŋ]   Near-open Front Unrounded

9. [ʒæʃ]   Near-open Front Unrounded   19. [θeb]   Close-mid Front Unrounded

10. [ðɪʔ]   Near-close Front Unrounded   20. [ʔæx]   Near-open Front Unrounded

Review of Vowels and Glides

Identify the vowels in the following exercise. This exercise contains all of the vowels that you have studied so far. These vowels are [i], [ɪ], [e], [ɛ], [æ], [ʌ], [ɑ], [ɔ], [o], [ʊ], and [u]. Respond by giving the non-technical name of the vowel.

Exercise 16.14: Recognizing Front Vowels

1. [sɛ]   Epsilon   3. [so]   O   5. [sɪ]   Small Capital I

2. [sɔ]   Open O   4. [sɑ]   Script A   6. [sʊ]   Upsilon

7. [sæ] Ash
8. [si] I
9. [sʌ] Turned V
10. [se] E
11. [su] U
12. [so] O
13. [lʊf] U
14. [lɛf] Epsilon
15. [lɑf] Script A
16. [lɪf] Small Capital I

17. [lɔf] Open O
18. [læf] Ash
19. [lif] I
20. [lɑf] Script A
21. [lʌf] Turned V
22. [lɛf] Epsilon
23. [lʊf] Upsilon
24. [lɔf] Open O
25. [tʰæd] Ash
26. [tʰid] I

27. [tʰed] E
28. [tʰod] O
29. [tʰɪd] Small Capital I
30. [tʰɛd] Epsilon
31. [tʰed] E
32. [tʰʌd] Turned V
33. [tʰud] U
34. [tʰɑd] Script A
35. [tʰʊd] Upsilon
36. [tʰʊd] Upsilon

Listen to the following exercise, and name which vowel glide you hear. Some of these glides are not found in English.

Exercise 16.15: Recognizing Vowel Glides

1. [soⁱ] i
2. [soᵘ] u
3. [soᵊ] ə
4. [dæᵘ] u
5. [beⁱ] ɪ
6. [toᵄ] ɚ
7. [giᵄ] ɚ
8. [bɛᵊ] ə
9. [nɑᵄ] ɚ
10. [kɑⁱ] ɪ
11. [doᵘ] u
12. [doᵘ] ʊ
13. [mæᵊ] ə
14. [kɑⁱ] i
15. [oⁱ] i
16. [iᵄ] ɚ
17. [aᵘk] u
18. [oᵘv] ʊ
19. [eᵆ] æ
20. [eᵄŋ] ɚ
21. [æⁱl] i

Give the full technical names of the vowel sounds in the following exercise. This exercise contains all of the vowels that you have learned.

Exercise 16.16: Full Technical Names of Vowels

1. [si] Close Front Unrounded
2. [sʊ] Near-close Back Rounded

194

3. [su]   Close Back Rounded

4. [sɛ]   Open-mid Front Unrounded

5. [sʌ]   Open-mid Back Unrounded

6. [so]   Close-mid Back Rounded

7. [sæ]   Near-open Front Unrounded

8. [sɑ]   Open Back Unrounded

9. [pɪt]   Near-close Front Unrounded

10. [pɔt]   Open-mid Back Rounded

11. [pʊt]   Near-close Back Rounded

12. [pet]   Close-mid Front Unrounded

13. [pɑt]   Open Back Unrounded

14. [pot]   Close-mid Back Rounded

15. [pit]   Close Front Unrounded

16. [pet]   Close-mid Front Unrounded

17. [dɪs]   Near-close Front Unrounded

18. [dos]   Close-mid Back Rounded

19. [dɛs]   Open-mid Front Unrounded

20. [dæs]   Near-open Front Unrounded

21. [muf]   Close Back Rounded

22. [mɔf]   Open-mid Back Rounded

23. [mef]   Close-mid Front Unrounded

24. [mæf]   Near-open Front Unrounded

25. [mʌf]   Open-mid Back Unrounded

26. [mʊf]   Near-close Back Rounded

27. [lin]   Close Front Unrounded

28. [lɑn]   Open Back Unrounded

29. [læn]   Near-open Front Unrounded

30. [lɪn]   Near-close Front Unrounded

31. [sɔf]   Open-mid Back Rounded

32. [sɛf]   Open-mid Front Unrounded

33. [sʌf]   Open-mid Back Unrounded

34. [suf]   Close Back Rounded

Table 16.1: Introductory Front Vowels Summary

IPA Symbol	Name	Technical Name	English Example	APA Symbol
i	I	Close Front Unrounded Vowel	elite	i
I	Small Capital I	Near-close Front Unrounded Vowel	bit	I
e	E	Close-mid Front Unrounded Vowel	eight	e
æ	Ash	Near-open Front Unrounded Vowel	bat	æ

Lesson 17: Laterals

Lesson Outline

Glossary

The **lateral** manner of articulation involves air passing by one or both sides of the tongue rather than over its center. If you examine the position of your tongue during the word-initial lateral in the words "log" and "leaf," you will notice that the tip of your tongue touches the alveolar ridge but the air stream is allowed to escape relatively freely past its sides. The most common lateral is the [l] such as in the words listed above.

Table 17.1 introduces the symbols for the lateral sounds discussed in this lesson. This chart is by no means exhaustive. Additional voiceless and retroflexed variations which are less common will be presented in later chapters.

Table 17.1: Laterals

		Tip-Dental	Tip-Alveolar	Blade-Alveopalatal	Retroflexed	Back-Velar
Approximant	Voiceless		l̥			ʟ̥
	Voiced	l̪	l ɫ	ʎ	ɭ	ʟ
Fricative	Voiceless		ɬ			
	Voiced		ɮ			
Affricate	Voiceless		tɬ			kɬ
	Voiced		dɮ			gɮ

Lateral Approximants

Laterals are classified as either approximants or fricatives. An **approximant** is a sound produced when an articulator approaches near enough to a point of articulation to redirect the air stream, but it does not significantly restrict it. Approximants differ from fricatives in that there is no audible turbulence produced by the articulator. The lateral sounds in the words "log" and "leaf" are approximants because the air stream is not audibly restricted. The articulation of approximants is not as open as that of vowels, however, since the air stream is narrowed or reduced somewhat. The most common laterals are approximants.

Alveolar Laterals

The lateral chart above contains two laterals at the alveolar position. These two laterals are produced at the same point of articulation, but with slightly different tongue configurations. Both of these laterals occur in English, but in different environments. **Clear L** [l], also simply called **L** [l], is articulated with the tip or blade of the tongue against the alveolar ridge and the back of the tongue lowered to a neutral position. This lateral is also called the High Tongue L by some linguists because the blade of the tongue remains high, close to the alveopalatal area before dropping down in the back. The Clear L is the principle lateral in Spanish and French. Clear L occurs in English word initially and when followed by a close front vowel, such as in the word "leaf." The **Dark L** [ɫ], also called velarized or pharyngealized L, is also articulated with the tip of the tongue against the alveolar ridge, but unlike Clear L, the back of the tongue is raised to some degree at the velar position. This tongue configuration, called velarization, will be dealt with more thoroughly in another lesson. This lateral is also called Low Tongue L because the blade of the tongue is lowered away from the alveopalatal area before being raised in the back. It often occurs word final in English, such as in the word "pool." Illustration 17.1 and Illustration 17.2 depict the different tongue configurations of Clear L and Dark L.

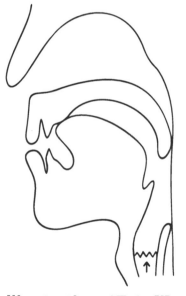

Illustration 17.1: [l]   **Illustration 17.2: [ɫ]**

The following exercise demonstrates Clear L and Dark L with common English words. As you listen for the different sound qualities, you will notice that the Clear L may have a certain "Spanish sound" associated with it. Follow along in the text to familiarize yourself with the symbols. Clear L will be given first and Dark L second.

Exercise 17.1: Recognizing [l] and [ɫ]

1. [lip ɫip]   3. [spɪl spɪɫ]

2. [pʰil pʰiɫ]   4. [lɪps ɫɪps]

5. [leⁱs ɬeⁱs]   8. [læb ɬæb]

6. [seⁱl seⁱɬ]   9. [lup ɬup]

7. [bɑl bɑɬ]   10. [pʰul pʰuɬ]

To pronounce Clear L [l], make sure that the blade of your tongue stays high and near (but not touching) the alveopalatal area. You can accomplish this by saying [l] and [i] at the same time. The back of your tongue will naturally drop to a neutral position. As we have mentioned before, most English speakers use [l] at the beginning of the word "leaf." Some people also use [l] when saying William. Say these words and isolate the laterals, keeping your tongue in the correct position. You may also try using a Spanish accent to reach the articulation of [l].

Dark L [ɬ] occurs at the end of words or syllables in the speech of most English speakers. You can feel its articulation by saying the word "pool" and prolonging the lateral at the end. You can also try saying [l] and [ʌ] at the same time. This will automatically give the correct tongue contour for [ɬ].

In many languages, such as Spanish and French, the Dark L does not occur. English speakers have a tendency to insert the Dark L at the end of words when speaking these languages. While the English speaker may be unaware of the difference, this marks his speech with a distracting accent. Practice the pronunciation of [l] and [ɬ] in the following exercise. Mimic each utterance.

Exercise 17.2: Producing [l] and [ɬ]

1. [ɑl ɑɬ]	6. [ili iɬi]	11. [lo ɬo]
2. [lɑ ɬɑ]	7. [el eɬ]	12. [olo oɬo]
3. [ɑlɑ ɑɬɑ]	8. [le ɬe]	13. [ul uɬ]
4. [il iɬ]	9. [ele eɬe]	14. [lu ɬu]
5. [li ɬi]	10. [ol oɬ]	15. [ulu uɬu]

Practice these laterals until you can recognize and reproduce them; then listen to the next exercise, and respond with Clear L or Dark L.

Exercise 17.3: Recognizing Clear L or Dark L

1. [ɑlɑ]	Clear L	3. [ɑlɑ]	Clear L	5. [ɬo]	Dark L
2. [ɑɬɑ]	Dark L	4. [iɬi]	Dark L	6. [olo]	Clear L

7.	[æɫæ]	Dark L	11.	[mɑl]	Clear L	15.	[tɑɫ]	Dark L
8.	[ɛlɛ]	Clear L	12.	[ɫete]	Dark L	16.	[lisu]	Clear L
9.	[ælɛ]	Clear L	13.	[lopɛz]	Clear L	17.	[tɑl]	Clear L
10.	[mɑɫ]	Dark L	14.	[kule]	Clear L	18.	[ɫopɛz]	Dark L

Producing [l̪] and [ɭ]

Just like other alveolar consonants that we have studied, laterals can be both fronted and retroflexed. It should not be difficult to produce these variations since you are already familiar with the concepts of fronting and retroflexion. Alveolar laterals are the only fronted and retroflexed sounds presented in this lesson, although these variations of other laterals are possible as well.

The fronted lateral is represented by adding a diacritic called a **Bridge** [̪] below the symbol [l̪]. A retroflexed lateral is symbolized by the addition of a **Right Hook** [̨] below the symbol. This symbol is known as **Right-tail L** [ɭ].

Practice your recognition of fronted and retroflexed laterals in the following exercise. Respond with "fronted," "alveolar," or "retroflexed."

Exercise 17.4: Recognizing Fronted, Alveolar, and Retroflexed Laterals

1.	[ɑl̪ɑ]	Fronted	6.	[l̪as]	Fronted	11.	[mil]	Alveolar
2.	[ɑlɑ]	Alveolar	7.	[fɛl̪]	Fronted	12.	[ɣol̪]	Fronted
3.	[ɑɭɑ]	Retroflexed	8.	[loʃi]	Retroflexed	13.	[doɭi]	Fronted
4.	[pɑl]	Alveolar	9.	[zolo]	Alveolar	14.	[ʃɑɭaɣ]	Retroflexed
5.	[tɑɭ]	Retroflexed	10.	[kɑɭɑ]	Retroflexed	15.	[ʒɛl̪ɛʒ]	Fronted

The Alveopalatal Lateral [ʎ]

The blade-alveopalatal lateral, commonly known as **Retracted L** [l̠], corresponds with the articulation of Enye [ñ]. Although this sound does not occur in normal English speech, it should not be too difficult to produce as you are already used to the articulation of the alveopalatal nasal.

Since the position of the tongue for an alveopalatal lateral [l̠] is only slightly higher than [i], it is often accompanied by an [i] glide at its onset or release. You can learn to articulate [l̪] by beginning with the vowel [i] and gradually closing your mouth until the blade of the tongue touches the alveopalatal point of articulation. Remember to keep the tip of your tongue tucked behind you lower teeth so that it doesn't cause you to say [l]. You can also start with [ñ] and switch to lateral articulation for [l̪].

The alveopalatal lateral [l̪] is often confused with Clear L. Listen for and mimic the difference between [ɫ], [l], and [l̪] in the following exercise.

Exercise 17.5: Producing [ɫ], [l], and [l̪]

1. [aɫ al al̪]	6. [iɫi ili il̪i]	11. [ɫo lo l̪o]
2. [ɫa la l̪a]	7. [eɫ el el̪]	12. [oɫo olo ol̪o]
3. [aɫa ala al̪a]	8. [ɫe le l̪e]	13. [uɫ ul ul̪]
4. [iɫ il il̪]	9. [eɫe ele el̪e]	14. [ɫu lu l̪u]
5. [ɫi li l̪i]	10. [oɫ ol ol̪]	15. [uɫu ulu ul̪u]

Practice distinguishing between [l] and [l̪] in the following exercise. Respond with "alveolar" or "alveopalatal."

Exercise 17.6: Recognizing Alveolar or Alveopalatal Laterals

1. [ala]	Alveolar	5. [fal̪]	Alveopalatal	9. [laŋ]	Alveolar
2. [al̪a]	Alveopalatal	6. [zɛl]	Alveolar	10. [ʒol̪]	Alveopalatal
3. [al̪a]	Alveopalatal	7. [kæl̪ɛm]	Alveopalatal	11. [sel̪iʃ]	Alveopalatal
4. [tala]	Alveolar	8. [ʃal]	Alveolar	12. [ŋalap]	Alveolar

Velar Lateral [ʟ]

The **Small Capital L [ʟ]** is articulated with the back of the tongue at the velar point of articulation. Do not confuse the velar lateral [ʟ] with the velarized lateral [ɫ]. The velarized lateral's primary articulation is between the tip of the tongue and the alveolar ridge. English has few, if any, examples of velar laterals. Some speakers may use a velar lateral in words like "milk" and "bulk" as the back-velar stop pulls the lateral farther back. More commonly, the tongue approaches the velar point of articulation but does not actually touch it. This produces a type of approximant which we will discuss in a later lesson.

To learn the articulation for Small Capital L [ʟ], say words that start with "gl," such as "glue" and "glean." Make sure that the tip of your tongue stays down behind your lower teeth as you release the back velar stop into a lateral. Lengthen the lateral and then isolate it to arrive at Small Capital L [ʟ]. The following exercise demonstrates this process. Listen to the exercise first, and then mimic it.

Exercise 17.7: Recognizing [ʟ]

1. a) [gʟu]   b) [gʟːu]   c) [ʟːu]   d) [ʟː]   e) [aʟa]

2. a) [gʟin]   b) [gʟːin]   c) [ʟːin]   d) [ʟː]   e) [aʟa]

Voiceless Laterals

By controlling the glottis, we can produce any lateral sound as either voiced or voiceless. Every voiced lateral has a voiceless counterpart. The audible difference between most voiceless laterals, however, is very slight. The only voiceless lateral approximants studied in this course are voiceless Clear L [l̥] and voiceless Small Capital L [ʟ̥]. Voiceless lateral fricatives will be discussed later.

In English, voiceless laterals are often found after voiceless aspirated stops. You can learn to articulate them by isolating them in those instances. The following exercise demonstrates [l̥] in common English words. The [ʟ̥] does not naturally occur in these words, but you can learn its articulation in the drill. Listen to the words, and practice them until you can hear and produce the voiceless [l̥].

Exercise 17.8: Producing [l̥]

1. a) [pl̥at]   b) [pl̥ːat]   c) [l̥ːa]   d) [l̥ː]   e) [al̥a]

2. a) [pl̥iz]   b) [pl̥ːiz]   c) [l̥ːi]   d) [l̥ː]   e) [il̥i]

3. a) [pl̥ʌk]   b) [pl̥ːʌk]   c) [l̥ːʌ]   d) [l̥ː]   e) [ʌl̥ʌ]

4. a) [kl̥ak]   b) [kl̥ːak]   c) [l̥ːa]   d) [l̥ː]   e) [al̥a]

5. a) [kl̥u]   b) [kl̥ːu]   c) [l̥ːu]   d) [l̥ː]   e) [ul̥u]

6. a) [kʟ̥u]   b) [kʟ̥ːu]   c) [ʟ̥ːu]   d) [ʟ̥ː]   e) [uʟ̥u]

7. a) [kʟ̥ʌk]   b) [kʟ̥ːʌk]   c) [ʟ̥ːʌ]   d) [ʟ̥]   e) [ʌʟ̥ʌ]

Respond to the next exercise with "voiced" or "voiceless."

Exercise 17.9: Recognizing Voiced or Voiceless Laterals

1. [a̯la] Voiceless	6. [l̥ak] Voiceless	11. [do̯li] Voiceless
2. [a̯la] Voiceless	7. [para̯l] Voiceless	12. [bulʌ] Voiced
3. [ala] Voiced	8. [mʌlʌn] Voiced	13. [zo̯luv] Voiceless
4. [ʌ̯lʌ] Voiceless	9. [ke̯lim] Voiceless	14. [salaf] Voiced
5. [tal] Voiced	10. [se̯lax] Voiceless	15. [ʃælfɛɹ] Voiced

Many people articulate both voiceless and voiced laterals together when trying to produce a voiceless lateral. Listen to the following exercise, and see if you can tell the difference between a voiced lateral, a voiceless lateral, and a voiced and voiceless lateral together. Respond with "voiced," "voiceless," or "both."

Exercise 17.10: Recognizing Voiced and Voiceless Laterals

1. [ala] Voiced	6. [a̯la] Voiceless	11. [u̯llu] Both
2. [a̯lla] Both	7. [pal] Voiced	12. [ŋulu] Voiceless
3. [a̯la] Voiceless	8. [so̯lo] Voiceless	13. [i̯lli] Both
4. [a̯lla] Both	9. [ʃɛlɛ] Voiced	14. [eleŋ] Voiced
5. [a̯lla] Both	10. [ʃɛ̯llɛ] Both	15. [o̯lo] Voiceless

Lateral Fricatives

Some laterals involve an audible restriction of the air stream. These laterals are classified as lateral fricatives. **Lateral fricatives** differ from other fricatives in that the center or tip of the tongue is raised to touch the point of articulation while the sides remain open allowing the air to escape. The shape of the tongue is exactly opposite from that of sibilants. Remember that sibilants are a type of fricative for which the sides of the tongue are raised and the air is channeled over the center. The following illustrations show a head-on view of the shape of the tongue for sibilants, flat fricatives, and laterals.

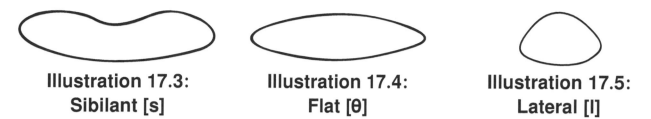

Illustration 17.3:
Sibilant [s]

Illustration 17.4:
Flat [θ]

Illustration 17.5:
Lateral [l]

The voiceless lateral fricative is symbolized by a symbol called **Belted L [ɬ]**. The voiced lateral fricative is represented by ligature of an L [l] and an Ezh [ʒ], sometimes referred to as **Lezh [ɮ]** or L-Ezh ligature.

Producing [ɬ] and [ɮ]

The articulation of lateral fricatives differs from that of lateral approximants only in that the openings where the air escapes along the sides of the tongue are restricted enough to cause audible turbulence. You can learn to pronounce the voiced, tip-alveolar lateral fricative [ɮ] by lengthening [l:] and gradually reducing the size of the air stream's outlet until you get friction. You may also try keeping your tongue somewhat relaxed while saying [l:], and applying greater force with the lungs. English speakers with a lisp will sometimes use [ɮ] is place of [z] in words like "zebra" and "zone."

To produce the voiceless tip-alveolar lateral fricative [ɬ], say a lengthened voiceless [l̥] and gradually close off the air stream's outlet until you get friction. People with a lisp will often use [ɬ] in place of [s] or [ʃ] in words like "sunshine" and "sleepy."

The following exercise demonstrates the production of [ɬ] and [ɮ]. Listen to and mimic each utterance.

Exercise 17.11: Producing [ɬ] and [ɮ]

1. [ala]
2. [al:ɮa]
3. [aɮa]
4. [ili]
5. [il:ɮi]
6. [iɮi]

7. [ulu]
8. [ul:ɮu]
9. [uɮu]
10. [al̥a]
11. [al̥:ɬa]
12. [aɬa]

13. [ili]
14. [il:ɬi]
15. [iɬi]
16. [ulu]
17. [ul:ɬu]
18. [uɬu]

Practice distinguishing between lateral fricatives and lateral approximants in the following exercise. Respond with "fricative" or "approximant."

Exercise 17.12: Recognizing Lateral Fricatives and Approximants

1.	[aʤa]	Fricative	6.	[aʒa]	Fricative	11.	[ŋaʤ]	Fricative
2.	[ala]	Approximant	7.	[tal]	Approximant	12.	[ʃalaʒ]	Approximant
3.	[aɬa]	Fricative	8.	[maɬam]	Fricative	13.	[ʒaŋ]	Fricative
4.	[aʤa]	Fricative	9.	[sal̩]	Approximant	14.	[l̩aʃ]	Approximant
5.	[al̩a]	Approximant	10.	[ɬav]	Fricative	15.	[ðalad]	Approximant

The following exercise contains grooved fricatives, flat fricatives, and lateral fricatives. Determine if each fricative is a lateral or not.

Exercise 17.13: Recognizing Laterals

1.	[aɬa]	Lateral	6.	[poʤ]	Lateral	11.	[xaz]	No
2.	[asa]	No	7.	[ɬeme]	Lateral	12.	[jaɬat]	Lateral
3.	[aza]	No	8.	[maθak]	No	13.	[ɛðɛŋ]	No
4.	[ŋaʤa]	Lateral	9.	[busu]	No	14.	[iɬu]	Lateral
5.	[kað]	No	10.	[ʤik]	Lateral	15.	[ŋaθo]	No

Lateral Affricates

In Lesson 9 we explained how stops can be released into fricatives to produce sound combinations that we call affricates. We have already dealt with stops released into flat fricatives and sibilants. Stops can also be released into lateral fricatives, creating **lateral affricates**. The table of phonetic symbols at the beginning of this lesson gives the lateral affricates which we will drill in this lesson. There are several other lateral affricate possibilities not listed, which include fronted and retroflexed affricates. These affricates are entirely possible, though not as common.

The stop/lateral combination [dl] is also very common in languages throughout the world, but this consonant cluster is not technically an affricate since the lateral release is an approximant and not a fricative.

The tip-alveolar lateral affricates [tɬ] and [dɮ] are produced quite easily. Simply articulate for the stop and then, while keeping the tip of your tongue against the alveolar ridge, lower the sides of your tongue to produce the lateral fricative. This same procedure applies for both voiced and voiceless affricates.

The velar-alveolar affricates [kɬ] and [gɮ] are produced by articulating the back-velar stop and tip-alveolar lateral at the same time so that when the stop is released, the lateral is already in articulation. The following exercise demonstrates lateral affricates. Listen to the sounds and mimic each utterance.

Exercise 17.14: Producing Lateral Affricates

1. a) [tʰɑ] b) [ɬɑ] c) [tɬɑ] d) [atɬɑ] e) [atɬ]

2. a) [dɑ] b) [ɮɑ] c) [dɮɑ] d) [adɮɑ] e) [adɮ]

3. a) [kʰɑ] b) [ɬɑ] c) [kɬɑ] d) [akɬɑ] e) [akɬ]

4. a) [gɑ] b) [ɮɑ] c) [gɮɑ] d) [agɮɑ] e) [agɮ]

The next exercise contains various stop/lateral combinations. Tell whether the combination in each utterance is an affricate or not. Remember that both the stop and the fricative of an affricate must share the same voicing characteristics.

Exercise 17.15: Recognizing Lateral Affricates

1. [adɮɑ] Affricate

2. [agɑ] No

3. [akɬɑ] Affricate

4. [nak] No

5. [agɮɑ] Affricate

6. [gadɮɑ] Affricate

7. [atɬɑ] Affricate

8. [taɬak] No

9. [ɬtak] No

10. [akɬak] Affricate

11. [maɮda] No

12. [atɬ] Affricate

It is often difficult to distinguish between [tɬ] and [kɬ], and between [dɮ] and [gɮ]. Practice distinguishing between these pairs in the next exercise. Respond with "alveolar" or "velar."

Exercise 17.16: Recognizing Alveolar and Velar Lateral Affricates

1. [adɮɑ] Alveolar

2. [agɮɑ] Velar

3. [akɬɑ] Velar

4. [atɬɑ] Alveolar

5. [adɮ] Alveolar

6. [akɬɑ] Velar

7. [gɮɑ] Velar

8. [atɬɑ] Alveolar

9. [akɬ] Velar

| 10. [agʤa] | Velar | 12. [adʤ] | Alveolar | 14. [atɬa] | Alveolar |
| 11. [gʤa] | Velar | 13. [akɬa] | Velar | 15. [atɬ] | Alveolar |

Follow the transcription in the next exercise and repeat each utterance after the recording.

Exercise 17.17: Producing Laterals

1. [aɬa]	9. [a̪laʤ]	17. [l̪aʤ]	25. [atɬa]
2. [ala]	10. [lal]	18. [laɬa]	26. [akɬakɬa]
3. [a̪la]	11. [aɬala̪la]	19. [aɬala̪la]	27. [adʤ]
4. [aʟa]	12. [a̪la̪l]	20. [l̪ala̪l]	28. [agʤa]
5. [ḁla]	13. [ɬaʤa]	21. [laʤa]	29. [kɬa]
6. [aɬa]	14. [laɬa]	22. [laɬ]	30. [gʤagʤ]
7. [aʤa]	15. [aʟal]	23. [a̪laɬaʤ]	31. [tɬatɬa]
8. [laɬa]	16. [ḁlaɬ]	24. [ɬal]	32. [adʤadʤ]

Table 17.2: Summary of Laterals

IPA Symbol	Name	Technical Name	English Example	APA Symbol
l̪	Fronted L	Voiced Tip-Dental Lateral Approximant		l̪
l̥	Voiceless L	Voiceless Tip-Alveolar Lateral Approximant	play	L
l	Clear L	Voiced Tip-Alveolar Lateral Approximant	leaf	lˆ
ɫ	Dark L	Voiced Tip-Alveolar Velarized Lateral Approximant	pool	lˇ

IPA Symbol	Name	Technical Name	English Example	APA Symbol
ɭ	Right-tail L	Voiced Tip-Retroflexed Lateral Approximant		!
l̠	Retracted L	Voiced Blade-Alveopalatal Lateral Approximant		ĩ
ʟ̥	Voiceless Small Capital L	Voiceless Back-Velar Lateral Approximant		
ʟ	Small Capital L	Voiced Back-Velar Lateral Approximant	milk	
ɬ	Belted L	Voiceless Tip-Alveolar Lateral Fricative		⌊
ɮ	Lezh	Voiced Tip-Alveolar Lateral Fricative		ɫ

Lesson 18:
Open Vowels and Length

Lesson Outline

Glossary Terms

This lesson introduces two new vowel sounds as well as a new phonetic concept called length. The vowels presented here will complete the number of open vowels drilled in this course.

Open Vowels

The new vowel sounds introduced in this lesson occur in English, but with less frequency than the other vowels we have studied. Their use is usually limited to certain dialects or phonetic environments. The open front unrounded vowel [a] is only found in diphthongs in most English dialects. Words like "how," "now," and "about" contain an [aᵘ] diphthong. Southern US dialects also tend to use the [a] in words like "I" and "pie"; whereas, the vowel and glide combination [ɑⁱ] is the standard pronunciation.[1] The open back unrounded vowel [ɒ] is often used in British dialects of English, and in some American dialects as well. They are often found in words like "our" and "father." The [ɒ] also may be used in place of the Open O [ɔ] in rapid speech, as in the word "call."

The bold symbols in the vowel chart below represent the new sounds introduced in this lesson. The difficulties in learning these sounds will be depend upon the individual's speech patterns. Some individuals will already produce one or both of these vowels in their normal speech, while others will have to work harder to learn them.

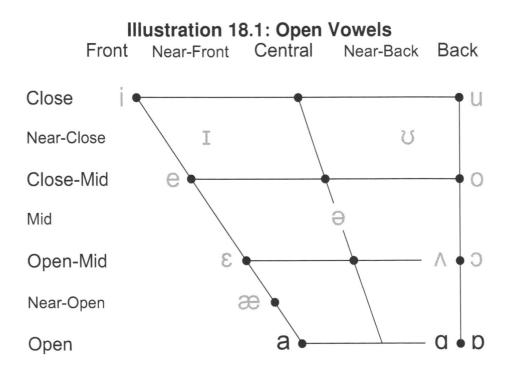

Illustration 18.1: Open Vowels

---

1 In standard American English, the diphthong [ʌⁱ] may occur before voiceless consonants, such as "ice" [ʌⁱs], and [ɑⁱ] occurs in all other environments, such as "eyes" [ɑⁱz] or "I" [ɑⁱ].

Illustration 18.2 below shows the approximate tongue position for both [a] and [ɒ]. Notice that the tongue is low for both sounds, but its highest point is in the front for [a] and in the back for [ɒ]. Also, the note that the lips were removed because [a] is unrounded, but [ɒ] is rounded.

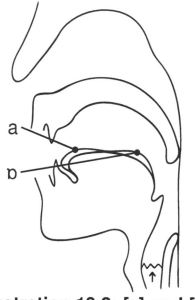

Illustration 18.2: [a] and [ɒ]

Producing [a]

The open, front unrounded vowel is called **Lowercase A** [a]. The [a] is difficult to isolate because English speakers normally glide [a] to [u]. One way to learn this vowel is to imagine being injured and say a lengthened, "ow!" Another way to learn this vowel is to imitate a southerner as he says "I want a piece of pie." This sound is also prevalent in a Bostonian accent. You may try to imitate a Bostonian as he says, "Park your car in Harvard Yard." You must make sure that you do not use [æ] or [ɑ].

The following exercise demonstrates the vowels Ash [æ], Lowercase A [a], and Script A [ɑ] in sentences. Notice that Lowercase A is somewhere between Ash and Script A. Follow the transcription, and repeat each utterance after the recording.

Exercise 18.1: Producing Open Vowels

1. [æææ aaa ɑɑɑ]

   a) [æ ˈwʌnə ˈpʰis ə pʰæ]

   b) [a ˈwʌnə ˈpʰis ə pʰa]

   c) [ɑ ˈwʌnə ˈpʰis ə pʰɑ]

2. [æææ aaa ɑɑɑ]

   a) [pʰæk jɨ kʰæ ɪn hævɨd jæd]

   b) [pʰak jɨ kʰa ɪn havɨd jad]

   c) [pʰɑk jɨ kʰɑ ɪn havɨd jɑd]

The following exercise contrasts [æ], [a] and [ɑ]. Listen to each utterance, and respond with "same" or "different."

Exercise 18.2: Recognizing Open Vowels

1. [las las] Same	7. [vas væs] Different	13. [θap θap] Same
2. [las læs] Different	8. [væs vas] Different	14. [θap θɑp] Different
3. [læs las] Different	9. [vas vas] Same	15. [θɑp θap] Different
4. [θap θap] Same	10. [las lɑs] Different	16. [vas vas] Same
5. [θap θæp] Different	11. [las lɑs] Different	17. [vas vas] Same
6. [θap θap] Same	12. [lɑs las] Different	18. [vɑs vas] Different

Listen to the following exercise and respond with the name of the vowel. This exercise will include Ash [æ], Lowercase A [a], and Script A [ɑ].

Exercise 18.3: Recognizing Open Vowels

1. [sæ] Ash	6. [zæs] Ash	11. [mɑʒ] Script A
2. [sa] Lowercase A	7. [θɑp] Script A	12. [mæʒ] Ash
3. [sɑ] Script A	8. [θæp] Ash	13. [ðan] Lowercase A
4. [zas] Lowercase A	9. [θap] Lowercase A	14. [ðæn] Ash
5. [zɑs] Script A	10. [mɑʒ] Script A	15. [ðan] Lowercase A

Producing [ɒ]

The open back unrounded vowel is called **Turned Script A [ɒ]**.[2] This vowel's sound is somewhere between [ɔ] and [ɑ]. To learn to produce the Turned Script A, say each vowel going down the back rounded column of the chart. Begin at the close, back rounded position and open your mouth a little wider for each sound until you reach the articulation for [ɒ]. The amount of lip rounding decreases as you approach the open position. For [ɒ], the lips should be nearly unrounded. Make sure, though, that your articulation is farther back than [ɑ]. You can also follow the same procedure beginning with the Ash [æ] and working your way back from a front unrounded position to a back unrounded position.

---

2 Be careful not to confuse the Turned Script A [ɒ] with the Turned A [ɐ], which is a near-open central vowel.

The following exercise compares the Turned Script A with similar vowels. Listen to the vowel qualities, and repeat each sound after the recording.

Exercise 18.4: Producing Open Vowels

1. [ɔɔɔ ɒɒɒ aɑɑ]

2. [pʰɔk jɨ kʰɔ ɪn hɔvɨd jɔd]

3. [pʰɒk jɨ kʰɒ ɪn hɒvɨd jɒd]

4. [pʰɑk jɨ kʰɑ ɪn hɑvɨd jɑd]

5. [aɑɑ ɒɒɒ ɔɔɔ]

6. It made me [lɑf] to see a [kɑf] go down the [pɑθ] to take a [bɑθ]

7. It made me [lɒf] to see a [kɒf] go down the [pɒθ] to take a [bɒθ]

8. It made me [lɔf] to see a [kɔf] go down the [pɔθ] to take a [bɔθ]

In the next exercise, you will hear these same three vowels contrasted. Listen to each utterance, and respond with "same" or "different."

Exercise 18.5: Recognizing Open Vowels

1. [lɒs lɒs] Same	7. [vɒs vɔs] Different	13. [θɑp θɒp] Different
2. [lɒs lɔs] Different	8. [vɒs vɒs] Same	14. [θɒp θɒp] Same
3. [lɒs lɒs] Same	9. [vɒs vɔs] Different	15. [θɑp θɒp] Different
4. [θɔp θɒp] Different	10. [lɒs las] Different	16. [vas vɒs] Different
5. [θɔp θɒp] Different	11. [lɒs lɒs] Same	17. [vɒs vas] Different
6. [θɔp θɒp] Different	12. [lɒs las] Different	18. [vɒs vɒs] Same

The next exercise includes [ɔ], [ɒ], and [ɑ]. Respond by giving the name of the vowel.

Exercise 18.6: Recognizing Open Vowels

1. [sɔ] Open O	3. [sɔ] Open O	5. [zɒs] Turned Script A
2. [sɒ] Turned Script A	4. [zas] Script A	6. [zɔs] Open O

7. [lɒp] Turned A	10. [dɔm] Open O	13. [kɑʒ] Script A
8. [lɑp] Script A	11. [dɒm] Turned Script A	14. [kɒʒ] Turned Script A
9. [lɑp] Script A	12. [dɔm] Open O	15. [kɑʒ] Script A

In the next exercise, practice the sentences, substituting [æ], [a], [ɑ], [ɒ], and [ɔ] in each frame. Mimic each utterance after the recording.

Exercise 18.7: Producing Open Vowels

1. [æææ aaa ɑɑɑ ɒɒɒ ɔɔɔ]

2. [pʰæk jɨ kʰæ ɪn hævɨd jæd]

3. [pʰak jɨ kʰa ɪn havɨd jad]

4. [pʰɑk jɨ kʰɑ ɪn hɑvɨd jɑd]

5. [pʰɒk jɨ kʰɒ ɪn hɒvɨd jɒd]

6. [pʰɔk jɨ kʰɔ ɪn hɔvɨd jɔd]

7. [æææ aaa ɑɑɑ ɒɒɒ ɔɔɔ]

8. It made me [læf] to see a [kæf] go down the [pæθ] to take a [bæθ]

9. It made me [laf] to see a [kaf] go down the [paθ] to take a [baθ]

10. It made me [lɑf] to see a [kɑf] go down the [pɑθ] to take a [bɑθ]

11. It made me [lɒf] to see a [kɒf] go down the [pɒθ] to take a [bɒθ]

12. It made me [lɔf] to see a [kɔf] go down the [pɔθ] to take a [bɔθ]

In the next exercise, respond by naming the vowel that you hear. This exercise will include [æ], [a], [ɑ], [ɒ], and [ɔ].

Exercise 18.8: Recognizing Open Vowels

1. [lɑk] Script A	4. [lɒk] Turned Script A	7. [zɔs] Open O
2. [lɒk] Turned Script A	5. [zæs] Ash	8. [zas] Lowercase A
3. [lak] Lowercase A	6. [zɑs] Script A	9. [gɔʒ] Open O

10. [gɑʒ] Script A   15. [θɑf] Script A   20. [zað] Script A

11. [gɒʒ] Turned Script A   16. [θɒf] Turned Script A   21. [pʰɒk] Turned Script A

12. [gæʒ] Ash   17. [zað] Lowercase A   22. [pʰɔk] Open O

13. [θaf] Lowercase A   18. [zæð] Ash   23. [pʰak] Lowercase A

14. [θɔf] Open O   19. [zæð] Ash   24. [pʰæk] Ash

Length

When we speak of **length** linguistically, we refer to the duration of time for which the articulation of a sound is held. Nearly all sounds can vary in length. Continuants, such as vowels, nasals, laterals, and fricatives, can be prolonged until the speaker is out of breath. Voiced stops, on the other hand, can be lengthened only until the chambers behind the articulator fill with air so that the air flow through the vocal cords is stopped. Voiceless stops can also be held for a brief period of time, but are inaudible until they are released. Flaps, which we will introduce in a later lesson, cannot be lengthened. When the articulation of a flap is held, it automatically becomes a different manner of articulation.

Do not confuse phonetically long and short vowels with the traditional English definition of long and short vowels. In English phonics you learned that the word "bait" contains a long vowel sound, while "bat" contains a short one. This is merely a difference in vowel quality and not of the duration of time that the sound is held. In phonetics, the terms "long" and "short" refer to the length of time that a sound is continued.

The length of a phonetic segment is relative to the length of the surrounding segments. In other words, to tell whether a sound is long or short, it must be compared to the length of adjacent sounds. In an utterance there is usually an average slot of time allotted for each sound. This determines the normal length for sounds within that utterance. A lengthened sound simply occupies more than one normal beat.

The official way to symbolize length in the IPA is to use a pair of triangles called the **Length Mark [ː]**. A **Colon [:]** is also used because of its practicality when typing. When three degrees of lengthening are present, a **Half-length Mark [ˑ]** is used to symbolize the degree of length between normal and full lengthening. If a sound is extra short, a **Breve [˘]** is placed above the symbol. The **Double-length Mark [ːː]** is used to indicate extra long phones.

Nearly all languages have examples of sounds which vary perceptibly in length. In some English dialects, vowels may have three different degrees of lengthening. Consider the words "bee," "bead," and "beat." All three of these words represent vowels with different lengths. The [iː] in "bee" is the longest, the [iˑ] in "bead" is half-long, and the [i] in "beat" is the shortest. This difference of vowel length is dependent upon whether the vowel comes before a voiceless consonant, a voiced consonant, or no consonant at all. There are no two English words that have a different meaning based only on vowel length. Therefore, length in English is not contrastive, meaning that it never makes a difference in the meaning of a word. In many other languages, however, the length of vowels is contrastive. In Khmuʔ, length is the only difference between [dɛk], meaning "little," and [dɛːk], meaning "flush at the end."

The following exercise demonstrates three different degrees of lengthening on vowels. Follow along in the text, and mimic each utterance as it builds up from a normal vowel to a fully lengthened one. Make sure that you do not change the vowel quality between the long and short vowels.

Exercise 18.9: Producing Lengthened Vowels

1. a) [si]   b) [siˑ]   c) [siː]   d) [sisiː]   e) [siːsi]

2. a) [se]   b) [seˑ]   c) [seː]   d) [seseː]   e) [seːse]

3. a) [sɑ]   b) [sɑˑ]   c) [sɑː]   d) [sasɑː]   e) [sɑːsɑ]

4. a) [so]   b) [soˑ]   c) [soː]   d) [sosoː]   e) [soːso]

5. a) [su]   b) [suˑ]   c) [suː]   d) [susuː]   e) [suːsu]

Listen to the vowels in the next exercise, and tell whether the vowel in the second syllable is lengthened or not.

Exercise 18.10: Recognizing Length

1. [babɑː] Lengthened	6. [seseː] Lengthened	11. [totoː] Lengthened
2. [babɑ] No	7. [nini] No	12. [totoː] Lengthened
3. [babɑ] No	8. [nini] No	13. [susuː] Lengthened
4. [seseː] Lengthened	9. [niniː] Lengthened	14. [susu] No
5. [sese] No	10. [toto] No	15. [susuː] Lengthened

Lengthened consonants can also be contrastive is some languages. In Finnish, for example, the length is the only phonetic difference between [mitæ], meaning "what" and [mitːæ] meaning "measurement." The following exercise demonstrates lengthened consonants. Follow along in the text, and mimic each utterance.

Exercise 18.11: Producing Lengthened Consonants

1. a) [ɑsɑ]   b) [ɑsːɑ]   c) [ɑsɑsːɑ]   d) [ɑsːɑsɑ]

2. a) [ɑvɑ]   b) [ɑvːɑ]   c) [ɑvɑvːɑ]   d) [ɑvːɑvɑ]

3. a) [ɑbɑ]   b) [ɑbːɑ]   c) [ɑbɑbːɑ]   d) [ɑbːɑbɑ]

4. a) [ɑtɑ]   b) [ɑtːɑ]   c) [ɑtɑtːɑ]   d) [ɑtːɑtɑ]

5. a) [ɑʃɑ]   b) [ɑʃːɑ]   c) [ɑʃɑʃːɑ]   d) [ɑʃːɑʃɑ]

In the following exercise, tell whether the lengthened sound is a vowel, a consonant, both, or neither.

Exercise 18.12: Recognizing Lengthened Vowels and Consonants

1. [babːɑ]	Consonant	7. [ninːi]	Consonant	13. [θatːɑ]	Consonant
2. [naːkɑ]	Vowel	8. [vːeːve]	Both	14. [tafːɑ]	Consonant
3. [ʒaʒːɑ]	Consonant	9. [sazːɑ]	Consonant	15. [loːgːo]	Both
4. [toːtːo]	Both	10. [luzuː]	Vowel	16. [sefe]	Neither
5. [susu]	Neither	11. [θiʃi]	Neither	17. [pakaː]	Vowel
6. [vaːva]	Vowel	12. [kakɑː]	Both	18. [bidːi]	Consonant

The following exercise contains examples of three contrastive degrees of lengthening on both vowels and consonants in Estonian. Listen to the recording and mimic each utterance.

Exercise 18.13: Estonian Mimicry

1. a) [sadɑ]   b) [saˑdɑ]   c) [saːdɑ]

2. a) [kɛdɑ]   b) [kʰeˑdan]   c) [kʰeːmɑ]

3. a) [kʰilo]   b) [kʰiˑlu]   c) [kʰiːlu]

4. a) [kʰolin]   b) [kʰoˑli]   c) [kʰoːli]

5. a) [tuli]   b) [tuˑlɛs]   c) [tuːli]

6. a) [vɨru]   b) [vɨˑras]   c) [vɨːraga]

7. a) [kæru]   b) [kæˑrit]   c) [kæːre]

8. a) [kɨha]   b) [nɨˑri]   c) [nɨːri]

9. a) [mɨra]   b) [mɨˑri]   c) [mɨːri]

10. a) [habe]   b) [hapˑe]   c) [hapːɪks]

11. a) [kate]   b) [katˑe]   c) [katːɪks]

12. a) [loku]   b) [lokˑus]   c) [lʊkːo]

13. a) [valan]   b) [valˑa]   c) [valːɑ]

14. a) [tome]   b) [tomˑalt]   c) [tomːɑ]

15. a) [kʰana]   b) [kʰanˑou]   c) [kʰanːo]

16. a) [nɑri]   b) [nɑri]   c) [nɑrːi]

17. a) [kʰaəsin]   b) [kʰaəsˑi]   c) [kʰaəsːi]

18. a) [kʰeha]   c) [kʰehːɑ]

19. a) [mɑja]   c) [mɑjːɑ]

20. a) [kʰɪvi]   c) [kʰɪvːi]

Table 18.1: Open Vowels Summary

IPA Symbol	Name	Technical Name	English Example	APA Symbol
a	Lowercase A	Open Front Unrounded Vowel	how	a
ɑ	Script A	Open Back Unrounded Vowel	father	ɑ
ɒ	Turned Script A	Open Back Rounded Vowel	**our** (British)	ɒ

Lesson 19: Flaps and Trills

Lesson Outline

Glossary

We have so far dealt only with stops, fricatives, nasals, and laterals. These manners of articulation involve a consciously controlled interaction between the articulator and point of articulation. In a stop, for instance, the articulator approaches the point of articulation, contacts it, and then is released in a concise movement. Flaps and trills are much less deliberate. Instead, they involve quick, flicking movements of a loosely held articulator against the point of articulation. The articulator actually only touches the point of articulation for a very brief period of time. In other ways, however, flaps and trills are articulated much the same as corresponding stops, nasals, or laterals.

Table 19.1 lists the symbols of the flaps, and Table 19.2 lists the symbols of trills that will be introduced in this lesson. The uvular point of articulation is the only point that has not been previously drilled in this course.

Table 19.1: Flaps

		Labiodental	Tip-Alveolar	Tip-Retroflexed
Flaps	Voiceless	v̬̊	ɾ̥	ɽ̊
	Voiced	v̬	ɾ	ɽ
Nasal Flaps	Voiceless		ň̥	
	Voiced		ň	
Lateral Flaps	Voiceless		ɺ̥	
	Voiced		ɺ	

Table 19.2: Trills

		Bilabial	Tip-Alveolar	Back-Uvular
Trills	Voiceless	ʙ̥	r̥	ʀ̥
	Voiced	ʙ	r	ʀ

The above chart of flapped and trilled sounds is not exhaustive. Many other consonants, including some fricatives, can be flapped by simply articulating them very rapidly. Fronted variations of the consonants above can also be flapped. Although these sounds are entirely possible, they are not found very frequently in languages. We have chosen the most common flaps to study here. To symbolize flapped phones that do not have a special symbol, place a **Breve** [˘] above the consonant symbol, such as [n̆]. Just like with vowels, breves indicate extra short articulation.

We will not present facial diagrams of most of the sounds discussed in this lesson since the static nature of the diagrams makes them incapable of showing the correct movement involved in a flap or trill. In a static representation, most flaps would look just like a stop or nasal.

Flaps

As we have already explained, the articulation of flaps is very similar to that of their corresponding stops, nasals, and laterals.[1] The main difference is that a **flap** is articulated with a quick, flicking movement of the articulator. In some environments, English speakers naturally replace stops with flaps when speaking quickly. If you were to say the sequence "bitter better butter battle" as fast as you could, you would notice that for each [t], the tongue barely touches the point of articulation before it bounces away again, creating an alveolar flap. The symbol for the alveolar flap is an "r" without the serif at the top and is commonly referred to as the **Fish-hook R** [ɾ].[2] A retroflexed flap is symbolized by a symbol called the **Right-tail R** [ɽ]. Listen to the next exercise as it demonstrates common English words, first with stops and then with flaps.

Exercise 19.1: Producing Stops and Flaps

1. [ˈbæ.tɚ] [ˈbæ.ɾɚ]

2. [ˈmʌ.di] [ˈmʌ.ɾi]

3. [ˈbɹɪ.t̩l] [ˈbɹɪ.ɾl̩]

4. [ˈtʰɚ.t̩l] [ˈtʰɚ.ɽl̩]

5. [ˈbɚ.di] [ˈbɚ.ɽi]

6. [ˈkʰɚ.d̩l] [ˈkʰɚ.ɽl̩]

7. [ˈmɪ.ni] [ˈmɪ.n̆i]

8. [ˈfʌ.ni] [ˈfʌ.n̆i]

9. [ˈtʰɛ.nɪs] [ˈtʰɛ.n̆ɪs]

---

1 Another term that may be encountered is *taps*. Many linguists use the terms *flaps* and *taps* interchangeably; however, some make a distinction between the two. These linguists contend that the articulator briefly touches the point of articulation when pronouncing a tap; whereas, when pronouncing a flap, the articulator moves toward the point of articulation but does not make contact. Linguists who make this distinction use the Fish-hook R [ɾ] to indicate a tip-alveolar tap and a small capital D [ᴅ] to indicate a tip-alveolar flap. For the purposes of this textbook, no distinction will be made between flaps and taps, and only the term *flap(s)* will be used in the text.

2 Although the alveolar flap [ɾ] is called a Fish-hook R, it sounds much more like the English "d" than it does the English "r."

Producing [ɾ] and [ɽ]

There are three different ways in which the tongue can move for flapped sounds produced at the alveolar ridge. If you say the word "Betty" [ˈbɛ.ɾi], you will notice that the tip of the tongue taps the alveolar ridge and then returns straight back down to its original position. If you say the word "Saturday" [ˈsæ.ɾɚ.ɾeⁱ], you will notice that for the first flap, the tongue flicks past the alveolar ridge as it moves backward. For the second flap [ɾeⁱ], the tongue flicks past the alveolar ridge as it moves toward the front of the mouth. These tongue movements are illustrated in the following diagram. Repeat each example word and see if you can feel the different types of movement.

| **Illustration 19.1:** | **Illustration 19.2:** | **Illustration 19.3:** |
| **Vertical Flap** | **Backward Flap** | **Forward Flap** |

In Illustration 19.1, the tongue taps the alveolar ridge and comes straight back down as in the word [ˈbɛ.ɾi]. In Illustration 19.2, the tongue flicks the alveolar ridge as it moves backward as in [ˈsæ.ɾɚ]. The tongue also flicks by the alveolar ridge as it moves forward in [ɾeⁱ], as shown in Illustration 19.3. You can learn to control the articulation of Fish-hook R [ɾ] by speeding up the pronunciation of certain practice words. Try saying "tada" [tʰəˈdɑ] several times increasing the speed until you get [tɾɑ]. Practice the same procedure with [gə ˈdɑ] and [dəˈdɑ]. Remember to relax the tip of your tongue a bit so that it can move freely. You may also try saying the words "auto" and "patty" quickly with a relaxed tongue.

Mimic the Fish-hook R [ɾ] in the following exercise. Remember not to try to control the articulation too much. A tightly controlled tongue will result in a stop instead of a flap.

Exercise 19.2: Producing [ɾ]

1. a) [ɑɾɑ]   b) [ɑɾ]   c) [ɾɑ]   d) [ɾɑɾɑɾ]

2. a) [iɾi]   b) [iɾ]   c) [ɾi]   d) [ɾiɾiɾ]

3. a) [eɾe]   b) [eɾ]   c) [ɾe]   d) [ɾeɾeɾ]

4. a) [oɾo]   b) [oɾ]   c) [ɾo]   d) [ɾoɾoɾ]

5. a) [uɾu]   b) [uɾ]   c) [ɾu]   d) [ɾuɾuɾ]

It can often be difficult to tell whether a sound is a flap or a stop. Remember that during the articulation of a stop, there is a buildup of pressure behind the articulator. There is no such pressure buildup with a flap, since the articulation is rapid and the tongue is somewhat relaxed. The following exercise contains both flaps and stops. Listen to each utterance, and identify the manner of articulation. Respond with "flap" or "stop."

Exercise 19.3: Recognizing Flaps and Stops

1.	[ɑɾɑ]	Flap	6.	[ete]	Stop	11.	[ɪɾi]	Flap
2.	[adɑ]	Stop	7.	[iɾɛ]	Flap	12.	[odo]	Stop
3.	[adɑ]	Stop	8.	[atɪ]	Stop	13.	[ɪɾɪ]	Flap
4.	[ɑɾɛ]	Flap	9.	[uro]	Flap	14.	[adɑ]	Stop
5.	[oɾo]	Flap	10.	[ɛde]	Stop	15.	[uru]	Flap

The difference between Fish-hook R [ɾ] and Right-tail R [ɽ] is the retroflexing of the tongue, and while the difference may be slight, being able to differentiate these sounds is necessary in some languages. Practice identifying these sounds in the following exercise. Respond with "alveolar" or "retroflexed."

Exercise 19.4: Recognizing Alveolar and Retroflexed Flaps

1.	[ɑɽɑ]	Retroflexed	5.	[ɑɾɑ]	Alveolar	9.	[iɽi]	Retroflexed
2.	[ɑɾɑ]	Alveolar	6.	[ɑɽɑ]	Retroflexed	10.	[ɛɽɛ]	Retroflexed
3.	[ɑɽɑ]	Retroflexed	7.	[ere]	Alveolar	11.	[ɪɾɪ]	Alveolar
4.	[ɑɾɑ]	Alveolar	8.	[oɽo]	Retroflexed	12.	[ɛɽɛ]	Retroflexed

The articulation of the Right-tail R [ɽ] is noticeably different from the articulation of the "r" sound in English, which is a glide symbolized by a Turned R [ɹ]. Although this sound has not yet been formally introduced, it should easy to differentiate these two sounds. Respond with "flap" or "approximant" in the following exercise.

Exercise 19.5: Recognizing Flaps and Approximants

1.	[ɑɾɑ]	Flap	3.	[ɑɹɑ]	Approximant	5.	[ɛɹɛ]	Approximant
2.	[ɑɹɑ]	Approximant	4.	[ɪɾe]	Flap	6.	[iɾɛ]	Flap

| 7. | [æɾæ] | Flap | 9. | [eɾi] | Flap | 11. | [ɑɾɑ] | Flap |
| 8. | [ɹɪ] | Approximant | 10. | [ɛɹæ] | Approximant | 12. | [ɹɛ] | Approximant |

Voiceless Flaps

All voiced flaps have voiceless counterparts; however, due to the short duration of flaps, it can be difficult to eliminate the voicing between two vowels. Most English speakers exclusively use voiced flaps. Consider the words "latter" and "ladder." In standard American English, both of these words are pronounced [ˈlæ.ɾɚ]. Remember that voicelessness is represented by placing an Under-ring [̥] beneath a symbol or an Over-ring [̊] above a symbol that has a descender.

Producing voiceless flaps is simply a matter of controlling the glottis. In order to eliminate the voicing, try saying [h] while articulating the flap. This section will focus on the alveolar and retroflexed flaps. The following exercise demonstrates [ɾ̥]. Mimic each utterance after the recording paying particular attention to your voicing.

Exercise 19.6: Producing [ɾ̥]

1.	a) [ɾ̥ɑ]	b) [ɑɾ̥]	c) [ɑɾ̥ɑ]	d) [ɾ̥ɑɾ̥ɑɾ̥]
2.	a) [ɾ̥i]	b) [iɾ̥]	c) [iɾ̥i]	d) [ɾ̥iɾ̥iɾ̥]
3.	a) [ɾ̥e]	b) [eɾ̥]	c) [eɾ̥e]	d) [ɾ̥eɾ̥eɾ̥]
4.	a) [ɾ̥o]	b) [oɾ̥]	c) [oɾ̥o]	d) [ɾ̥oɾ̥oɾ̥]
5.	a) [ɾ̥u]	b) [uɾ̥]	c) [uɾ̥u]	d) [ɾ̥uɾ̥uɾ̥]

The following exercise contrasts voiced and voiceless flaps. Respond after each utterance with "voiced" or "voiceless." Do not look at the text.

Exercise 19.7: Recognizing Voiced and Voiceless Flaps

1.	[ɑɾɑ]	Voiced	6.	[mɑɾɑ]	Voiced	11.	[ɪɾ̥ɪ]	Voiceless
2.	[ɑɾ̥ɑ]	Voiceless	7.	[ɑɾ̥ɑs]	Voiceless	12.	[sɑɾɪk]	Voiced
3.	[ɑɾ̥ɑ]	Voiceless	8.	[geɾ]	Voiced	13.	[teɾi]	Voiced
4.	[sɑɾ]	Voiced	9.	[ɾ̥ɪz]	Voiceless	14.	[poɾ̥ɑ]	Voiceless
5.	[ɾ̥ɑp]	Voiceless	10.	[veɾ̥]	Voiceless	15.	[oɾo]	Voiced

Now, practice differentiating between [ɾ̥] and [ɽ̥] in the following exercise. Respond with "alveolar" or "retroflexed."

Exercise 19.8: Recognizing Voiceless Alveolar and Retroflexed Flaps

1.	[ɑɽ̥ɑ]	Retroflexed	5.	[ɑɾ̥ɑ]	Alveolar	9.	[eɽ̥e]	Retroflexed
2.	[ɑɾ̥ɑ]	Alveolar	6.	[ɑɽ̥ɑ]	Retroflexed	10.	[ʊɽ̥ʊ]	Retroflexed
3.	[ɑɾ̥ɑ]	Alveolar	7.	[ɛɽ̥ɛ]	Retroflexed	11.	[æɾ̥æ]	Alveolar
4.	[ɑɽ̥ɑ]	Retroflexed	8.	[iɾ̥i]	Alveolar	12.	[ɑɽ̥ɑ]	Retroflexed

Producing Nasal and Lateral Alveolar Flaps

Most linguists agree that flapped nasals and laterals are simply nasals and laterals of extremely short duration. The only particular difficulty that most English speakers have in producing these flaps is in relaxing the tongue to the point that it can flap instead of creating an ordinary nasal or lateral consonant.

No special symbol has been decided upon by linguists to represent an alveolar nasal flap, so the Breve [˘] above an "n" is commonly used. The alveolar lateral flap, on the other hand, has been given a symbol called the **Turned Long-leg R [ɺ]**.[3]

You can feel the **Flapped N [n̆]** by saying the words "Minnie" and "penny" very rapidly. To pronounce a lateral flap [ɺ], quickly say the words "Millie" and "valley." Make sure that you do not insert an alveolar flap [ɾ] in place of the nasals and laterals.

Listen to the nasal and lateral sounds in the following exercise, and determine if each utterance contains a flapped phone or not.

Exercise 19.9: Recognizing Flaps

1.	[ɑɺɑ]	Flapped	6.	[zɑnɑ]	No	11.	[lɑs]	No
2.	[ɑlɑ]	No	7.	[mɑnɑs]	No	12.	[ɑnɑks]	No
3.	[ɑn̆ɑ]	Flapped	8.	[dɑn̆ɑ]	Flapped	13.	[tɑɺɑp]	Flapped
4.	[pɑɺɑ]	Flapped	9.	[fɑl]	No	14.	[ɑlɑps]	No
5.	[ɑɺɑf]	Flapped	10.	[ɑn̆ɑ]	Flapped	15.	[fɑn̆ɑ]	Flapped

---

3 Even though the symbol chosen to represent a lateral flap [ɺ] is a modified "r," this phone has no inherent r-like quality.

Labiodental Flaps [ⱱ]

The final flap that will be introduced in this lesson is the labiodental flap, which is symbolized by combining a V [v] with the Fish-hook R [ɾ] into a symbol called **Right Hook V** [ⱱ].[4] This phone is quite rare, being restricted to a few African languages.

The labiodental flap is articulated by the lower lip flicking outward briefly striking the upper teeth. When repeating the following utterances, be careful not to accidentally pronounce a [b]. As with all flaps, the articulator must flick past the point of articulation quickly.

Exercise 19.10: Producing [ⱱ] and [ⱱ̥]

1. [vavavavava]

2. [ⱱavaⱱavaⱱa]

3. [fafafafafa]

4. [ⱱ̥avⱱ̥avaⱱ̥a]

Trills

A **trill** is a rapid series of vibrations of an articulator against a point of articulation. These vibrations are not brought about by controlled muscular movements. Instead, the pressure of the air stream passing between the articulator and the point of articulation causes the articulator to "flutter" back and forth. Some linguists describe the articulator during a trill as "flapping in the breeze." It is important to realize that the articulator must be relaxed for this to occur. A trill cannot be produced by consciously trying to articulate a quick series of stops or flaps. The muscles serve only to hold the articulator in the correct position so that the passing air will cause it to flutter against the point of articulation.

Alveolar Trills [r]

The **alveolar trill** is symbolized simply by a **Lowercase R** [r].[5] Many people are already able to produce the alveolar trill [r]. This sound is commonly made by children when

---

4   Another symbol for labiodental flaps that may be encountered is the V with Curl [ⱴ]. A voiceless labiodental flap can be symbolized either by placing an under-ring below the Right Hook V [ⱱ̥] or by adding a breve above an "f" [f̆].

5   The Lowercase R [r] is intended only to represent alveolar trills; however, it is quite common to encounter this symbol being used incorrectly to represent the English "R."

imitating machine guns, cars, or airplanes. However, if you have trouble with this trill, you can learn to produce it by repeating "butter up" faster and faster until you get [brʌp]. Some people will find it easier to learn [r] after [p]. Do the same procedure with the phrase "put it on" so that you get [prɑn]. Remember to relax the tip of your tongue so that the air stream can cause it to flutter.

To produce the voiceless tip-alveolar trill [r̥], practice the same phrases as above, only this time in a whisper.

Once you have learned the articulation of [r] and [r̥], mimic the trills in the following exercise.

Exercise 19.11: Producing [r] and [r̥]

1. a) [ɑrɑ]   b) [rɑrɑr]   c) [ɑr̥ɑ]   d) [r̥ɑr̥ɑr̥]
2. a) [ɛrɛ]   b) [rɛrɛr]   c) [ɛr̥ɛ]   d) [r̥ɛr̥ɛr̥]
3. a) [iri]   b) [ririr]   c) [ir̥i]   d) [r̥ir̥ir̥]
4. a) [uru]   b) [rurur]   c) [ur̥u]   d) [r̥ur̥ur̥]

The following exercise contains both [r] and [r̥]. Respond with "voiced" or "voiceless."

Exercise 19.12: Recognizing Voiced and Voiceless Trills

1. [ɑrɑ]   Voiced   6. [ir̥ip]   Voiceless   11. [kæræk]   Voiced
2. [ɑr̥ɑ]   Voiceless   7. [mor̥ak]   Voiceless   12. [sore]   Voiced
3. [ɑrɑ]   Voiced   8. [ur̥u]   Voiceless   13. [nir̥usk] Voiceless
4. [vɑrɑf] Voiced   9. [lɛsɛr]   Voiced   14. [ɛrɛ]   Voiced
5. [pere]   Voiced   10. [ɛr̥ex]   Voiceless   15. [dær̥om]   Voiceless

Practice distinguishing between trills and flaps. Respond to each utterance in the following exercise with "flap" or "trill."

Exercise 19.13: Recognizing Flaps and Trills

1. [ɑrɑ]   Trill   4. [vɑrɑf]   Trill   7. [mor̥ak]   Trill
2. [ɑɾɑ]   Flap   5. [peɾe]   Flap   8. [uru]   Flap
3. [ɑɾɑ]   Flap   6. [ir̥ip]   Trill   9. [lɛsɛr]   Trill

10. [ɛɾex]	Flap	12. [sore]	Flap	14. [ɛɾɛ]	Trill
11. [kæræk]	Trill	13. [nirusk]	Flap	15. [dærom]	Flap

Bilabial Trills [ʙ]

The **bilabial trill** [ʙ] and voiceless bilabial trill [ʙ̥] may be less common than most other trills, so we will not spend a great deal of time on it in this course. They are symbolized by a **Small Capital B** [ʙ]. However, it does occur in some languages, so you should be familiar with its articulation. It should not be particularly difficult to produce if you keep your lips relaxed. Many times people say a lengthened bilabial trill [ʙ:] to indicate that they are shivering. You can also produce [ʙ̥] by imitating the voiceless snort of a horse. Try saying the following sequences.

Exercise 19.14: Producing [ʙ]

1. a) [ʙɑ]   b) [ɑʙ]   c) [ɑʙɑ]   d) [ʙɑʙɑʙ]

2. a) [ʙ̥ɑ]   b) [ɑʙ̥]   c) [ɑʙ̥ɑ]   d) [ʙ̥ɑʙ̥ɑʙ̥]

Uvular Trills [ʀ]

A **uvular trill** may prove difficult for some English speakers, as it is produced as the uvula flutters against the back of the tongue, creating a sound almost like gargling.

The symbol for a uvular trill is called **Small Capital R** [ʀ]. Illustration 19.4 shows the position of the tongue and uvula during a uvular trill.

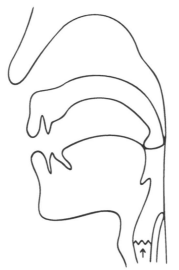

Illustration 19.4: Uvular Trill

To produce the uvular trill, start with [ɣ] and gradually move your tongue back until you feel the uvula begin to vibrate against the back of the tongue. You may have to practice this several times until you can get a smooth trilling sound. You may also try snoring artificially to get the feel of the articulation for [ʀ], since snoring uses the same articulation (except with an ingressive air stream and voicelessness). Once you have learned to produce the voiced uvular trill [ʀ], simply eliminate the voicing to produce its voiceless counterpart [ʀ̥]. You may also try saying [x] and then move the articulation farther back. Remember to keep your articulators relaxed for these sounds. Listen to the uvular trills in the following exercises, and mimic each utterance.

Exercise 19.15: Producing [ʀ]

1. a) [aʀa]   b) [aʀ]   c) [ʀa]   d) [ʀaʀaʀ]

2. a) [ɛʀɛ]   b) [ɛʀ]   c) [ʀɛ]   d) [ʀɛʀɛʀ]

3. a) [iʀi]   b) [iʀ]   c) [ʀi]   d) [ʀiʀiʀ]

4. a) [uʀu]   b) [uʀ]   c) [ʀu]   d) [ʀuʀuʀ]

In the following exercise, repeat each utterance after the recording.

Exercise 19.16: Producing [ʀ̥]

1. a) [aʀ̥a]   b) [aʀ̥]   c) [ʀ̥a]   d) [ʀ̥aʀ̥aʀ̥]

2. a) [ɛʀ̥ɛ]   b) [ɛʀ̥]   c) [ʀ̥ɛ]   d) [ʀ̥ɛʀ̥ɛʀ̥]

3. a) [iʀ̥i]   b) [iʀ̥]   c) [ʀ̥i]   d) [ʀ̥iʀ̥iʀ̥]

4. a) [uʀ̥u]   b) [uʀ̥]   c) [ʀ̥u]   d) [ʀ̥uʀ̥uʀ̥]

In the next exercise, tell whether the trills are alveolar trills or uvular trills. Respond with "alveolar" or "uvular."

Exercise 19.17: Recognizing Alveolar and Uvular Trills

1. [ara]   Alveolar   5. [laʀaf]   Uvular   9. [jaʀam]   Uvular

2. [aʀa]   Uvular   6. [mir̥ip]   Alveolar   10. [fɛʀi]   Uvular

3. [ar̥a]   Alveolar   7. [loʀu]   Uvular   11. [koruz]   Alveolar

4. [paʀas]   Uvular   8. [bare]   Alveolar   12. [mir̥ɛs]   Alveolar

In the following exercise, try to use the new manners of articulation to mimic the recording.

Exercise 19.18: Producing [ɾ̥, ɽ̥, r, ɽ, ʀ, and ʀ̥]

1. "Rowdy red riders raised a ruckus."

2. ɾowdy ɾed ɾiders ɾaised a ɾuckus.

3. ɽowdy ɽed ɽiders ɽaised a ɽuckus.

4. rowdy red riders raised a ruckus.

5. ɽowdy ɽed ɽiders ɽaised a ɽuckus.

6. ʀowdy ʀed ʀiders ʀaised a ʀuckus.

7. ʀ̥owdy ʀ̥ed ʀ̥iders ʀ̥aised a ʀ̥uckus.

Table 19.3: Flaps and Trills Summary

IPA Symbol	Name	Technical Name	English Example	APA Symbol
ɾ̥	Voiceless Fish-Hook R	Voiceless Tip-Alveolar Flap		ť
ɾ	Fish-Hook R	Voiced Tip-Alveolar Flap	butter	ď
ɽ̥	Voiceless Right-Tail R	Voiceless Tip-Retroflexed Flap		Ṛ̌
ɽ	Right-Tail R	Voiced Tip-Retroflexed Flap	Satur**d**ay	ř
ŋ̥	Voiceless Flapped N	Voiceless Tip-Alveolar Nasal Flap		Ň
ŋ	Flapped N	Voiced Tip-Alveolar Nasal Flap	mini	ň

IPA Symbol	Name	Technical Name	English Example	APA Symbol
ɺ̥	Voiceless Turned Long-Leg R	Voiceless Tip-Alveolar Lateral Flap		Ľ
ɺ	Turned Long-Leg R	Voiced Tip-Alveolar Lateral Flap	valley	Ǐ
v̥, f̆	Voiceless Right Hook V, Extra Short F	Voiceless Labiodental Flap		f̆
ⱱ	Right Hook V	Voiced Labiodental Flap		v̆
ʙ̥	Voiceless Small Capital B	Voiceless Bilabial Trill		
ʙ	Small Capital B	Voiced Bilabial Trill		
r̥	Voiceless Lowercase R	Voiceless Tip-Alveolar Trill		R̃
r	Lowercase R	Voiced Tip-Alveolar Trill		r̃
ʀ̥	Voiceless Small Capital R	Voiceless Back-Uvular Trill		R̰̃
ʀ	Small Capital R	Voiced Back-Uvular Trill		r̰̃

Lesson 20:
Central Vowels and Approximants

Lesson Outline

Glossary

In this lesson, you will learn to recognize two new vowel sounds and a new manner of articulation. Both vowels introduced are in the central position and occur frequently in English. The approximants introduced are also common English sounds.

Central Vowels

Although the central vowels in focus occur quite frequently in English, it is often difficult for English speakers to identify them. **Central vowels** are articulated by the mid section of the tongue modifying the air stream. In English, their use is usually limited to unstressed syllables, where the vowel sound is naturally reduced to a central quality like [ɨ] or [ə]. This phenomena is referred to as **vowel reduction**. Consider the word "enemy" [ˈɛnəˌmi]. If this word is pronounced in a relaxed, natural manner, the vowel in the unstressed syllable is reduced to [ə]. Only by over-articulating the word do we hear the expected [ʌ] or [ɛ] in the second syllable. This same phenomenon can be observed in the word "possess" [pʰəˈzɛs]. Here the first vowel is reduced from [o] to [ə]. The stressed syllable maintains its [ɛ] quality. In these cases the speaker is usually unaware of the vowel reduction, believing that he is actually producing a different vowel. Note that not all languages reduce vowels in the same way, and some languages do not reduce vowels at all.

The bold symbols in the chart below represent the sounds introduced in this lesson. The close central unrounded vowel is called Barred I [ɨ]. The mid central unrounded vowel is called Schwa [ə].

Illustration 20.1: English Central Vowels

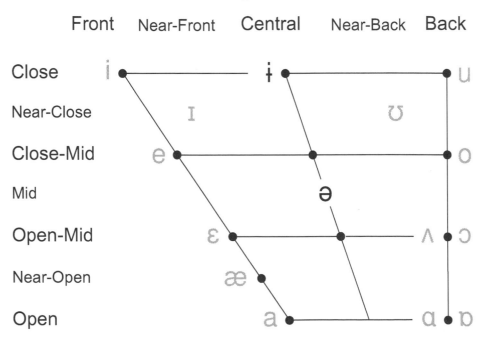

Illustration 20.2 pictures the approximate position of the tongue for four central and back unrounded vowels. Note that this diagram shows only the different positions of the tongue, while in reality the entire lower jaw would be repositioned for each sound.

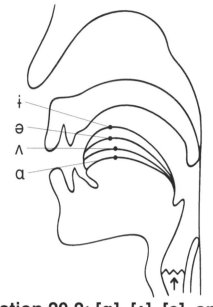

Illustration 20.2: [ɑ], [ʌ], [ə], and [ɨ]

Producing [ə]

The **Schwa** [ə] is a mid central unrounded vowel and by far the most common vowel in spoken English. As we have already mentioned, the use of Schwa in English is usually restricted to unstressed syllables, where it occurs due to vowel reduction. Exercise 20.1 demonstrates common English words pronounced with and without vowel reduction. The first time the words are given they will be pronounced normally, with [ə] in the unstressed syllable. The second time they will be over-articulated to eliminate vowel reduction. Listen to the exercise once, and then mimic.

Exercise 20.1: Recognizing [ə]

1. a) [pʰəˈzɛs]　　　　　　　　b) [pʰoᵘˈzɛs]

2. a) [bəˈlun]　　　　　　　　b) [bɑˈlun]

3. a) [ˈsæləd]　　　　　　　　b) [ˈsælɪd]

4. a) [səˈlut]　　　　　　　　b) [sʌˈlut]

5. a) [ˈdɑⁱ.mənd]　　　　　　b) [ˈdɑⁱ.mʌnd]

6. a) [dəˈstɹɛs]　　　　　　　b) [dɪˈstɹɛs]

7. a) [dəˈfaⁱ]   b) [diˈfaⁱ]

8. a) [bəˈfoˠ]   b) [biˈfoˠ]

9. a) [dəˈzaⁱn]   b) [diˈzaⁱn]

10. a) [bəˈsaⁱdz]   b) [biˈsaⁱdz]

11. a) [dəˈlɪv.ɚ]   b) [diˈlɪv.ɚ]

12. a) [bəˈliv]   b) [biˈliv]

13. a) [dəˈmænd]   b) [diˈmænd]

14. a) [bəˈkʌz]   b) [biˈkʌz]

15. a) [ˈsoᵘ.fəz]   a) [ˈsoᵘ.fʌz]

16. a) [dəˈziz]   b) [dɪˈziz]

The Schwa [ə] is produced with the tongue and other facial features in a relaxed, central position. You can learn to recognize and reproduce the Schwa by prolonging and isolating the reduced vowel in unstressed syllables. You may also try beginning with the open back vowel [ɑ] and, while keeping your tongue stationary, slowly close your mouth, resulting in [ɑ], [ʌ], and [ə]. Do not let your tongue slip back so that you get [ʊ], however. The following exercise demonstrates [ɑ], [ʌ], [ə], and [ʊ]. Mimic each utterance after the recording.

Exercise 20.2: Producing [ɑ], [ʌ], [ə], and [ʊ]

1. [ɑ]	6. [pʰʌt]	11. [lək]	16. [tʰʊk]
2. [ʌ]	7. [pʰət]	12. [lʊk]	17. [ʃak]
3. [ə]	8. [pʰʊt]	13. [tʰak]	18. [ʃʌk]
4. [ʊ]	9. [lak]	14. [tʰʌk]	19. [ʃək]
5. [pʰat]	10. [lʌk]	15. [tʰək]	20. [ʃʊk]

Learning to distinguish between the Schwa and other vowels like [ɪ], [ɛ], [ʌ], and [ʊ] can be a challenge for some people. The next exercise contrasts [ə] with other similar vowels. Each utterance will be given twice. Respond with "same" or "different."

Exercise 20.3: Recognizing Central Vowels

1.	[səl səl]	Same	9.	[səz sɛz]	Different	17.	[səl səl]	Same
2.	[səl sɪl]	Different	10.	[ʒən ʒɛŋ]	Different	18.	[sʌl səl]	Different
3.	[səl səl]	Same	11.	[ʒɛŋ ʒən]	Different	19.	[ŋəm ŋʊm]	Different
4.	[gəm gɪm]	Different	12.	[ʒən ʒən]	Same	20.	[ŋʊm ŋəm]	Different
5.	[gəm gəm]	Same	13.	[pʰəð pʰʌð]	Different	21.	[ŋəm ŋəm]	Same
6.	[gɪm gəm]	Different	14.	[pʰəð pʰəð]	Same	22.	[rəd rʊd]	Different
7.	[sɛz səz]	Different	15.	[pʰəð pʰəð]	Same	23.	[rəd rəd]	Same
8.	[səz səz]	Same	16.	[sʌl səl]	Different	24.	[rəd rʊd]	Different

Now practice identifying the vowels. The next exercise contains [ɪ], [ɛ], [ʌ], [ə], and [ʊ]. Respond by giving the name of the vowel that you hear.

Exercise 20.4: Recognizing Central Vowels

1.	[səl]	Schwa	7.	[zʌp]	Turned V	13.	[tʰəf]	Schwa
2.	[sʌl]	Turned V	8.	[zəp]	Schwa	14.	[tʰʌf]	Turned V
3.	[səl]	Schwa	9.	[zɛp]	Epsilon	15.	[tʰəf]	Schwa
4.	[mɪŋ]	Small Capital I	10.	[ŋɪŋ]	Small Capital I	16.	[zɛm]	Epsilon
5.	[mɛŋ]	Epsilon	11.	[ŋʌŋ]	Turned V	17.	[zəm]	Schwa
6.	[məŋ]	Schwa	12.	[ŋɛŋ]	Epsilon	18.	[zɪm]	Small Capital I

Producing [ɨ]

The **Barred I** [ɨ] is a close central unrounded vowel and also occurs in unstressed syllables in English. It usually occurs where close or near-close vowels are reduced to a central quality, especially when followed by an alveolar consonant, such as in the word "roses" [roᵘzɨz]. Not all English speakers reduce such vowels exactly the same way, however. A Schwa [ə] may also be pronounced instead.

Because Schwa [ə] and Barred I [ɨ] are both used only in unstressed syllables and are not believed to be the correct vowel, it can be difficult for English speakers to distinguish between the two. When pronouncing [ɨ], the tongue is almost completely touching the roof of the mouth. To practice saying and hearing these two vowels, try saying the phrase "Rosa's roses" [ˈroᵘ.zə ˈroᵘ.zɨz].

The following exercise demonstrates some common English words with near-close vowels reduced to [ɨ]. The first time the words are given they will contain [ɨ] in the unstressed syllables. The second time they will contain the vowel that is considered the supposed proper sound for the word. Listen to the exercise once, and then mimic. Repeat each word just as it is transcribed, regardless of whether you normally pronounce it that way or not.

Exercise 20.5: Producing [ɨ]

1. a) [ˈɹoᵘzɨz]   b) [ˈɹoᵘzɪz]

2. a) [ˈdʌ.zɨnz]   b) [ˈdʌ.zɪnz]

3. a) [ˈbɪz.nɨs]   b) [ˈbɪz.nɪs]

4. a) [ˈiŋ.glɨʃ]   b) [ˈiŋ.glɪʃ]

5. a) [ˈhɪn.d͡ʒɨz]   b) [ˈhɪn.d͡ʒɪz]

6. a) [ˈkeˠ.ɹɨt]   b) [ˈkeˠ.ɹɪt]

7. a) [ˈeⁱ.d͡ʒɨz]   b) [ˈeⁱ.d͡ʒɪz]

8. a) [ˈrʌ.ʃɨn]   b) [ˈrʌ.ʃɪn]

9. a) [ˈæ.rɨk]   b) [ˈæ.rɪk]

10. a) [dɨˈziz]   b) [dɪˈziz]

You can learn to control the pronunciation of Barred I [ɨ] by beginning with [ɑ] and working your way up the chart through [ʌ], [ə], and finally [ɨ]. It is important to make sure that your tongue remains relatively stationary during this sequence. Only the jaw should move up and down. You may also try moving your tongue forward and backward between [i] and [u] to find [ɨ] between the two. Practice the sequences in the following exercise. Mimic each utterance.

Exercise 20.6: Producing [ɑ], [ʌ], [ə], and [ɨ]

1. [ɑ]   2. [ʌ]   3. [ə]   4. [ɨ]

5.	[pʰɑt]	8.	[pʰɨt]	11.	[lək]	14.	[tʰʌk]
6.	[pʰʌt]	9.	[lɑk]	12.	[lɨk]	15.	[tʰək]
7.	[pʰət]	10.	[lʌk]	13.	[tʰak]	16.	[tʰɨk]

Now practice distinguishing between [ɨ] and other similar vowels. Respond in the next exercise with "same" or "different."

Exercise 20.7: Recognizing Central Vowels

1.	[sɨf sɨf]	Same	10.	[zɛn zɨn]	Different	19.	[ʃʊfɨ ʃʊfɨ]	Same
2.	[sɪf sɨf]	Different	11.	[zɨn zɨn]	Same	20.	[ʃʊfʊ ʃʊfɨ]	Different
3.	[sɨf sɪf]	Different	12.	[zɨn zɛn]	Different	21.	[ʃʊfɨ ʃʊfɨ]	Same
4.	[bɨd bɨd]	Same	13.	[bʌda bɨda]	Different	22.	[zɨnʌ zʊnʌ]	Different
5.	[bɨd bɪd]	Different	14.	[bɨda bʌda]	Different	23.	[zɨnʌ zʊnʌ]	Different
6.	[bɨd bɨd]	Same	15.	[bɨda bɨda]	Same	24.	[zɨnʌ zɨnʌ]	Same
7.	[lɨk lɛk]	Different	16.	[lasɨ lasʌ]	Different	25.	[sɨn sən]	Different
8.	[lɛk lɨk]	Different	17.	[lasɨ lasʌ]	Different	26.	[sɨn sɨn]	Same
9.	[lɨk lɨk]	Same	18.	[lasɨ lasɨ]	Same	27.	[sən sɨn]	Different

The next exercise includes [ɨ], [ə], [ɪ], [ɛ], and [ʊ]. Respond by naming the vowel.

Exercise 20.8: Recognizing Central Vowels

1.	[sɨ]	Barred I	7.	[lək]	Schwa	13.	[mɨn]	Barred I
2.	[sɪ]	Small Capital I	8.	[bɨs]	Barred I	14.	[gəv]	Schwa
3.	[sɛ]	Epsilon	9.	[frf]	Small Capital I	15.	[tɨx]	Barred I
4.	[sɨf]	Barred I	10.	[vʊf]	Upsilon	16.	[lʊx]	Upsilon
5.	[fən]	Schwa	11.	[kɛd]	Epsilon	17.	[bɨm]	Barred I
6.	[nʊm]	Upsilon	12.	[dək]	Schwa	18.	[mək]	Schwa

Mimic the utterances in the following exercise.

Exercise 20.9: Producing Central Vowels

1. [nʌp]	9. [gʌs]	17. [dʌfʌ]	25. [sʌpɨ]
2. [nəp]	10. [gəs]	18. [dəfʌ]	26. [səpɨ]
3. [nɨp]	11. [gɨs]	19. [dɨfʌ]	27. [sɨpɨ]
4. [nʊp]	12. [gʊs]	20. [dʊfʌ]	28. [sʊpɨ]
5. [dʌt]	13. [dʌfɑ]	21. [sʌpə]	29. [vʌrʊ]
6. [dət]	14. [dəfɑ]	22. [səpə]	30. [vərʊ]
7. [dɨt]	15. [dɨfɑ]	23. [sɨpə]	31. [vɨrʊ]
8. [dʊt]	16. [dʊfɑ]	24. [sʊpə]	32. [vʊrʊ]

Central Approximants

In Lesson 17, approximants were introduced. **Central approximants**[1] are phones in which the air stream is reduced, but not obstructed enough to cause audible turbulence. The articulation of approximants, therefore, is not as open as that of vowels, but not as close as that of fricatives and other consonants. Because this distinction is very slight, central approximants are often wrongly classified as vowels or fricatives.

Lateral approximates have already been studied at length. Central approximants are similar in many aspects; however, unlike lateral approximants, for which the air stream is directed around the sides of the tongue, central approximants involve passage of the air stream over the center of the tongue.

English Approximants

English speakers are already familiar with three approximants; however, they can be difficult to distinguish from their vowel counterparts. The three English approximants are listed in Table 20.1 below. The first symbol [ɹ] is the "r" sound in the word "red." The [j] represents what is normally considered a "y" in English, such as the word "yes." The [w] sounds like the English "w."

---

1 Central approximants are commonly referred to simply as approximants.

Table 20.1: English Approximants

	Alveolar	Palatal	Labial-Velar[2]
Voiceless	ɹ̥	j̊	w̥
Voiced	ɹ	j	w

As already mentioned, approximants involve greater constriction between the articulator(s) and point(s) of articulation than vowels, but not as much constriction as fricatives. One way to picture the articulation of approximants in relation to that of vowels and fricatives is to extend the top of the vowel chart upward to include sounds produced with a more closed position than the close vowels [i] and [u]. Illustration 20.3 pictures the different manners of articulations produced as the tongue moves upward, closer to the palate. Note that as the tongue raises, more of the tongue modifies the air stream, and therefore, the point of articulation moves back slightly. As is customary with vowel charts, symbols on the left side of the dot are unrounded, and symbols on the right are rounded. Also, as with all charts, the position of the symbols is merely an approximation.

Illustration 20.3: Comparison of Consonant and Vowel Heights

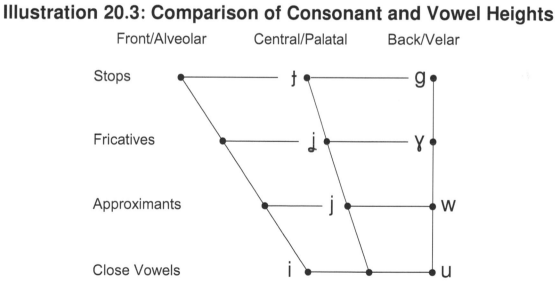

Central approximants also differ from vowels in that they are non-syllabic. Instead of constituting the nucleus of a syllable as vowels do, central approximants usually function as peripheral elements of syllables. Because of this similarity to vowel glides, approximants are often wrongly classified as such.[3]

---

2 Labial-velar approximants are double articulated phones. The air stream is modified at both the labial and velar points of articulation.

3 The term "semi-vowel," which is another name for vowel glides, is also often wrongly used to classify approximants.

As stated previously in this book, English contains very few actual on-glides. English usually uses approximants in such situations. Consider the word "ye" [ji]. When spoken slowly, one can feel the tongue moving downward slightly from the palatal approximant to the vowel. The symbol **J** [j] representing palatal approximants may be confusing to English speakers, but many European languages pronounce the letter "j" as English speakers pronounce "y."

Another common approximant in English is the double articulated labial-velar approximant **W** [w]. This sound is quite similar to the vowel [u], but the tongue and lips are closer to the points of articulation. The word "woo" [wuː][4] demonstrates the difference between the vowel [u] and the consonant [w]. When pronouncing this word, the one should be able to feel the lips separate when transitioning from the approximant to the vowel. The tongue also lowers slightly, but this is more difficult to notice. This distinction, though subtle, is important because some languages use on-glides instead of approximants. An English speaker imposing his or her own habits onto such a language would have an accent noticeable to native speakers.

The alveolar approximant is represented by a **Turned R** [ɹ].[5] The [ɹ] can be difficult for speakers of other languages, and English speakers often confuse the alveolar approximant [ɹ] with the rhotacized Schwa [ɚ] and rhotacized Turned Epsilon [ɝ]. It helps to remember that approximants are non-syllabic, and, in English, usually precede vowels. To hear the difference, slowly say the word "rear" [ɹiɚ] repeatedly. The tongue is closer to the roof of the mouth and less retroflexed when pronouncing the approximant. Also, native English speakers naturally round and protrude their lips when pronouncing [r]. This habit must be overcome to produce the pure sound.

Exercise 20.10: Recognizing Central Approximants

1. [ji]	ye	4. [ɹiɚ]	rear	7. [ɹɑt]	rot	10. [waʊ]	wow
2. [wi]	we	5. [jɑt]	yacht	8. [waɪ]	why	11. [ɹut]	root
3. [ɹid]	read	6. [wɑt]	watt	9. [ju]	you	12. [woʊ]	woe

Non-English Approximant

Many other approximants can be heard in the various languages of the world. Unfamiliar approximant may be learned simply by lowering fricatives or raising vowels. Table 20.2 below lists common approximants found in foreign languages.

---

4   An approximant may also be pronounced at the end of the word as well, i.e., [wuːw].

5   Though the Turned R [ɹ] may be alveolar, it is usually slightly retroflexed and, therefore, more alveopalatal.

Table 20.2: Non-English Approximants

	Bilabial	Labiodental	Retroflexed	Velar	Labial-Palatal[6]
Voiceless	β̞̊	ʋ̥	ɻ̊	ɰ̊	ɥ̊
Voiced	β̞	ʋ	ɻ	ɰ	ɥ

The **bilabial approximant** [β̞] does not have a separate symbol. The Beta [β] is used with a **Down Tack** [̞] diacritic indicating lowering. Like all diacritics, Down Tacks may be placed above or below a symbol. The bilabial approximant [β̞] is very similar to the [w] except that the lips do not round and the tongue does not raise when pronouncing [ʋ].

The labiodental approximant is represented by a symbol called **Cursive V** [ʋ]. This phone sounds similar to the voiced labiodental fricative [v].

The retroflexed approximant is symbolized the a **Turned R with Right Tail** [ɻ]. This is the same as an alveolar approximant but with a Right Tail [̢] indicating retroflexion. This phone sounds similar to the voiced retroflexed fricative [ʐ].

The symbol for the velar approximant is a **Turned Long Leg M** [ɰ]. To pronounce [ɰ] the back of the tongue is raised more than a [u], but the tongue is not as close to the roof of the mouth as it is when pronouncing a Gamma [ɣ]. This phone is similar to the [w]; however, the lips remain unrounded when pronouncing [ɰ]. The [ɰ] is found in Irish dialects.

Another approximant is the double articulated, labial-palatal approximant, symbolized by **Turned H** [ɥ]. This phone is articulated with the lips rounded and the mid section of the tongue is raised near the roof of the mouth. The [ɥ] sounds similar to the rounded I [y], which is studied in later lessons. The Turned H is common in French.

Voiceless Approximants

The concept of voiceless approximants is no different from that of other voiceless sounds. The glottis must be controlled so that the vocal cords are inactive during the approximant. Many English speakers produce voiceless approximants in their normal speech. Consider the words "wear" and "where." People who pronounce these words differently pronounce a voiceless approximant [w̥] at the beginning of the word "where." Other speakers produce voiceless approximants in words like "cute" [kj̊ut] and "quick" [kw̥ɪk].[7] The following exercise contrasts voiceless approximants with voiced approximants in

---

6 Labial-palatal approximants are double articulated phones.

7 Note that when diacritics are applied above a symbol, any floating dots are removed, e.g., "j" [j] becomes dotless "j" [ȷ].

English words. Follow along in the text, and pay particular attention to the voicing of the glides.

Exercise 20.11: Producing Voiceless Approximants

1. [kj̊ut kjut]   4. [fj̊u fju]   7. [pj̊u pju]

2. [kw̥ɪk kwɪk]   5. [sw̥it swit]   8. [kw̥æk kwæk]

3. [tɹ̥ɪk tɹɪk]   6. [tɹ̥it tɹit]   9. [tɹ̥æk tɹæk]

To produce voiceless approximants, it may be helpful to think "h" while saying the approximant. For example, instead of saying "you," think "h" and say "hyou." Be sure that you do not say a voiced and voiceless approximant together, such as [j̊ju]. Mimic the voiceless approximants in the following exercise.

Exercise 20.12: Producing Voiceless Approximants

1. [jɑ j̊ɑ]   7. [ju j̊u]   13. [jaᵁ j̊aᵁ]

2. [wɑ w̥ɑ]   8. [wu w̥u]   14. [waᵁ w̥aᵁ]

3. [ɹɑ ɹ̥ɑ]   9. [ɹu ɹ̥u]   15. [ɹaᵁ ɹ̥aᵁ]

4. [ji j̊i]   10. [jɑⁱ j̊ɑⁱ]   16. [jɑˤ j̊ɑˤ]

5. [wi w̥i]   11. [wɑⁱ w̥ɑⁱ]   17. [weˤ w̥eˤ]

6. [ɹi ɹ̥i]   12. [ɹɑⁱ ɹ̥ɑⁱ]   18. [ɹɑˤ ɹ̥ɑˤ]

In the following exercise, tell whether the approximants are voiced or voiceless.

Exercise 20.13: Recognizing Voiced and Voiceless Approximants

1. [j̊ɑ] Voiceless   6. [ɹɑ] Voiced   11. [jɛv] Voiced

2. [wɑ] Voiced   7. [we] Voiced   12. [w̥osto] Voiceless

3. [jɑ] Voiced   8. [iw̥o] Voiceless   13. [ɹiˈɑtʃ] Voiced

4. [ow̥o] Voiceless   9. [j̊ava] Voiceless   14. [wetse] Voiced

5. [ɹ̥i] Voiceless   10. [j̊atʃɛ] Voiceless 15. [ɹ̥agɑz] Voiceless

Table 20.3: Central Vowels and Approximants

IPA Symbol	Name	Technical Name	English Example	APA Symbol
ɨ	Barred I	Close Central Unrounded Vowel	English	ɨ
ə	Schwa	Mid Central Unrounded Vowel	ahead	ə
β̥	Voiceless Lowered Beta	Voiceless Bilabial Approximant		
β	Lowered Beta	Voiced Bilabial Approximant		
ʋ̥	Cursive V	Voiceless Labiodental Approximant		
ʋ	Cursive V	Voiced Labiodental Approximant		
ɹ̥	Voiceless Turned R	Voiceless Alveolar Approximant		R
ɹ	Turned R	Voiced Alveolar Approximant	red	r
ɻ̥	Voiceless Turned R with Right Tail	Voiceless Retroflexed Approximant		Ṛ
ɻ	Turned R with Right Tail	Voiced Retroflexed Approximant		r̩
j̊	Voiceless Dottless J	Voiceless Palatal Approximant	cute	Y
j	J	Voiced Palatal Approximant	yes	y

IPA Symbol	Name	Technical Name	English Example	APA Symbol
ɰ̥	Voiceless Turned Long Leg M	Voiceless Velar Approximant		
ɰ	Turned Long Leg M	Voiced Velar Approximant		
ɥ̥	Voiceless Turned H	Voiceless Labial-Palatal Approximant		
ɥ	Turned H	Voiced Labial-Palatal Approximant		
ʍ̥	Voiceless W	Voiceless Labial-Velar Approximant	q**u**it	ʍ
w	W	Voiced Labial-Velar Approximant	**w**e	w

Lesson 21: Alveopalatal Stops

Lesson Outline

Glossary

Thus far you have studied stops produced only at the labial, dental, alveolar, and velar points of articulation. As mentioned in Lesson 1, stops may be produced at any point along the roof of the mouth. In this lesson you will learn some stops produced at the alveopalatal point of articulation.

The two alveopalatal stops that will be studied are commonly called **Retracted T** [t̠] and **Retracted D** [d̠]. Alveopalatal stops are symbolized by placing a Minus Sign below [ˍ] or above [ˉ] the symbol of the corresponding alveolar stop. The **Minus Sign** [ˍ] indicates that a phone is retracted (or backed), usually meaning that the tongue is slightly farther back in the mouth than usual.[1] This diacritic can also be applied to other symbols besides stops.

A diacritic is used to indicate an alveopalatal stop instead of a unique symbol because the distinction in sound between alveolar and alveopalatal stops is minor; however, some languages do make a strong distinction between dentalized and alveopalatal stops.

These sounds are not found in English as distinct phones, but English speakers may occasionally pronounce alveopalatal stops in place of alveolar stops in rapid speech. This is especially common when a stop is followed by an alveopalatal phone. For example, the word "church" may be rendered [t͡ʃʰɚt͡ʃ].

Table 21.1 gives the symbols for the stops introduced in this lesson along with similar stops introduced previously.

Table 21.1: Introducing Alveopalatal Stops

	Tip-Dental	Tip-Alveolar	Blade-Alveopalatal	Tip-Retroflexed
Aspirated	t̪ʰ	tʰ	t̠ʰ	ʈʰ
Voiceless	t̪	t	t̠	ʈ
Voiced	d̪	d	d̠	ɖ

Illustration 21.1 below shows the position of the tongue for alveopalatal stops. The blade is the articulator for these sounds, the tip of the tongue being down behind the lower teeth. Notice that the articulation of these stops is identical to that of Enye [ñ], except that for the stops the velic is closed.[2]

---

1   The Minus Sign [ˍ] diacritic must not be confused with the Bridge [ˍ], which indicates fronting or dentalizing.

2   Some linguists interpret the Enye [ñ] as alveopalatal, but others interpret it as palatal. Officially, the IPA symbolizes an alveopalatal nasal as a Retracted N [n̠] and an Enye as a palatal nasal [ɲ].

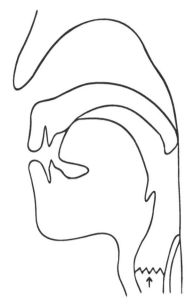

Illustration 21.1: Voiced Alveopalatal Stop [d̪]

Producing Alveopalatal Stops

When producing alveopalatal stops, it is important to make sure that the tip of your tongue stays tucked behind your lower teeth so that the blade can act as the articulator.

You are already familiar with the sounds [ʃ], [ʒ], [ñ], and [ʎ], all of which are produced at the alveopalatal point of articulation. You can use your familiarity with the articulation of these sounds to help you learn the new alveopalatal sounds. Remember that alveopalatal nasals and laterals are often accompanied by a palatal approximant [j] since the tongue is very near the position for [j] during their release. You will find that the corresponding stops [t̪] and [d̪] are usually accompanied by an approximant as well. However, although the [j] quality is usually present in alveopalatal consonants, it is not technically considered a part of the consonant's articulation. You must be careful not to confuse alveopalatal consonants with an alveolar phone followed by an approximant, such as [dja].

To produce [d̪], begin by saying [ñ] and convert the sound from a nasal to a stop by closing the velic. Practice this by saying the following sequence: [aña aña aña ad̪a ad̪a ad̪a aña ad̪a aña ad̪a aña ad̪a]. You may also try the same procedure with [ʒ] and [d̪].

The primary difference between the articulation of [t̪] and [d̪] is voicing. Practice controlling your voicing by saying the sequence [ad̪a ad̪a ad̪a at̪a at̪a at̪a ad̪a at̪a ad̪a at̪a ad̪a at̪a]. Practice aspirated and unaspirated alveopalatal stops by saying [at̪a at̪a at̪a at̪ʰa at̪ʰa at̪ʰa at̪a at̪ʰa at̪a at̪ʰa at̪a at̪ʰa]. Try saying the words "cheap" and "jeep" with the alveopalatal stops [t̪] and [d̪] instead of with affricates.

The following exercise contrasts alveolar stops with alveopalatal stops. Practice the sounds until you can recognize and reproduce them easily.

Exercise 21.1: Producing Alveopalatal Stops

1. [atʰɑ at̯ʰɑ]	7. [etʰe et̯ʰe]	13. [ʊtʰʊ ʊt̯ʰʊ]
2. [ata at̯a]	8. [ete et̯e]	14. [ʊtʊ ʊt̯ʊ]
3. [adɑ ad̯ɑ]	9. [ede ed̯e]	15. [ʊdʊ ʊd̯ʊ]
4. [itʰi it̯ʰi]	10. [otʰo ot̯ʰo]	16. [utʰu ut̯ʰu]
5. [iti it̯i]	11. [oto ot̯o]	17. [utu ut̯u]
6. [idi id̯i]	12. [odo od̯o]	18. [udu ud̯u]

In the following sentences, replace the alveolar stops with alveopalatal stops. This will give practice using alveopalatal stops in conjunction with other sounds.

1. ten tough turkeys taste terrible.

2. t̯ʰen t̯ʰough t̯ʰurkeys t̯ʰaste t̯ʰerrible.

3. t̯en t̯ough t̯urkeys t̯aste t̯errible.

4. dear daddy don't do that.

5. d̯ear d̯add̯y d̯on't d̯o that.

Recognizing Alveopalatal Stops

Although producing alveopalatal stops may be relatively easy, many people find it difficult to distinguish between alveopalatal and alveolar stops. The following exercise contrasts these stops. Respond with "same" or "different." When identifying alveopalatal stops, remember that the alveopalatal sounds are often accompanied by an approximant.

Exercise 21.2: Recognizing Alveopalatal Stops

1. [ad̯a ad̯a]	Same	4. [ŋat̯a ŋat̯a]	Same	7. [vlatʰa vlatʰa]	Different
2. [ada ad̯a]	Different	5. [ŋad̯a ŋada]	Different	8. [vlata vlat̯a]	Different
3. [at̯a ata]	Different	6. [ŋatʰa ŋatʰa]	Same	9. [vlata vlat̯a]	Different

10. [ðæt̪ɛ ðæt̪ɛ]	Same	12. [ðæd̪ɛ ðæd̪ɛ]	Same	14. [hot^hox hot^hox]	Different
11. [ðæd̪ɛ ðæd̪ɛ]	Different	13. [hot̪ox hotox]	Different	15. [hodox hodox]	Same

In the next exercise, respond by naming the point of articulation that you hear. Respond with "alveolar" or "alveopalatal."

Exercise 21.3: Recognizing Alveolar and Alveopalatal Stops

1. [at̪a]	Alveopalatal	6. [rad̪ʌ]	Alveopalatal	11. [at̪ɑʊ]	Alveopalatal
2. [ata]	Alveolar	7. [at^haθ]	Alveopalatal	12. [flɛtʌ]	Alveolar
3. [ada]	Alveolar	8. [ʒɛt^haŋ]	Alveolar	13. [ʌdʌ]	Alveolar
4. [ðad̪a]	Alveopalatal	9. [fut̪o]	Alveopalatal	14. [θad̪o]	Alveopalatal
5. [zɛda]	Alveolar	10. [vid̪an]	Alveopalatal	15. [at^haʃ]	Alveopalatal

Tell whether the sounds in the following exercise are alveopalatal or velar.

Exercise 21.4: Recognizing Alveopalatal and Velar Stops

1. [ðæt̪a]	Alveopalatal	5. [sakaf]	Velar	9. [vrad̪a]	Alveopalatal
2. [zad̪is]	Alveopalatal	6. [mat̪añ]	Alveopalatal	10. [aðkaθ]	Velar
3. [ŋagam]	Velar	7. [oʒga]	Velar	11. [hækɛl]	Velar
4. [d̪aða]	Alveopalatal	8. [ligom]	Velar	12. [lat̪al]	Alveopalatal

Alveopalatal stops can often be confused with the alveopalatal affricates [tʃ] and [dʒ]. Practice distinguishing between these sounds in the following exercise. Respond with "stop" or "affricate."

Exercise 21.5: Recognizing Stops and Affricates

1. [zad̪a]	Stop	5. [θat̪av]	Stop	9. [metʃeʒ]	Affricate
2. [zadʒa]	Affricate	6. [satʃaʃ]	Affricate	10. [dʒuð]	Affricate
3. [sataʃ]	Stop	7. [ŋad̪al]	Stop	11. [zot̪u]	Stop
4. [ad̪aŋ]	Stop	8. [zodʒu]	Affricate	12. [ʒed̪o]	Stop

In the next exercise, practice distinguishing between voiced and voiceless alveopalatal stops. Remember to listen only for the stop. Do not let the other consonants confuse you.

Exercise 21.6: Recognizing Voiced and Voiceless Alveopalatal Stops

1. [θad̠o] Voiced	5. [at̠ʰaʃ] Voiceless	9. [vrad̠a] Voiced
2. [vid̠an] Voiced	6. [θat̠av] Voiceless	10. [θat̠av] Voiceless
3. [at̠aɹ] Voiceless	7. [lat̠al] Voiceless	11. [ʒed̠o] Voiced
4. [ðad̠a] Voiced	8. [ŋat̠añ] Voiceless	12. [ŋad̠al] Voiced

In the next exercise respond with "aspirated" or "unaspirated."

Exercise 21.7: Recognizing Aspirated and Unaspirated Alveopalatal Stops

1. [at̠ʰoð] Aspirated	6. [zat̠aŋ] Unaspirated	11. [at̠ʰaθ] Aspirated
2. [at̠oð] Unaspirated	7. [ŋat̠ʰa] Aspirated	12. [ðet̠ʰof] Aspirated
3. [ʃot̠ʰav] Aspirated	8. [θaŋt̠ʰa] Aspirated	13. [ŋoʒt̠o] Unaspirated
4. [sat̠ʰa] Aspirated	9. [vlat̠a] Unaspirated	14. [t̠ʰaθaθ] Aspirated
5. [nat̠al] Unaspirated	10. [et̠e] Unaspirated	15. [mat̠ad] Unaspirated

As previously mentioned, alveopalatal stops are often accompanied by an approximant during their release. These stops can be easily confused with alveolar stops followed by an approximant. The following exercise contains both alveopalatal stops and alveolar stops followed by approximants. Respond with "alveopalatal" or "alveolar."

Exercise 21.8: Recognizing Alveopalatal and Alveolar Stops

1. [ad̠a] Alveopalatal	6. [ñad̠aŋ] Alveopalatal	11. [d̠eme] Alveopalatal
2. [adja] Alveolar	7. [ðedje] Alveolar	12. [djil] Alveolar
3. [atja] Alveolar	8. [mat̠af] Alveopalatal	13. [nodju] Alveolar
4. [ʒat̠a] Alveopalatal	9. [ŋoʒt̠o] Alveopalatal	14. [lat̠o] Alveopalatal
5. [ʒatja] Alveolar	10. [zetjo] Alveolar	15. [mod̠ol] Alveopalatal

In the next exercise, we will combine all of the stops charted in Table 21.1 above. Respond by giving the name of the symbol.

Exercise 21.9: Recognizing [t̠ʰ], [t̠], [d̠], [tʰ], [t], [d], [t̠ʰ], [t̠], [d̠], [t̠ʰ], [t̠], and [d̠]

1.	[at̠ʰa]	t̠ʰ	9.	[atʰa]	tʰ	17.	[pad̠a]	d̠
2.	[atʰa]	tʰ	10.	[ad]	d	18.	[pat̠a]	t̠
3.	[at̠a]	t̠	11.	[at̠ʰ]	t̠ʰ	19.	[d̠apa]	d̠
4.	[ad̠a]	d̠	12.	[at]	t	20.	[tʰapa]	tʰ
5.	[at̠a]	t̠	13.	[t̠a]	t̠	21.	[dapa]	d
6.	[ad̠a]	d̠	14.	[da]	d	22.	[lad̠a]	d̠
7.	[ada]	d	15.	[t̠a]	t̠	23.	[atal]	t
8.	[ata]	t	16.	[pat̠ʰa]	t̠ʰ	24.	[lata]	t

Table 21.2 below summarizes the sounds introduced in this lesson and gives the alternate symbols sometimes used to represent them.

Table 21.2: Alveopalatal Stops Summary

IPA symbol	Name	Technical Name	English Example	APA symbol
t̠ʰ	Aspirated Retracted T	Voiceless Aspirated Blade-Alveopalatal Stop		t̃ʰ
t̠	Retracted T	Voiceless Blade-Alveopalatal Stop		t̃
d̠	Retracted D	Voiced Blade-Alveopalatal Stop		d̃

Lesson 22:
Vowel and Glide Clusters

Lesson Outline

Glossary

Thus far all of the vowels you have learned have been single vowels or vowels separated by consonants or glides. In this lesson we will introduce sequences of adjacent vowels called vowel clusters, as well as adjacent vowel glides called glide clusters. These phonetic features are relatively common throughout the languages of the world, and it is very important that you be familiar with both their sound and articulation.

Vowel Clusters

A **vowel cluster** is two or more syllabic vowel sounds occurring together in a sequence with no intervening consonants. Vowel clusters differ from vowels with glides in that vowel glides are non-syllabic, while both sounds in a vowel cluster carry syllabicity. The sequence [ɑⁱ] consists of one syllable, but the corresponding vowel cluster [ɑ.i] is two separate syllables.

Vowel clusters are very common in languages like Tahitian and many indigenous languages of North America. English speakers do not naturally say vowel clusters. English speakers always insert either an approximant or glottal stop between two vowels. For example, "poet" [ˈpoᵘ.wɨt], "eon" [ˈi.jɑn], and "uh-oh" [ˈʌʔoᵘ] all contain consonants separating the vowels and are therefore not vowel clusters.

Representing Vowel Clusters

Vowel clusters should be represented by writing the symbols for both vowels with a syllable division separating the two, such as [ɑ.i]. The syllable break is important because it is common for linguists not to distinguish vowel glides from syllabic vowels, and therefore two vowels side-by-side would be ambiguous. Table 22.1 gives examples of vowel glides and corresponding vowel clusters. This table is by no means exhaustive, as any combination of vowels can be articulated in any sequence to form a vowel cluster.

Table 22.1: Vowel Cluster Symbolization

Vowel Glide	Vowel Cluster
[ɑⁱ]	[ɑ.i]
[ɑᵘ]	[ɑ.u]
[ⁱɑ]	[i.ɑ]
[ᵘɑ]	[u.ɑ]

Recognizing Vowel Clusters

The following exercise demonstrates the differences in pronunciation between vowels with approximants, vowels with glides, and vowel clusters. Pay particular attention to the number of syllables in each utterance. Listen to the sounds first, and then mimic.

Exercise 22.1: Producing Approximants, Vowel Glides, and Vowel Clusters

Approximants	Vowel Glide	Vowel Clusters
1. [njʌ]	7. [nⁱʌ]	13. [ni.ʌ]
2. [kʰjɛ]	8. [kʰⁱɛ]	14. [kʰi.ɛ]
3. [bju]	9. [bⁱu]	15. [bi.u]
4. [fwɑ]	10. [fᵘɑ]	16. [fu.ɑ]
5. [nwʌ]	11. [nᵘʌ]	17. [nu.ʌ]
6. [mwi]	12. [mᵘi]	18. [mu.i]

In many situations, distinguishing between vowel clusters and vowel glides can be challenging. Practice differentiating between these types of sequences in the following exercise. Remember to listen for the number of syllable beats during the vowel sequence. Respond with "glide" or "cluster."

Exercise 22.2: Recognizing Glides and Clusters

1. [mɑⁱ]	Glide	8. [mⁱɑ]	Glide	15. [mɑᵊ]	Glide
2. [mɑ.i]	Cluster	9. [o.us]	Cluster	16. [wɑⁱ]	Glide
3. [mi.ɑ]	Cluster	10. [soᵘ]	Glide	17. [bzoᵘ]	Glide
4. [bⁱu]	Glide	11. [goᵘ]	Glide	18. [di.ɑ]	Cluster
5. [bi.u]	Cluster	12. [tʰɑ.iʒ]	Cluster	19. [ᵘɑlp]	Glide
6. [su.o]	Cluster	13. [dⁱoᵘ]	Glide	20. [ɪf]	Glide
7. [ni.æ]	Cluster	14. [mɑ.ə]	Cluster	21. [fi.e]	Cluster

It can be sometimes difficult to tell whether a sequence is composed of two separate vowels or one long vowel. In terms of duration, vowel clusters and lengthened vowels may occupy roughly the same amount of time. However, it is important to remember that vowel clusters differ from lengthened vowels in that a lengthened vowel represents a single prolonged syllable, while each vowel in a cluster represents a separate syllable. It is entirely possible for two vowels that are exactly the same to occur together with separate syllable beats, making the sequence a cluster rather than a lengthened vowel. A cluster consisting of two identical vowels is often called a **re-articulated vowel**. In such cases, the quality of the vowel may remain the same throughout the entire sequence, but the presence of two syllable beats, and very often a change of stress within the cluster, constitutes the re-articulation.

The following exercise contains utterances consisting of multiple syllables. Focus on the vowels in the second syllable of each word and respond with "lengthened" or "re-articulated."

Exercise 22.3: Recognizing Lengthened and Re-articulated Vowels

1.	[moˈpʰɑ.ɑ]	Re-articulated	6.	[sɑˈmu.u]	Re-articulated	11. [juˈkʰæ.æ]	Re-articulated
2.	[moˈpʰɑː]	Lengthened	7.	[liˈsoː]	Lengthened	12. [juˈkʰæː]	Lengthened
3.	[moˈpʰɑ.ɑ]	Re-articulated	8.	[liˈso.o]	Re-articulated	13. [diˈse.e]	Re-articulated
4.	[sɑˈmuː]	Lengthened	9.	[liˈso.o]	Re-articulated	14. [diˈse.e]	Re-articulated
5.	[sɑˈmuː]	Lengthened	10. [juˈkʰæː]	Lengthened	15. [diˈseː]	Lengthened

As we have already stated, any combination of vowel sounds may be articulated sequentially to form a vowel cluster. In some languages, vowel clusters have been known to consist of more than two vowels. The following exercise contains vowel sequences of one, two, and three syllables. Remember that vowel glides are non-syllabic. Do not confuse two vowels and a glide for a three-syllable vowel cluster. Listen to the glided vowels and vowel clusters in the following exercise, and tell how many syllables you hear. Respond with "one," "two," or "three."

Exercise 22.4: Recognizing the Number of Syllables

1.	[mo.ɑ]	two	6.	[no.u.o]	three	11. [wɑ.ʌ.æ]	three
2.	[i.e.o]	three	7.	[wɑ.u.je]	three	12. [e.e]	two
3.	[ɛ.ʌⁱ]	two	8.	[ro.ʌ.ɔ]	three	13. [jɛᵘ]	one
4.	[woⁱ]	one	9.	[oᵘ.jɑ]	two	14. [i.e.ɛp]	three
5.	[o.wi]	two	10. [oⁱ.ʊᵘ]	two	15. [u.oᵘ]	two

Producing Vowel Clusters

When producing vowel clusters, you must make sure that no unwanted transitional sounds are inserted between the vowels. As stated earlier, English speakers break up the cluster with an approximant, as in the sequence [uwo]. Another common error is to place a glottal stop between the vowels, such as [uʔo]. These habits prevent many speakers from pronouncing clusters correctly, since by definition a vowel cluster has no intermediate consonants separating the vowels. It is important that you learn to eliminate the transitional sounds and still pronounce each vowel with its own syllable beat.

The following exercise builds pronunciation from vowels separated by glides and glottal stops to pure vowel clusters. Follow along in the text, and mimic each utterance.

Exercise 22.5: Producing Vowel Clusters

1. [e.jo.wi]	4. [o.we.jʌ]	7. [ɔ.wɑ.jæ]	10. [i.jʊ.wa]	13. [u.wo.we]
2. [eʔoʔi]	5. [oʔeʔʌ]	8. [ɔʔɑʔæ]	11. [iʔʊʔa]	14. [uʔoʔe]
3. [e.o.i]	6. [o.e.ʌ]	9. [ɔ.ɑ.æ]	12. [i.ʊ.a]	15. [u.o.e]

In the next exercise, tell whether the vowels are separated by a glide, a stop, or neither.

Exercise 22.6: Recognizing Vowel Clusters

1. [o.ᵘɑ]	Glide	5. [oʔi]	Stop	9. [e.ʊᵘ.æ]	Glide
2. [i.e]	Neither	6. [ɑ.juᵘo]	Glide	10. [i.ɛ.e]	Neither
3. [uʔe]	Stop	7. [iᵊ.æ]	Glide	11. [ʊʔuʔo]	Stop
4. [ɑ.ʊ.i]	Neither	8. [u.ʌ.ɑ]	Neither	12. [æ.u.ə]	Neither

Just as each vowel in a cluster carries its own beat, it may also have its own level of stress. The primary stress can occur on the first syllable, the second syllable, or on both syllables equally. The placement of stress often affects the sound of vowel clusters, causing them to be confused with glides. Watch the stress patterns on the vowel clusters in the following exercise and mimic each utterance.

Exercise 22.7: Demonstrating Stress Placement

1. [ˈeˈo]	3. [ˈe.o]	5. [ɑˈi]
2. [eˈo]	4. [ˈɑˈi]	6. [ˈɑ.i]

7. [ˈuˈɑ]   11. [iˈɛ]   15. [ˈo.u]

8. [uˈɑ]   12. [ˈi.ɛ]   16. [ˈæˈɛ]

9. [ˈu.ɑ]   13. [ˈoˈu]   17. [æˈɛ]

10. [ˈiˈɛ]   14. [oˈu]   18. [ˈæ.ɛ]

Mimic the vowel clusters in the following exercise. Pay attention to the stress patterns, and make sure that you do not insert any transitional stops or approximants.

Exercise 22.8: Producing Vowel Clusters

1. [tu.oˈtu.o.ɑ]   6. [sɑ.eˈtɑ.ʌ.ʊ]   11. [mʊ.ʌ.iˈmi.ɔ]

2. [le.oˈlo.ɔ.ʌ]   7. [ju.oˈɑ.tu.o]   12. [lɛ.u.ʊˈsɪ.æ]

3. [sɑ.ɑˈmʌ.ɑ.o]   8. [so.ɔ.ʌˈle.e]   13. [so.e.eˈvɑ.u.ɑ]

4. [mʊ.uˈlo.u.u]   9. [tʌ.ɑ.eˈlɑ.i]   14. [ni.o.uˈri.ɛ.e]

5. [lʌ.ɔˈmʊ.ʌ.ɔ]   10. [lɔ.ʊ.ɑˈmʊ.ɨ]   15. [lɔ.æ.aˈɑ.o.e.i]

Glide Clusters

Just as it is possible for two vowels to occur together with no intervening sounds, it is also possible for two vowel glides to occur together with no sounds between. This means that more than one glide can precede or follow the syllabic sound of a syllable. A series of adjacent glides occurring in the same syllable is called a **glide cluster**.

While both sounds in a vowel cluster are syllabic, both sounds in a glide cluster are non-syllabic. A glide cluster, therefore, can be described more accurately as a sequence of adjacent, non-syllabic vowel sounds preceding or following a syllabic sound. Glide clusters do not occur normally in English.

Glide clusters are represented by writing the symbols for both glide sounds in order, such as [ᵘⁱɑ]. Sometimes the sounds in a glide cluster occur in rapid sequence and sometimes simultaneously, making it difficult to tell which is the initial sound. Represent simultaneous clusters by first writing the sound that occurs more toward the front of the oral cavity.

Because glide clusters do not occur in English, they can be difficult to learn. However, pronouncing glide clusters is essentially the same as saying multiple vowels quickly. The following exercise demonstrates single glides, glide clusters, and glides in two separate syllables. Follow along in the text, and mimic each utterance.

Exercise 22.9: Producing Glide Clusters

1. a) [ᵘɛk]   b) [ᵃˊɛk]   c) [ᵘᵃˊɛk]   d) [ᵘᵃˊ.ɛk]

2. a) [ᵘæp]   b) [ᵃˊæp]   c) [ᵘᵃˊæp]   d) [ᵘᵃˊ.æp]

3. a) [faⁱ]   b) [faᵃˊ]   c) [faⁱᵃˊ]   d) [fa.ⁱᵃˊ]

4. a) [tʰaᵘ]   b) [tʰaᵃˊ]   c) [tʰaᵘᵃˊ]   d) [tʰa.ᵘᵃˊ]

5. a) [faⁱ]   b) [faᵉ]   c) [faⁱᵊ]   d) [fa.ⁱᵊ]

6. a) [baⁱ]   b) [baᵘ]   c) [baⁱᵘ]   d) [ba.ⁱu]

Practice distinguishing between single glides and glide clusters in the next exercise. Respond with "glide" or "glide cluster."

Exercise 22.10: Recognizing Glides and Glide Clusters

1. [ʔaⁱ]   Glide   6. [waᵃˊ]   Glide   11. [smaⁱᵃˊ]   Glide Cluster

2. [aᵘᵃˊ]   Glide Cluster   7. [tʰaⁱᵊ]   Glide Cluster   12. [ᵘaʃ]   Glide

3. [ᵘᵃˊak]   Glide Cluster   8. [tʰaⁱ]   Glide   13. [ᵘoⁱ]   Glide

4. [ᵃˊak]   Glide   9. [ᵘⁱaʃ]   Glide Cluster   14. [ᵘᵃˊʊdʒ]   Glide Cluster

5. [pʰlaⁱᵃˊ]   Glide Cluster   10. [doⁱᵘ]   Glide Cluster   15. [ⁱaⁱ]   Glide

In the next exercise, tell what type of cluster you hear. Respond with "vowel cluster" or "glide cluster."

Exercise 22.11: Recognizing Vowel Clusters and Glide Clusters

1. [mo.a]   Vowel Cluster   7. [tᵘᵃˊi]   Glide Cluster   13. [væ.el]   Vowel Cluster

2. [di.u]   Vowel Cluster   8. [ᵃˊu.ot]   Vowel Cluster   14. [e.o.ux]   Vowel Cluster

3. [ʔaᵘᵃˊ]   Glide Cluster   9. [lⁱᵘak]   Glide Cluster   15. [mᵘᵃˊæk]   Glide Cluster

4. [ⁱa.i]   Vowel Cluster   10. [li.a.ik]   Vowel Cluster   16. [du.o.e]   Vowel Cluster

5. [ᵘⁱaⁱ]   Glide Cluster   11. [blo.i]   Vowel Cluster   17. [maⁱᵃˊ]   Glide Cluster

6. [ᵘᵃˊug]   Glide Cluster   12. [ko.ex]   Vowel Cluster   18. [soᵘᵊk]   Glide Cluster

Lesson 23:
Palatal and Uvular Consonants

Lesson Outline

Glossary

You have already studied many sounds produced at the velar point of articulation. In this lesson you will focus on sounds produced slightly before and slightly behind the velum. You will recall from Lesson 1 that the area immediately in front of the velum is called the hard palate. This is the palatal point of articulation. The area immediately behind the **velum** is called the uvular point of articulation. The articulator for palatal sounds is usually the mid part of the tongue, while for velar and uvular sounds, the back of the tongue is the articulator.

Palatal and Uvular Consonants

Palatal and uvular consonants can be referred to as fronted and retracted (or backed) velar sounds. You must be careful, however, not to confuse back-velar sounds, in which the back of the tongue touches the velar point of articulation, with backed velar sounds, where the back of the tongue touches the uvular point of articulation.

The consonant chart below introduces the symbols for palatal and uvular sounds. This chart is by no means exhaustive, since voiceless counterparts of the palatal and uvular nasals and laterals presented are also possible. The palatal and uvular fricatives and stops can also be combined to create affricates.

Table 23.1: Palatal, Velar, and Uvular Stops and Fricatives

		Mid-Palatal	Back-Velar	Back-Uvular
Stops	Voiceless Aspirated	cʰ	kʰ	qʰ
	Voiceless	c	k	q
	Voiced	ɟ	g	ɢ
Fricatives	Voiceless	ç	x	χ
	Voiced	ʝ	ɣ	ʁ

Several new symbols are introduced in Table 23.1 above. Voiceless palatal stops are symbolized by a **Lowercase C [c]**, and uvular stops are symbolized by a **Lowercase Q [q]**. Even though these symbols are from the English alphabet, they do not sound anything like the English letters. Voiced palatal and uvular stops are symbolized by **Dotless Barred J [ɟ]** and **Small Capital G [ɢ]** respectively.

Voiceless palatal fricatives are symbolized by a symbol called **C Cedilla [ç]**. Voiceless uvular fricatives are symbolized by the Greek letter **Chi [χ]**. Voiced palatal fricatives are represented by a symbol called **Curly Tail J** [ʝ], and voiced uvular fricatives are represented by an **Inverted Small Capital R** [ʁ].

The following facial diagrams illustrate the position of the tongue for the articulation of palatal, velar, and uvular stops. Study the diagrams to familiarize yourself with the new points of articulation. For the corresponding fricatives, the articulation is the same except for a small gap between the articulator and point of articulation. Palatal and uvular nasals are produced with the same tongue position, but the velic must be open.

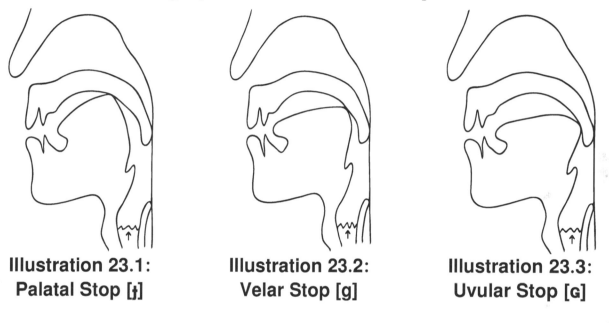

| Illustration 23.1: | Illustration 23.2: | Illustration 23.3: |
| Palatal Stop [ɟ] | Velar Stop [g] | Uvular Stop [ɢ] |

Producing Palatal and Uvular Consonants

Slight variations of velar phones are common in English. Velar consonants followed by front vowels may be produced more toward the front of the velum, nearer to the palatal point of articulation, but this movement must be exaggerated in order to reach the hard palate. Velar consonants adjacent to back vowels may be closer to the uvular point of articulation in anticipation of the proceeding vowel, but again, this movement must be exaggerated in order to reach the uvula. You can feel this difference by saying the words in Table 23.2 below.

Table 23.2: Comparison of Palatal, Velar, and Uvular Stops

Palatal	Velar	Uvular
"key" [cʰi]	"cop" [kʰɑp]	"caw" [qʰɔ]
"creep" [cʰɹip]	"crop" [kʰɹɑp]	"craw" [qɹɔ]
"geek" [ɟik]	"guck" [gʌk]	"gawk" [ɢɔk]

The voiceless palatal fricative [ç] occurs in English words when an "h" precedes a palatal approximant [j] or the close front vowel [i], such as in the words "hue" [çju] and "he" [çi]. To become familiar with the palatal fricative, try prolonging the word "hue" and concentrate on the height and position of the tongue.

Another way to gain a feel for the articulation of palatal and uvular sounds is by beginning with [x] and moving your tongue forward and backward so that you "hiss" the sequences [x ç x χ x ç x χ x]. You should hear the pitch move up and down during this sequence. This change of pitch is due to the altered size of the oral cavity. As the tongue moves forward, the size of the oral cavity is reduced, creating a higher resonance. When the tongue moves back, the oral cavity is enlarged, creating a lower sound. This difference in pitch can be very helpful in differentiating between palatal and uvular sounds.

Beginning with [x], try hissing the song "London Bridge is Falling Down" as if you were whistling the tune with the back of your tongue. The last three syllables, "fair la-dy," consist of the palatal fricative [ç], the velar fricative [x], and the uvular fricative [χ], respectively. This same procedure can be used to learn the articulation of [ʝ], [ɣ], and [ʁ].

You may also try imitating a donkey's "hee-haw," replacing [h] with [x]. Push the articulation of the last syllable back as far as possible. This will produce both [ç] and [χ]. Try the same procedure using voicing.

Once you have learned to control the use of the palatal and uvular points of articulation with stops and fricatives, you will have no trouble with the production of palatal and uvular nasals, laterals, and approximants. Mimic the consonants in the following exercise. Make sure, however, that you do not pronounce the palatal sounds with the same articulation as alveopalatal consonants.

Exercise 23.1: Producing Palatal and Uvular Stops and Fricatives

1.	a) ici	aka	ɔqɔ		3.	a) içi	axa	ɔχɔ
	b) ici	iki	iqi			b) içi	ixi	iχi
	c) aca	aka	aqa			c) aça	axa	aχa
	d) ɔcɔ	ɔkɔ	ɔqɔ			d) ɔçɔ	ɔxɔ	ɔχɔ
2.	a) iɟi	aga	ɔɢɔ		4.	a) iʝi	aɣa	ɔʁɔ
	b) iɟi	igi	iɢi			b) iʝi	iɣi	iʁi
	c) aɟa	aga	aɢa			c) aʝa	aɣa	aʁa
	d) ɔɟɔ	ɔgɔ	ɔɢɔ			d) ɔʝɔ	ɔɣɔ	ɔʁɔ

Recognizing Palatal and Uvular Consonants

Using palatal and uvular consonants in the place of velar consonants makes no difference in the meaning of English words. In some languages, however, these sounds can be contrastive. In such languages it is very important to be able to distinguish between palatal, velar, and uvular consonants. The following exercises will help you to develop an ear for these sounds. Listen to the following exercise, and respond by telling whether the pairs of sounds are the same or different.

Exercise 23.2: Recognizing Palatal and Uvular Consonants

1. [ɑcɑ ɑcɑ] Same	8. [ɑɢɑ ɑɟɑ] Different	15. [ɑça ɑça] Same
2. [ɑcɑ ɑqɑ] Different	9. [ogo oɢo] Different	16. [ɑɣ ɑɣ] Same
3. [ɑqɑ ɑcɑ] Different	10. [ɟa ɟa] Same	17. [ɑʁɑ ɑɟɑ] Different
4. [oqo oqo] Same	11. [iɟi igi] Different	18. [oʁo oɣo] Different
5. [ko qo] Different	12. [iɟo iɢo] Different	19. [ɑɢɑ ɑgɑ] Different
6. [ikɪ ikɪ] Same	13. [xa xa] Same	20. [ɑɴ ɑɴ] Same
7. [ɑɟa ɑɢɑ] Different	14. [ɑç ɑχ] Different	21. [iɲi iɴi] Different

Listen to the following exercise and respond by telling whether the stops that you hear are palatal or uvular.

Exercise 23.3: Recognizing Palatal and Uvular Stops

1. [ɑcɑ] Palatal	6. [ʃɑcɑ] Palatal	11. [dɑχɑ] Uvular
2. [ɑqɑ] Uvular	7. [æqæf] Uvular	12. [dɑçɑ] Palatal
3. [ɑcɑ] Palatal	8. [æcæf] Palatal	13. [mɑχ] Uvular
4. [ʃɑcɑ] Palatal	9. [æqæf] Uvular	14. [mɑχ] Uvular
5. [ʃɑqɑ] Uvular	10. [dɑχɑ] Uvular	15. [mɑç] Palatal

In the following exercise, tell whether the stops are velar or uvular.

Exercise 23.4: Recognizing Velar and Uvular Stops

1. [ɑgɑ] Velar	2. [ɑɢɑ] Uvular	3. [ɑgɑ] Velar

4. [nogos] Velar   8. [sæɢo] Uvular   12. [ɣab]   Velar

5. [sɑɢaf] Uvular   9. [gomi] Velar   13. [poɣoz] Velar

6. [ɢaz]   Uvular   10. [laʁɑ] Uvular   14. [iʁip]   Uvular

7. [migæ]   Velar   11. [aʁan] Uvular   15. [jaɣæ]   Velar

Listen to the following exercise, and respond by telling whether the stops are palatal or velar.

Exercise 23.5: Recognizing Palatal and Velar Stops

1. [ɑcɑ]   Palatal   6. [mɑɟɑ] Palatal   11. [miɣ]   Velar

2. [ɑkɑ]   Velar   7. [lixot] Velar   12. [laɣo]   Velar

3. [ɑkɑ]   Velar   8. [tuço] Palatal   13. [ɲom]   Palatal

4. [niɟil] Palatal   9. [dɑçe] Palatal   14. [ŋom]   Velar

5. [ægæt]   Velar   10. [miɟ]   Palatal   15. [iɲed]   Palatal

Tell whether the stops in the following exercise are palatal, velar, or uvular.

Exercise 23.6: Recognizing Palatal, Velar, and Uvular Stops

1. [ɑcɑ]   Palatal   8. [ɟɑ]   Palatal   15. [vaŋ]   Velar

2. [ɑkɑ]   Velar   9. [ʁɑ]   Uvular   16. [oʁaz] Uvular

3. [ɑqɑ]   Uvular   10. [noqo] Uvular   17. [eke]   Velar

4. [ɑɢ]   Uvular   11. [moco] Palatal   18. [nuɴu] Uvular

5. [ɑx]   Velar   12. [sogo] Velar   19. [ɑcɑ]   Palatal

6. [ɑɟ]   Palatal   13. [sɑçɑ] Palatal   20. [mokɑ] Velar

7. [gɑ]   Velar   14. [ɑɲaf] Palatal   21. [ɑqav] Uvular

The next exercise contains alveopalatal and palatal stops. Respond by naming the point of articulation.

Exercise 23.7: Recognizing Alveopalatal and Palatal Stops

1.	[acɑ]	Palatal	5.	[baña]	Alveopalatal	9.	[o̠lo]	Alveopalatal
2.	[ad̠ɑ]	Alveopalatal	6.	[aɲal]	Palatal	10.	[d̠im]	Alveopalatal
3.	[aɟa]	Palatal	7.	[vit̠a]	Alveopalatal	11.	[ecot]	Palatal
4.	[saɲ]	Palatal	8.	[gaʎa]	Palatal	12.	[aɟef]	Palatal

Palatal and Uvular Affricates

As you have already learned, palatal or uvular stops and fricatives can be combined to create affricates. The most common combinations are homorganic, where both the stop and fricative share the same point of articulation. It is also possible, however, to produce heterorganic affricates by combining palatal or uvular stops with fricatives of any other point of articulation.

Palatal and uvular affricates should not be particularly difficult to produce, but differentiating between palatal, velar, and uvular affricates can be a challenge. The following exercise contains homorganic palatal, velar, and uvular affricates. Listen to each utterance, and respond by naming the point of articulation.

Exercise 23.8: Recognizing Palatal, Velar, and Uvular Affricates

1.	[acça]	Palatal	7.	[sa.qχa] Uvular		13.	[akxɑ]	Velar
2.	[akxɑ]	Velar	8.	[ma.qχa]Uvular		14.	[naqχ]	Uvular
3.	[agɣa]	Velar	9.	[a.kxaf]	Velar	15.	[acça]	Palatal
4.	[aɢʁa]	Uvular	10.	[la.ɟʝal]	Palatal	16.	[zaɟʝ.as] Palatal	
5.	[agɣ]	Velar	11.	[aɢʁ.fa]	Uvular	17.	[fa.gɣav]Velar	
6.	[ɟʝa]	Palatal	12.	[kagɣ]	Velar	18.	[aqχa]	Uvular

Palatal, Velar, and Uvular Nasals and Laterals

In addition to stops and fricatives, nasals and laterals can also be formed at the palatal and uvular points of articulation. These phones are made in exactly the same way as their alveolar counterparts, except that the tongue is positioned farther back in the mouth. This will feel quite awkward to an English speaker at first, and he will naturally try to move the tongue toward the alveolar ridge, but such habits must be overcome in order to correctly pronounce these sounds. Table 23.3 below lists the symbols used to represent these sounds.

Table 23.3: Palatal, Velar, and Uvular Nasals and Laterals

	Mid-Palatal	Back-Velar	Back-Uvular
Nasals	ɲ	ŋ	ɴ
Lateral Approximants	ʎ	ʟ	

Palatal nasals are represented by a symbol called **Left-tail N (at left)** [ɲ]. It may help to remember this symbol as the combination of a "j" and an "n." The uvular nasals are symbolized by a **Small Capital N** [ɴ]. To learn how to pronounce these phones, try pronouncing a lengthened Eng [ŋ:] and move the tongue forward and backward.

The palatal lateral approximant is symbolized by a **Turned Y** [ʎ]. This sound is quite difficult for English speakers to hear and pronounce. When pronouncing this sound, one must ensure that the air steam flows laterally around the sides of the tongue.

The velar lateral approximant is represented by a **Small Capital L** [ʟ]. This too is awkward to pronounce at first. To produce this sound, start by pronouncing a lengthened Eng [ŋ:] and then redirect the air stream from going through the velic to moving around the sides of the tongue. Though the sides of the tongue may move slightly, be careful not to move the tongue forward.

After practicing forming these new sounds, listen to and mimic the exercise below.

Exercise 23.9: Producing Palatal, Velar, and Uvular Nasals and Laterals

1. a) iɲi   aŋa   ɔɴɔ   2. a) iʎi   aʟa

    b) iɲi   iŋi   iɴi   b) iʎi   iʟi

    c) aɲa   aŋa   aɴa   c) aʎa   aʟa

    d) ɔɲɔ   ɔŋɔ   ɔɴɔ   d) ɔʎɔ   ɔʟɔ

Practice control over the production of all of the phones learned in this lesson. Mimic each utterance in the following exercises.

Exercise 23.10: Mimicry

Palatal	Velar	Uvular
1. cream colored cittens	kream kolored kittens	qream qolored qittens
2. ɟooey ɟreen ɟrapes	gooey green grapes	ɢooey ɢreen ɢrapes
3. çrotchety çueen çatherine	xrotchety xueen xatherine	χrotchety χueen χatherine
4. ʝary ʝrinds ʝears	ɣary ɣrinds ɣears	ʁary ʁrinds ʁears
5. diɲ dɔɲ sɔɲ	diŋ dɔŋ sɔŋ	diɴ dɔɴ sɔɴ
6. ʎittʎe ʎarry ʎaughs	ʟittʟe ʟarry ʟaughs	

In the following exercise, repeat each utterance after the recording.

Exercise 23.11: Mimicry

1. [cɑˈqɑ]	9. [qɨˈqɑ]	17. [ɟaˈɢa]
2. [qʌˈcə]	10. [ŋɛˈcʊ]	18. [ɟuˈɢa]
3. [ʝuˈʎæ]	11. [ʟɔˈgɨ]	19. [xæˈɟɛ]
4. [ɢoˈʎɑ]	12. [cæˈqi]	20. [ɟɛˈɟe]
5. [cɔˈqɨ]	13. [qaˈçe]	21. [ʁaˈɣɑ]
6. [ʟeˈɲa]	14. [χɛˈɴʌ]	22. [ɢoˈɟa]
7. [qaˈce]	15. [qaˈcu]	23. [ɢaˈɢχ]
8. [cɛˈçæ]	16. [ɲuˈʝa]	24. [ɴɛˈcæ]

Table 23.4 below summarizes the sounds and symbols learned in this lesson.

Table 23.4: Palatal and Uvular Consonants Summary

IPA Symbol	Name	Technical Name	English Example	APA Symbol
c	C	Voiceless Mid-Palatal Stop		̣k̢

IPA Symbol	Name	Technical Name	English Example	APA Symbol
ɟ	Barred Dotless J	Voiced Mid-Palatal Stop		ĝ
q	Q	Voiceless Back-Uvular Stop		ḳ
ɢ	Small Capital G	Voiced Back-Uvular Stop		ġ
ç	C Cedilla	Voiceless Mid-Palatal Fricative	**h**ue	x̧
ʝ	Curly-Tail J	Voiced Mid-Palatal Fricative		ĝ̇
χ	Chi	Voiceless Back-Uvular Fricative		x̣
ʁ	Inverted Small Capital R	Voiced Back-Uvular Fricative		ġ̣
ɲ	Left-Tail N (at left)	Voiced Mid-Palatal Nasal		ñ
ɴ	Small Capital N	Voiced Back-Uvular Nasal		ṇ̇
ʎ	Turned Y	Voiced Mid-Palatal Lateral Approximant		
ʟ	Small Capital L	Voiced Back-Velar Lateral Approximant		

Lesson 24: Nasalized Vowels

Lesson Outline

Glossary

All of the vowels that we have studied so far have been produced with the velic closed, the resonance occurring strictly in the oral cavity. In this lesson we will introduce vowels produced with the velic partially open, allowing the sound to resonate in both the oral and nasal cavities at the same time. Sounds which involve both oral and nasal resonation are said to be **nasalized**, while those involving strictly oral resonation are said to be **non-nasalized**, or oral sounds.

Nasalization

The distinction between nasal sounds and nasalized sounds is very important. Nasals are sounds in which the air stream is completely blocked at some point in the oral cavity and redirected through the nasal cavity. For nasals no air escapes through the mouth because it is completely blocked by an articulator. For nasalized sounds, on the other hand, the air stream is not blocked in the oral cavity. The oral cavity remains the primary channel of articulation. The velic is lowered, however, allowing the nasal cavity to act as a secondary channel of articulation. This means that the air stream, instead of exiting the mouth only, exits through the nose as well. Illustration 24.1 and Illustration 24.2 picture the difference between nasal and nasalized articulation.

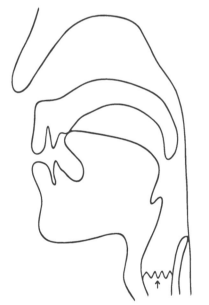 

Illustration 24.1: Nasal Consonant   **Illustration 24.2: Nasalized Vowel**

Understanding Nasalization

Vowels are the most commonly nasalized sounds and will therefore occupy the main focus of this lesson. However, most continuants (sounds produced with incomplete closure) can be nasalized. For voiceless consonants like [f] and [s], the acoustic quality added by nasalization is slight. For voiced consonants like [v] and [z], on the other hand, nasalization may change the sound significantly. Nasalized consonants are not drilled in this lesson, but you should be aware that they do occur.

It is important to note that nasalized sounds are articulated primarily in the oral cavity. While different vowel qualities can be produced by altering the size and shape of the oral cavity, the size and shape of the nasal cavity are essentially fixed. A speaker can control whether or not a vowel is nasalized, but cannot produce different vowel sounds by changing the size or shape of the nasal cavity itself. Therefore, nasalization is viewed as a modification of vowels, rather than unique vowel sounds.

Degrees of Nasalization

There may be different degrees of nasalization depending on the size of the velic opening. Sounds produced with the velic only slightly open are referred to as lightly nasalized, while those produced with a large velic opening are referred to as heavily nasalized. The following facial diagrams illustrate the position of the velum for different degrees of nasalization.

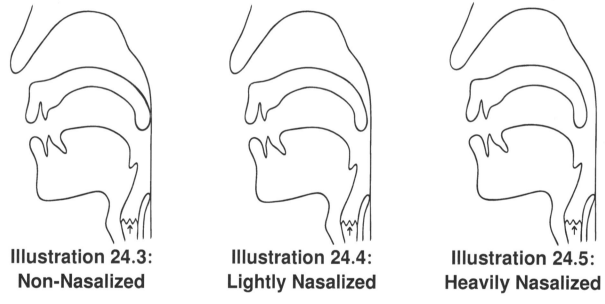

Illustration 24.3:
Non-Nasalized

Illustration 24.4:
Lightly Nasalized

Illustration 24.5:
Heavily Nasalized

Nasalization is represented by placing a **Tilde Above** [˜] a symbol (for example, [ɑ̃]) or a **Tilde Below** [˷] a symbol that has an ascender (for example, [ʎ̰]). If three different degrees of nasalization are present in a language, an **ogonek** [˛] (or Polish hook), can be used in conjunction with the tilde to represent heavy nasalization (for example, [ą̃]).

Nasalized Vowels

Nasalized vowels are found contrastively in some languages. This means that the meaning of a word can change depending on whether a vowel is oral or nasalized. Although nasalized vowels occur quite frequently in English, they make no difference in the meaning of words. Most English speakers nasalize vowels that occur next to nasal consonants like [m] and [n]. In these cases, the velic simply opens in anticipation of the nasal consonant. This happens automatically with no conscious thought from the speaker.

To determine if a vowel is nasalized, hold your nose closed with your thumb and finger as you pronounce the vowel. If the vowels are purely oral, their sound will not be affected by the closure. If they are nasalized, you will feel the pressure and vibration of the air stream in the nasal cavity. Prolong the vowel sound if you are still unsure if it is nasalized.

Say the pairs of words in Table 24.1 below, and try to detect the difference between the vowels in the first column and those in the second column.

Table 24.1: Comparison of Oral and Nasal Vowels

Oral	Nasal
"beat" [bit]	"mean" [mĩn]
"bit" [bɪt]	"min" [mĩn]
"bet" [bɛt]	"men" [mɛ̃n]
"bat" [bæt]	"man" [mæ̃n]
"pot" [pʰɑt]	"mom" [mɑ̃m]
"boot" [but]	"moon" [mũn]

Producing Nasalization

Although most English speakers produce both nasalized and oral vowels in their normal speech, it is necessary to practice in order to be able to control their production in any environment. You can practice gaining control of the velic by saying sequences of stops and nasals since the only physical difference between homorganic stops and nasals is the position of the velic. Say the word "hidden" without putting a vowel between the [d] and [n] of the last syllable, such as [hɪd.n̩]. Repeat the last syllable several times so that you get the sequence [dn̩dn̩dn̩dn̩dn̩]. You should be able to feel the velic opening and closing during this sequence. Try the same procedure with the sequences [bm̩bm̩bm̩bm̩bm̩] and [gŋ̩gŋ̩gŋ̩gŋ̩gŋ̩].

Say the sequence [mĩmĩmĩmĩmĩ], making sure that the velic does not close between the consonants. Prolong the last vowel and then, while making sure that the velic does not close, isolate the vowel [ĩ]. Test the vowel to see if it is nasalized by holding your nose closed with your fingers. Try the same procedure with other vowels such as [ɑ] and [u], and other nasals like [n] and [ŋ].

Most people find it relatively easy to produce nasalized vowels next to nasal consonants. Producing them next to oral sounds, however, is much more difficult. You can practice this by isolating the nasalized vowel with the procedure described above, and inserting an oral sound before it.

Practice mimicking the sequences in the following exercise. You must concentrate on opening your velic after the oral consonant.

Exercise 24.1: Producing Nasalized Vowels

1.	[mĩmĩmĩ]	[mĩ:]	[ĩ:]	[bĩ:]
2.	[mɛ̃mɛ̃mɛ̃]	[mɛ̃:]	[ɛ̃:]	[bɛ̃:]
3.	[næ̃næ̃næ̃]	[næ̃:]	[æ̃:]	[dæ̃:]
4.	[nɑ̃nɑ̃nɑ̃]	[nɑ̃:]	[ɑ̃:]	[dɑ̃:]
5.	[ŋõŋõŋõ]	[ŋõ:]	[õ:]	[gõ:]
6.	[ŋũŋũŋũ]	[ŋũ:]	[ũ:]	[gũ:]

Use a mirror to watch the movement of your velic and practice saying sequences of oral and nasalized vowels such as [ĩ i ĩ i ĩ i ĩ i ĩ], [ɑ̃ ɑ ɑ̃ ɑ ɑ̃ ɑ ɑ̃ ɑ ɑ̃], and [ũ u ũ u ũ u ũ u]. Practice nasal and oral vowels with all of the basic vowels on the chart.

Practice mimicking the vowels in the following exercise. Make sure that the oral vowels are pronounced purely oral. Test your pronunciation by closing off your nose with your fingers.

Exercise 24.2: Producing Nasalized and Oral Vowels

1.	[mi]	7.	[bɛ]	13.	[nɑ]	19.	[go]
2.	[mĩ]	8.	[bɛ̃]	14.	[nɑ̃]	20.	[gõ]
3.	[bi]	9.	[næ]	15.	[dɑ]	21.	[ŋu]
4.	[bĩ]	10.	[næ̃]	16.	[dɑ̃]	22.	[ŋũ]
5.	[mɛ]	11.	[dæ]	17.	[ŋo]	23.	[gu]
6.	[mɛ̃]	12.	[dæ̃]	18.	[ŋõ]	24.	[gũ]

Recognizing Nasalized Vowels

It can often be more difficult to identify nasalized vowels than non-nasalized vowels because their quality is altered slightly by the resonation in the nasal cavity. Nasalized vowels are often perceived as being produced at a lower position than they actually are. The following exercise demonstrates the oral and nasalized counterparts of each vowel that has been introduced, beginning with [i] and going around the chart. First listen to the different quality added by nasalization, and then try mimicking each vowel.

Exercise 24.3: Demonstration of Oral and Nasalized Vowels

1. [i ĩ]	6. [a ã]	11. [o õ]
2. [ɪ ɪ̃]	7. [ɑ ɑ̃]	12. [ʊ ʊ̃]
3. [e ẽ]	8. [ɒ ɒ̃]	13. [u ũ]
4. [ɛ ɛ̃]	9. [ʌ ʌ̃]	14. [ɨ ɨ̃]
5. [æ æ̃]	10. [ɔ ɔ̃]	15. [ə ə̃]

Listen to the vowels in the next exercise and respond with "same" or "different."

Exercise 24.4: Recognizing Nasalized and Oral Vowels

1. [bɑ bɑ]	Same	6. [ʔɑ ʔɑ]	Same	11. [mek mẽk]	Different
2. [sɑ sɑ̃]	Different	7. [zu zũ]	Different	12. [võᵘt voᵘt]	Different
3. [lɑ̃ lɑ]	Different	8. [læ̃f læf]	Different	13. [pæ̃k pæ̃k]	Same
4. [tʰɔ̃ tʰɔ̃]	Same	9. [vus vũs]	Different	14. [lin lĩn]	Different
5. [bẽⁱ beⁱ]	Different	10. [dʊg dʊg]	Same	15. [gõk gõk]	Same

In the following exercise, respond by telling whether the vowels that you hear are nasalized or oral.

Exercise 24.5: Recognizing Nasalized and Oral Vowels

1. [bĩ]	Nasalized	4. [lɑ]	Oral	7. [zup]	Oral
2. [si]	Oral	5. [do]	Oral	8. [mẽk]	Nasalized
3. [ʔĩf]	Nasalized	6. [lɑ̃m]	Nasalized	9. [tʰɔ̃]	Nasalized

10. [tĩf]	Nasalized	14. [ʒɛʒ]	Oral	18. [ʔɔ̃x]	Nasalized
11. [se]	Oral	15. [fã̃ŋ]	Nasalized	19. [mæ̃gz]	Nasalized
12. [kɑx]	Oral	16. [kil]	Oral	20. [dʊg]	Oral
13. [gõk]	Nasalized	17. [ðəʃ]	Oral	21. [tʰʊ̃θ]	Nasalized

Practice identifying the nasalized vowels in the following exercise. This exercise may contain any of the vowels that have been introduced so far. Respond by giving the name of each vowel. Do not let the combinations of consonants distract you.

Exercise 24.6: Name the Vowel

1. [ʔã]	Script A	11. [õg]	O	21. [lãm]	Script A
2. [ʔʌ̃]	Turned V	12. [zə̃s]	Schwa	22. [tĩf]	I
3. [ʔũ]	U	13. [mẽk]	E	23. [zõg]	Open O
4. [sĩ]	I	14. [zbɛ̃g]	Epsilon	24. [bẽi]	E
5. [sã]	Script A	15. [klĩm]	Small Capital I	25. [gɛ̃dʒ]	Epsilon
6. [sẽ]	E	16. [hæ̃sks]	Ash	26. [svĩt]	I
7. [tʊ̃k]	Upsilon	17. [ʃẽvz]	E	27. [ɹũð]	U
8. [æ̃l]	Ash	18. [spʌ̃ft]	Turned V	28. [tʃʰõŋ]	O
9. [mɔ̃d]	Open O	19. [bvĩg]	I	29. [nĩf]	I
10. [tʰɔ̃]	Open O	20. [jãuk]	Lowercase A	30. [frə̃]	Schwa

Mimic each sound in the following exercise.

Exercise 24.7: Producing Nasalized Vowels

1. [iʔĩ]	5. [eʔẽ]	9. [ɛʔɛ̃]
2. [ihĩ]	6. [ehẽ]	10. [ɛhɛ̃]
3. [iĩ]	7. [eẽ]	11. [ɛɛ̃]
4. [ĩi]	8. [ẽe]	12. [ɛ̃ɛ]

13. [æʔæ̃]   21. [ʌʔʌ̃]   29. [ʊʔʊ̃]

14. [æhæ̃]   22. [ʌhʌ̃]   30. [ʊhʊ̃]

15. [ææ̃]   23. [ʌʌ̃]   31. [ʊʊ̃]

16. [æ̃æ]   24. [ʌ̃ʌ]   32. [ʊ̃ʊ]

17. [ɑʔɑ̃]   25. [oʔõ]   33. [uʔũ]

18. [ɑhɑ̃]   26. [ohõ]   34. [uhũ]

19. [ɑɑ̃]   27. [oõ]   35. [uũ]

20. [ɑ̃ɑ]   28. [õo]   36. [ũu]

In the following exercise, repeat each sound after the recording.

Exercise 24.8: Producing Nasalized Vowels

1. [tõsɑɛ]   5. [swisɑ̃ɛ]   9. [nũsɑɛ]

2. [tosɑ̃ɛ]   6. [swĩsɑɛ]   10. [tʌ̃sɑɛ]

3. [tõsɑ̃ɛ]   7. [nũsɑɛ]   11. [tʌsɑ̃ɛ]

4. [swĩsɑɛ]   8. [nusɑ̃ɛ]   12. [tʌ̃sɑ̃ɛ]

Lesson 25:
Double Articulations and Prenasalization

Lesson Outline

Glossary

As we have seen in previous lessons, the articulation of consonants involves some degree of closure between an articulator and a point of articulation. It is possible for two such closures to occur at the same time. A sound consisting of two simultaneous closures of the same manner of articulation and the same voicing are called **double articulations**. Both sounds involved in double articulation are usually of equal or nearly equal prominence. The most common double articulated consonants are stops, although double nasals also occur in some languages. Double fricatives and even double affricates are possible, but rare.

Double Articulations

Double articulations are most often composed of labial and velar closures. These are described as **labial-velar articulations**. **Labial-alveolar articulations** and **labial-alveopalatal articulations** do occur in some languages, but are much less common. Just as affricates, double articulations can be symbolized by placing a **Tie Bar Above** [͡] (or Double Breve) or a **Tie Bar Below** [͜] the symbols of both consonants involved, such as [k͡p] or [g͜b]. Table 25.1 below gives the symbols for the sounds introduced in this lesson.

Table 25.1: Introducing Double Articulations

		Labio-Alveolar	Labio-Velar
Stops	Voiceless	t͡p	k͡p
	Voiced	d͡b	g͜b
Nasals	Voiced	n͡m	ŋ͡m

For double articulations, the closure produced farther back is represented first. This is because the sound produced closest to the origin of the air stream is usually heard first, especially in sequences where the double articulation occurs word medial.

The consonants involved in a double articulation occur simultaneously rather than sequentially as in other types of consonant clusters. Even consonant clusters with close transition are sequential; though the sounds may overlap slightly, neither the initiations nor releases of the two articulations occur at the same time. In double articulations, on the other hand, either the initiations or the releases (or both in some cases) occur at the same time. They are articulated together as a unit rather than as separate sounds. Functioning as a unit, the double articulation takes roughly the normal time slot of one consonant, whereas a sequential consonant cluster takes as many slots as consonants in the cluster.

Illustrations 25.1–25.3 below picture individually articulated labial and velar consonants in contrast with double articulated labial and velar consonants.

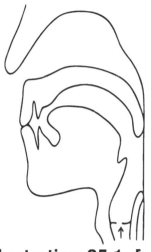 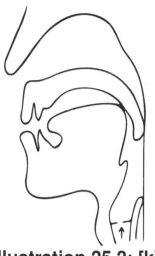 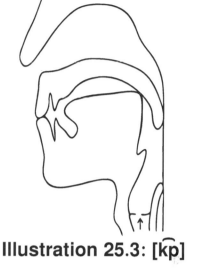

Illustration 25.1: [p]　　**Illustration 25.2: [k]**　　**Illustration 25.3: [k͡p]**

Producing Double Articulation

In order to produce double articulated consonants, you must learn to form and release two consonant closures at the same time. Begin by saying the following sequences faster and faster until the sounds are run together. This will eliminate the vowel between the [g] and [b], and result in double articulation. You will probably find the labio-velar articulations easiest, so practice them until you can articulate them easily before moving on to the labio-alveolar articulations. Mimic each utterance after the recording.

Exercise 25.1: Producing Double Articulations

1. ['bʌgʌ 'bʌgʌ 'bʌgʌ 'bʌgʌ 'g͡bʌg 'g͡bʌg 'g͡bʌg 'g͡bʌg]

2. ['pʌkʌ 'pʌkʌ 'pʌkʌ 'pʌkʌ 'k͡pʌk 'k͡pʌk 'k͡pʌk 'k͡pʌk]

3. ['mʌŋʌ 'mʌŋʌ 'mʌŋʌ 'mʌŋʌ 'ŋ͡mʌŋ 'ŋ͡mʌŋ 'ŋ͡mʌŋ 'ŋ͡mʌŋ]

4. ['daba 'daba 'daba 'daba 'd͡bad 'd͡bad 'd͡bad 'd͡bad]

5. ['tapa 'tapa 'tapa 'tapa 't͡pat 't͡pat 't͡pat 't͡pat]

6. ['nama 'nama 'nama 'nama 'n͡man 'n͡man 'n͡man 'n͡man]

Sometimes people produce double stops when trying to imitate a chicken clucking. Say the following sequence of double stops after the recording, making it sound as if you were imitating a chicken. When you can produce [k͡p] easily, substitute other double articulations.

7. [k͡pək k͡pək k͡pək k͡pək k͡pək k͡pək k͡pək k͡pək]

8. [g͡bəg g͡bəg g͡bəg g͡bəg g͡bəg g͡bəg g͡bəg g͡bəg]

Another way to learn to produce double articulations is to say the following sequences of English words and change the syllable boundaries, making the last consonant of the first syllable part of the second syllable. Repeat each utterance after the recording.

Exercise 25.2: Producing Double Articulations

1. [bɪg ˈboⁱ]
2. [bɪgː ˈboⁱ]
3. [bɪː ˈg͡boⁱ]
4. [ˈg͡boⁱ]
5. [ˈg͡bo ˈg͡ba ˈg͡bi ˈg͡bu]

6. [meⁱk ˈpʰeⁱst]
7. [meⁱkː ˈpʰeⁱst]
8. [meⁱː k͡peⁱst]
9. [k͡peⁱst]
10. [k͡pe k͡pa k͡pi k͡pu]

11. [bɹiŋ ˈmaⁱn]
12. [bɹiŋː ˈmaⁱn]
13. [bɹiː ŋ͡maⁱn]
14. [ŋ͡maⁱn]
15. [ŋ͡ma ŋ͡mo ŋ͡mi ŋ͡mu]

Say the following sentences using double articulations at the beginning of each word. Follow the pseudo transcription.

Exercise 25.3: Producing Double Articulations

1. **ŋ͡m**ake **ŋ͡m**y **ŋ͡m**onkey **ŋ͡m**ind **ŋ͡m**other.

2. **k͡p**eter **k͡p**ik͡per **k͡p**icked a **k͡p**eck of **k͡p**ickled **k͡p**ek͡pers.

3. The **g͡b**ig **g͡b**ad **g͡b**oy **g͡b**ent **g͡b**illy's **g͡b**ike.

Recognizing Double Articulations

When listening for double articulations in word medial and word final positions, keep in mind that the articulation closest to the back of the oral cavity is usually heard first and can obscure the sound of the labial articulation. This is because the air stream coming from the lungs is acted upon first by the articulation closest to its origin. It will help immensely if you are able to watch the speaker's mouth and see the labial articulation. The articulation closest to the front of the oral cavity may sound predominant in word initial double articulations.

The acoustic difference between double articulations and single articulations is often very slight. It may require much practice to be able to recognize them well. The following exercise contains both double and single articulations. Listen to the pairs of utterances, and respond with "same" or "different."

Exercise 25.4: Recognizing Single and Double Articulations

1.	[ag͡ba ag͡ba]	Same	8.	[ama aŋ͡ma]	Different	15. [iŋ͡me ime]	Different
2.	[ag͡ba aba]	Different	9.	[ugu ugu]	Same	16. [aka ak͡pa]	Different
3.	[ak͡pa aka]	Different	10.	[ik͡pi ipi]	Different	17. [iŋ͡mo iŋ͡mo]	Same
4.	[aŋ͡ma aŋ͡ma]	Same	11.	[ʌbʌ ʌgbʌ]	Different	18. [egbʌ egbʌ]	Same
5.	[aka ak͡pa]	Different	12.	[aŋ͡ma aŋa]	Different	19. [iŋo iŋ͡mo]	Different
6.	[ebe ebe]	Same	13.	[uŋu uŋu]	Same	20. [ʊk͡pu ʊk͡pu]	Same
7.	[oŋo oŋo]	Same	14.	[oga og͡ba]	Different	21. [ik͡pe ik͡pe]	Same

The following exercise contains labio-alveolar double articulations in addition to labio-velar sounds. Respond with "double" if you hear double articulation, and "single" if you hear single consonants.

Exercise 25.5: Recognizing Single and Double Articulations

1.	[aba]	Single	7.	[ɛd͡bɛ]	Double	13.	[ænæ]	Single
2.	[aŋ͡ma]	Double	8.	[ede]	Single	14.	[od͡bi]	Double
3.	[aŋ͡ma]	Double	9.	[iŋ͡mo]	Double	15.	[aŋ͡ma]	Double
4.	[ʊt͡pu]	Double	10.	[oga]	Single	16.	[ete]	Single
5.	[æba]	Single	11.	[apa]	Single	17.	[ɛt͡pæ]	Double
6.	[ot͡pə]	Double	12.	[ɔk͡pa]	Double	18.	[obo]	Single

It is also important to be able to distinguish between double articulated consonants and consonant clusters with close transition. Listen to the consonants in the next exercise, and respond with "simultaneous" for double articulations and "sequential" for consonant clusters. This exercise also contains labio-alveolar articulations.

Exercise 25.6: Recognizing Simultaneous and Sequential Stop Clusters

1. ['sak.pʰa] Sequential   6. [deg'bo]   Sequential   11. [a.xɛ'g͡bu] Simultaneous

2. [sa'k͡pa]   Simultaneous 7. [vʌ'k͡pak] Simultaneous 12. [an͡ma]   Simultaneous

3. [zoᵘ'gbo] Simultaneous 8. [ʃu'ŋ͡mə]   Simultaneous 13. [kʰot'pʊʒ] Sequential

4. [tʰi'ŋ͡mi] Simultaneous 9. [ʒæ'd͡bi]   Simultaneous 14. [dɔŋ'mən]   Sequential

5. [tʰɛŋ'man] Sequential   10. [ɹik'pʰeⁱs] Sequential   15. [ɣæᵉ'k͡pɛʔ] Simultaneous

Tell whether the following double articulations are voiced or voiceless.

Exercise 25.7: Recognizing Voiced and Voiceless Double Articulations

1. [sa'k͡pa]   Voiceless   5. [ʌg͡bʌ]   Voiced   9. [a.xɛ'g͡bu]   Voiced

2. [ɛd͡bɛ]   Voiced   6. [ʃə'n͡mæ]   Voiced   10. [ðu'd͡bəʒ]   Voiced

3. [ɔk͡pa]   Voiceless   7. [kʰo'k͡pʊʒ] Voiceless 11. [ne'f͡pɛr]   Voiceless

4. [ʊt͡pu]   Voiceless   8. [ɛt͡pæ]   Voiceless 12. [ma'k͡pas]   Voiceless

Double Articulations with Modified Release

When double stops are released, they are often accompanied by a slight pop or click caused by a movement of the tongue during the release. Study Illustration 25.4 and Illustration 25.5 below. The dotted lines represent the position the tongue moves to as the sound is released. Notice that in Illustration 25.4 the tongue moves forward during the release, pressurizing the air between the velar and labial points of articulation. When this pressure is released, it can sound like a small burst or pop.

In Illustration 25.5, the tongue moves backward during the release, creating a vacuum between the labial and velar articulations. This can cause it to sound similar to an implosive articulation at its release.

Although the acoustic difference added by these tongue movements may be slight, you should be aware of their affect on double articulations and be able to produce either type of release.

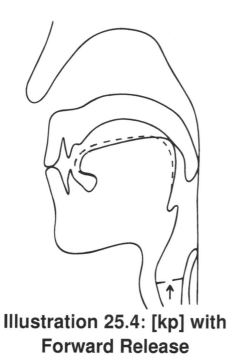

Illustration 25.4: [kp] with Forward Release

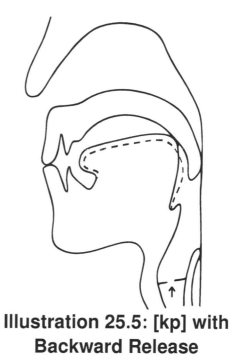

Illustration 25.5: [kp] with Backward Release

Practice your pronunciation of double articulations in the initial, medial, and final positions by mimicking the utterances in the following exercise.

Exercise 25.8: Producing Double Articulations

1. [aŋ͡mæ]	13. [ŋ͡ma]	25. [aŋ͡m]
2. [agbæ]	14. [gba]	26. [agb]
3. [ak͡pæ]	15. [k͡pa]	27. [ak͡p]
4. [eŋ͡mɪ]	16. [ŋ͡mɔ]	28. [eŋ͡m]
5. [egbɪ]	17. [gbɔ]	29. [egb]
6. [ek͡pɪ]	18. [k͡pɔ]	30. [ek͡p]
7. [uŋ͡ma]	19. [ŋ͡mʊ]	31. [uŋ͡m]
8. [ugba]	20. [gbʊ]	32. [ugb]
9. [uk͡pa]	21. [k͡pʊ]	33. [uk͡p]
10. [æŋ͡mə]	22. [ŋ͡mʌ]	34. [ɔŋ͡m]
11. [ægbə]	23. [gbʌ]	35. [ɔgb]
12. [æk͡pə]	24. [k͡pʌ]	36. [ɔk͡p]

Prenasalization

In some languages, stops and affricates are often preceded by a brief nasal onset called **prenasalization**. In a prenasalized sound, the velic opens a brief moment before the stop is released. Prenasalization differs from a consonant cluster involving a nasal followed by a stop in that the nasal onset for prenasalization is much less prominent than an ordinary consonant. The nasalization and the stop function together as a unit, much like double articulations, with both sounds occurring in the same syllable.

Unlike double articulations, prenasalized consonants tend to share the same point of articulation, but differ in their manner of articulation and sometimes in voicing. The nasal sound is usually voiced, whereas the stop may be either voiced or voiceless. Also, the nasal sound is not as prominent as the following stop or affricate, whereas both sounds in a double articulation carry the same degree of prominence.

Prenasalized sounds are symbolized by a superscript nasal symbol placed before the symbol of the stop or affricate involved, such as [ᵐb], [ⁿdʒ], or [ᵑg].

Mimic the prenasalized consonants in the following exercise. Be careful not to produce syllabic nasals such as [m̩.ba] or [n̩.da].

Exercise 25.9: Producing Prenasalized Consonants

1. [ᵐba]	5. [ᵐbi]	9. [ᵐbo]	13. [ᵐbu]
2. [ⁿda]	6. [ⁿd̪i]	10. [ᴺɢoᵘ]	14. [ⁿdu]
3. [ⁿdʒa]	7. [ⁿdʒi]	11. [ⁿdʒo]	15. [ⁿdʐu]
4. [ᵑga]	8. [ᵑgi]	12. [ᵑgo]	16. [ᵑgu]

The following exercise contrasts prenasalized consonants with consonant clusters and syllabic nasals. Determine if each utterance is prenasalized or not.

Exercise 25.10: Recognizing Prenasalized Sounds

1. [ⁿda]	Prenasalized	6. [ŋ̩.gʌ]	No	11. [ŋ̩.kadð]	No
2. [m̩.ba]	No	7. [ⁿdiç]	Prenasalized	12. [ᵑkif]	Prenasalized
3. [aŋga]	No	8. [ən̩.qoɣ]	No	13. [ⁿt̪oc]	Prenasalized
4. [ᵐbu]	Prenasalized	9. [ⁿdʒadʒ]	Prenasalized	14. [n̩.tədʒ]	No
5. [ⁿdʒo]	Prenasalized	10. [n̩.doks]	No	15. [ᵐᴺbɢug]	Prenasalized

Table 25.2 below gives alternative symbols for the double articulations introduced in this lesson.

Table 25.2: Double Articulations

IPA Symbol	Name	Technical Name	English Example	APA Symbol
k͡p		Voiceless Labial-velar Double Stop		ᵏp
g͜b		Voiced Labial-velar Double Stop		ᵍb
ŋ͡m		Voiced Labial-velar Double Nasal		ⁿm
t͡p		Voiceless Labial-alveolar Double Stop		ᵗp
d͡b		Voiced Labial-alveolar Double Stop		ᵈb
n͡m		Voiced Labial-alveolar Double Nasal		ⁿm

Lesson 26:
Front Rounded and Back Unrounded Vowels

Lesson Outline

Glossary

As was explained in Lesson 10, it is possible for any vowel to be produced with either rounded or unrounded lips. In English, front and central vowels are unrounded, while the majority of back vowels are rounded. In other languages, rounded and unrounded vowels can conform to different patterns. In languages like French and German, for example, front rounded vowels occur quite frequently. Vietnamese and Turkish, on the other hand, contain many back unrounded vowels. In this lesson you will learn to control lip rounding on front and back vowels.

The following vowel chart presents several front rounded vowels and back unrounded vowels in addition to the vowels that you have already studied. These symbols augment the inventory of English vowels in the International Phonetic Alphabet. Many more vowels remain, but due to time constraints, no further vowels will be studied in detail in this textbook.

Illustration 26.1: Non-English Front and Back Vowels

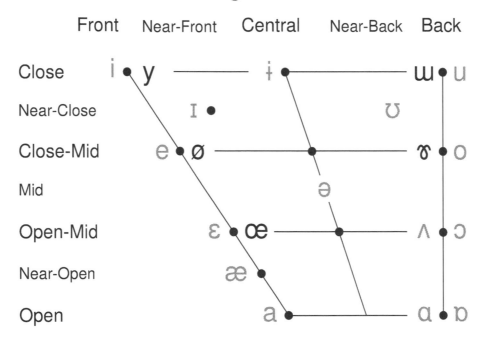

Front Rounded Vowels

When producing front rounded vowels, remember that the position of the tongue for each front rounded vowel is the same as that of its unrounded counterpart. Only the condition of the lips changes. The configuration of the lips for each front rounded vowel is the same as the back rounded vowel of the same height. For example, to produce the front rounded vowel [y], the tongue is in the same position as for [i], while the lips are rounded as for the close back vowel [u]. As with all other vowels, you must be careful not to glide front rounded vowels.

Producing [y]

The close, front rounded vowel is symbolized by a **Lowercase Y** [y]; however, this sound has little in common with the English "y."[1] A good way to achieve the articulation of [y] is to begin with [u] and move your tongue forward to the [i] position while keeping your lips rounded. Move your tongue slowly back and forth between these positions several times. This technique is called **slurring**. Practice slurring between [u] and [i] until you can easily keep your lips rounded to produce [y]. Practice isolating [y] in the following drill.

1. [uːyː y y y]

You may also try slurring with the lips instead of the tongue. Keep your tongue from moving while you begin with [i] and practice rounding and unrounding your lips. Then isolate [y].

2. [iːyː y y y]

Practice saying the phrase, "He sees three mean bees," with tightly rounded lips.

3. [ˈçyˈsyzˈθɹyˈmynˈbyz]

Often the best way to learn the articulation of a new sound is by mimicry. Listen carefully to the vowels in the following exercise and repeat the sentences after the recording. Follow the transcription.

Exercise 26.1: Producing [i], [u] and [y]

1. [i] "Fleece the geese."

2. [u] "Fluce the goose."

3. [y] "Fl**y**ce the g**y**se."

Producing [ø]

The rounded counter part to [e] is called the **Slashed O** [ø].[2] The [ø] is a close-mid front rounded vowel. To learn the articulation of this vowel, practice the same slurring

---

1 Do not confuse the Lowercase Y [y] with the Small Capital Y [ʏ]. The [ʏ] is a near-close near-front rounded vowel. Also, the English "y" consonant sound is represented by the approximant Lowercase J [j].

2 Do not confuse the Slashed O [ø] with the Barred O [ɵ]. The [ɵ] is a close-mid central rounded vowel.

procedure as with the previous vowel. Slur between the vowels [o] and [e], keeping your lips rounded. Repeat the slur several times, and then isolate the front rounded vowel.

1. [oːøː ø ø ø]

Now practice the rounded and unrounded slur between [e] and [ø]. Remember to keep your tongue from moving during this exercise.

2. [eːøː ø ø ø]

Say the phrase, "Kate bakes eight cakes," with rounded lips on each vowel. The lip rounding for [ø] will be slightly less than for [y].

3. [ˈkʰøtˈbøksˈʔøtˈkʰøks]

Mimic the sentences in the following exercise. Practice careful lip rounding as you repeat each utterance.

Exercise 26.2: Producing [e], [o], and [ø]

1. [e] "Make the cake."

2. [o] "Moke the coke."

3. [ø] "Møke the cøke."

Producing [œ]

The open-mid front rounded vowel is symbolized by the **Lowercase O-E Ligature** [œ].[3] It is the rounded counterpart to Epsilon [ɛ]. This vowel is lower and produced with slightly less lip rounding than [ø]. Practice the same slurring procedure as used above, this time slurring between [ɔ], [ɛ], and [œ].

Begin with [ɔ], and keep your lips rounded as you glide toward [œ]. Isolate the rounded vowel, and repeat it several times.

1. [ɔːœː œ œ œ]

Slur between the front rounded and unrounded positions.

2. [ɛːœː œ œ œ]

Say the phrase, "Shred Ted's red sled," with slightly rounded lips.

3. [ˈʃɹœdˈtœdzˈɹœdˈslœd]

---

3   Do not confuse the Lowercase O-E Ligature [œ] with the Small Capital O-E Ligature [ɶ]. The [ɶ] is an open front rounded vowel.

Repeat each utterance in the following exercise.

Exercise 26.3: Producing [œ]

1. [ɛ] "Check the deck."

2. [ɔ] "Chalk the dock."

3. [œ] "Chœck the dœck."

Repeat each of the following utterances after the recording.

Exercise 26.4: Producing [y], [ø], and [œ]

1. [ny]	7. [dy]	13. [θyz]
2. [nø]	8. [dø]	14. [θøz]
3. [nœ]	9. [dœ]	15. [θœz]
4. [sy]	10. [ly]	16. [ʒyf]
5. [sø]	11. [lø]	17. [ʒøf]
6. [sœ]	12. [lœ]	18. [ʒœf]

Recognizing Front Rounded Vowels

The shape of the lips affects the sound of vowels to a great degree. English speakers often find it difficult to identify vowels which do not conform to the English lip rounding patterns. Since front rounded vowels do not occur in English, you may have to practice a good deal to be able to identify their positions. Listen to the vowels in the following exercise, and respond with "same" or "different."

Exercise 26.5: Recognizing Front Rounded Vowels

1. [ŋyʃ ŋyʃ]	S	6. [ŋyʃ ŋyʃ]	S	11. [gøf gøf]	S
2. [ŋiʃ ŋyʃ]	D	7. [lu'byt lu'bit]	D	12. [gef gef]	S
3. [ŋiʃ ŋiʃ]	S	8. [lu'bit lu'bit]	S	13. [gøf gef]	D
4. [ŋyʃ ŋiʃ]	D	9. [lu'bit lu'byt]	D	14. [gef gøf]	D
5. [ŋyʃ ŋiʃ]	D	10. [gøf gef]	D	15. [gef gøf]	D

16. [vəˈʒøm vəˈʒøm] S   26. [koˈθœʔ koˈθœʔ] S   36. [ɣøʒ ɣœʒ]   D

17. [vəˈʒøm vəˈʒem] D   27. [koˈθœʔ koˈθɛʔ] D   37. [ɣyʒ ɣyʒ]   S

18. [vəˈʒem vəˈʒøm] D   28. [nɨz nyz]   D   38. [ɣøʒ ɣœʒ]   D

19. [lœð lœð]   S   29. [nœz nœz]   S   39. [ɣœʒ ɣəʒ]   D

20. [lɛð lɛð]   S   30. [nuz nyz]   D   40. [θøz θøz]   S

21. [lœð lɛð]   D   31. [nɨz nɨz]   S   41. [iz yz]   D

22. [lœð lœð]   S   32. [nəz nøz]   D   42. [mœk mɨk]   D

23. [lɛð lœð]   D   33. [nœz nəz]   D   43. [lɛð lœð]   D

24. [lœð lɛð]   D   34. [ɣyʒ ɣuʒ]   D   44. [koˈθœʔ koˈθɛʔ] D

25. [koˈθœʔ koˈθœʔ] S   35. [ɣœʒ ɣœʒ]   S   45. [nɨz nɨz]   S

The following exercise contains both rounded and unrounded front vowels. Listen carefully to each utterance, and respond with "rounded" or "unrounded."

Exercise 26.6: Recognizing Rounded and Unrounded Front Vowels

1. [ŋyf]   Rounded   7. [ɹøz]   Rounded   13. [mœm] Rounded

2. [sig]   Unrounded   8. [ʒið]   Unrounded   14. [tyk] Rounded

3. [mœl]   Rounded   9. [dœf]   Rounded   15. [ŋeð] Unrounded

4. [døz]   Rounded   10. [geʃ] Unrounded   16. [θøm] Rounded

5. [kex]   Unrounded   11. [sɛm] Unrounded   17. [lef] Unrounded

6. [lip]   Unrounded   12. [vib] Unrounded   18. [kyp] Rounded

In the following exercise, give the names for the vowel sound that you hear. This exercise contains the three front rounded vowels that we have introduced and their unrounded counterparts.

Exercise 26.7: Recognizing Front Rounded Vowels

1. [i]   I   3. [y]   Y   5. [œ]   OE Ligature

2. [ø]   Slashed O   4. [ɛ]   Epsilon   6. [e]   E

7. [sy]	Y	11. [sɛ]	Epsilon	15. [nœg]	OE Ligature
8. [sœ]	OE Ligature	12. [sø]	Slashed O	16. [døf]	Slashed O
9. [sɛ]	Epsilon	13. [zyf]	Y	17. [sil]	I
10. [si]	I	14. [lem]	E	18. [nɛv]	Epsilon

Back Unrounded Vowels

English speakers produce most back vowels with rounded lips. Many languages, however, have primarily unrounded back vowels. Do not let your English habits keep you from pronouncing these vowels correctly. Remember that back unrounded vowels should be produced with lip rounding similar to the corresponding front vowel of the same height.

Producing [ɯ]

The close back unrounded vowel is represented by a **Turned M** [ɯ]. This vowel is produced with the tongue in the same position as for [u] but with unrounded lips.

To learn to produce Turned M [ɯ], practice slurring between the front unrounded vowel [i] and the back unrounded vowel [ɯ]. Make sure that your lips remain unrounded as your tongue moves to the back position. Practice this sequence several times, and then practice the back unrounded vowel in isolation.

1. [iːɯː ɯ ɯ ɯ]

Slur between the back rounded [u] and the back unrounded [ɯ]. Make sure that your tongue does not move during this sequence. Then isolate the unrounded vowel.

2. [uːɯː ɯ ɯ ɯ]

Say the sentence, "Two shooters shoot through a goose," with unrounded lips. You may find it helpful to smile as you say the words. This keeps the lips from becoming rounded.

3. [ˈtʰɯˈʃɯ.tɝz ˈʃɯtˈθɹɯʔəˈgɯs]

Mimic the phrases in the following exercise. Watch your lips with a mirror to make sure that they are unrounded.

Exercise 26.8: Producing [i], [u], and [ɯ]

1. [i] "Fleece the geese."

2. [u] "Fluce the goose."

3. [ɯ] "Flɯce the gɯse."

Producing [ɤ]

The close-mid back unrounded vowel is represented by a symbol called **Ram's Horns** [ɤ]. This is the rounded counterpart to [o], and is produced with the tongue in the same position as for [o]. To learn to produce this sound, practice slurring between front unrounded vowel [e] and the corresponding back unrounded position [ɤ]. Repeat this procedure several times.

1. [eːɤː ɤ ɤ ɤ]

Now slur between [o] and [ɤ]. Be careful to keep your tongue from moving.

2. [oːɤː ɤ ɤ ɤ]

Say the phrase, "Joe go blow snow," with unrounded lips. Remember to smile as you say the words.

3. [ˈdʒɤˈgɤˈblɤˈsnɤ]

Watch your lips in a mirror as you mimic the following phrases.

Exercise 26.9: Producing [e], [o], and [ɤ]

1. [e] "Make the cake."

2. [o] "Moke the coke."

3. [ɤ] "Mɤke the cɤke."

Repeat each utterance after the recording.

Exercise 26.10: Producing [ɯ], [ɤ], and [ɨ]

1. [nɯ]   3. [nɨ]   5. [sɤ]

2. [nɤ]   4. [sɯ]   6. [sɨ]

7. [lɯ]	10. [θɯz]	13. [ʒɯf]
8. [lɚ]	11. [θɚz]	14. [ʒɚf]
9. [lɨ]	12. [θɨz]	15. [ʒɨf]

Recognizing Back Unrounded Vowels

It may require a good deal of practice for English speakers to be able to recognize back unrounded vowels as they do not usually occur in normal English speech. The following exercises are designed to help develop your ability to identify back unrounded vowels.

Listen to the pairs of utterances in the following exercises, and respond with "same" or "different."

Exercise 26.11: Recognizing Back and Central Vowels

1. [nɯ nɯ] Same	11. [nɚ nɚ] Same	21. [mof mɚf] Different
2. [nɯ nu] Different	12. [no nɚ] Different	22. [zuʒ zuʒ] Same
3. [nɯ nɨ] Different	13. [sə sɚ] Different	23. [zəʒ zɚʒ] Different
4. [sɨ sɨ] Same	14. [sə sə] Same	24. [zɯʒ zɨʒ] Different
5. [sɯ su] Different	15. [sɚ so] Different	25. [ʃɨŋ ʃɨŋ] Same
6. [su su] Same	16. [lok lok] Same	26. [ʃɚŋ ʃʌŋ] Different
7. [lɯk lɯk] Same	17. [lək lɚk] Different	27. [ʃɚŋ ʃoŋ] Different
8. [lɯk luk] Different	18. [lɚk lʌk] Different	28. [duθ duθ] Same
9. [lɯk lɨk] Different	19. [mɯf muf] Different	29. [dəθ dɚθ] Different
10. [nɚ no] Different	20. [mof mof] Same	30. [dɚθ dɚθ] Same

Listen carefully to the vowel sounds in the following exercise, and respond with "rounded" or "unrounded."

Exercise 26.12: Recognizing Back Rounded and Unrounded

| 1. [nuf] Rounded | 3. [mɯl] Unrounded | 5. [kɚx] Unrounded |
| 2. [sog] Rounded | 4. [doz] Rounded | 6. [lɚp] Unrounded |

7. [ɹuz]	Rounded	11. [sɯm]	Unrounded	15. [ŋwð]	Unrounded
8. [ʒwð]	Unrounded	12. [vɯb]	Unrounded	16. [θum]	Rounded
9. [zof]	Rounded	13. [mum]	Rounded	17. [lɤf]	Unrounded
10. [gɤʃ]	Unrounded	14. [tɤk]	Unrounded	18. [kop]	Rounded

In the following exercise, back unrounded vowels will be given along with several other similar vowel sounds. Respond by giving the name of the vowel that you hear.

Exercise 26.13: Recognizing Back and Central Vowels

1. [ɯ]	Turned M	7. [ə]	Schwa	13. [ə]	Schwa
2. [u]	U	8. [ɯ]	Turned M	14. [ɯ]	Turned M
3. [o]	O	9. [ɨ]	Barred I	15. [ʌ]	Turned V
4. [ɤ]	Ram's Horns	10. [ɤ]	Ram's Horns	16. [ɤ]	Ram's Horns
5. [ʌ]	Turned V	11. [u]	U	17. [ɨ]	Barred I
6. [o]	O	12. [ɯ]	Turned M	18. [ɯ]	Turned M

In the following exercise, listen to the vowel sounds and tell whether they are rounded or unrounded. This exercise contains all of the front rounded and back unrounded vowels that have been presented in this lesson along with other similar vowels.

Exercise 26.14: Recognizing Rounded and Unrounded Vowels

1. [gɯm]	Unrounded	9. [bes]	Unrounded	17. [ðʌʒ]	Unrounded
2. [suf]	Rounded	10. [xuŋ]	Rounded	18. [neð]	Unrounded
3. [dɨb]	Unrounded	11. [tɛb]	Unrounded	19. [tɯk]	Unrounded
4. [vɤz]	Unrounded	12. [zøf]	Rounded	20. [kiv]	Unrounded
5. [ɹoʔ]	Rounded	13. [num]	Rounded	21. [gox]	Rounded
6. [dʌv]	Unrounded	14. [kɤk]	Unrounded	22. [ʃɤθ]	Unrounded
7. [pil]	Unrounded	15. [mœt]	Rounded	23. [nov]	Rounded
8. [lyd]	Rounded	16. [gom]	Rounded	24. [tɨd]	Unrounded

Identify the vowel sounds in the following exercise. This exercise contains all of the basic vowels presented in this course. Respond by giving the name of each vowel.

Exercise 26.15: Name the Vowel

1. [i]	I	12. [o]	O	23. [æ]	Ash
2. [ʊ]	Upsilon	13. [y]	Y	24. [y]	Y
3. [ø]	Slashed O	14. [ɯ]	Turned M	25. [ɔ]	Open O
4. [œ]	OE Ligature	15. [e]	E	26. [ɤ]	Ram's Horns
5. [ɤ]	Ram's Horns	16. [u]	U	27. [ʊ]	Upsilon
6. [ɛ]	Epsilon	17. [e]	E	28. [ɯ]	Turned M
7. [ɯ]	Turned M	18. [y]	Y	29. [u]	U
8. [i]	I	19. [ɪ]	Small Capital I	30. [ə]	Schwa
9. [ʌ]	Turned V	20. [ə]	Schwa	31. [e]	E
10. [ə]	Schwa	21. [i]	I	32. [ɔ]	Open O
11. [ɤ]	Ram's Horns	22. [ɑ]	Script A	33. [ʊ]	Upsilon

In the following exercise, repeat each utterance after the recording.

Exercise 26.16: Producing Front Rounded and Back Unrounded Vowels

1. [sisy]	[sesø]	[sɛsœ]	[susɯ]	[sosɤ]
2. [vivy]	[vevø]	[vɛvœ]	[vuvɯ]	[vovɤ]
3. [xixy]	[xexø]	[xɛxœ]	[xuxɯ]	[xoxɤ]
4. [yfif]	[øfef]	[œfɛf]	[ɯfuf]	[ɤfof]
5. [ymim]	[ømem]	[œmɛm]	[ɯmum]	[ɤmom]

The following table summarizes the sounds and symbols introduced in this lesson.

Table 26.1: Non-English Front and Back Vowels

IPA Symbol	Name	Technical Name	English Example	APA Symbol
y	Lowercase Y	Close Front Rounded Vowel		ü
ø	Slashed O	Close-mid Front Rounded Vowel		ö
œ	Lowercase O-E Ligature	Open-mid Front Rounded Vowel		ɔ̈
ɯ	Turned M	Close Back Unrounded Vowel		ï
ɤ	Ram's Horns	Close-mid Back Unrounded Vowel		ë

Lesson 27:
Transition and Release

Lesson Outline

Glossary

Consonants are defined not only by their articulators but also in the way that their articulators are released and in the types of transitions that link them to other consonants. There are several different ways in which the articulators can separate after pronouncing a consonant. This separation is referred to as their release. The different ways in which the articulators move from one consonant to the next are called transitions. To avoid a distracting accent, it is very important to be able to recognize these features and be able to reproduce them accurately.

The Release of Consonants

The **release** of consonants describes the interaction between the articulator and point of articulation immediately following the closure of a consonant. Consonants which occur at the ends of utterances can be either released or unreleased. In other words, the articulator may move away from the point of articulation (released), or it may remain stationary (unreleased).

Released Consonants

There are several different ways in which consonants, and stops in particular, may be released. If a stop is voiceless, it may be followed by aspiration and described as an **aspirated release**, or it may be released audibly without significant air flow and described simply as a **regular release**.

Voiced consonants may be released in several ways. Like voiceless stops, they can be followed by a regular release or a puff of air similar to aspiration. In voiced stops, the aspiration-like puff is described as **breathiness**, and can be transcribed by adding a **Superscript Hooktop H** [ʱ] after the consonant, such as [abʱ].[1] A voiced consonant may also be released as the vocal chords are still vibrating and, therefore, generate a short vowel sound, often identified as a Schwa [ə]. This type of release is known as **voiced release** and is represented by a **Superscript Schwa** [ᵊ] following the consonant, such as [abᵊ].

The difference between a voiced aspirated release and voiced release is that the vocal chords are slightly farther apart when producing voiced aspiration than they are when producing a voiced release. Also, a larger amount of air generally escapes when aspiration occurs.

Consonants can also be released into a nasal or lateral. This is transcribed simply by placing after the consonant a superscript symbol, such as **Superscript N** [ⁿ], **Superscript M** [ᵐ], or **Superscript L** [ˡ]. For example, the English word "cotton" could be pronounced as [ˈkʰɑ.tⁿn̩]

---

1 Voiced aspiration is usually referred to as breathy voice or murmur and will be studied at length in a later lesson.

and "bottle" could be transcribed as ['bɑ.tʰl̩]. These English examples end with a syllabic consonant, but not all languages have a full nasal or lateral after a release. Often, nasal and lateral releases are voiced, but they can also be voiceless. To indicate voiceless nasal or later release, simply add an Under- or Over-ring diacritic to the superscript symbol (for example, [n̥]).

Unreleased Consonants

If at the end of an utterance, the articulator and point of articulation either maintain contact or separate inaudibly, the final sound is said to be **unreleased**. An unreleased sound is represented by placing a superscript diacritic called **Corner** [˺] after the consonant, as in [ɑp˺].[2]

Table 27.1 below lists the different types of releases and their symbolization.

Table 27.1: A Comparison of (Un)Releases

	Unreleased	Regular Release	Aspirated Release	Voiced Release	Nasal Release	Lateral Release
Voiceless	ɑp˺	ɑp	ɑpʰ		ɑpⁿ̥	ɑpˡ̥
Voiced	ɑb˺	ɑb	ɑbʰ	ɑbə	ɑbᵐ	ɑbˡ

Stops are not the only sounds which may be unreleased. Nasals and laterals are also commonly unreleased in English. In French, on the other hand, most utterance-final nasals and laterals are spoken with a voiced release. The following exercise demonstrates English words with different types of release. Follow the recording, and mimic each word.

Exercise 27.1: Producing Released and Unreleased Consonants

1. [stɑpʰ]
2. [stɑp]
3. [stɑp˺]
4. [pʰɑtʰ]
5. [pʰɑt]
6. [pʰɑt˺]
7. [sɑkʰ]
8. [sɑk]
9. [sɑk˺]
10. [bɑbə]
11. [bɑb]
12. [bɑb˺]
13. [bæədə]
14. [bæəd]
15. [bæəd˺]
16. [bɪgə]
17. [bɪg]
18. [bɪg˺]
19. [sæəmə]
20. [sæəm]
21. [sæəm˺]
22. [boʊnə]
23. [boʊn]
24. [boʊn˺]
25. [sɔŋə]
26. [sɔŋ]
27. [sɔŋ˺]
28. [tʰɒlə]
29. [tʰɒl]
30. [tʰɒl˺]

2   The Corner [˺]diacritic is also referred to as Upper Right-hand Corner or Left Angle Above.

It is important to note that as we speak of released and unreleased sounds, we refer only to those sounds which occur in the utterance-final position. Listen to the final sounds in the following words and respond with "released" or "unreleased."

Exercise 27.2: Recognizing Released and Unreleased Consonants

1. [gæbᵊ]	Released	9. [poᶦdᵊ]	Released	17. [vob˺]	Unreleased
2. [bɨkʰ]	Released	10. [kolɪk˺]	Unreleased	18. [ɸit˺]	Unreleased
3. [xʊd]	Released	11. [lo.ʌpʰ]	Released	19. [ɑzim˺]	Unreleased
4. [pikun˺]	Unreleased	12. [tʃhɔŋᵊ]	Released	20. [mĩðɛp]	Released
5. [sɪbʰ]	Released	13. [sɛdm̩˺]	Unreleased	21. [ædᶦ]	Released
6. [ʒɛbᵐ]	Released	14. [mɛɬ]	Released	22. [ʃul˺]	Unreleased
7. [ɹuᵊp˺]	Unreleased	15. [tɬɑt]	Released	23. [jeɡ̚ən]	Released
8. [seᶦd˺]	Unreleased	16. [ɣʊᵘkʰ]	Released	24. [pjɛt˺]	Unreleased

The next exercise contains word-final sounds with regular release and aspirated release. Respond by telling which type of release you hear.

Exercise 27.3: Recognizing Aspirated Release and Regular Release

1. [ɸatʰ]	Aspirated	6. [djɛtʰ]	Aspirated	11. [θʌbʰ]	Aspirated
2. [tsɨpʰ]	Aspirated	7. [xɹop]	Regular	12. [ðəp]	Regular
3. [sic]	Regular	8. [jɛstoq]	Regular	13. [ʃɛst]	Regular
4. [mʊqʰ]	Aspirated	9. [eikɑdʰ]	Aspirated	14. [nɛkʰ]	Aspirated
5. [ʔutʃit]	Regular	10. [ŋokʰ]	Aspirated	15. [lipʰ]	Aspirated

The following exercise includes voiced release and regular release. Tell which type of release you hear.

Exercise 27.4: Recognizing Voiced Release and Regular Release

1. [zubᵊ]	Voiced	3. [dʊg]	Regular	5. [n̩nɛd]	Regular
2. [ʃɨbun]	Regular	4. [gɔmᵊ]	Voiced	6. [ʔorɛʎᵊ]	Voiced

7. [θɔɢ]	Regular	10. [lʊd]	Regular	13. [pagedᵊ]	Voiced
8. [refɑmᵊ]	Voiced	11. [næbᵊ]	Voiced	14. [vlɑʃim]	Regular
9. [hoɟ]	Regular	12. [mɑdɑŋᵊ]	Voiced	15. [ɬɔrigᵊ]	Voiced

Unreleased stops, and particularly voiceless stops, can be difficult to distinguish. One tendency of English speakers, for example, is to confuse an unreleased [t] with a Glottal Stop [ʔ]. Listen carefully to the final unreleased sounds in the next exercise, and respond by telling what stop is being unreleased.

Exercise 27.5: Recognizing Unreleased Stops

1. [jodʼ]	D	6. [spokʼ]	K	11. [tɨqʼ]	Q
2. [χœtʼ]	T	7. [bzitʼ]	T	12. [tsygʼ]	G
3. [nɔɣəbʼ]	B	8. [bʊʔʼ]	?	13. [muiʔʼ]	?
4. [bɔgʼ]	G	9. [n̩dɪdʼ]	D	14. [ŋæpʼ]	P
5. [lupʼ]	P	10. [dʒʌbʼ]	B	15. [ʐøtʼ]	T

Transition

A **consonant cluster** is made up of two or more consonants that occur adjacently with no intervening vowels. When studying consonant clusters, you must understand how the articulators transition from the first consonant to the second. The act of changing from the articulation of one consonant to another is called **transition**.

Close Transition

There are several different types of transition that can take place between consonants. In affricates the first consonant is released directly into the second with no intervening sounds. A consonant cluster formed with no audible space between the consonants is said to have **close transition**. The second sound is formed before the first one is released.

Consider the word "cupcake," [kʰʌpkʰeⁱk]. Notice that if the words are pronounced in a normal, relaxed manner there is no space between the [p] and the [k]. The articulation for [k] is formed while the [p] is still unreleased. As soon as [p] is released, the [k] is heard. This type of transition parallels the unreleased consonants introduced earlier in this chapter, except that it occurs between contiguous consonants rather than utterance-final.

Close transition is left unmarked in phonetic transcription. In a consonant cluster, if open transition is not specifically indicated, the transition is assumed to be close.

Open transition

Open transition occurs when a transient sound such as aspiration or a short vowel occurs between the two consonants of a consonant cluster. There is a brief period of time between the release of the first consonant and the onset of the second. In voiceless stops, this transitional sound is heard as aspiration. This type of transition occurs in English when syllables such as "cup" and "cake" are over-articulated, resulting in an aspirated [pʰ] at the end of "cup." A phonetic transcription would look like [kʰʌpʰkʰeⁱk].

Clusters of voiced consonants often have an open transition consisting of a short, central vowel such as schwa. This type of transition typifies the accent of Italians speaking English as a second language. Consider the words "big boy." An English speaker would normally pronounce these words with close transition between [g] and [b]. An Italian person, on the other hand, may insert a short vowel between these consonants, forming a voiced transition such as [bɪgᵊboⁱ]. Many oriental speakers who have difficulty pronouncing English consonant clusters insert a short Schwa between the consonants as in the word "stop," resulting in [sᵊtɑp]. Voiced consonants can also transition with aspiration, but this is quite rare.

Table 27.2 compares the different types of transition for voiced and voiceless consonants.

Table 27.2: Comparing Transitions

	Open Transition	Close Transition
Voiceless	apʰka	apka
Voiced	abᵊda	abda

The next exercise demonstrates English words pronounced with close and open transition. Mimic each word after the recording.

Exercise 27.6: Producing Close and Open Transition

1.	sɪkmæn	"sick man"	4.	hɑpʰtʰoᵘd	"hop toad"	7.	spidbʌmp	"speed bump"
2.	sɪkʰmæn	"sick man"	5.	hɔgbæk	"hog back"	8.	spidᵊbʌmp	"speed bump"
3.	hɑptʰoᵘd	"hop toad"	6.	hɔgᵊbæk	"hog back"	9.	sneⁱk	"snake"

10. sᵊneⁱk   "snake"   11. mæsk   "mask"   12. mæsᵊk   "mask"

Tell whether the utterances in the following exercise have open or close transition.

Exercise 27.7: Recognizing Close or Open Transition

1.	[nɔgba]	Close	8.	[nambo]	Close	15. [ŋokbe]	Close
2.	[nɔgᵊba]	Open	9.	[ʃukʰpʰɔ]	Open	16. [baɖᵊga]	Open
3.	[θʌpʰtʰʌʃ]	Open	10.	[jʊbdø]	Close	17. [gʊdga]	Close
4.	[tatpo]	Close	11.	[xamna]	Close	18. [ʃutʰbaʌ̯]	Open
5.	[dadᵊba]	Open	12.	[xamᵊna]	Open	19. [dɛdga]	Close
6.	[ðækʰtʰe]	Open	13.	[ɸodᵊʟɛŋ]	Open	20. [gøɬdᵊbæg]	Open
7.	[sədᵊɢi]	Open	14.	[ʔœtɟa]	Close	21. [sædᵊtʰeⁱl]	Open

Lesson 28:
States of the Glottis

Lesson Outline

Glossary

The concept of voicing was introduced in Lesson 2. Remember that voicing originates in the glottis and is created by the vibration of the vocal cords as the air stream passes through the larynx. Whether or not the vocal cords vibrate depends on the position of the vocal cords and the amount of tension applied to them. These conditions are described as **states of the glottis**.

States of the Glottis

Different degrees of voicing are possible depending on the state of the glottis. If the glottis is completely relaxed, the vocal cords will be spread apart, allowing air to pass between them with no vibration or resonance. This state is known as voiceless. As the vocal cords are tensed and drawn together, the vibration increases until **modal voice** is reached. This state, known as voiced, is that of optimal tension for smooth vibration. If the tension continues to increase, the vibrations decrease until the vocal cords are so tense that the air stream is blocked and the vocal cords are again unable to vibrate. Between these two extremes there lies a whole range of vocal activity which depends on the measure of tension applied to the vocal cords.

Two different states of the glottis have already been introduced: voiceless and voiced. Table 28.1 lists some of the states of the glottis introduced in this lesson; however, not all states of the glottis have official symbols to represent them, and some diacritics have multiple functions.

Table 28.1: Common States of the Glottis

	Voiced	Voiceless	Breathy	Creaky	Stiff	Slack	Whispered
Vowel	ɑ	ɑ̥	ɑ̤	ɑ̰			ɑ̣
Vd. Consonant	b		b̤	b̰	b̩	b̞	ḍ
Vl. Consonant		t			t̩	t̞	ṭ
Nasal Consonant	ŋ	ŋ̊	ŋ̤	ŋ̃	ŋ̆	ŋ̥	ṅ

The states of the glottis introduced in this lesson are conditions that can apply to all vowels and to many consonants. Except for the whispered state, all of the states of the glottis have been found to contrast word meanings in languages throughout the world. They are also often applied as speech styles, affecting the articulation of speech as a whole.

For each different state of the glottis, specific diacritics are added to the base symbol. Table 28.2 below gives the diacritics for each state.

Table 28.2: Symbolizing the States of the Glottis

Name	Diacritic	Function	Example
Under-Ring	̥	Voiceless, Slack Voice	ạ̥ ḅ̥
Over-Ring	̊	Voiceless, Slack Voice	ẙ g̊
Subscript Wedge	̬	Voiced, Stiff Voice	s̬ t̬
Superscript Wedge	̌	Voiced, Stiff Voice	p̌ š
Diaeresis Below	̤	Breathy	a̤ b̤
Diaeresis Above	̈	Breathy	ÿ ṅ̈
(Superscript) Hooktop H	ɦ, ʱ	Breathy	ɦɑ bʱ
Tilde Below	̰	Creaky	a̰ b̰
Tilde Above	̃	Creaky	ỹ d̃
Dot Below	.	Whispered	ạ ṇ
Dot Above	˙	Whispered	ẏ ċ

Voiceless

The **voiceless** state occurs when the vocal cords are spread apart and relaxed so that they do not vibrate. The air stream is allowed to pass through relatively unimpeded. The most common voiceless sounds are consonants such as stops, fricatives, and sonorants, although many languages contain voiceless vowels as well.

There are two ways to indicate that a sound is voiceless. Because the IPA is based on European alphabets, some symbols are inherently voiceless, such as [f], [s], and [k]. Other symbols, however, do not have voiced counterparts; therefore, voicelessness can be represented by either placing an **Under-ring** [̥] beneath a symbol (for example, [ḁ]) or an **Over-ring** [̊] above a symbol that has a descender (for example, [ŋ̊]).

Voiceless vowels are found in languages such as Japanese and several indigenous North American languages.

Breathy

Breathy sounds involve partial voicing. This occurs when the glottis is slightly more tensed than for voiceless sounds, yet more relaxed than for voiced sounds. With the vocal cords only slightly tensed, they remain far enough apart that the air stream is allowed to pass through more freely than for voiced sounds, but still causes some vibration. Breathy voice is perceived auditorily as being halfway between voiceless and voiced.

Breathiness can be found as a feature in both consonants and vowels. Vowels are the most common breathy sounds, although certain languages in India have a set of breathy stops as well. In many languages, breathy voice is used to distinguish meaning. It is also used as an over all speech style. Breathy consonants will be studied in more depth in a later lesson.

The IPA symbolizes breathy voice by placing a **Diaeresis** [̈] beneath [a̤] or above [ÿ] a symbol. If a breathy vowel exists whose quality is predictable, such as one that always precedes and matches a voiced vowel, the **Hooktop H** [ɦ] can be used; that is, [a̤a] could be represented as [ɦa].[1]

The following exercise contrasts breathy voice with other states of the glottis. Respond by telling whether the pairs of utterances are the same or different.

Exercise 28.1: Recognizing Breathy Voice

1.	[sɑm sɑ̤m]	Different	6.	[ð̤am ðam]	Different	11.	[rɔ̤ʂ rɔʂ]	Different
2.	[sɑ̤m sɑ̤m]	Same	7.	[pʰetʃ pʰe̤tʃ]	Different	12.	[zɑbβ zɑbβ]	Same
3.	[sɑm sɑm]	Same	8.	[tiv ti̤v]	Different	13.	[d̤apf d̤apf]	Different
4.	[foʃ fo̤ʃ]	Different	9.	[βʊx βʊx]	Same	14.	[ʒɔ̤ʤ ʒɔʤ]	Different
5.	[mɛʒ mɛʒ]	Same	10.	[ʔe̤ks ʔe̤ks]	Same	15.	[ʔɨft ʔɨft]	Same

In the next exercise, tell whether the utterances are breathy or not.

Exercise 28.2: Recognizing Breathy Voice

1.	[sɑ̤m]	Breathy	5.	[dam]	No	9.	[ʔʌʂ]	No
2.	[sam]	No	6.	[z̤ɔks]	Breathy	10.	[ñ̤ñad]	No
3.	[sam]	No	7.	[tʃʰɔ̤ʔ]	Breathy	11.	[ŋe̤ŋg]	Breathy
4.	[mɛdʒ]	Breathy	8.	[lekx]	No	12.	[rər]	No

---

1 The Hooktop H [ɦ] is the voiced counterpart to H [h].

| 13. [xųnʔ] | Breathy | 15. [f̪.taʃ] | No | 17. [ʃɑ̤n] | Breathy |
| 14. [ʒa̤dʒ] | Breathy | 16. [ze̤r] | Breathy | 18. [s̪ɨ̤ʃ] | Breathy |

To produce breathy sounds, exhale while holding the vocal cords in a relaxed manner as they are for [h]. Tense them slightly until a small amount of voicing occurs. Make sure that the vocal cords are more relaxed than for modal voice. Breathy voice can also be achieved by imitating certain speech styles, such as "spookiness" or "sultry glamor."

Exercise 28.3: Producing Breathy Voice

1. a) [sɑ]   b) [sɑ̤]   c) [sɑsɑ̤]   d) [sɑ̤sɑsɑ̤]

2. a) [ni]   b) [nį̤]   c) [nini̤]   d) [ni̤nini̤]

3. a) [fu]   b) [fṳ]   c) [fufṳ]   d) [fṳfufṳ]

4. a) [ŋo]   b) [ŋo̤]   c) [ŋoŋo̤]   d) [ŋo̤ŋoŋo̤]

5. a) [tsɔ]   b) [tsɔ̤]   c) [tsɔtsɔ̤]   d) [tsɔ̤tsɔtsɔ̤]

Breathy stops are often spoken of as voiced aspirated stops since the short, breathy release of these sounds delays voice onset time, similar to aspiration. Describing these sounds as voiced aspirated is technically a contradiction, however, because breathiness and voicing are glottal states that cannot coexist.

Voiced

Voiced phones are produced when the vocal cords have optimal tension applied to them for a smooth and even vibration along their entire length. This is called modal voice. Voiced sounds are common in every language. Voiced vowels are more common than vowels with any other type of glottal activity.

Voicing is usually assumed to be an intrinsic quality of the base symbol. There is no special diacritic to add voicing to an inherently voiceless symbol. Examples of voiced phones are [b], [v], [ʒ] and [ɣ].

In the following exercise, respond by telling whether the vowels are breathy or voiced.

Exercise 28.4: Recognizing Breathy Voice

| 1. [na̤f] | Breathy | 3. [son] | Voiced | 5. [tseʔ] | Voiced |
| 2. [naf] | Voiced | 4. [zi̤ɬ] | Breathy | 6. [dʒṳl] | Breathy |

7.	[tʰo̤ks]	Breathy	10. [ræʁ]	Voiced	13. [ʔo̤dz]	Breathy
8.	[ɸi̤ñ]	Breathy	11. [mʌnŋ]	Voiced	14. [sumn]	Voiced
9.	[dibz]	Voiced	12. [ðɑ̤pɸ] Breathy		15. [glɛd͡b]	Voiced

Creaky

Creaky voice involves a slower, more irregular vibration of the vocal cords than with voiced sounds. This state of the glottis occurs when the vocal cords have increased tension applied to them so that they cannot vibrate smoothly along their entire length. The glottis is relaxed just enough so that the vocal cords do not close completely. If any more tension were applied, a glottal stop would be formed. Creaky voice is characterized by a rough or forced vocal resonance.

The creaky state of the glottis is sometimes used as an over all speech style in languages like English, but it can be used to distinguish meaning as well. When used contrastively, creaky voice is usually applied to vowels and other sonorants. Some major languages that use creaky vowels contrastively are Burmese, Vietnamese, and Hmong.

The IPA symbolizes creaky voice by a **Tilde [̰]** beneath [ɑ] or [g̰] above a symbol.[2] Creaky voice is also referred to as **laryngealization**.

The following exercise contrasts creaky voice with other states of the glottis. Respond by telling whether the pairs of utterances are the same or different.

Exercise 28.5: Recognizing Creaky Voice

1. [sɑm sɑ̰m]	Different	6. [ð̰ɑm ðɑm]	Different	11. [ro̰s ros]	Different
2. [sɑ̰m sɑ̰m]	Same	7. [pʰetʃ pʰḛtʃ]	Different	12. [zɑbβ zɑbβ]	Same
3. [sɑm sɑm]	Same	8. [tiv tḭv]	Different	13. [ɗɑpf ɗɑ̰pf]	Different
4. [foʃ fo̰ʃ]	Different	9. [βʊx βʊx]	Same	14. [ʒo̰ʤ ʒoʤ]	Different
5. [mɛʒ mɛʒ]	Same	10. [ʔə̰ks ʔə̰ks]	Same	15. [ʔɨft ʔɨft]	Same

Respond to each utterance in the following exercise by telling if it is creaky or not.

Exercise 28.6: Recognizing Creaky Voice

---

2   Unfortunately, the tilde is also used to represent nasalization. Usually, the tilde below represents creaky voice and the tilde above represents nasalization. Also, a tilde above an N [ñ], normally represents an alveopalatal or palatal nasal.

1. [sa̰m]	Creaky	7. [tʃʰɔ̰ʔ]	Creaky	13. [χṵnʔ]	Creaky
2. [sɑm]	No	8. [lekx]	No	14. [ʒa̰dʒ]	Creaky
3. [sɑm]	No	9. [ʔʌs̩]	No	15. [ftaʃ]	No
4. [mɛ̰dʒ]	Creaky	10. [n̥ñad]	No	16. [zḛr]	Creaky
5. [dɑm]	No	11. [ŋə̰ŋg]	Creaky	17. [ʃɑ̰n]	Creaky
6. [z̰ɔks]	Creaky	12. [rər]	No	18. [s̰ɨʃ]	Creaky

Creaky voice can be produced by prolonging a voiced vowel and gradually tightening the vocal cords until a creaky quality is reached. Read the following sentences with creaky voice to imitate someone waking out of bed.

Exercise 28.7: Producing Creaky Voice

1. I am so sleepy.

2. Rising at sunrise is a chore.

3. The creaky, croaky crawdad crawled across a creek.

In the next exercise, repeat each utterance after the recording.

Exercise 28.8: Producing Creaky Voice

1. a) [sɑ]	b) [sɑ̰]	c) [sɑsɑ̰]	d) [sɑ̰sɑsɑ̰]
2. a) [ni]	b) [nḭ]	c) [ninḭ]	d) [nḭninḭ]
3. a) [fu]	b) [fṵ]	c) [fufṵ]	d) [fṵfufṵ]
4. a) [ŋo]	b) [ŋo̰]	c) [ŋoŋo̰]	d) [ŋo̰ŋoŋo̰]
5. a) [tsɔ]	b) [tsɔ̰]	c) [tsɔtsɔ̰]	d) [tsɔ̰tsɔtsɔ̰]

The following exercise contains vowels with four different states of the glottis. Respond by naming the state of the glottis that is applied to each utterance.

Exercise 28.9: Recognizing Voiceless, Breathy, Voiced, and Creaky Vowels

1. [sɑm]	Voiced	3. [dʒi̥]	Voiceless	5. [sa̰m]	Creaky
2. [dʒṳl]	Breathy	4. [ŋə̤ŋg]	Breathy	6. [n̩.dok]	Voiced

7.	[tʃʰɔʔ]	Creaky	13.	[ðɔ̰pɸ]	Breathy	19.	[mɛm̰n̰]	Creaky
8.	[tʃʰɔ̥]	Voiceless	14.	[m̥.bɑ̰ts]	Voiceless	20.	[n̥.strɛ̥]	Voiceless
9.	[ŋɪmb̰]	Voiced	15.	[tsɔ̰r]	Creaky	21.	[pθʊ̈r]	Breathy
10.	[ⁿglɛ̰d͡b]	Creaky	16.	[nḭ]	Creaky	22.	[ʐɔ̰wg]	Creaky
11.	[sɑ̰]	Creaky	17.	[ɸi̤ñ]	Breathy	23.	[ⁿgɱeˀ]	Voiced
12.	[mɑ̤ðz]	Breathy	18.	[mʌnŋ˺]	Voiced	24.	[fṳl]	Breathy

Stiff and Slack Voice

The **Stiff voice** state of the glottis occurs when the opening of the glottis and vocal cords are stiffer than normal. No official symbol has been chosen to represent stiff voice, but a **Subscript Wedge** [ˌ] or a **Superscript Wedge** [ˇ] is often used for this purpose (for example, [ab̌a]).[3]

The opposite of stiff voice is slack voice (also called lax voice). **Slack voice** occurs when the opening vocal chords is slightly wider than normal. Though no official symbol exists for the slack voice state of the glottis, the Under-ring [̥] and Over-ring [˚] are frequently used (for example, [ab̥a]). This can cause confusion because these symbols usually represent voicelessness. If these diacritics occur with a voiceless consonant or a voiced consonant that has a voiceless counterpart, they will likely indicate slack voice. Like stiff voice, slack voice only occurs in consonants.

English speakers often find it difficult to identify stiff and slack voice consonants from their modal voiced and voiceless counterparts. Many Asian languages contrast slack and stiff voice along with other states of the glottis.

Whisper

The **whispered** state of the glottis occurs when the vocal cords are tensed too much to allow them to vibrate, yet a small space is left between them through which air is allowed to pass. This state of the glottis applies mostly to vowels and a few other sonorants.

Whispered vowels are auditorily similar to voiceless vowels in that there is no vocal resonance. The restriction to the air stream, however, causes them to have a hissing sound not present in voiceless vowels. Many people learning to produce voiceless vowels have a tendency to say whispered vowels instead.

---

3   The Subscript Wedge [ˌ] officially indicates voicing (though it is rarely used for this purpose since most symbols have a voiced counterpart) for example, a voiced palatal lateral fricative could be symbolized as [ʎ̝].

Although whispering occurs quite commonly as a speech style, it is not used in the normal speech of any language. Therefore, whispering is not normally transcribed. However, the IPA extension diacritic **Dot Below** [.] is used to indicated whispering in speech pathology (for example, [ɑ̣]). Like all diacritics, the Dot can also be placed above a symbol with a descender if necessary (for example, [ġ]).

Glottal Closure

If the glottis is tensed even further than for a whisper, a state is eventually reached in which the vocal cords are drawn so tightly together that no air can pass between them. This state corresponds with the conditions required to produce a glottal stop, although the glottal stop is not technically a state of the glottis. The glottal stop is a separate consonant which uses the vocal cords as its articulator.

The **glottal** state of complete closure is the exact opposite of that of voicelessness, since for voiceless sounds the vocal cords are relaxed and apart. However, sounds made with this state of the glottis, like the glottal stop for example, will be perceived auditorily as voiceless since no air passes through the vocal cords.

States of the Glottis as Speech Styles

Each of the states of the glottis introduced in this lesson can be applied not only to individual segments or syllables, but also to speech as a whole. Any specific phonetic characteristic that is applied to speech as a whole, and is not used to distinguish the meaning of individual words, is called a speech style. The breathy, voiced, creaky, and whispered glottal states occur quite frequently in English as speech styles. Other speech styles will be introduced later in this course.

Lesson 29:
Implosives

Lesson Outline

Glossary Terms

Implosives are sounds which involve an **ingressive air stream**. The concept of the air stream was introduced in Lesson 1. Without the movement of air in the vocal tract, no speech sounds could occur. The muscles or organs that set that air in motion are called air stream mechanisms. There are three different air stream mechanisms in the speech tract, each capable of moving air either outward or inward. These mechanisms are the lungs, the glottis, and the tongue. For all of the phones drilled so far in this course, the air stream originates in the lungs and is moved outward by the diaphragm and muscles of the rib cage. This type of air stream is called egressive pulmonic. For implosive sounds, the air stream is set in motion by the glottis and moves inward. This is described as **ingressive glottalic air**.

Implosives occur contrastively in approximately 10–15% of the world's languages. Stops are the most common implosive sounds, but some languages contain implosive affricates as well.

The IPA indicates that a sound is implosive with an **upper right hook** on the base symbol (for example [ɓ]). The official symbols for voiceless implosive stops do not correspond with those for egressive voiceless stops. Voiceless implosives are represented by placing an Under-ring [̥] beneath or an Over-ring [̊] above the symbol for the voiced implosive at the same point of articulation (for example, [ɓ̥] or [ɠ̊]).[1] Table 29.1 below gives the implosive symbols that will be drilled in this lesson.

Table 29.1: Implosives

	Bilabial	Tip-Alveolar	Mid-Palatal	Back-Velar	Back-Uvular
Voiceless	ɓ̥	ɗ̥	ʄ̥	ɠ̊	ʛ̥
Voiced	ɓ	ɗ	ʄ	ɠ	ʛ

Most of the symbol names are intuitive. The bilabial implosive is **Hooktop B** [ɓ], and the alveolar implosive is **Hooktop D** [ɗ]. The symbol for the palatal implosive is a bit ambiguous, but it is usually considered a **Hooktop Barred Dotless J** [ʄ]. The velar and uvular implosives are **Hooktop G** [ɠ] and **Hooktop Small Capital G** [ʛ] respectively.

For the articulation of a voiceless implosive consonant, the glottis must be completely closed while at the same time there is a complete closure in the oral cavity, as for a stop. The glottis is pulled downward, which rarefies[2] the air between the glottis and the articulators. When the articulation is released, a sudden burst of air rushes inward to fill the vacuum

---

1   The IPA had dedicated symbols for voiceless implosives (i.e., [ƥ] [ƭ] [ƈ] [ƙ] [ʠ]), but they were withdrawn in 1993.

2   Rarification is the opposite of compression. It is used in linguistics to describe a partial vacuum condition between two articulations.

created by the downward movement of the glottis. Illustration 29.1 pictures the action of the glottis and the direction of the air stream for a voiceless implosive.

Voiced implosives are more common than their voiceless counterparts. For voiced implosives to occur, there must be enough air passing through the vocal cords to produce vibrations. For this to occur, the glottis is not completely closed while it is being pulled downward, as it is for voiceless implosives. This allows enough egressive pulmonic air to escape upward between the vocal cords to produce voicing. Thus, voiced implosives actually use a combination of ingressive glottalic air and egressive pulmonic air. Illustration 29.2 pictures voiced implosive articulation.

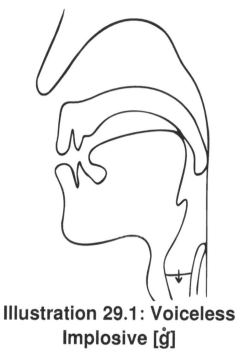

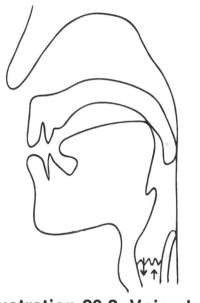

Illustration 29.1: Voiceless Implosive [g̊]

Illustration 29.2: Voiced Implosive [ɠ]

Producing Implosives

Most people find voiced implosives easier to produce than voiceless ones. To start with the voiced velar implosive [ɠ], try to imitate the "glug, glug" of water being poured from a bottle: [ɠəʔ ɠəʔ ɠəʔ ɠəʔ].

In the same way, you may be able to produce the voiced velar implosive [ɠ] by imitating the croaking of a bull frog: [ɠəʔ ɠəʔ ɠəʔ ɠəʔ] If this helps you to articulate the velar implosive, try the other implosives [ɓ], [ɗ], [ʄ], and [ʛ] by analogy.

To produce voiceless implosives, try whispering the exercises above. Practice this until you can do it with [ɓ̥], [ɗ̥], [ʄ̥], [g̊], and [ʛ̥], then work on using voiced vowels between the voiceless implosives.

Practice saying the sentences after the recording in the following exercise. Practice these until the implosive sounds come naturally for you.

Exercise 29.1: Producing Implosives

1. ɓig ɓad ɓoy
2. ɠooey ɠreen ɠrapes
3. ɗoes ɗotty ɗream

4. ɓeter ɓiɓer ɓicked ɓeɓɓers
5. ɠatherine ɠicked the ɠing
6. ɗake ɗommy ɗo the ɗrain

English speakers often confuse implosives with double articulated stops. The following exercise contrasts egressive double articulations with implosive articulations.

Exercise 29.2: Implosive and Egressive Double Articulations

1. a) [ak͡pa]   b) [akɓa]

2. a) [at͡pa]   b) [atɓa]

3. a) [ag͡ba]   b) [agɠa]

4. a) [ad͡ba]   b) [adɗa]

Recognizing Implosives

Throughout this course, most of the implosive sounds are articulated clearly and put between vowels for easier recognition. In actual languages, however, the implosives may not be articulated as distinctly, or may be surrounded by other sounds that disguise their distinctive sound. In such cases the implosives will be harder to recognize. In the following exercise, practice recognizing implosives by stating whether each pair of utterances are the same or different.

Exercise 29.3: Recognizing Implosives

1. [aɓi aɓi]	Same	5. [aɢə aɢə]	Different	9. [aɓɔ aɓɔ]	Same
2. [aɓi abi]	Different	6. [ʊɓʌ ʊɓʌ]	Same	10. [ɗa ɗa]	Different
3. [ga ɠa]	Different	7. [aɗɛ aɗɛ]	Same	11. [aɠɨ aɠɨ]	Same
4. [ɗu du]	Different	8. [ɪɟə ɪɟə]	Different	12. [ɨɟɨ ɨɟɨ]	Same

13. [udɪ udɪ]   Different   14. [eɢɛ eɢɛ]   Different   15. [æro æro]   Same

Tell whether the stops in the following exercise are implosives or not.

Exercise 29.4: Recognizing Implosives

1. [abɑ]   No
2. [aɓɑ]   Implosive
3. [ɗa]   Implosive
4. [nado]   No
5. [ɛtæ]   No
6. [lore]   No

7. [ɢif]   Implosive
8. [ŋurʊ]   No
9. [uɗʊ]   Implosive
10. [sʌɟə]   Implosive
11. [lɑpu]   No
12. [aɓɑ]   Implosive

13. [æɠɪ]   Implosive
14. [ɓo]   Implosive
15. [suda]   No
16. [mebas]   No
17. [ʊɠam]   Implosive
18. [goŋ]   No

Voiceless implosives are not only more difficult to produce, but also more difficult to recognize than their voiced counterparts. The following exercise contains both voiced and voiceless implosives. Respond to each utterance by telling whether the stops that you hear are voiced or voiceless.

Exercise 29.5: Recognizing Voiced and Voiceless Implosives

1. [ɓ̥əf]   Voiceless
2. [ʔoɗaŋ]   Voiced
3. [ɠ̥em]   Voiceless
4. [ɗar]   Voiced

5. [aɓaɲ]   Voiceless
6. [aɠ̥a]   Voiceless
7. [ɗ̥ɪʃ]   Voiceless
8. [oba?]   Voiced

9. [ɓ̥el]   Voiceless
10. [aɠev]   Voiced
11. [bʌβ]   Voiced
12. [ɗ̥uv]   Voiceless

Practice articulating the implosives in the following exercise. Follow the text as you repeat each utterance after the recording.

Exercise 29.6: Producing Implosive Stops

1. a) [ɓa]   b) [aɓ]   c) [ɓaɓ]   d) [ɓaɓaɓ]
2. a) [ɓa]   b) [aɓ]   c) [ɓaɓ]   d) [ɓaɓaɓ]
3. a) [ɓa]   b) [aɓ]   c) [ɓaɓ]   d) [ɓaɓaɓ]
4. a) [ɗa]   b) [aɗ]   c) [ɗaɗ]   d) [ɗaɗaɗ]

5. a) [ɗɑ]   b) [ɑɗ]   c) [ɗɑɗ]   d) [ɗɑɗɑɗ]

6. a) [ɗɑ]   b) [ɑɗ]   c) [ɗɑɗ]   d) [ɗɑɗɑɗ]

7. a) [ɠɑ]   b) [ɑɠ]   c) [ɠɑɠ]   d) [ɠɑɠɑɠ]

8. a) [ɠɑ]   b) [ɑɠ]   c) [ɠɑɠ]   d) [ɠɑɠɑɠ]

9. a) [ɠɑ]   b) [ɑɠ]   c) [ɠɑɠ]   d) [ɠɑɠɑɠ]

10. a) [ɓ̥ɑ]   b) [ɑɓ̥]   c) [ɓ̥ɑɓ̥]   d) [ɓ̥ɑɓ̥ɑɓ̥]

11. a) [ɓ̥ɑ]   b) [ɑɓ̥]   c) [ɓ̥ɑɓ̥]   d) [ɓ̥ɑɓ̥ɑɓ̥]

12. a) [ɓ̥ɑ]   b) [ɑɓ̥]   c) [ɓ̥ɑɓ̥]   d) [ɓ̥ɑɓ̥ɑɓ̥]

13. a) [ɗ̥ɑ]   b) [ɑɗ̥]   c) [ɗ̥ɑɗ̥]   d) [ɗ̥ɑɗ̥ɑɗ̥]

14. a) [ɗ̥ɑ]   b) [ɑɗ̥]   c) [ɗ̥ɑɗ̥]   d) [ɗ̥ɑɗ̥ɑɗ̥]

15. a) [ɗ̥ɑ]   b) [ɑɗ̥]   c) [ɗ̥ɑɗ̥]   d) [ɗ̥ɑɗ̥ɑɗ̥]

16. a) [ɠ̊ɑ]   b) [ɑɠ̊]   c) [ɠ̊ɑɠ̊]   d) [ɠ̊ɑɠ̊ɑɠ̊]

17. a) [ɠ̊ɑ]   b) [ɑɠ̊]   c) [ɠ̊ɑɠ̊]   d) [ɠ̊ɑɠ̊ɑɠ̊]

18. a) [ɠ̊ɑ]   b) [ɑɠ̊]   c) [ɠ̊ɑɠ̊]   d) [ɠ̊ɑɠ̊ɑɠ̊]

   Many people learning to articulate implosives for the first time have a tendency to produce instead a consonant cluster consisting of a glottal stop and an egressive stop instead. Even if there is no trouble producing them, hearing the difference between implosives and such consonant clusters when the implosives are lightly articulated can be difficult, as in either case glottal closure is involved. The utterances in the following exercise contain implosives and other consonant clusters. Listen to each utterance, and tell whether the stops you hear are implosives or consonant clusters. Do not look at the text.

Exercise 29.7: Recognizing Implosives and Consonant Clusters

1. [ɗɑ]   Implosive   5. [ʔdæn]   CC   9. [ʔdʊβ]   CC

2. [ʔdɑ]   CC   6. [ɠiv]   Implosive   10. [ʔpeθ]   CC

3. [ʔgʌ]   CC   7. [ɗɑr]   Implosive   11. [ɠuɣ]   Implosive

4. [ɓ̥ɛz]   Implosive   8. [bʊn]   Implosive   12. [ʔkɑŋ]   CC

The following exercise combines all of the implosive sounds drilled in this lesson. Listen carefully to each utterance, and respond by naming the consonant you hear.

Exercise 29.8: Reviewing Implosives

1.	[aɗa]	ɗ	7.	[ba.u]	ɓ	13.	[g̊ul]	g̊
2.	[aɓa]	ɓ	8.	[oɗʌ]	ɗ	14.	[doʔo]	ɗ
3.	[aɗa]	ɗ	9.	[mɔg̊e]	g̊	15.	[o.əg̊ə]	g̊
4.	[aɠa]	ɠ	10.	[ɠola]	ɠ	16.	[ɗap]	ɗ
5.	[eɓ̥o]	ɓ̥	11.	[ɠɔŋ]	ɠ	17.	[g̊uŋu]	g̊
6.	[lʊɠʌ]	ɠ	12.	[aɓa]	ɓ	18.	[ɓ̥er]	ɓ̥

The following table summarizes the sounds and symbols presented in this lesson and gives alternate symbols for each.

Table 29.2: Implosives Summary

IPA Symbol	Name	Technical Name	English Example	APA Symbol
ɓ̥	Voiceless Hooktop B	Voiceless Bilabial Implosive		ƥ
ɓ	Hooktop B	Voiced Bilabial Implosive		ɓ
ɗ̥	Voiceless Hooktop D	Voiceless Tip-alveolar Implosive		ƭ
ɗ	Hooktop D	Voiced Tip-alveolar Implosive		ɗ
ʄ̥	Voiceless Hooktop Barred Dotless J	Voiceless Palatal Implosive		ƈ

IPA Symbol	Name	Technical Name	English Example	APA Symbol
ʄ	Hooktop Barred Dotless J	Voiced Palatal Implosive		ʄ
ɠ̥	Voiceless Hooktop G	Voiceless Velar Implosive		ƙ
ɠ	Hooktop G	Voiced Velar Implosive		ɠ
ʛ̥	Voiceless Hooktop Small Capital G	Voiceless Uvular Implosive		q̓
ʛ	Hooktop Small Capital G	Voiced Uvular Implosive		g̓

Lesson 30:
Breathy Consonants and Consonant Clusters

Lesson Outline

Glossary

You may be more familiar with some phonetic features than others based on whether or not they are common in your native language. The breathy consonants reviewed in this lesson will be easy to identify, but much more difficult to produce. English speakers sometimes produce breathy consonants, but only when mimicking a specific speech style. It is never used to distinguish meaning. In some languages, however, the difference between two words could be the breathiness of a single consonant. Once learned, this feature will go a long way to improving your speech skills in languages where it is contrastive.

Breathy Consonants

Breathy sounds are produced when the vocal cords are more relaxed than for modal voice, allowing a greater volume of air to flow through with less vibration. This state of the glottis was introduced with vowels in Lesson 28. Breathy voice can be applied to consonants as well. Nearly any voiced sound can also be produced with breathy voice. Breathy voice involves some audible vocal activity, but not as much as for modal voice. Consonants produced with breathy voice are characterized by a windy quality.

Breathy stops are very important in several languages of India and Nepal, where they are often used contrastively to distinguish word meanings. In English, breathiness is usually an over all speech style. Breathy consonants are also referred to as **murmured** consonants.

As mentioned previously, the diacritic for breathy consonants is a **Diaeresis** [..] below [b̤] or above [g̈] a voiced symbol. A breathy stop or affricate may also be written with a **Superscript Hooktop H** [ʱ], such as [bʱ], because most linguists consider voiced aspiration identical to breathiness. For simplicity, the Diaeresis will be used throughout the remainder of this chapter.

Table 30.1 below lists a few examples of breathy consonant symbolization.

Table 30.1: Breathy Consonant Examples

	Bilabial	Alveolar	Alveopalatal	Retroflexed	Palatal	Velar	Uvular
Breathy Stops	b̤	d̤	d̈	ḍ̈	ɟ̈	g̈	ɢ̤
Breathy Fricatives	β̈	z̤	ʒ̈	ʐ̤	ʝ̈	ɣ̈	ʁ̤
Breathy Nasals	m̤	n̤	ñ̈	ɳ̈	ɲ̈	ŋ̈	ɴ̤

The effect of breathiness on voiced stops is very similar to that of aspiration on voiceless ones in that it delays the full onset of voicing. Some linguists, therefore, refer to breathy stops as voiced aspirated stops. The voiced and breathy glottalic states, however, are two separate conditions that cannot coexist. The vocal cords vibrate evenly along their entire length during voiced sounds. During a breathy sound, however, the front part of the vocal cords vibrate loosely, while in the back the vocal cords are spread apart and do not vibrate at all. For this reason, breathy stops should not be described as voiced aspirated.

Producing Breathy Consonants

Continuants, such as fricatives, nasals, and laterals, are not difficult to produce with breathy voice. The glottal activity involved in producing these consonants is no different than that of breathy vowels. The glottis must be relaxed slightly more than for normal voicing so that the air stream passes through more freely. Breathy stops, however, can be more challenging to produce since the flow of the air stream is interrupted. Most of the drills in this lesson are dedicated to practicing breathy stops.

To produce breathy stops, relax the glottis and say a voiced stop while expelling more air than usual from the lungs. This should result in a puff of air similar to aspiration on a voiceless stop. Be careful not to add so much extra air that it adds another syllable to the utterance, as in [bəhɑ].

Say the word "rabbit" with a voiced stop, then add an [h] after the [b]. Combine the two sounds until you can pronounce the [b] as a breathy stop, then replace [b] with breathy stops [d̤] and [g̈]. Follow the transcription in the next exercise, and repeat each utterance after the recording.

Exercise 30.1: Producing Breathy Consonants

1. Rabbit   ['ɹæ.bɪt]

2. Rab.hit   ['ɹæb.hɪt]

3. Ra.bhit   ['ɹæ.b̤ɪt]

4. Ra.dhit   ['ɹæ.d̤ɪt]

5. Ra.ghit   ['ɹæ.g̈ɪt]

Repeat each utterance after the recording in the following exercise. In this exercise, make sure that the vowel following the breathy consonant is voiced instead of breathy.

Exercise 30.2: Producing Breathy Consonants

1. ['beⁱ.bi] ['b̤eⁱ.bi] ['b̤eⁱ.b̤i]

2. ['do.do] ['d̤o.do] ['d̤o.d̤o]

3. ['gɑ.gɑ] ['g̈ɑ.gɑ] ['g̈ɑ.g̈ɑ]

4. b̤illy's b̤ig b̤lue b̤ike

5. d̥on't d̥unk d̥onuts   6. g̊ooey g̊reen g̊rapes

Recognizing Breathy Consonants

Breathy consonants are characterized by a softer quality then their voiced counterparts. They may be thought of as having a windy or half whispered sound. Breathy speech is also often associated with spookiness or sultry glamor.

The following exercise contrasts breathy and voiced stops. Listen to each pair of utterances in the following exercise, and tell whether they are the same or different.

Exercise 30.3: Recognizing Breathy Consonants

1.	[b̥ɑ] [b̥ɑ]	Same	5.	[d̥is] [dis]	Different	9.	[ɪg̊æ] [ɪgæ]	Different
2.	[β̥o] [β̥o]	Different	6.	[b̥e] [b̥e]	Same	10.	[od̥ɑ] [odɑ]	Different
3.	[g̊ʊ] [gʊ]	Different	7.	[og̊ʊ] [og̊ʊ]	Same	11.	[b̥ə] [b̥ə]	Same
4.	[b̥o] [b̥o]	Same	8.	[dɔf] [d̥ɔf]	Different	12.	[ɴɛ] [ɴ̥ɛ]	Different

In the next exercise, respond to each utterance by telling whether the phone is breathy or voiced.

Exercise 30.4: Recognizing Breathy and Voiced Consonants

1.	[b̥ɑ]	Breathy	6.	[ʑ̊ɛ]	Breathy	11.	[b̥ʊⁱ]	Breathy
2.	[du]	Voiced	7.	[b̥aⁱ]	Breathy	12.	[v̥ɑᵘ]	Breathy
3.	[bi]	Voiced	8.	[ʁʌ]	Voiced	13.	[ɣ̊wə]	Breathy
4.	[d̥a]	Breathy	9.	[g̊ɛᵘ]	Breathy	14.	[bɔ]	Voiced
5.	[go]	Voiced	10.	[gɑ]	Voiced	15.	[d̥ʊᵘ]	Breathy

It may be difficult at times to distinguish between breathy stops and voiceless aspirated stops. In the following exercise, listen to each utterance, and tell whether the stop is breathy or voiceless.

Exercise 30.5: Recognizing Breathy and Voiceless Aspirated Stops

1.	[b̥a.i]	Breathy	2.	[tʰɑs]	Voiceless	3.	[kʰo]	Voiceless

4.	[d̤ef]	Breathy	7.	[pʰin]	Voiceless	10.	[kʰɛl]	Voiceless
5.	[g̈er]	Breathy	8.	[d̤a]	Breathy	11.	[b̤æʔ]	Breathy
6.	[b̤an]	Breathy	9.	[tʰɛm]	Voiceless	12.	[g̈as]	Breathy

One mistake that learners often make when producing breathy stops is over-emphasizing the breathiness, adding an [h] after the stop. This adds an extra syllable to the original sound. Care must be taken to make a smooth transition from the breathy stop to the voiced vowel without breaking up the syllable pattern. Practice recognizing incorrect transitions in the next exercise. Respond by telling whether each utterance contains one syllable or two.

Exercise 30.6: Recognizing Correct Transition

1.	[b̤ɑ]	One	5.	[ɢə.he]	Two	9.	[b̤ɨ.hu]	Two
2.	[b̤ə.hɑ]	Two	6.	[ɟ̈ɨ]	One	10.	[r̤œ]	One
3.	[g̈ə]	One	7.	[b̤ə.hæ]	Two	11.	[d̤ɯ]	One
4.	[d̤o]	One	8.	[ɟ̈ə.hɪ]	Two	12.	[ɟ̈ɨ.hy]	Two

The following exercise contains words from the Nepali language in which breathy consonants are used to distinguish meaning. Follow the transcription, and repeat each utterance after the recording.

Exercise 30.7: Nepali Breathy Stops

1.	[ˈtʰulo]	"big"	8.	[ˈb̤atθʰ]	"cooked rice"
2.	[ˈd̤ulo]	"dust"	9.	[ˈbɑri]	"field"
3.	[ˈduŋgɑ]	"boat"	10.	[ˈb̤ɑɾi]	"luggage"
4.	[ˈd̤uŋgɑ]	"stone"	11.	[ˈdani]	"giver"
5.	[ˈdɑn]	"offering"	12.	[ˈd̤ani]	"rich man"
6.	[ˈd̤ɑn]	"rice paddy"	13.	[ˈdɑ.i]	"elder brother"
7.	[ˈbatθʰ]	"talking"	14.	[ˈd̤ɑ.i]	"midwife"

Consonant Clusters

A **cluster** is a group of adjacent sounds which are of the same phonetic category and have no intervening or transitional sounds. Therefore, a **consonant cluster** consists of two or more consecutive consonants with no intervening vowels or semivowels.

Consonant clusters can be very difficult to pronounce. Whether a combination of consonants is difficult for you to produce or not depends largely on your native language habits. In some languages, the majority of consonants are clustered, while in others consonant clusters rarely occur. In this lesson several types of clusters will be introduced to improve your awareness of the different combinations you may encounter.

A consonant cluster may be composed of a series of consonants of any manner of articulation, or a mixture of several manners. Affricates are a type of consonant cluster consisting of a stop followed by a fricative. Longer clusters involving more manners of articulation will be drilled in this lesson.

Recognizing Consonant Clusters

You will remember from Lesson 27 that it is common for a short vowel, such as Schwa [ə], to occur between voiced consonants, especially stops. At times, sequences of consonants will be encountered which sound very similar to consonant clusters, but the consonants are actually separated by a transitional element such as a short vowel or an approximant release. It is important to be able to determine whether a group of sounds is really a consonant cluster or not. In the following exercise, practice distinguishing consonant clusters from sequences broken up by vowels and approximants. Respond to each utterance by determining if the group of consonants is a consonant cluster or not.

Exercise 30.8: Recognizing Consonant Clusters

1. [ɑ.gdɑ] Consonant Cluster

2. [ɑ.gᵊdɑ] No

3. [bᵊdaŋ] No

4. [splo] Consonant Cluster

5. [pʰə.tʰɑ] No

6. [ɑ.dzɣa] Consonant Cluster

7. [ptɑ]   Consonant Cluster

8. [ptkoɲ] Consonant Cluster

9. [gᵊkʊŋ] No

10. [ʔɑlmk] Consonant Cluster

11. [ʃᵊsʊ]   No

12. [dᵊʒɑk] No

A consonant cluster can be either **monosyllabic** or **polysyllabic** based on the number and type of consonants included. In the English word "strengths," transcribed [sɹɛŋθs], there are two consonant clusters even though the word consist of only one syllable. Now consider the Salish word [xɬp'χʷɬtʰɬpʰɬːskʷʰt͡s'], which means "He possessed a bunchberry plant." Even though this word consists of several syllables, the entire utterance is one consonant cluster since there are no vowels separating the consonants. The syllable boundaries occurring between the consonants do not interrupt the continuity of the cluster. Notice, however, that in a polysyllabic cluster, each syllable must contain a sonorant or some similar continuant to carry the syllable beat.

In the following exercise, practice identifying how many syllables each consonant cluster contains. Respond by giving the number of syllables.

Exercise 30.9: Recognizing Syllable Boundaries in Consonant Clusters

1. [ʔoks.tχ] Two
2. [ʃẓ.vfʂ] Two
3. [skr̥ʃk] One
4. [kʃm̩.kfʂ] Two
5. [kʰ l̩m.pʃ.tfχ] Three
6. [pʰṣ.dʒ] Two
7. [ɢɣʒ.kɬ.dv̩.fʂk] Four
8. [ŋẓs.ʃʒ] Two
9. [kɬʰptk.stɬ] Two
10. [ðɣz.pl̩z] Two
11. [pr̥t͡sk] One
12. [pʰ.tʰ.fʃk] Three

Producing Consonant Clusters

Learning to produce complex consonant clusters is simply a matter of practice and perseverance. The following exercise contains English sentences in which the first letter of each word has been substituted with a consonant cluster. Practice reading these sentences until you can read them smoothly.

Exercise 30.10: Producing Consonant Clusters

1. **ptkw**een **ptk**atherine **ptk**an **ptk**ick a **ptk**ranky **ptk**ing

2. **kfs**ister **kfs**ue **kfs**ews **kfs**atin **kfs**ocks

3. **kɬʰft**iny **kɬʰft**im **kɬʰft**ook a **kɬʰftɹ**ain **kɬʰft**o **kɬʰft**oronto.

4. **ʒgʀ**ooey **ʒgʀɹ**een **ʒgʀɹ**apes

5. **pʰfskɹ**anberries, **pʰfskɹ**abapples, and **pʰfskɹ**ackers

The following exercise contains real words from several languages, each containing consonant clusters. Follow the transcription and read each word before starting the recording. After each utterance, compare your pronunciation with that of the recording.

Exercise 30.11: Producing Consonant Clusters

1. [ʃtvɚtⁱ]

2. [ˈnukstx]

3. [gɣbɚdɣɣnis]

4. [bɚt'q'ɛli]

5. [ˈekʰtʰkʰ]

6. [m̩ts'vɚtnɛɹi]

7. [pr̩t͡skʏna]

8. [ˈitʰkʰpʃ̩]

9. [oˈʔolɛptʃkiç]

10. [ʒbl̩ŋknutje]

11. [ɔpskɚbʎiʋaɲɛ]

12. [aˈklokʃtʰpʰtʃʰkʰ]

Lesson 31: Ejectives

Lesson Outline

Glossary

Ejectives are sounds which involve an **egressive glottalic air stream**. The concept of glottalic air stream was introduced in Lesson 29. Glottalic air is set in motion by the glottis and can move either outward or inward. The implosive sounds studied in Lesson 29 involve ingressive glottalic air, which means that the glottis moves downward and draws air inward. Ejectives are just the opposite. The glottis is completely closed and at the same time there is a closure in the oral cavity. When the glottis moves upward, the air between the glottis and the articulators is compressed. As the articulation is released this pressurized air is rapidly expelled from the oral cavity, creating an ejective puff of air. Ejectives are also referred to as explosives or glottalized consonants.

Most ejectives in the languages of the world are ejective stops. Some languages also have ejective affricates, and a few have have ejective fricatives.

Ejectives are found in about 20% of languages in the world. They are common languages as diverse as Thai, Georgian, Quechua, and several languages indigenous to North America.

Ejectives are represented by placing an **Apostrophe [']** after a voiceless consonant (for example, [t'], [ts'], or [x']). The following chart gives symbols for the ejective sounds introduced in this lesson. This chart is by no means exhaustive. Nearly all stops and affricates, as well as a few fricatives, can be produced as ejectives.

Table 31.1 lists some examples of ejective consonants. Many other ejectives occur in spoken languges. Also, ejective affricates can be hetorogranic, but for simplicity, only homorganic affricates are listed below.

Table 31.1: Ejective Consonant Examples

	Bilabial	Alveolar	Alveopalatal	Retroflexed	Palatal	Velar	Uvular
Ejective Stops	p'	t'	t̠'	ʈ'	c'	k'	q'
Ejective Fricatives	ɸ'	s'	ʃ'	ʂ'	ç'	x'	χ'
Ejective Affricates	pɸ'	ts'	tʃ'	ʈʂ'	cç'	kx'	qχ'

Ejectives are unlike implosives in that the vocal cords must be completely closed while the glottis is being raised to compress the air stream. It is impossible, therefore, to articulate a voiced ejective, since no air passes between the vocal cords during ejective articulation. It is also important to note that the velic must be closed during the articulation of an ejective.

The following facial diagrams compare the articulation of [t], [t'], and [ʔ]. Notice that for [t'], the glottis is closed and the air stream arrow is drawn through the vocal cords. This indicates that the glottis is the air stream mechanism.

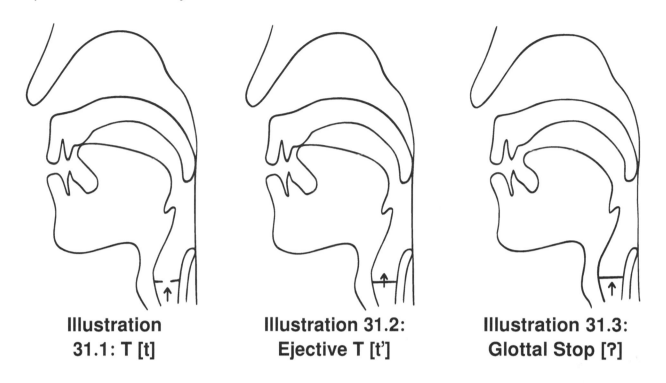

Illustration 31.1: T [t]

Illustration 31.2: Ejective T [t']

Illustration 31.3: Glottal Stop [ʔ]

Producing Ejectives

Learning to produce ejectives is relatively easy. Stops are probably the easiest sounds to learn as ejectives. Remember to practice only with voiceless sounds, as it is not possible to produce a voiced ejective.

Watch your instructor produce several ejective stops. Notice how the larynx is raised just before the release of the consonant. You can practice this muscle movement by pretending to spit a small bit of grass off the tip of your tongue. Protrude your tongue tip between your lips and draw it in sharply, blowing the imaginary fragment away. If you can produce a glottalic air stream like this, try doing the same with [p], [t], and [k].

Hold your breath and say [k] several times in a row, loud enough so that someone sitting next to you could hear it.

Another suggestion is to expel all of the air from your lungs and then try to say [k]. This will result in using the glottis to produce the air necessary for this sound.

Repeat the following set of sentences after the recording, pronouncing all of the voiceless stops as ejectives.

Exercise 31.1: Producing Ejectives

1. **p'**eter **p'ip'**er **p'**icked **p'ep'**ers

2. **k'**atherine **k'ik'**ed the **k'**ing

3. t'ake t'ommy t'o the t'rain

4. s'is'ter s'ue s'its s'ewing s'ocks

5. f'ive f'unny f'oxes f'uss

6. tʃ'ew tʃ'unky tʃ'ocolate tʃ'ips

Recognizing Ejectives

Ejectives are usually distinguishable by the sharp burst of air that accompanies their release. This burst is a characteristic of the glottalic air stream that produces ejectives.

It is not usually difficult to distinguish between ejectives and voiced pulmonic stops. Ejectives may easily be confused, however, with voiceless unaspirated stops. Practice identifying the ejectives in the following exercise. Respond to each pair of utterances by telling whether they are the same or different.

Exercise 31.2: Recognizing Ejectives

1.	[at'ɑ atɑ]	Different	8.	[ɪk'ɤ ɪk'ɤ]	Same	15. [nɑp'o nɑp'o]	Same
2.	[kom k'om]	Different	9.	[ap'ɛ apɛ]	Different	16. [ʟœtɬʊ ʟœtɬ'ʊ]	Different
3.	[pɑ pɑ]	Same	10.	[ɪtə ɪtə]	Same	17. [opu op'u]	Different
4.	[ti t'i]	Different	11.	[ok'am ok'am]	Same	18. [k'es kes]	Different
5.	[t'aʔ taʔ]	Different	12.	[p'æ pæ]	Different	19. [ɔp' ɔp]	Different
6.	[at'ə at'ə]	Same	13.	[at'ɨ atɨ]	Different	20. [ŋot'ɨ ŋot'ɨ]	Same
7.	[ʊkʌ ʊk'ʌ]	Different	14.	[ʁe ʁe]	Same	21. [ʃn̩kx' ʃn̩kx']	Same

Listen carefully to each utterance in the next exercise, and determine if each utterance contains an ejective stop or not.

Exercise 31.3: Recognizing Ejective Stops

1.	[atɑ]	No	4.	[nɑko]	No	7.	[k'ɨf]	Ejective
2.	[at'ɑ]	Ejective	5.	[æp'ɑ]	Ejective	8.	[ŋupʊ]	No
3.	[k'ɑ]	Ejective	6.	[lope]	No	9.	[ut'ʊ]	Ejective

10. [pʼɑn]	Ejective	13. [ætɪ]	No	16. [metʼɑs]	Ejective
11. [lɑpu]	No	14. [pʼo]	Ejective	17. [ʊtʼɑm]	Ejective
12. [ɑkʼɑ]	Ejective	15. [akɛʔ]	No	18. [poŋ]	No

The next exercise involves ejective affricates as well as stops. Determine if each utterance contains an ejective phone or not.

Exercise 31.4: Recognizing Ejective Stops and Affricates

1. [tsʼoŋ]	Ejective	5. [pfʰuʃ]	No	9. [ka]	no
2. [tsɑv]	No	6. [ksʼef]	Ejective	10. [psʼɑʔ]	Ejective
3. [tʃʼɪɲ]	Ejective	7. [kil]	No	11. [kθʰen]	No
4. [tʼɛ]	Ejective	8. [tsʰu]	No	12. [tθʼɑʔ]	Ejective

The following exercise contains all of the ejective sounds drilled in this lesson. Listen carefully to each utterance, and respond by giving the name of each ejective sound.

Exercise 31.5: Recognizing Ejective Consonants

1. [pʼɑn]	pʼ	6. [atʼɨ]	tʼ	11. [kʼo]	kʼ
2. [kʼɑ]	kʼ	7. [tsʼoŋ]	tsʼ	12. [okʼɑm]	kʼ
3. [tʼaʔ]	tʼ	8. [ʊtʼɑm]	tʼ	13. [ksʼef]	ksʼ
4. [tʃʼɪɲ]	tʃʼ	9. [psʼɑʔ]	psʼ	14. [ŋotʼɨ]	tʼ
5. [kʼɨf]	kʼ	10. [tθʼɑʔ]	tθʼ	15. [tʼo]	tʼ

The following exercise focuses on the production of ejective sounds. Follow the text, and repeat each utterance after the recording.

Exercise 31.6: Producing Ejective Consonants

1. a) [pʼɑ]	b) [ɑpʼ]	c) [pʼɑpʼ]	d) [pʼɑpʼɑpʼ]
2. a) [tʼɑ]	b) [ɑtʼ]	c) [tʼɑtʼ]	d) [tʼɑtʼɑtʼ]
3. a) [kʼɑ]	b) [ɑkʼ]	c) [kʼɑkʼ]	d) [kʼɑkʼɑkʼ]
4. a) [psʼɑ]	b) [ɑpsʼ]	c) [psʼɑpsʼ]	d) [psʼɑpsʼɑpsʼ]

5. a) [ts'ɑ]   b) [ɑts']   c) [ts'ɑts']   d) [ts'ɑts'ɑts']

6. a) [ks'ɑ]   b) [ɑks']   c) [ks'ɑks']   d) [ks'ɑks'ɑks']

7. a) [x'ɑ]   b) [ɑx']   c) [x'ɑx']   d) [x'ɑx'ɑx']

Lesson 32:
Tongue Root Placement

Lesson Outline

Glossary

Changing the size and shape of the pharyngeal cavity affects how vowels and other sonorants resonate, thus changing their quality of sound. The size and shape of the pharyngeal cavity is affected by the position of the tongue root. If the tongue root is pushed farther forward than normal, the size of the pharyngeal cavity is expanded. Likewise, if the tongue root is pulled farther backward than normal, the pharyngeal cavity becomes smaller. Understanding the positions of the tongue root, therefore, are important in knowing how sonorants are produced and modified. **Tongue root placement** describes how the root of the tongue is positioned in relationship to the pharyngeal walls and the position of the larynx.

There are three recognized positions of the tongue root. They are advanced tongue root, neutral tongue root, and retracted tongue root. Vowels with different tongue root placement have been found contrastively in several African and Asian languages.

The following facial diagram illustrates the position of the tongue for advanced, neutral, and retracted tongue root.

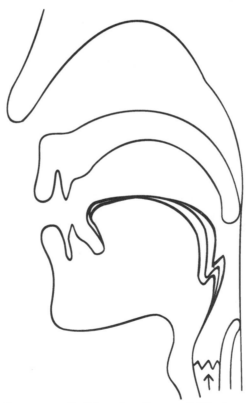

Illustration 32.1: Advanced, Neutral, and Retracted Tongue Root

The positions of the tongue root are symbolized by subscript diacritics, [ɑ̟] or [ɑ̠], beneath the base symbol pointing to the direction in which the tongue is moved. Neutral tongue root is considered the normal or default position of the tongue and is left unmarked.

Advanced Tongue Root

Advanced tongue root occurs when the pharyngeal cavity is enlarged by moving the base of the tongue forward, away from the back of the throat. Advanced tongue root is symbolized by placing a **Tack Left** [̯] below a symbol, such as [ɑ̟]. The larynx is usually lowered as well. Advanced tongue root is abbreviated **+ATR** .

Producing Sounds with Advanced Tongue Root

When a voice teacher asks a student to "open up" for a richer tone, advanced tongue root is actually the condition desired. To produce sounds with advanced tongue root, try saying a vowel while practicing anything that makes the pharyngeal cavity larger such as lowering the jaw or changing the shape of the tongue. You may try lowering your larynx to get a "woofy" sound.

It may also help to practice saying vowels while yawning. This pushes the tongue root forward, opening up the pharyngeal cavity more than for a normal vowel.

Practice the following sequence of vowels with neutral and advanced tongue root position. Pay particular attention to the forward and backward movement of the tongue root.

[ɑɑ̟ɑɑ̟ɑɑ̟ɑɑ̟ɑɑ̟]

Follow the text of the following exercise and repeat each utterance after the recording.

Exercise 32.1: Producing Vowels with Advances Tongue Root

1. a) [ɑ]   b) [ɑ̟]   c) [mɑmɑ]   d) [mɑ̟mɑ̟]

2. a) [i]   b) [i̟]   c) [sisi]   d) [si̟si̟]

3. a) [ɛ]   b) [ɛ̟]   c) [gɛgɛ]   d) [gɛ̟gɛ̟]

4. a) [o]   b) [o̟]   c) [lolo]   d) [lo̟lo̟]

5. a) [u]   b) [u̟]   c) [vuvu]   d) [vu̟vu̟]

Recognizing Sounds with Advanced Tongue Root

Vowels produced with advanced tongue root are usually characterized by a hollow sound. Advanced tongue root vowels often involve breathy voice as well, and usually have a lower pitch.

Practice identifying advanced tongue root in the following exercise. Respond after each pair of utterances by telling whether they are the same or different.

Exercise 32.2: Recognizing Advanced Tongue Root

1. [pʰɑ̟ pʰɑ̟]   Same
5. [wɑ wɑ̟]   Different
9. [ŋɑ̟ᵊ ŋɑ̟ᵊ]   Same

2. [pʰɑ̟ pʰɑ]   Different
6. [dʒjᵊ dʒiᵊ]   Different
10. [doᵘ dɑ̟ᵘ]   Different

3. [tʃɑ̟ tʃo]   Different
7. [pwɑ̟ pwɑ̟]   Same
11. [ʒβɪ̟ ʒβɪ̟]   Same

4. [njᵘ njᵘ]   Same
8. [klɛ̟ klɛ̟]   Same
12. [mɑ̟̃ᵘ mɑ̃ᵘ]   Different

In the following exercise, tell whether the vowels that you hear have advanced or neutral tongue root.

Exercise 32.3: Recognizing Advanced and Neutral Tongue Root

1. [pʰɑ]   Neutral
5. [grʉ]   Advanced
9. [t'ex]   Neutral

2. [pʰɑ̟]   Advanced
6. [mɑ̃ᵘ]   Neutral
10. [p'oj]   Neutral

3. [dʒjᵊ]   Advanced
7. [lɑ̟]   Advanced
11. [mɑ̟n]   Advanced

4. [ⁿto]   Neutral
8. [ŋɑ̟w]   Advanced
12. [vɛ̟n]   Advanced

Neutral Tongue Root

Neutral tongue root occurs when the tongue root is in its most relaxed, natural position for speech. This position is directly between that of advanced and retracted tongue root and is considered to be the normal or default tongue root position for most speech sounds.

All of the vowels which have been introduced in previous lessons are produced with neutral tongue root. The position of the tongue varies slightly, however, depending on the vowel being produced.

Retracted Tongue Root

Retracted tongue root involves moving the tongue root farther back toward the rear of the pharyngeal wall than its normal position for vowels. This reduces the size of the pharyngeal cavity, altering the vowel's original quality. This tongue root position is actually partial pharyngealization and may sometimes border on full pharyngealization.

Retracted tongue root is abbreviated **–ATR**. The IPA symbolizes retracted tongue root with a subscript **Right Tack** [̠], such as [ɑ̠]. This diacritic is the exact opposite of that used to denote advanced tongue root.

Producing Sounds with Retracted Tongue Root

Retracted tongue root vowels are produced by constricting the pharyngeal cavity with the root of the tongue. This can be done by beginning from the position of the pharyngeal fricative **Reversed Glottal Stop** [ʕ], for which the tongue root is the articulator, and partially opening the gap between the tongue root and the back of the throat.

Another way to learn to produce retracted tongue root vowels is to pretend you are choking on the back of your tongue while pronouncing a vowel.

Practice the following sequence of vowels with neutral and retracted tongue root positions. Pay particular attention to the forward and backward movement of the tongue root.

[ɑɑ̠ɑɑ̠ɑɑ̠ɑɑ̠ɑɑ̠]

Follow the text in the following exercise, and repeat each utterance after the recording.

Exercise 32.4: Producing Vowels with Retracted Tongue Root

1. a) [ɑ]   b) [ɑ̠]   c) [mɑmɑ]   d) [mɑ̠mɑ̠]

2. a) [i]   b) [i̠]   c) [sisi]   d) [si̠si̠]

3. a) [ɛ]   b) [ɛ̠]   c) [gɛgɛ]   d) [gɛ̠gɛ̠]

4. a) [o]   b) [o̠]   c) [lolo]   d) [lo̠lo̠]

5. a) [u]   b) [u̠]   c) [vuvu]   d) [vu̠vu̠]

Recognizing Sounds with Retracted Tongue Root

Retracted tongue root vowels are characterized by a choked sound. They usually involve creaky voice and may also have a higher pitch than the surrounding sounds.

The following exercise contains vowels with retracted and neutral tongue root positions. Practice identifying the retracted tongue root vowels. Respond by telling whether each pair of utterances is the same or different.

Exercise 32.5: Recognizing Retracted Tongue Root

1. [pʰa̱ pʰa]	Different	5. [gɾɑl gɾɑl]	Different	9. [ʈʂy̱ ʈʂy̱]	Same
2. [pʰa̱ pʰa̱]	Same	6. [ni nɪ̱]	Different	10. [tʃʙᵘ tʃʙ̱ᵘ]	Different
3. [moⁱ mo̱ⁱ]	Different	7. [wa̱ᵊŋ wa̱ᵊŋ]	Same	11. [ʂa̱ʔ ʂa̱ʔ]	Same
4. [sɑɢ sɑɢ]	Same	8. [t'æ̱kˡ t'æ̱kˡ]	Same	12. [do̱ᵘ doᵘ]	Different

In the following exercise, respond by telling whether the vowel that you hear has retracted or neutral tongue root.

Exercise 32.6: Recognizing Retracted and Neutral Tongue Root

1. [pʰa̱]	Retracted	5. [bo̱ᵘ]	Retracted	9. [ʀɑɹ]	Neutral
2. [pʰa]	Neutral	6. [stwʌ̱]	Retracted	10. [χi]	Neutral
3. [doᵘ]	Neutral	7. [tʰoʔ]	Neutral	11. [mo̱ⁱ]	Retracted
4. [t'æ̱k]	Retracted	8. [ʌy̱]	Retracted	12. [vɾɑ̱d]	Retracted

The following exercise contains vowels with advanced, neutral, and retracted tongue root placement. Respond to each utterance by naming the position of the tongue root. Review this and the previous exercises until you are confident in identifying and producing all three tongue root positions.

Exercise 32.7: Recognizing Tongue Root Placement

1. [pʰa̟]	Advanced	6. [ŋa̟w]	Advanced	11. [mo̱ⁱ]	Retracted
2. [pʰa̱]	Retracted	7. [wa̟]	Advanced	12. [ʂɑʔ]	Neutral
3. [pʰa]	Neutral	8. [bʊ]	Neutral	13. [ɾœʟ]	Neutral
4. [fy̱]	Retracted	9. [koᵊn]	Neutral	14. [mã̟ᵘ]	Advacned
5. [ø̈ɹ]	Neutral	10. [nɪ̟ᵘ]	Advanced	15. [tʰo̱ʔ]	Retracted

Lesson 33: Secondary Articulations

Lesson Outline

Glossary

Remember that for a consonant to be produced, it is necessary for an articulator to approach near enough to a point of articulation that the air stream is significantly modified or obstructed. During the production of most consonants, only one articulator is active. It is possible, however, for more than one articulator to be engaged at the same time, creating a condition known as co-articulated consonants. One type of co-articulated consonants, known as **double articulation**, was introduced in Lesson 26. Another type of co-articulated consonants, called **secondary articulation**, involves both a primary and a secondary articulator. While the primary articulator forms the main consonant, an additional articulator also shapes or modifies the air stream, forming a secondary consonant simultaneous with the first.

Consider the English word "view." Notice how during the initial [v] the blade of the tongue is raised toward the hard palate forming the approximant [j]. This is an example of secondary articulation since both sounds occur simultaneously. Contrast this with the [v] in the word "voodoo," where the secondary articulation is absent.

Primary and secondary articulations differ in their manner of articulation. The **primary consonant** is usually a sound which involves significant air stream modification, such as a stop, fricative, or nasal. The **secondary consonant** is usually a more open sound, such as an approximant. The secondary articulation therefore always sounds less prominent than the primary consonant, since there is less impedance. Both the primary and secondary articulation share the same voicing characteristics. Either both sounds are voiced or both are voiceless.

There are six common secondary articulations. These are termed labialization, palatalization, velarization, labial-palatalization, labial-velarization, and pharyngealization. All involve approximant articulation.

Primary and secondary articulations can be released either simultaneously or sequentially. Secondary articulations are usually released after the primary consonant, giving the sound a strong glided quality. A secondary articulation consisting of an approximant, therefore, may sound very much like a vowel glide.

Secondary articulations are represented by placing a superscript approximant symbol of the appropriate place of articulation after the symbol of the primary consonant. A palatalized [d], for example, is represented as [dʲ]. When a consonant must have a series of superscript symbols, such as an ejective Apostrophe ['] or a Raised H [ʰ], in addition to secondary articulation, the symbol of the secondary articulation belongs closest to the base consonant symbol, for example [pʷʰ] represents a labialized aspirated P. The Table 33.1 below gives the symbols for the six secondary articulations. Note that some symbols have multiple meanings.

Table 33.1: Secondary Articulators

Symbol	Point(s) of Articulation
w	Labial
j	Palatal
ɣ	Velar
ɥ	Labial, Palatal
w	Labial, Velar
ʕ	Pharyngeal

It is important to distinguish between a secondary articulation and a double articulation. A secondary articulation always sounds less prominent and its manner of articulation is always different from that of its primary consonant. In a double articulation, on the other hand, both consonants share the same manner of articulation and are of equal or nearly equal prominence.

Labialization

Labialization occurs when the lips are rounded during the articulation of a separate primary consonant. This occurs in the English words "quick" [kʷwɪk] and "Guam" [gʷwɑm]. Notice in these words how the lips round while the first consonant is pronounced. This rounding of the lips before the [w] approximant is labialization.

Labialization is symbolized by placing a **Superscript W** [ʷ] after the main consonant symbol. It should be noted that the W [w] is actually a double articulated labial-velar approximant, but the Superscript W [ʷ] can represent both labialization and labial-velarization. The latter will be discussed later on, but it is important to remember not to raise the back of the tongue unnecessarily when labializing a phone.

All consonants, including bilabials, can be labialized by simply rounding the lips. The following facial diagrams illustrate a [k] both with and without labialization. Notice in the diagram of [kʷ], that the labialization involves much less restriction than the primary articulation [k].

Illustration 33.1: [k]

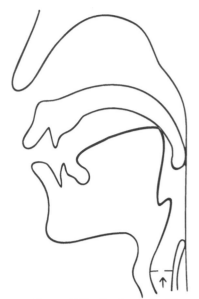

Illustration 33.2: Labialized [kʷ]

Producing Labialization

Producing labialized consonants is usually easy. Simply round the lips while saying the primary sound. Remember that the articulation may be released simultaneously or sequentially. A sequential release is very similar in sound to a vowel glide. In the following exercise, focus on releasing both articulations simultaneously. Repeat each utterance after the recording.

Exercise 33.1: Producing Labialization

1. a) [apʷa]   b) [pʷa]   c) [apʷ]   d) [pʷapʷapʷ]

2. a) [adʷa]   b) [dʷa]   c) [adʷ]   d) [dʷadʷadʷ]

3. a) [akʷa]   b) [kʷa]   c) [akʷ]   d) [kʷakʷakʷ]

4. a) [asʷa]   b) [sʷa]   c) [asʷ]   d) [sʷasʷasʷ]

5. a) [axʷa]   b) [xʷa]   c) [axʷ]   d) [xʷaxʷaxʷ]

Repeat each of the following sentences after the recording, labializing the initial consonant of each word. Remember to release the labialization simultaneously with the primary consonant.

Exercise 33.2: Producing Labialization is Sentences.

1. **pʷeter pʷipʷer pʷicked a pʷeck of pʷickled pʷeppʷers.**

2. **ʒ**ʷany **ʒ**ʷebras **ʒ**ʷip and **ʒ**ʷoom.

3. **k**ʷeen **k**ʷatherine **k**ʷan **k**ʷick a **k**ʷranky **k**ʷing.

Recognizing Labialization

Labialization is characterized by a rounded quality that affects the sound of the primary consonant. Since labialization sounds similar to a vowel glide, it is often easier to recognize labialization by sight than by sound. Practice recognizing labialization in the following exercise. Listen to each pair of utterances, and respond by telling whether they are the same or different.

Exercise 33.3: Recognizing Labialized and Non-labialized Sounds

1. [adʷɑ adʷɑ]	Same	5. [ke kʷe]	Different	9. [otʷɑ otʷɑ]	Same
2. [abɑ abʷɑ]	Different	6. [osʷʌ osʌ]	Different	10. [edi edʷi]	Different
3. [atʷʰɑ atʰɑ]	Different	7. [ɪgʷɑ ɪgʷɑ]	Same	11. [aʃʷɑ aʃʷɑ]	Same
4. [ʌpʷʌ ʌpʷʌ]	Same	8. [ʒʷi ʒʷi]	Same	12. [bʷa ba]	Different

It is important to be able to distinguish between labialization and the labial approximant W [w]. Labialization affects the sound quality of the primary consonant, while in an approximant, more of the labialized sound comes after the consonant. In the following exercise, some of the consonants are labialized while others are followed by approximants or vowel glides. Respond after each pair of utterances by telling whether they are the same or different.

Exercise 33.4: Recognizing Labialization and Vowel Glides

1. [apʷɑ apwɑ]	Different	5. [ʃʷe ʃʷe]	Same	9. [gwʌ gʷʌ]	Different
2. [dʷɑ dʷɑ]	Same	6. [ɑvʷɚ ɑvʷɚ]	Same	10. [tʷi tᵘi]	Different
3. [imwa imʷɑ]	Different	7. [pʷɔ pʰwɔ]	Different	11. [øðʷɑ øðᵘɑ]	Different
4. [ozᵘə ozwe]	Different	8. [eʒʷi eʒʷi]	Same	12. [pʷɑ pʷɑ]	Same

The following exercise contains labialized consonants and non-labialized consonants Respond by telling whether each consonant is labialized or not.

Exercise 33.5: Recognizing Labialization

1. [adʷa] Labialized   5. [gʊ]   No   9.   [eʒʷi] Labialized

2. [ada] No   6. [avʷa] Labialized   10. [ʃwe] No

3. [adwa] No   7. [ty]   No   11. [tʷi] Labialized

4. [ʃʷe] Labialized   8. [mʷa] Labialized   12. [ʒo]   No

Palatalization

Palatalization involves raising the blade of the tongue toward the hard palate during a primary articulation. Palatalization produces the approximant [j] as the secondary sound. The initial "v" in the English word "view" [vʲju] is an example of palatalization. Palatalized sounds are very common in Russian, where they are referred to as soft consonants. Palatalization is symbolized by placing a **Superscript J** [ʲ] after the main consonant symbol.

Nearly any phone can be palatalized, with the exception of certain pharyngeal consonants and palatal consonants since the palatal place of articulation is already engaged.

The following facial diagrams depict [m] with and without palatalization. Notice that for [mʲ] the blade of the tongue is near the hard palate.

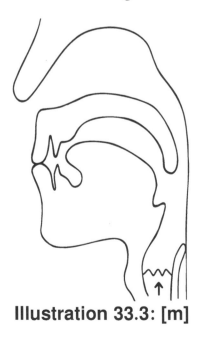

Illustration 33.3: [m]

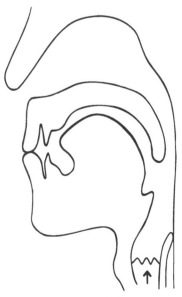

Illustration 33.4: Palatalized [mʲ]

Producing Palatalization

To produce a palatalized sound, form a primary articulation and then raise the blade of the tongue toward the hard palate as for the approximant [j]. Another way to learn to palatalize sounds is to think about saying the vowel [i] at the same time you say the primary consonant.

Practice the palatalized sounds in the following exercise. Repeat each sound after the recording.

Exercise 33.6: Producing Palatalization

1. a) [abⁱɑ]   b) [bⁱɑ]   c) [abⁱ]   d) [bⁱabⁱabⁱ]

2. a) [adⁱɑ]   b) [dⁱɑ]   c) [adⁱ]   d) [dⁱadⁱadⁱ]

3. a) [akⁱɑ]   b) [kⁱɑ]   c) [akⁱ]   d) [kⁱakⁱakⁱ]

4. a) [asⁱɑ]   b) [sⁱɑ]   c) [asⁱ]   d) [sⁱasⁱasⁱ]

5. a) [axⁱɑ]   b) [xⁱɑ]   c) [axⁱ]   d) [xⁱaxⁱaxⁱ]

In the following sentences, practice palatalizing each initial consonant. Repeat each sentence after the recording.

Exercise 33.7: Producing Palatalization is Sentences

1. **pʲ**eter **pʲip**ʲer **pʲ**icked a **pʲ**eck of **pʲ**ickled **pʲepp**ʲers.

2. **zʲ**any **zʲ**ebras **zʲ**ip and **zʲ**oom.

3. **kʲ**een **kʲ**atherine **kʲ**an **kʲ**ick a **kʲ**ranky **kʲ**ing.

Recognizing Palatalization

Palatalization is usually released after the primary consonant. This makes the palatalization sound very similar to an [i] or [ɨ] glide or the approximant [j]. Notice in the word "view" that the glided sound continues after the [v] is released.

The following exercise contains both palatalized and non-palatalized consonants. Practice recognizing palatalized sounds by telling whether each utterance is the same or different.

Exercise 33.8: Recognizing Palatalized and Non-palatalized Sounds

1.	[adʲɑ adʲɑ]	Same	5.	[asʲe ɑse]	Different	9.	[tʲe tʲe]	Same
2.	[ɑdɑ adʲɑ]	Different	6.	[etʲo etʲo]	Same	10.	[akʲɑ akʲɑ]	Same
3.	[kɑ kʲɑ]	Different	7.	[ne nʲe]	Different	11.	[afmʲɛ afmʲɛ]	Same
4.	[afmʲɛ afmʲɛ]	Same	8.	[əpʲɑ əpɑ]	Different	12.	[ɯzɛ ɯzʲɛ]	Different

In the next exercise, practice distinguishing between palatalized consonants and consonants followed by vowel glides or approximants. The vowel glides and approximants will sound more separated from the consonant than the palatalization. Respond by telling whether each pair of words is the same or different.

Exercise 33.9: Recognizing Palatalization and Glides

1.	[adʲo adʲo]	Same	5.	[asʲe asje]	Different	9.	[tʲe tje]	Different
2.	[adʲo adʲo]	Different	6.	[ivʲo ivʲo]	Same	10.	[afmʲɛ afmʲɛ]	Same
3.	[mja mʲa]	Different	7.	[ʔafʲə ʔafʲə]	Same	11.	[nʲɨ nʲɨ]	Same
4.	[osʲɑ osʲɑ]	Same	8.	[dʲœ djœ]	Different	12.	[asje asʲe]	Different

It is important that you learn to distinguish between palatalized sounds, non-palatalized sounds, and consonants followed by vowel glides. Respond after each utterance by telling whether it is palatalized or not.

Exercise 33.10: Recognizing Palatalization

1.	[adʲɑ]	Palatalized	5.	[asʲe]	Palatalized	9.	[əpja]	No
2.	[adʲɑ]	Palatalized	6.	[mjɔ]	No	10.	[dju]	No
3.	[adɑ]	No	7.	[etʲo]	Palatalized	11.	[ɪvʲo]	Palatalized
4.	[ɚdja]	No	8.	[əp'ɑ]	No	12.	[nʲe]	Palatalized

Velarization

For **velarization**, the back of the tongue is raised toward the velum, similar to the articulation of the close back unrounded vowel, Turned M [ɯ]. The Dark l [ɫ] is an English example of velarization because the tip of the tongue touches the alveolar ridge and the back of the tongue approaches the velum. This changes the shape of the oral cavity, modifying the over all sound of the primary consonant. Velarized sounds are common in Russian and are referred to as hard consonants.

The only consonants which can be velarized are those whose articulators are toward the front of the oral cavity. Consonants produced at the velar point of articulation cannot be velarized because the velar point of articulation is already engaged.

Velarization is represented by placing a **Superscript Gamma** [ˠ] after the symbol of the primary consonant, such as [dˠ]. Another method of representation, used most frequently with laterals, is to place a **Middle Tilde** [~] through the main symbol, as in the Dark L [ɫ]. However, the Middle Tilde can indicate either velarization or pharyngealization.

The following facial diagrams illustrate a velarized and a non-velarized [d]. Notice that the velar closure is not close enough to create a fricative.

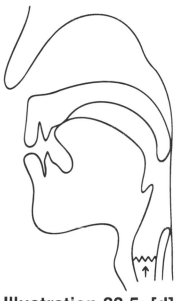

Illustration 33.5: [d]

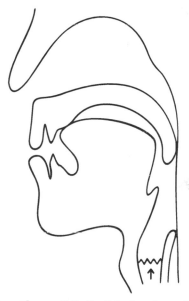

Illustration 33.6: Velarized [dˠ]

Producing Velarization

For velarization, the position of the back of the tongue is similar to that of the vowels U [u] and Turned M [ɯ], as well as that of the labial-velar approximant [w]. One difficulty when learning to velarize sounds is to keep from rounding your lips. Practice keeping your lips unrounded while saying English words that have [w] approximants, such as "twinkle," "swing," and "Dwight."

Practice velarizing consonants in the following exercise. Repeat each utterance after the recording.

Exercise 33.11: Producing Velarization

1. a) [abˠa]   b) [bˠa]   c) [abˠ]   d) [bˠabˠabˠ]

2. a) [adˠa]   b) [dˠa]   c) [adˠ]   d) [dˠadˠadˠ]

3. a) [aɬa]   b) [ɬa]   c) [aɬ]   d) [ɬaɬaɬ]

4. a) [azˠa]   b) [zˠa]   c) [azˠ]   d) [zˠazˠazˠ]

5. a) [anˠa]   b) [nˠa]   c) [anˠ]   d) [nˠanˠanˠ]

Practice velarization in the following sentences. Follow the transcription, and repeat each utterance after the recording.

Exercise 33.12: Producing Velarization in Sentences

1. **pˠeter pˠipˠer pˠicked a pˠeck of pˠickled pˠeppˠers.**

2. **zˠany zˠebras zˠip and zˠoom.**

3. **ɬittɬe ɬouɬou ɬicked ɬots of ɬicorice.**

Recognizing Velarization

Velarization does not involve lip rounding, so it should be fairly easy to distinguish between velarization and approximants and vowel glides. Because velarization is created with the back of the tongue behind the primary articulator (i.e., the tip of the tongue), it will be more difficult to distinguish it from ordinary non-velarized sounds.

The following exercise contains velarized and non-velarized consonants. Listen to each pair of utterances, and respond by telling whether they are the same or different.

Exercise 33.13: Recognizing Velarized and Non-velarized Sounds

1. [atˠa atˠa]	Same	5. [imˠo imˠo]	Same	9. [cˠo.i co.i]	Different
2. [atˠa ata]	Different	6. [ʔɛθi ʔɛθˠi]	Different	10. [ʔotˠe ʔote]	Different
3. [bˠa bˠa]	Same	7. [ɬæ.a læ.a]	Different	11. [sˠa.o sˠa.o]	Same
4. [ɬe le]	Different	8. [aʒˠo aʒˠo]	Same	12. [iʒu iʒˠu]	Different

In the following exercise, respond by telling whether each consonant is velarized or is followed by an approximant. Answer with "velarized" or "approximant."

Exercise 33.14: Recognizing Velarization and Approximants

1. [atˠɑ] Velarized
2. [atwɑ] Approximant
3. [awɑ] Approximant
4. [ʔanˠi] Velarized

5. [bwɑ.æ] Approximant
6. [ɛpˠi] Velarized
7. [ʃˠɔ.ə] Velarized
8. [ʔɛθwi] Approximant

9. [ɬæ.a] Velarized
10. [imˠo] Velarized
11. [oɟwʌ] Approximant
12. [ɟwu.u] Approximant

Labial-Palatalization

As its name suggests, labial-palatalization involves both labialization and palatalization at the same time. For this to occur, the lips must be rounded and the blade of the tongue raised toward the hard palate at the same time that the primary articulated consonant is produced. **Labial-palatalization** is represented by a **Superscript Turned H** [ᶣ] after the main consonant, as in [dᶣ]. As you may remember, the Turned H [ɥ] is a labial-palatal approximant.

Any sound that can be palatalized can also be labial-palatalized. Facial diagrams of labial-palatalized sounds are not included as no new articulator configuration is introduced.

Producing Labial-Palatalization

If you can produce labialization and palatalization separately, it should not be difficult to combine them to produce labial-palatalized sounds. Since the close front rounded vowel [y] involves lip rounding and a slight palatal closure, it may help to think of producing this vowel at the same time as a primary articulation.

Follow the transcription in the following exercise, and repeat each utterance after the recording.

Exercise 33.15: Producing Labial-palatalization

1. a) [apᶣɑ]   b) [pᶣɑ]   c) [apᶣ]   d) [pᶣapᶣapᶣ]
2. a) [adᶣɑ]   b) [dᶣɑ]   c) [adᶣ]   d) [dᶣadᶣadᶣ]
3. a) [akᶣɑ]   b) [kᶣɑ]   c) [akᶣ]   d) [kᶣakᶣakᶣ]
4. a) [asᶣɑ]   b) [sᶣɑ]   c) [asᶣ]   d) [sᶣasᶣasᶣ]
5. a) [axᶣɑ]   b) [xᶣɑ]   c) [axᶣ]   d) [xᶣaxᶣaxᶣ]

Practice labial-palatalizing the first consonant of each word in the following sentences. Repeat each sentence after the recording.

Exercise 33.16: Practicing Secondary Articulation

1. pᶣeter pᶣipᶣer pᶣicked a pᶣeck of pᶣickled pᶣeppᶣers.

2. zᶣany zᶣebras zᶣip and zᶣoom.

3. kᶣeen kᶣatherine kᶣan kᶣick a kᶣranky kᶣing.

Recognizing Labial-Palatalization

Labial-palatalization usually involves a delayed release much like that of palatalization. This gives the secondary articulation a strong glided sound. Labial-palatalization is often characterized by a sound similar to the close front rounded vowel [y].

It can be very easy to confuse labial-palatalization with either palatalization or labialization. The following exercise contains all three secondary articulations. Practice identifying the labial-palatalized sounds. Respond to each pair of utterances by telling whether they are the same or different.

Exercise 33.17: Recognizing Labial-palatalized, Palatalized, and Labialized phones

1.	[adᶣɑ adᶣɑ]	Same	6.	[emᶣɔk emᶣɔk]	Same	11.	[sᶣu.ə? sᶣu.ə?]	Same
2.	[adᶣɑ adʲɑ]	Different	7.	[udʷə udᶣə]	Different	12.	[ɢoʷ.ɑ ɢᶣo.ɑ]	Different
3.	[xᶣɑ xᶣɑ]	Same	8.	[æɟʲ æɟʲ]	Same	13.	[ðᶣæ ðᶣæ]	Same
4.	[pᶣe.o pᶣe.o]	Same	9.	[kᶣi kʲi]	Different	14.	[arʲɛ arᶣɛ]	Different
5.	[ogᶣɑ ogʷɑ]	Different	10.	[nᶣɑ?ɛ nʲɑ?ɛ]	Different	15.	['ɨⁿdᶣʌ 'ɨⁿdʷʌ]	Different

Listen carefully to each word in the following exercise, and determine if each utterance contains a labial-palatalized phone or not.

Exercise 33.18: Recognizing Labial-palatalization

1.	[adɑ]	No	3.	[xᶣɑ]	Labial-palatalized	5. [pᶣã.o] Labial-palatalized
2.	[adᶣɑ]	Labial-palatalized	4.	[upa]	No	6. [ʃɔ.ɔ] No

7.	[ðiʔɛ̰]	No	9.	[kᶣʰɑʔ]	Labial-palatalized	11.	[lᶣo]	Labial-palatalized
8.	[bᶣe]	Labial-palatalized	10.	[xᶣɪʔɪ]	Labial-palatalized	12.	[ʟu.o]	No

Labial-Velarization

Labial-velarization also involves two simultaneous secondary articulations. For this type of secondary articulation, the lips are rounded and the back of the tongue is raised at the velar point. In essence, this manner of secondary articulation simply combines the labialization and velarization introduced earlier in this chapter.

As with velarization, only sounds made toward the front of the mouth can be labial-velarized. All consonants that can be velarized can also be labial-velarized.

As mentioned earlier, labial-velarization is symbolized with a **Superscript W** [ʷ] after the main symbol, such as [kʷ], which is the same as labialization. The reason for this is that it is very unlikely for labial-velarization and labialization to be used contrastively, therefore most linguists do not bother to differentiate between these two types of secondary articulation.

Producing Labial-Velarization

To produce labial-velarization, think of saying the W [w] approximant or a close back rounded vowel U [u] at the same time as a primary articulation. Make sure that your lips are as rounded as they should be for [w] and [u]. Remember to practice labial-velarization with consonants produced toward the front of the oral cavity.

Practice saying the labial-velarized sounds in the following exercise. Repeat each sound after the recording.

Exercise 33.19: Producing Labial-velarization

1. a) [ɑpʷɑ] b) [pʷɑ] c) [ɑpʷ] d) [pʷɑpʷɑpʷ]
2. a) [ɑdʷɑ] b) [dʷɑ] c) [ɑdʷ] d) [dʷɑdʷɑdʷ]
3. a) [ɑlʷɑ] b) [lʷɑ] c) [ɑlʷ] d) [lʷɑlʷɑlʷ]
4. a) [ɑzʷɑ] b) [zʷɑ] c) [ɑzʷ] d) [zʷɑzʷɑzʷ]
5. a) [ɑnʷɑ] b) [nʷɑ] c) [ɑnʷ] d) [nʷɑnʷɑnʷ]

Recognizing Labial-Velarization

Labial-velarization can be distinguished from labialization by a more restricted quality. Although the difference may be slight, it is important to be aware of the condition that is occurring and be able to imitate it well.

Practice identifying the labial-velarization in the following exercise. This exercise contains labial-velarization and labialization. Respond to each pair of utterances by telling whether they are the same or different.

Exercise 33.20: Recognizing Labial-velarized and Labialized Sounds

1. [ɑnɑ ɑnʷɑ]   Different   5. [ʒʷi ʒʷi]   Same   9. [ʃʷe ʃʷe]   Same

2. [ɑzʷɑ ɑzʷɑ]   Same   6. [ðʷo.u ðʷo.u]   Same   10. [aβʷo aβʷo]   Same

3. [osʷʌ osʷʌ]   Same   7. [ɔvʷa ɔva]   Different   11. [fɑʔ fʷɑʔ]   Different

4. [ɑʒi ɑʒʷi]   Different   8. [tʷiʀ tʷiʀ]   Same   12. [ɔmʷɑ ɔmɑ]   Different

Determine whether each utterance in the following exercise contains a labial-velarized phone or not.

Exercise 33.21: Recognizing Labial-velarization

1. [osʷʌ] Labial-velarized   5. [oɫʊ] No   9. [taʀ] No

2. [ɑzʷɑ] Labial-velarized   6. [sʲa.e] No   10. [fʷaʔ] Labial-velarized

3. [ɑzɑᵊ] No   7. [osʷʌ] Labial-velarized   11. [kemf] No

4. [aβʷo] Labial-velarized   8. [ʒʷɪx] Labial-velarized   12. [zʷɪʔi] Labial-velarized

Pharyngealization

Pharyngealization involves retracting the root of the tongue toward the back of the throat, as for a pharyngeal approximant. This manner of secondary articulation is very similar to velarization, except that it occurs farther back in the vocal tract.

Pharyngealization is symbolized by placing a **Superscript Reverse Glottal Stop** [ˤ] after the base consonant symbol, for example [dˤ]. The **Reverse Glottal Stop** [ʕ] is a pharyngeal fricative. The following facial diagrams illustrate the articulation of a non-pharyngealized [d] and pharyngealized [dˤ].

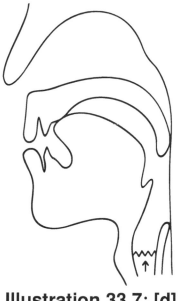

Illustration 33.7: [d]

**Illustration 33.8:
Pharyngealized [dˤ]**

Producing Pharyngealization

The position of the tongue for pharyngealization is very similar to retracted tongue root placement. The root of the tongue is close enough to the back wall of the pharynx to restrict the air stream, but not close enough to create much friction. When producing pharyngealization, it may be helpful to think of choking yourself with your tongue while pronouncing the primary articulation.

Practice the pharyngealized sounds in the following exercise. Repeat each utterance after the recording.

Exercise 33.22: Producing Pharyngealization

1. a) [abˤɑ]   b) [bˤɑ]   c) [abˤ]   d) [bˤabˤabˤ]

2. a) [adˤɑ]   b) [dˤɑ]   c) [adˤ]   d) [dˤadˤadˤ]

3. a) [alˤɑ]   b) [lˤɑ]   c) [alˤ]   d) [lˤalˤalˤ]

4. a) [anˤɑ]   b) [nˤɑ]   c) [anˤ]   d) [nˤanˤanˤ]

5. a) [azˤɑ]   b) [zˤɑ]   c) [azˤ]   d) [zˤazˤazˤ]

Recognizing Pharyngealization

Pharyngealization is characterized by a quality similar to that of retracted tongue root. When the pharyngealization is released after the primary articulation, a slight glided sound will be present.

The following exercise contains pairs of pharyngealized and non-pharyngealized consonants. Respond after each pair of words by telling whether they are the same of different.

Exercise 33.23: Recognizing Pharyngealized and Non-pharyngealized Phones

1. [adˤa adˤa] Same
2. [adˤa ada] Different
3. [za zˤa] Different
4. [unˤʌ unˤʌ] Same

5. [erɛ erˤɛ] Different
6. [aʒˤa aʒˤa] Same
7. [ivˤə ivˤə] Same
8. [ətˤʌ ətˤʌ] Same

9. [aβˤa aβa] Different
10. [zˤe zˤe] Same
11. [ʃa ʃˤa] Different
12. [dˤa da] Different

In the following exercise, determine whether the consonants are pharyngealized or not.

Exercise 33.24: Recognizing Pharyngealization

1. [adˤa] Pharyngealized
2. [ada] No
3. [aʃˤa] Pharyngealized
4. [atˤa] Pharyngealized

5. [ata] No
6. [erˤɛ] Pharyngealized
7. [eɠo] No
8. [alˤa] Pharyngealized

9. [unˤʌ] Pharyngealized
10. [fˤo] Pharyngealized
11. [oda] No
12. [qeʲ] No

The following exercise contains all of the secondary articulations introduced in this lesson. Respond by naming the type of secondary articulation applied to each consonant.

Exercise 33.25: Recognizing Secondary Articulations

1. [atʷa] Labialized
2. [aɫa] Velarized
3. [atᶶa] Labial-palatalized
4. [adʲa] Palatalized

5. [aʃˤa] Pharyngealized
6. [aʒˠa] Velarized
7. [anʷa] Labial-velarized
8. [amʲa] Palatalized

9. [apᶶa] Labial-palatalized
10. [akʷa] Labialized
11. [afˤa] Pharyngealized
12. [abʲa] Palatalized

Table 33.2 gives a summary of the sounds and symbols introduced in this lesson.

Table 33.2: Secondary Articulations Summary

IPA Symbol	Name	Technical Name	English Example	APA Symbol
ʷ	Superscript W	Labial Secondary Articulation or Labial-velar Secondary Articulation	**qu**ick	
ʲ	Superscript J	Palatal Secondary Articulation	**v**iew	
ˠ	Superscript Gamma	Velar Secondary Articulation		
ᶣ	Superscript Turned H	Palatal-velar Secondary Articulation		
ˤ	Superscript Reversed Glottal Stop	Pharyngeal Secondary Articulation		

Lesson 34:
Fortis and Lenis Articulation

Lesson Outline

Glossary Terms

Fortis and lenis articulation involves the intensity of articulation, or the amount of articulatory strength applied to an individual consonant. This distinction does not involve a new manner of articulation, but rather added conditions that can be applied to any of the consonants already studied in this course.

Fortis and Lenis Articulation

The distinction between fortis and lenis articulation is a combination of several articulatory conditions such as tenseness of the articulators, varied air pressure, length, varied degrees of voicing, and length of aspiration. Depending on the language and the phonetic environment, there are often variations in exactly which of these conditions determine the difference between fortis and lenis consonants.

In English, voiced stops are more often lenis while voiceless stops tend to be fortis. This difference can be heard when the words "fan" and "van" are whispered in a sequence. Although the whispered state of the glottis eliminates all voicing, the "f" and "v" are still distinguishable. Although many phonological factors are involved, the fortis/lenis condition of these sounds help make this distinction possible.

Symbolizing Fortis and Lenis

Neither fortis nor lenis are normally symbolized in written transcription. This is because there is no single phonological element that defines fortis or lenis. Rather, it is the general impression to the hearer that a sound is stronger (fortis) or weaker (lenis). Although the IPA has no dedicated symbol which represents fortis and lenis, the IPA extension symbol for strong articulation **Double Vertical Lines** [„] is often placed below or above a symbol to indicate fortis (for example, [t̬] or [g̈]).[1] The APA lenis diacritic, **Scribble** [ ], is still in common use among linguists today, and can be placed above or below a consonant to indicate lenis articulation (for example, [ŋ̞] or [ç̑]). Occasionally, the IPA extension diacritic for weak articulation **Corner Below** [ˏ] is also used to for lenis, such as [t̡].

Alternatively, fortis and lenis are contrasted by lengthening or doubling a phonetic symbol. For example, [pː sː nː] or [pp ss nn] could represent fortis articulation and [p s n] could represent lenis in this case. It is also common to use the voiceless diacritics with voiced symbols to indicate lenis articulation. For example, if fortis articulation were transcribed as [p k s], lenis articulation would be [b̥ g̊ z̥]. However, this notation is identical to slack voice notation and, therefore, could be confusing.

---

1 The Double Vertical Lines [„] diacritic is also used to indicate faucalized supra-glottal phonation.

Producing Fortis and Lenis Consonants

Fortis articulation is produced when the the organs of the speech tract move with greater energy or force than usual. It also involves an increased build-up of air pressure behind the articulators, which can produce the various articulatory conditions that were mentioned above. In producing fortis consonants, try to make the entire articulation more tensed than normal without relying on a single phonetic feature such as voicing or aspiration to create the distinction.

Lenis articulation is produced in just the opposite way of fortis articulation. The muscles of the speech tract operate with somewhat lesser force, producing a condition in which a consonant is perceived as being softer or less forceful. Try to make the articulatory organ softer or more fluid to create this distinction. Again, do not rely simply on voicing or aspiration to constitute lenis articulation.

In some languages, such as Korean, the difference between fortis and lenis articulation is just as important as the difference between voicing and voicelessness. Korean contrasts three different types of voiceless stops which include fortis, lenis, and aspirated. The Korean words "daughter" [t̰al], "moon" [t̤al], and "mask" [tʰal] are examples of contrastive fortis and lenis articulation.[2]

Practice producing fortis consonants in the following exercise. Repeat each utterance after the recording.

Exercise 34.1: Producing Fortis Consonants

1. a) [pa]	b) [p̈a]	c) ['pa.p̈a]	d) ['p̈a.pap̈]
2. a) [ba]	b) [b̰a]	c) ['ba.b̰a]	d) ['b̰a.bab̰]
3. a) [ka]	b) [k̰a]	c) ['ka.k̰a]	d) ['k̰a.kak̰]
4. a) [ga]	b) [g̈a]	c) ['ga.g̈a]	d) ['g̈a.gag̈]
5. a) [sa]	b) [ṣa]	c) ['sa.ṣa]	d) ['ṣa.saṣ]
6. a) [za]	b) [z̰a]	c) ['za.z̰a]	d) ['z̰a.zaz̰]
7. a) [la]	b) [l̰a]	c) ['la.l̰a]	d) ['l̰a.lal̰]
8. a) [na]	b) [n̰a]	c) ['na.n̰a]	d) ['n̰a.nan̰]

---

2 As mentioned above, "fortis" and "lenis" are general terms which describe the impression of the listener. More precise terms, such as "stiff voice" and "slack voice" are usually used to define such differences. The terms "fortis" and "lenis" are rarely used by linguists today.

Practice producing lenis consonants in the following exercise. Repeat each utterance after the recording.

Exercise 34.2: Producing Lenis Consonants

1. a) [pɑ]   b) [p̬ɑ]   c) [ˈpɑ.p̬ɑ]   d) [ˈp̬ɑ.pɑp̬]

2. a) [bɑ]   b) [b̥ɑ]   c) [ˈbɑ.b̥ɑ]   d) [ˈb̥ɑ.bɑb̥]

3. a) [kɑ]   b) [k̬ɑ]   c) [ˈkɑ.k̬ɑ]   d) [ˈk̬ɑ.kɑk̬]

4. a) [gɑ]   b) [g̥ɑ]   c) [ˈgɑ.g̥ɑ]   d) [ˈg̥ɑ.gɑg̥]

5. a) [sɑ]   b) [s̬ɑ]   c) [ˈsɑ.s̬ɑ]   d) [ˈs̬ɑ.sɑs̬]

6. a) [zɑ]   b) [z̥ɑ]   c) [ˈzɑ.z̥ɑ]   d) [ˈz̥ɑ.zɑz̥]

7. a) [lɑ]   b) [l̥ɑ]   c) [ˈlɑ.l̥ɑ]   d) [ˈl̥ɑ.lɑl̥]

8. a) [nɑ]   b) [n̥ɑ]   c) [ˈnɑ.n̥ɑ]   d) [ˈn̥ɑ.nɑn̥]

Recognizing Fortis and Lenis Consonants

The acoustic differences between fortis and lenis consonants can be very subtle. When learning to identify fortis and lenis consonants, keep in mind that this distinction is not determined solely by aspiration or voicing, although variations of both of these conditions may function as contributors.

Fortis consonants are recognized by more forceful articulator movement and air stream expulsion, while lenis consonants are just the opposite. The pairs of words in the following exercise contrast fortis and lenis consonants. Listen carefully to each pair, and respond by telling whether they are the same or different.

Exercise 34.3: Recognizing Fortis and Lenis Articulation

1. [ap̈ɑ ap̈ɑ]   Same   6. [k̥ouʊ k̥ou]   Different   11. [ig̈e ig̈e]   Same

2. [ap̈ɑ ap̈ɑ]   Different   7. [ɔg̈o ɔg̈o]   Different   12. [aд̈ɑ aд̈ɑ]   Different

3. [ʌd̈ɑ ʌd̈ɑ]   Different   8. [n̈øɴ n̈øɴ]   Same   13. [d̈uwa d̈uwɑ] Same

4. [as̈ɛ as̈ɛ]   Different   9. [ʈal ʈal]   Different   14. [ræñ ræñ]   Same

5. [ad̈ɑ ad̈ɑ]   Same   10. [əβ̈ɛ əβ̈ɛ]   Same   15. [ʈɪl ʈɪl]   Different

16. [ɓʷʊf ɓʷʊf] Same   18. [k̬ʰæʔ k̬ʰæʔ] Different   20. [op̈eʔ op̈eʔ] Different

17. [ʂɚ ʂ̈ɚ] Different   19. [t̬ʰɨv t̬ʰɨv] Same   21. [t̬ʰʊp˥ t̬ʰʊp˥] Different

In the following exercise, tell whether the consonants that you hear are fortis or lenis.

Exercise 34.4: Recognizing Fortis and Lenis Consonants

1. [ak̬ɑ] Fortis

2. [ak̬ɑ] Lenis

3. [d̥ʊ.əᵘ] Lenis

4. [ɛʒ̈æ] Fortis

5. [ig̈ʌ] Fortis

6. [ɓo̥ᵊ] Fortis

7. [dˠaʔ] Lenis

8. [ʌm̥œ] Forits

9. [at̬ʼɑ] Fortis

10. [uk̬ʼo.u] Lenis

11. [p̌aⁱ] Lenis

12. [ʔuɟ̈o] Fortis

13. [ʔɛ̬d̥o] Lenis

14. [t̬ᵘʰwɑʔ] Fortis

15. [ʟ̈ɹ.e] Fortis

Lesson 35: Clicks

Lesson Outline

Glossary Terms

Clicks are speech sounds produced with a lingual ingressive air stream. **Lingual ingressive air** is set in motion by the tongue and moves inward. Clicks are the only sounds produced with lingual ingressive air.

Table 35.1 lists the symbols for all the clicks found in the languages of the world. Not all of these symbols have been officially added to the IPA, but they are listed here for completeness. Only the most common clicks will be studied in detail.

Table 35.1: Clicks

	Bilabial	Dental	Alveolar	Retroflexed	Palatal
Central	⊙	|	!¹	ʮ²	ǂ
Lateral		|||	||		ǂǂ
Flapped			!¡		

To produce the lingual ingressive air stream necessary for clicks, the back of the tongue raises to form a complete closure at either the velar or uvular point of articulation. Simultaneously, another stop is formed toward the front of the oral cavity by the tip of the tongue or the lips. This forms a double stop, but rather than both articulations being released at once, the body of the tongue is lowered or retracted, forming a partial vacuum between the two closures. When the articulator in the front of the oral cavity is released, air rushes into the mouth to fill the vacuum. This sudden burst of inward air creates the distinctive "click" sound.

The closure at the back of the oral cavity is usually closer to the uvular point of articulation than the velar point. This closure can also be produced with an open velic, resulting in nasal clicks. The consonant articulated more toward the front of the oral cavity may be released either with a central release or a lateral release, making lateral clicks possible as well. Although clicks could be pronounced at any point in a word, they are only found at the beginning of syllables.

Clicks are contrastive within the alphabets of many languages of southern and eastern Africa. In the Khoisan and Bantu language families, clicks are particularly prevalent. The !Xóõ language, for example, has fifty click phonemes. Nearly seventy percent of the words in the dictionary of this language begin with a click.

---

1 The Exclamation Point [!] represents both alveolar and alveopalatal click phones because they are not contrastive in any language. Also, some phoneticians use a Stretched C [Ɔ] to represent this phoneme.

2 The Double Exclamation Point [!!] is also used to symbolize a retroflexed click.

Clicks occur occasionally in English, although not as a part of normal words. Their use in English is usually restricted to special expressions such as a show of pity (written as "tsk, tsk") or the noise sometimes used to get a horse to quicken its pace (often spelled "tchlick").

The IPA symbols given in Table 35.1 above are voiceless. Voiced clicks are symbolized by adding a voiced symbol before the click symbol, for example [g!] or [ɢǁ]. The two symbols can be linked together with a Tie Bar, for example [g͡!]. Clicks can also be nasalized. This is represented by adding the appropriate nasal symbol before the click, such as [ŋʘ] or [ŋ̊ʘ]. Clicks can have many other phonetic features, such as aspiration [kǁʰ], breathy voice [gǂʱ], or an ejective quality [q|']. Some of these features are even occasionally combined together. For example, a click phoneme found in the !Xóõ language contains ingressive nasal air flow and aspiration, transcribed as [↓ŋ̊ʘʰ]. Clicks can also be released into fricatives, such as [ǂx].

Any click from the chart above can be either voiced or voiceless. For voiced clicks, a combination of lingual ingressive and pulmonic egressive air is used. As the click is articulated, enough pulmonic air is allowed to pass through the vocal cords to produce voicing. This air builds up behind the velar closure and is released after the release of the click. For voiceless clicks, the lingual air stream is the only air in motion. Any of the voiceless clicks presented can also be aspirated.

The following facial diagrams illustrate the articulation of voiced and voiceless alveolar clicks. Notice the small arrow indicating the backward movement of the tongue. Also notice that for the voiceless click there is no arrow below the glottis.

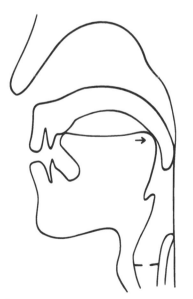 

Illustration 35.1: Voiceless Click   **Illustration 35.2: Voiced Click**

Producing Clicks

Most of the clicks presented in this lesson are rather simple to produce. A bilabial click, for example, is nothing more than a kiss, while the dental click [|] is quite similar to the expression "tsk, tsk, tsk."

The action of the tongue that produces the inward air stream for clicks may be thought of as a sucking action similar to that of a baby sucking a bottle. If this action is imitated while saying [t], the result will be the alveolar click [!]. Once the proper tongue action is achieved, it is a simple matter to change the point of articulation to pronounce any of the clicks on the chart above.

The clicks that will be studied below are the most common clicks in spoken languages. These clicks are the bilabial click (symbolized by a **Bull's Eye** [☉]), the dental click (called **Pipe** [|]), the alveolar or alveopalatal click (represented by an **Exclamation Point** [!]), the palatal or palatalalveolar click (called **Double-barred Pipe** [ǂ]), and the alveolar lateral click (symbolized by a **Double Pipe** [‖]).

Voiceless clicks are the easiest to learn to produce. The following exercise contains only voiceless clicks from the chart above. Follow the transcription, and repeat each utterance after the recording.

Exercise 35.1: Producing Voiceless Clicks

16. a) [☉ɑ]   b) [ɑ☉ɑ]   c) [aŋ̊☉ɑ]   d) [ɑ☉xɑ]

17. a) [|ɑ]   b) [ɑ|ɑ]   c) [aŋ̊|ɑ]   d) [ɑ|xɑ]

18. a) [!ɑ]   b) [ɑ!ɑ]   c) [aŋ̊!ɑ]   d) [ɑ!xɑ]

19. a) [ǂɑ]   b) [ɑǂɑ]   c) [aŋ̊ǂɑ]   d) [ɑǂxɑ]

20. a) [‖ɑ]   b) [ɑ‖ɑ]   c) [aŋ̊‖ɑ]   d) [ɑ‖xɑ]

Once the proper articulation for voiceless clicks is learned, it is only a matter of practice to add the voicing and produce the voiced counterpart of any of the clicks introduced. The following exercise contains voiced clicks at the same points of articulation as the clicks practiced above. Follow the transcription, and repeat each utterance after the recording.

Exercise 35.2: Producing Voiced Clicks

21. a) [g☉ɑ]   b) [ɑg☉ɑ]   c) [aŋ☉ɑ]   d) [ɑg☉xɑ]

22. a) [g|ɑ]   b) [ɑg|ɑ]   c) [aŋ|ɑ]   d) [ɑg|xɑ]

23. a) [g!ɑ]   b) [ag!ɑ]   c) [aŋ!ɑ]   d) [ag!xɑ]

24. a) [g‡ɑ]   b) [ag‡ɑ]   c) [aŋ‡ɑ]   d) [ag‡xɑ]

25. a) [g‖ɑ]   b) [ag‖ɑ]   c) [aŋ‖ɑ]   d) [ag‖xɑ]

Recognizing Clicks

Clicks are distinctly characterized by a sharp popping sound created by the inward rush of air at their release. Each click has a different type of pop based on the shape of the tongue and the size of the cavity between the first and second closure. Alveolar and retro-flexed clicks sound similar to a cork being pulled from an empty bottle. Some languages may employ a speech style that lessens the sharpness of clicks.

Distinguishing clicks from other manners of articulation is not usually difficult. Distinguishing one click from another, however, may take some practice. The following exercise contains voiced and voiceless clicks. Respond by telling whether the pairs of clicks are the same or different.

Exercise 35.3: Recognizing Voicing with Clicks

26. [aŋ! aŋ!]   Same   29. [‖ɑ ‖ɑ]   Same   32. [taʘa taʘa]   Same

27. [a‡a ag‡a]   Different   30. [sag!a sa!a]   Different   33. [a!xa ag!xa]   Different

28. [aʘha aʘha]   Same   31. [‖ap ‖ap]   Same   34. [g‡ɑ? ‡ɑ?]   Different

In the following exercise, respond by telling whether each click is voiced or voiceless.

Exercise 35.4: Recognizing Voiced and Voiceless Clicks

35. [aŋ!]   Voiceless   39. [ʔog‖a]   Voiced   43. [ɛɢ!e]   Voiced

36. [ag!a]   Voiced   40. [i‡ɛ]   Voiceless   44. [‡oʔ]   Voiceless

37. [aŋʘa]   Voiced   41. [ŋ̊ʘap]   Voiceless   45. [g‡a]   Voiced

38. [‖i]   Voiceless   42. [ʔa‖u]   Voiceless   46. [ugʘʌ]   Voiced

The following exercise contains clicks at the bilabial, dental, alveolar, and alveopalatal, points of articulation. Respond by giving the point of articulation for the click that you hear, as well as telling if the click is retroflexed or lateral.

Exercise 35.5: Recognizing Clicks

47. [ɑ!ɑ]   Alveolar   52. [ɑʘɑ]   Bilabial   57. [k|ʰɑ]   Dental

48. [ʘɑ]   Bilabial   53. [ɪ|i]   Dental   58. [!ɑⁱ]   Alveolar

49. [ɑǂɑ]   Alveopalatal   54. [ɑ!ɚ]   Alveolar   59. [ɑŋǂɑ]   Alveopalatal

50. [‖ɑ]   Alveolar Lateral 55. [ɑɢʘɑ] Bilabial   60. [‖ɯ]   Alveolar Lateral

51. [ɡ!ʰɑ]   Alveolar   56. [ɑǂɑ]   Alveopalatal   61. [ɑʘɑ]   Bilabial

The following table summarizes the sounds and symbols introduced in this lesson.

Table 35.2: Clicks Summary

IPA Symbol	Name	Technical Name	English Example	APA Symbol
ʘ	Bull's Eye	Voiceless Bilabial Click		p←
|	Pipe	Voiceless Dental Click	*tsk*	t←
‖‖	Triple Pipe	Voiceless Dental Lateral Click		
!, C	Exclamation Point, Stretched C	Voiceless Alveolar/Alveopalatal Click		t̃←
!i	Exclamation Point-Inverted Exclamation Point Digraph	Voiceless Alveolar Flapped Click		t̆←
˞, !!	Rhotacized Exclamation Point, Double Exclamation Point	Voiceless Retroflexed Click		
‖	Double Pipe	Voiceless Alveolar Lateral Click	*tchlick*	tʟ←

IPA Symbol	Name	Technical Name	English Example	APA Symbol
ǂ	Double-barred Pipe	Voiceless Palatoalveolar Click		t̼←
ǂǂ	Double Double-barred Pipe	Voiceless Lateral Palatalveloar Click		k̥ɬ←

Lesson 36:
Speech Styles

Lesson Outline

Glossary Terms

In order to speak a language with a good accent, all of the phonetic segments and variations which we have studied throughout this course must be carefully noted and applied. Recognizing and reproducing the individual segments of a language, however, is not enough to perfect a native-like accent. Each language is spoken with its own distinctive style which is applied to speech as a whole and affects the sound of every phonetic segment in an utterance. The articulatory variations which create these styles are called **speech styles**.

Speech styles are determined by the position and range of motion of the articulatory organs as well as other variables such as volume, timing, glottal activity, and pitch modulation. Most of these conditions and the symbolization for each have already been introduced as applying to individual segments. As speech styles, however, they are used on a broader spectrum, shading or coloring one's entire speech. In some languages, for example, a speaker may always have slightly rounded lips, or may always speak with fronted or backed tongue. In another language, all of the sounds may be slightly retroflexed. While making no difference in the meaning of words, these variations are very important for a good over-all accent.

A language can employ more than one speech style at the same time. A rounded lip style, for example, can occur together with breathiness, set jaw, or any speech style other than one involving the lips.

Speech styles may be dictated by languages, dialects, speakers, moods, and social environments. It is important to be aware of when speech styles are used to reflect the mood or social situation of a speaker rather than as a characteristic of the language as a whole.

Once it has been determined that a certain speech style exists in a language, it is not necessary to continue notations of the articulatory characteristic involved. However, it is important to note speech styles and cite the situations where they are used.

The following list gives a short description of several possible articulatory conditions that constitute common speech styles. This list is not exhaustive, however. Keep in mind that nearly any condition that can accompany vowels and consonants can be used as a speech style.

Position of the Tongue

Several speech styles can be created by the body of the tongue being placed either forward or backward from its normal position while speaking. This subsequently causes all of the consonants and vowels to be slightly more fronted or backed than what is considered normal.

There are three main tongue positions that can be used as speech styles. These are **fronted tongue style**, **backed tongue style**, and **retroflexed tongue style**.

Fronted tongue style involves speech produced with the body of the tongue held farther forward than normal, while backed tongue style is just the opposite, with the tongue being held farther toward the back of the throat. Retroflexed tongue style occurs when the tip of the tongue remains slightly curled during normal speech. This results in each of the consonants and vowels of the utterance having a retroflexed quality.

Practice producing the following sentences with each of the speech styles listed above. Read the sentences first with fronted tongue style, then with backed tongue style, and finally with retroflexed tongue style. Repeat each utterance after the recording.

Exercise 36.1: Producing Fronted, Backed, and Retroflexed Tongue Style

1. Laugh while you can because it will be just as funny when you learn my language.

2. The more you mimic the more you learn.

3. Although it takes a while, you have to learn the style to make the native smile.

Position of the Lips

Another condition that affects speech is the shape of the lips. The lips may be either spread, rounded, or squared. The spread and rounded lip configurations have already been introduced.

The **spread lip style** is created when the lips are relatively flat and do not protrude at all. This lip configuration is called unrounded when referring to vowels. Smiling when speaking may help you produce this speech style.

The shape of the lips for **rounded lip style** corresponds directly to that of rounded vowels. This speech style causes most of the consonants and even vowels which are normally unrounded to have a measure of lip rounding.

The lips often take on a squared shape as extra tightness causes them to protrude farther than for normal lip rounding. This is called **squared lip style**.

Practice the spread, rounded, and squared lip speech styles with the following sentences. Follow the transcription and repeat each sentence after the recording.

Exercise 36.2: Producing Spread, Rounded, and Squared Lip Style

1. Laugh while you can because it will be just as funny when you learn my language.

2. The more you mimic the more you learn.

3.   Although it takes a while, you have to learn the style to make the native smile.

Position of the Jaw

Languages also differ in the range of motion permitted to the jaw. If the jaw is allowed to open freely with each articulation, the sounds will have an over all open quality. If the jaw is limited in its vertical range of motion, the sounds of the language will have a restricted quality. This condition may even cause vowel possibilities to be restricted to those with close tongue position.

There are two different speech styles based on jaw movement. These are termed **free jaw style** and **set jaw style**. For free jaw style, the jaw is allowed a wide range of motion for articulation. For set jaw style, the movement of the jaw is restricted to a very narrow range of motion.

Practice saying the following sentences, first with free jaw style and then with set jaw.

Exercise 36.3: Producing Free and Set Jaw Style

1.   Laugh while you can because it will be just as funny when you learn my language.

2.   The more you mimic the more you learn.

3.   Although it takes a while, you have to learn the style to make the native smile.

State of the Glottis

The states of the glottis were introduced in Lesson 28. Each of the glottal states except whispered can be found contrastively in languages throughout the world. More often, however, glottalic states are used as speech styles. In English, for example, breathy voice is often used for telling spooky stories, while creaky voice is used as a speech style when one is tired or physically strained.

Breathy voice, **creaky voice**, and **whisper** are all states of the glottis that are often used as speech styles. The articulatory conditions that produce these styles have already been discussed.

Practice saying the following sentences with breathy voice, creaky voice, and whisper. Follow the transcription and repeat each sound after the recording.

Exercise 36.4: Producing Breathy, Creaky, and Whispered Style

1. Laugh while you can because it will be just as funny when you learn my language.

2. The more you mimic the more you learn.

3. Although it takes a while, you have to learn the style to make the native smile.

Position of the Velic

The normal position of the velic can vary from one language to another. In some languages, the velic is held in a closed position for all but nasal consonants. Other languages tend to let the velic remain partly open more often than what may be considered normal, giving more of the vowels and consonants a nasalized quality.

The speech styles which result from the positions of the velic are called **nasalized style** and **non-nasalized style**. A language with non-nasalized style may have virtually no nasalized vowels and fewer nasal consonants than most other languages. In languages with nasalized style, the number of nasalized vowels and nasal consonants will be greater than average.

Read the following sentences first with nasalized style and then with non-nasalized style.

Exercise 36.5: Producing Nasalized and Non-nasalized Style

1. Laugh while you can because it will be just as funny when you learn my language.

2. The more you mimic the more you learn.

3. Although it takes a while, you have to learn the style to make the native smile.

Speed

Languages may differ in the speed with which they are spoken. Some languages are characterized by a slow, methodical style. This is called **slow speech style**. Other languages tend to be spoken more quickly. This is called **rapid speech style**. The speed with which a language is spoken can have a strong effect on other phonetic features as well, such as vowel reduction and syllable timing.

Practice varying your speed by reading the following sentences, first with slow speech style and then with rapid speech style.

Exercise 36.6: Producing Slow and Rapid Style

1. Laugh while you can because it will be just as funny when you learn my language.

2. The more you mimic the more you learn.

3. Although it takes a while, you have to learn the style to make the native smile.

Pitch Variation

The relative pitch patterns of a language, whether tonal or intonational, may vary in the distance permitted between pitch levels. In some languages, the pitch may be restricted to a narrow range of modulation while in others a broad range is permitted. These conditions are called **wide range style** and **narrow range style**.

Another form of pitch modulation is monotone, in which little or no pitch variation occurs at all throughout an entire phrase. This is called **monotone style**. Truly monotone speech is actually quite rare, however.

In the following exercise, practice using each of the speech style described above. Repeat each sentences after the recording.

Exercise 36.7: Producing Wide Range, Narrow Range, and Monotone Style

1. Laugh while you can because it will be just as funny when you learn my language.

2. The more you mimic the more you learn.

3. Although it takes a while, you have to learn the style to make the native smile.

Volume

How loudly or softly a person speaks can also affect the sound of a language as a whole. Some languages will always be spoken relatively quietly while others may sound more loud than normal. This is called **soft speech style** and **loud speech style**.

Differences in the volume of a language may be a characteristic of the language as a whole, or can be affected by such factors as age, sex, or social status.

Correctly mimicking the natural volume of a language is very important. Speaking loudly when a language should have soft speech style may make native listeners feel threatened or uncomfortable. Likewise, in a language with loud speech style, quiet speech may come across as an indication of weak character or of even seductive intent.

Practice controlling your volume by reading the following sentences, first with loud speech style and then with soft speech. Repeat each utterance after the recording.

Exercise 36.8: Producing Loud and Soft Style

1. Laugh while you can because it will be just as funny when you learn my language.

2. The more you mimic the more you learn.

3. Although it takes a while, you have to learn the style to make the native smile.

Appendix

Glossary

Advanced tongue root
n. The position of the tongue root considered farther forward than normal during the pronunciation of a vowel

Affricate
n. Consonant cluster consisting of a stop followed by a fricative
See Tie Bar.

Air stream
n. A stream of air set in motion to produce a speech sound

Air stream mechanism
n. The physiological structure involved in creating air flow

Alveolar
adj. Adjective form of the point of articulation alveolar ridge

Alveolar ridge
n. The ridge behind the upper teeth

Alveolar trill
n. Sound in which the tip of the tongue touches the alveolar ridge more than once in a rapid sequence

Alveolo-palatal
adj. The description of a phone articulated with the blade of the tongue at the alveopalatal region and touching the hard palate simultaneously
See Curly-tail C [ɕ] and Curly-tail Z [ʑ].

Alveopalatal
adj. Adjective form of the point of articulation alveopalatal region [depreciated]
See postalveolar.

Alveopalatal region
n. The area of the roof of the mouth located between the alveolar ridge and the hard palate

Apical
adj. A phone articulated primarily with the tip of the tongue, optionally symbolized with an Inverted Bridge [̺]

Apostrophe [']
n. Diacritic used to denote ejective sounds

Approximant
n. Manner of articulation involving less friction than fricatives but more than vowels

Articulator
n. Movable part(s) of the speech apparatus which are raised to meet the points of articulation

Articulatory phonetics
n. The study of how the interaction of different human physiological structures produce speech sounds

Ash [æ]
n. Near-open front unrounded vowel

Aspirated release
n. A type of consonant release involving aspiration

Aspiration
n. A burst of air accompanying the release of a stop or the closure of some obstruents

Back
n. The articulator directly behind the mid used as active articulator in back velar sounds and for the articulation of some vowels
adj., n. The position of a vowel when articulated with the back part of the tongue

Backed tongue style
n. Speech style in which the body of the tongue is farther back than normal

Barred I [ɨ]
n. Close central unrounded vowel

Belted L [ɬ]
n. Voiceless tip-alveolar lateral fricative

Beta [β]
n. Voiced Bilabial fricative

Bilabial approximant [β̞]
n. Approximant produced at the bilabial pint of articulation
See Approximant.

Bilabial trill
n. Trill produced at the bilabial point of articulation
See Trill.

Blade
n. The active articulator behind the tip used for blade alveopalatal sounds and for the articulation of some vowels; interacts with the alveolar ridge and palate
See Laminal.

Breathy
adj. Used to describe sound produced with breathy voice
See Breathy Voice.

Breathy voice
n. State of the glottis in which there is more tension applied to the vocal cords than for voicelessness, but not as much as for Modal Voice; enough tension applied to the vocal cords to produce minimal voicing
See Murmured.

Breve [˘]
n. Superscript diacritic used to indicate that a sound is shorter than normal

Bridge [̪]
n. Subscript diacritic used to denote fronting

Bull's Eye [⊙]
n. Voiceless Bilabial click

C Cedilla [ç]
n. Voiceless palatal fricative

Cavity
n. Areas or chambers in the vocal apparatus which determine the resonant quality of speech sounds

Central
adj., n. The position of a vowel when articulated with the mid section of the tongue

Central approximant
n. Approximant produced with the air flow directed over the center of the tongue
See Approximant.

Central oral sonorant
n. Speech sounds having significant resonant properties, produced in the oral cavity with the air flow directed over the center of the tongue

Chi [χ]
n. Voiceless uvular fricative

Clear L [l]
n. Voiced tip-alveolar lateral

Click
n. Speech sounds produced with lingual ingressive air

Close
adj., n. Describing the height position of the tongue when pronouncing vowels with the tongue very close to the roof of the mouth

Close-mid
adj., n. Describing the height position of the tongue when pronouncing vowels with the tongue slightly closer to the roof of the mouth than the mid position

Close transition
n. A type of transition between two consonants in which the first consonant is released directly into the second, i.e., no intervening vowel or approximant occurs
See Transition.

Cluster
n. A series of adjacent phonetic segments of the same category with no intervening sounds

Colon [:]
n. An alternate diacritic used to indicate lengthening
See Length Mark.

Complex contour
n. A tone contour involving more than one direction of tone movement in a single syllable

Consonant cluster
n. A series of adjacent consonants with no intervening vowels

Continuant
n. Phone produced with incomplete closure of the speech apparatus (as opposed to stops) and can therefore be prolonged, such as [ɑ], [s], [m] or [l]
See Stop and Obstruent.

Continuous line contour system
n. Method of pitch representation which involves continuous lines

Contoured tone
n. Tone pattern that contains pitch glides; changes in tone level can occur within syllable

Corner [˺]
n. Diacritic used to indicated that a sounds in unreleased (e.g., [d˺])

Corner Below [˛]
n. IPA diacritic for weak articulation; sometimes used to refer to Lenis

Creaky voice
n. Glottal state between Modal voice and Glottal closure

Curly-tail C [ɕ]
n. voiceless alveolo-palatal fricative

Curly-tail J [ʝ]
n. Voiced back-palatal fricative

Curly-tail Z [ʑ]
n. voiced alveolo-palatal fricative

Cursive V [ʋ]
n. Voiced labiodental approximant

Dark L [ɫ]
n. Voiced tip-alveolar lateral

Dental
adj. Adjective form of the point of articulation teeth

Dentalized
adj. A change in articulation to a dental phone, symbolized by a Bridge [̪]

Diaeresis [̈]
n. Subscript diacritic used to indicate breathiness

Digraph
n. A pair of symbols written side-by-side to represent a phoneme, such as "th" in English
n. A misnomer for Ash [æ]

Dot Below [̣]
n. IPA extension diacritic to indicate whispered articulation in speech pathology
n. Diacritic used in APA to indicate retroflexion [depreciated]

Dotless Barred J [ɟ]
n. Voiced palatal stop

Double articulation
n. Consonant cluster involving two simultaneous articulation of the same manner
See Tie Bar.

Double Pipe [ǁ]
n. Voiceless alveolar lateral click

Double Vertical Lines [̎]
n. Diacritic used to denote fortis articulation

Double-barred Pipe [ǂ]
n. Voiceless palatoalveolar click

Double-length mark [ː ː]
n. Diacritic used to indicate extra long sounds

Down Tack [̞]
n. Diacritic used to indicate that a vowel is lowered slightly from its normal position

E [e]
n. Close-mid front unrounded vowel

Egressive
adj. Outward air stream, also referred to as exhaling

Egressive glottalic air
n. Air stream set in motion by the glottis and moves outward

Egressive pulmonic
n. Air stream which originates in the lungs and moves outward

Ejective
adj., n. Consonant produced with Egressive Glottalic air

Eng [ŋ]
n. Voiced back-velar nasal

Enye [ñ]
n. Voiced blade-alveopalatal nasal (APA symbol) [depreciated]
See Retracted N [n̠] and Left-tail N (at left).

Esh [ʃ]
n. Voiceless tip or blade-alveopalatal fricative

Eth [ð]
n. Voiced tip-dental fricative

Exclamation Point [ǃ]
n. Voiceless alveopalatal/alveolar click
See Stretched C [ɕ].

Ezh [ʒ]
n. Voiced tip or blade-alveopalatal fricative

F [f]
n. Voiceless labiodental fricative

Facial diagram
n. Static representations of the speech mechanism

Fish-Hook R [ɾ]
n. Voiced tip-alveolar flap

Flapped N [ň]
  n. Voiced Tip-alveolar nasal flap
Flaps
  n. Manner of articulation involving a loosely
  controlled, rapid flicking motion by the articulator
Flat fricative
  n. Fricative produced with the tongue flat (not
  cupped or humped) across its body laterally (e.g.,
  [θ] as opposed to [ş])
  See Grooved articulation and Sibilant.
Fortis
  n. Sounds articulated more forcefully than normal
Frame
  n. Group of syllables having consistent, known
  phonetic characteristics; used for comparing
  syllables of unknown characteristics
Free jaw style
  n. Speech style which involves free or unrestricted
  jaw movement
Fricative
  n. A phone created by friction of the air stream in
  the speech apparatus
Front
  adj., n. The position of a vowel when articulated
  with the front part of the tongue
Fronted
  adj. Used to describe sounds produced with the
  tongue pushed farther forward than normal
Fronted N [ṇ]
  n. Voiced fronted tip-alveolar nasal; produced
  slightly farther forward than the alveolar point of
  articulation
Fronted tongue style
  n. Speech style involving the body of the tongue
  being pushed farther forward than normal
Full Stop [.]
  n. Diacritic used to represent a syllable break
  See Period.
Gamma [ɣ]
  n. Voiced back-velar fricative
Glide cluster
  n. A series of adjacent glides
Glided pitch
  n. Pitch which moves up, down, or both within a
  single syllable

Glottal
  adj. Pertaining to the glottis
Glottal stop [ʔ]
  n. Glottal stop
  n. Glottal consonant produced by stoppage of air
  stream at glottis
Glottis
  n. Area surrounding and including vocal cords
Grooved articulation
  adj., n. Articulation which involves a groove down
  the center of the tongue, usually applicable to
  fricatives (e.g., [ş] as opposed to [θ])
  See Flat fricatives and Sibilants.
Half-length mark [ˑ]
  n. Diacritic used to denote less than normal length
Height
  n. The position of the tongue in the articulation of
  vowels
Heterorganic
  adj. Referring to two phones (e.g., affricates,
  double stops) which do not share the same point
  of articulation
Homorganic
  adj. Referring to two phones (e.g., affricates,
  double stops) which share the same point of
  articulation
Hooktop B [ɓ]
  n. Voiced bilabial implosive
Hooktop Barred Dotless J [ʄ]
  n. Voiced palatal implosive
Hooktop D [ɗ]
  n. Voiced tip-alveolar implosive
Hooktop G [ɠ]
  n. Voiced back-velar implosive
Hooktop H [ɦ]
  n. Voiced glottal fricative
  n. Indicates breathy voice
Hooktop Small Capital G [ʛ]
  n. Voiced uvular implosive
I [i]
  n. Close front unrounded vowel
I Off-glide [ⁱ]
  n. Non-syllabic tongue movement away from a
  primary vowel and toward the position of [i]

I On-glide [ⁱ]
> n. Non-syllabic tongue movement from the [i] position toward a primary vowel's position

Implosive
> n. Stop produced with ingressive glottalic air stream

Ingressive air stream
> n. Air stream which moves inward

Ingressive glottalic air
> n. Air stream that is set in motion by the glottis and moves inward

Interdental
> adj. Used to describe the point of articulation for tip-dental sounds

Intonation
> n. Relative pitch which is used to affect the implied meaning of a sentence or phrase

Intonational language
> n. Languages in which relative pitch affects the meaning of a phrase or sentence rather than the definition of individual words

Inverted Breve [̯]
> n. Diacritic indicating non-syllabic phone

Inverted Bridge [̺]
> n. Diacritic indicating apical articulation

Inverted Small Capital R [ʁ]
> n. Voiced back-uvular fricative

J [j]
> n. Voiced palatal approximant

Juncture
> n. An audible pause between two phones

L [l]
> n. Voiced tip-alveolar lateral

Labial
> adj. Adjective form of the point of articulation lip

Labial-palatalization
> n. Secondary articulation involving simultaneous labial and palatal secondary articulations; symbolized by a Superscript Turned H [ᶣ]
> See Secondary Articulation.

Labial-velarization
> n. Secondary articulation involving simultaneous labial and velar secondary articulations; symbolized by a Superscript W [ʷ]
> See Secondary Articulation.

Labialization
> n. Secondary articulation involving a lip rounding; symbolized by a Superscript W [ʷ]
> See Secondary Articulation.

Labio-alveolar articulation
> n. Secondary articulation involving simultaneous labial and alveolar secondary articulations
> See Secondary Articulation.

Labio-alveopalatal articulation
> n. Secondary articulation involving simultaneous labial and alveopalatal secondary articulations
> See Secondary Articulation.

Labio-velar articulation
> n. Pair of sounds involving simultaneous labial and velar closures

Laminal
> adj. A phone articulated primarily with the blade of the tongue, optionally symbolized with a Square [̻]

Laryngealization
> n. Sometimes used to describe the creaky state of the glottis
> See Creaky Voice.

Larynx
> n. Organ which houses the vocal cords

Lateral
> n. "L-like" sound in which the air stream passes around one or both sides of the tongue but not over the center

Lateral affricate
> n. Combination of stop and lateral fricative

Lateral fricative
> n. Lateral which involve audible friction

Lateral oral sonorant
> n. Lateral consonant which are produced in the oral cavity and have some degree of resonance

Left-tail N (at left) [ɲ]
> n. Voiced palatal nasal

Length
> n. The duration of time for which an articulation is pronounced

Length Mark [ː]
> n. Diacritic used to indicate lengthening

Lenis
> n. Pertaining to softer articulation

Level tone
n. Tone that does not rise or fall

Lezh [ɮ]
n. Voiced tip-alveolar lateral fricative

Ligature
n. A symbol composed of two or more characters bound by a stroke or bar (e.g., [æ] and [k͡p])

Lingual ingressive air
n. Air stream set in motion by the tongue and moves inward

Liquid
n. A class of consonants containing both laterals and rhotics
See Lateral and Rhotic.

Long glide
n. Tone glide ranging from high to low or from low to high

Loud speech style
n. Speech style involving more volume than normal

Low Vertical Line [ˌ]
n. Diacritic used to indicate that a consonant is syllabic

Lowercase A [a]
n. Open front unrounded vowel

Lowercase C [c]
n. Voiceless palatal stop

Lowercase O-E Ligature [œ]
n. Open-mid front rounded vowel

Lowercase Q [q]
n. Voiceless uvular stop

Lowercase R [r]
n. Voiced tip-alveolar trill

Lowercase Y [y]
n. Close front rounded vowel

M [m]
n. Voiced bilabial nasal

Manner of articulation
n. Interaction and degree of impedance of the organs involved in making speech sounds

Meng [ɱ]
n. Voiced labiodental nasal

Mid
n. Portion of the tongue directly under the hard palate that acts as the active articulator in palato-alveolar sounds

adj., n. Describing the height position of the tongue when pronouncing vowels with the tongue mid-way between the open and close positions

Middle Tilde [~]
n. Diacritic used to indicate velarization

Minimal pair
n. Pairs of sounds which have only one phonetic difference (e.g., [pʰɑ] and [pɑ])

Minus Sign [_]
n. Diacritic used to denote that a sounds is alveopalatal

Modal voice
n. A state of the glottis involving optimal tension for smooth vibration

Monosyllabic
adj. Pertaining to a single syllable

Monotone style
n. Speech style involving no tone fluctuation

Murmured
adj. A state of the glottis known as breathy voice
See Breathy voice

N [n]
n. Voiced tip-alveolar nasal

Narrow range style
n. Speech style in which a very narrow range of tone fluctuation exists

Nasal
n. A sound produced with the entire air stream exiting through the nasal cavity

Nasal cavity
n. The cavity between the nares (nostrils) and the velic

Nasalized
adj. Involving partial velic opening; sounds which resonate in both the oral and nasal cavities

Nasalized style
n. Speech style involving nasalization

Near-close
adj., n. Describing the height position of the tongue when pronouncing vowels with the tongue slightly farther from the roof of the mouth than the close position

Near-open

adj., n. Describing the height position of the tongue when pronouncing vowels with the tongue slightly closer to the roof of the mouth than the open position

Neutral tongue root

n. Describes the normal position of the tongue root for relaxed speech, i.e., not retracted or advanced

Non-nasalized

adj. Sounds which are strictly oral, involving no velic opening at all

Non-nasalized speech style

n. Speech style involving strictly oral sounds, i.e., no velic opening

Non-sonorant

adj. Sounds characterized by a very low degree of resonance and turbulent airflow, such as [p] or [v]

Nucleus

n. The center of a syllable carrying the main beat; the syllabic

Obstruent

n. Sound which involves complete or partial obstruction of the air stream, such as [t] or [s]

Ogonek [˛]

n. Diacritic used in conjunction with above tilde to denote strong nasalization (also known as Polish Hook)

On-glide

n. Non-syllabic movement of the tongue toward a primary vowel position

Open

adj. A vowel pronounced with the tongue far from the roof of the mouth

Open O [ɔ]

n. Open-mid back rounded vowel

Open transition

n. A transition between two consonants which includes a short vowel or aspiration

Open-mid

adj., n. Describing the height position of the tongue when pronouncing vowels with the tongue slightly father from the roof of the mouth than the mid position

Oral cavity

n. The mouth, when used as an articulator

Over-ring [˚]

n. Diacritic used to indicate voicelessness; used only on symbols with a descender (e.g., [ŋ̊])

Palatal

adj. Adjective form of the point of articulation palate

Palatalization

n. Secondary articulation involving a palatal approximant; symbolized by a Superscript J [ʲ]
See Secondary Articulation.

Palate

n. The relatively flat region extending from the edge of the alveopalatal region to the soft palate

Period [.]

n. Diacritic used to represent a syllable break
See Full Stop.

Pharyngeal cavity

n. Area of the throat located above the larynx and below the uvula

Pharyngealization

n. Secondary articulation which involves a pharyngeal approximant; symbolized by a Superscript Reverse Glottal Stop [ˤ]
See Secondary Articulations.

Phi [ɸ]

n. Voiceless bilabial fricative

Phones

n. Speech sounds

Phonetics

n. The study of human speech sounds

Phrase stress

n. Pertains to the most prominent syllable of a phrase or sentence

Pipe [|]

n. Voiceless Dental click

Pitch

n. The perceived melody that accompanies speech
See Tone.

Pitch levels

n. Perceived levels of pitch relative to surrounding pitch

Plosive

n. Oral stops; sometimes used to refer to stops in general
See Stop.

Point of articulation
n. Point of contact where an obstruction occurs within the vocal apparatus

Polysyllabic
n. Pertaining to multiple syllables

Postalveolar
n. The region of the roof of the mouth behind the alveolar ridge
adj. Pertaining to the postalveolar region
See alveopalatal.

Prenasalization
n. Short nasal onset, usually connected with voiced stops

Primary consonant
n. Most prominent consonant of a Double Articulation
See Double Articulation.

Primary stress
n. Most prominent level of stress

Pulmonic
adj. Sounds created by the lungs, may be either egressive or ingressive

Pure vowel
n. Non-glided vowel

R-colored vowel
n. Vowel containing some rhoticity (retroflexion), generally symbolized with a Right Hook [˞]

Raised Circle [°]
n. Used to indicate phrase stress

Ram's Horns [ɤ]
n. Close-mid back unrounded vowel

Rapid speech style
n. Speech style which involves greater speed than usual

Re-articulated vowel
n. A vowel cluster made up of two vowels of the same quality

Registered tone
n. Tone pattern that contains no glides, i.e., only level tones are used; all changes in pitch level occurs between syllables

Regular release
n. Type of release in which the articulator and point of articulation separate audibly, but without voicing or aspiration; contrast with unreleased, voiced release, and aspirated release

Release
n. Refers to the manner in which the articulator and point of articulation separate

Retracted D [d̠]
n. Voiced blade-alveopalatal stop

Retracted L [l̠]
n. Voiced blade-alveopalatal lateral

Retracted N [n̠]
n. Voiced blade-alveopalatal nasal

Retracted T [t̠]
n. Voiceless blade-alveopalatal stop

Retracted tongue root
n. The position of the tongue root considered farther backward than normal during the pronunciation of a vowel

Retroflex hook
n. Diacritic indicating that a sound is retroflexed (e.g., [ɖ])

Retroflexed
adj. Describing a condition in which the tongue tip curls upward and backward

Retroflexed tongue style
n. Speech style which involves retroflexion

Reverse Glottal Stop [ʕ]
n. Voiced pharyngeal fricative

Rhotacized Reversed Epsilon [ɝ]
n. Open-mid front unrounded vowel with rhoticity

Rhotacized Schwa [ɚ]
n. Mid central unrounded vowel with rhoticity

Rhotacized Schwa Off-glide [ᵊ˞]
n. Non-syllabic tongue movement away from another vowel position and toward the mid central unrounded position with rhoticity

Rhotacized Schwa On-glide [ᵊ˞]
n. Non-syllabic tongue movement from the mid central unrounded position to another vowel position

Rhotic
"R-like" consonants including trills; flaps; alveolar and retroflexed approximants; velar, uvular, and glottal fricatives and approximants
See Liquids.

Rhythm
n. The rhythm with which a language is spoken

Right Hook [˞]
n. Used to denote retroflexion

Right Hook [˞]
n. Used in IPA to denote rhoticity of vowels

Right Hook V [ⱱ]
n. Voiced bilabial flap

Right Tack [˗]
n. Diacritic used to denote retracted tongue root

Right-tail [̢]
n. Used in IPA to denote retroflexion

Right-tail D [ɖ]
n. Voiced retroflexed tip-alveolar stop

Right-tail L [ɭ]
n. Voiced retroflexed tip-alveolar lateral

Right-tail N [ɳ]
n. Voiced retroflexed tip-alveolar nasal

Right-tail R [ɽ]
n. Voiced retroflexed tip-alveolar flap

Right-tail S [ʂ]
n. Voiceless retroflexed tip-alveolar fricative

Right-tail T [ʈ]
n. Voiceless retroflexed tip-alveolar stop

Right-tail Z [ʐ]
n. Voiced retroflexed tip-alveolar fricative

Root
n. Base of tongue, located below back articulator; used as active articulator in pharyngeal consonants

Rounded
adj. Used to describe the shape of the lips when forming a circular opening

Rounded lip style
n. Speech style which involves lip rounding

Rounding
n. Rounding of the lips when applied to a vowel or consonant

Schwa [ə]
n. Mid central unrounded vowel

Schwa Off-glide [ᵊ]
n. Non-syllabic movement of the tongue away from another vowel position toward the mid central unrounded position

Scribble [̰]
n. Diacritic indicating that a sound is Lenis (APA symbol)
See Lenis Articulation.

Secondary articulation
n. A consonant (usually approximant) articulated simultaneously with another consonant, but with less prominence

Secondary consonant
n. Approximant involved in secondary articulation
See Secondary Articulation.

Secondary stress
n. Level of stress less prominent than Primary stress and more prominent than all other levels present

Set jaw style
n. Speech style in which the jaw is allowed less range of motion than normal

Short glide
n. Tone glide not traversing the full scale (e.g., gliding from low to mid or mid to high)

Sibilant
n. Grooved fricatives (e.g., [ʂ] as opposed to [θ])
See Grooved articulation and Flat fricative.

Slack voice
n. State of the glottis occurring when the vocal cords are slightly more relaxed than for modal voice

Slashed O [ø]
n. Close-mid front rounded vowel

Slow speech style
n. Speech style involving slower speech than normal

Slurring
n. Tongue movement between one vowel and another; used to locate and practice the position of new vowel sounds

Small Capital B [ʙ]
n. Voiced bilabial trill

Small Capital G [ɢ]
n. Voiced uvular stop

Small Capital I [ɪ]
n. Near-close front unrounded vowel

Small Capital L [ʟ]
n. Voiced velar nasal

Small Capital N [ɴ]
n. Voiced uvular nasal

Small Capital R [ʀ]
n. Voiced uvular trill

Soft speech style
n. Speech style involving less volume than normal

Sonorant
n. Phone produced with significant resonance and minimal impedance, such as [ɑ], [n], or [l]

Speech apparatus
n. All parts of human anatomy used to produce speech

Speech style
n. Characteristic applied to one's entire speech in certain situations or environments

Spread lip style
n. Speech style involving spread lips

Square [̻]
n. The diacritic indicating laminal (blade) articulation

Squared lip style
n. Speech style involving squared lips

State of the glottis
n. Describes the posture and activity of the vocal cords during a sound

Stiff voice
n. State of the glottis occurring when the vocal cords are slightly stiffer than for modal voice

Stop
n. Phones created by complete impedance of the air stream

Stretched C [C]
n. Alternate symbol for a voiceless alveopalatal/alveolar click
See Exclamation Point [!]

Stress
n. The degree of emphasis or prominence that sets one syllable apart from surrounding syllables

Stress mark
n. Used to indicate stress placement (e.g., [pɑˈpɑ])

Stress-timed
n. Used to describe languages in which the rhythm is based on stressed syllables
See Syllable Timed.

Subscript Wedge [̬]
n. Indicates that a sound is voiced

Superscript Gamma [ˠ]
n. The symbol indicating velarized articulation
See Secondary articulation

Superscript H [ʰ]
n. The symbol used to indicate aspiration (e.g., [pʰ])

Superscript Hooktop H [ʱ]
n. Sometimes used to represent breathiness; also known as voiced aspiration

Superscript J [ʲ]
n. The symbol indicating palatal articulation
n. Sometimes used in place of [ⁱ] [depreciated]
See Secondary articulation.

Superscript L [ˡ]
n. The symbol indicating lateral release

Superscript M [ᵐ]
n. The symbol indicating bilabial nasal release

Superscript N [ⁿ]
n. The symbol indicating bilabial nasal release

Superscript R [ʳ]
n. Alternative symbol for indicating rhoticity
See R-colored vowel.

Superscript Reverse Glottal Stop [ˤ]
n. The symbol indicating pharyngealized articulation
See Secondary articulation.

Superscript Schwa [ᵊ]
n. mid central unrounded vowel glide

Superscript Turned H [ᶣ]
n. The symbol indicating palatal-velar articulation
n. Sometimes used to represent a rounded [j] approximant
See Secondary articulation.

Superscript W [ʷ]
n. The symbol indicating labial articulation
n. The symbol indicating labial-velar articulation
n. Sometimes used to represent U glides [ᵘ]
See Secondary articulation.

Superscript Wedge [̌]
n. Diacritic used by IPA to indicate rising tone; used by APA to represent alveopalatal fricatives and affricates

Syllabic
adj., n. The syllable nucleus, or the phone which occupies the resonant peak of the syllable

Syllabification
n. The process of separating individual syllables

Syllable

n. A sound or group of sounds which is an uninterrupted unit and carries its own beat

Syllable boundary

n. The non-nucleus point between phones which divides syllables

Syllable-timed

adj. Used to describe languages in which the rhythm is based on individual syllables
See Stress Timed.

Tack Left [ˌ]

n. Diacritic used to denote advanced tongue root

Teeth

n. Teeth, when used as an articulator

Tertiary stress

n. Stress of the third level of prominence; used when four levels of stress are recognized
See also Primary and Secondary Stress.

Theta [θ]

n. Voiceless tip-dental fricative

Tie bar

n. Diacritic used to link sounds (e.g., affricates [t͡s] and double articulations [k͡p])
See Tie Bar Above and Tie Bar Below.

Tie Bar Above [◌͡◌]

n. Used to link symbols with descenders (e.g., [ɡ͡ɣ])

Tie Bar Below [◌͜◌]

n. Used to link symbols with ascenders (e.g., [b͜d])

Tilde [◌̃], [◌̰], or [~]

n. Diacrtic used to indicate nasalization, creaky voice, velarization or pharyngealization, and, formerly, alveopalatal articulation
See Tilde Above, Tilde Below, Middle Tilde, and Enye [ñ].

Tilde Above [◌̃]

n. Used to denote nasalization

Tilde Below [◌̰]

n. Used to denote creaky voice

Tip

n. The tip of the tongue, articulator for the tip-dental, and tip-alveolar consonants
See apical.

Tonal language

n. Languages in which tone is used to distinguish a lexical difference between two words

Tone

n. Pitch used to affect the lexical meaning of words or syllables; sometimes used interchangeably with "pitch"
See Pitch.

Tone diacritics

n. Superscript diacritics used to indicate tone levels and glides

Tone letter

n. A symbol used to indicated tone levels and glides

Tone number

n A superscript number used to indicate tone levels and glides

Tongue

n. The tongue, when used as an active articulator
See also the five parts of the tongue (e.g., Tip, Blade, Mid, Back, Root).

Tongue root placement

n. Describes the position of the tongue root during a sound
See Advanced, Neutral, and Retracted tongue root.

Tooth [◌̪]

n. Subscript diacritic used to indicate fronting, or dentalization, (e.g., [t̪])
See Bridge.

Transition

n. Used to describe the way the articulators transition from one articulation to the next in a consonant cluster

Trill

n. Manner of articulation which involves a rapid series of vibration between an articulator and point of articulation

Turned A [ɐ]

n. Near-open central vowel (can be either rounded or unrounded)

Turned H [ɥ]

n. Voiced labial-palatal approximant

Turned Long Leg M [ɰ]

n. Voiced velar approximant

Turned Long-leg R [ɺ]

n. Voiced alveolar lateral flap

Turned M [ɯ]

n. Close back unrounded vowel

Turned R [ɹ]
:   n. Voiced alveolar approximant

Turned R with Right Tail [ɻ]
:   n. Voiced retroflexed alveolar approximant

Turned Script A [ɒ]
:   n. Open back rounded vowel

Turned V [ʌ]
:   n. Open-mid back unrounded vowel

Turned Y [ʎ]
:   n. Voiced blade-palatal nasal

U [u]
:   n. Close back rounded vowel

U Off-glide [ᵘ]
:   n. Non-syllabic movement of the tongue from any other vowel position toward the [u] position

U On-glide [ᵘ]
:   n. Non-syllabic movement of the tongue from the [u] position to another vowel position

Under-ring [̥]
:   n. Diacritic used to indicate voicelessness

Unreleased
:   adj. Utterance-final consonant in which the articulators remain together for a time after articulation, or separate inaudibly

Unrounded
:   adj. Phones produced without lip rounding

Upper lip
:   n. Used as a point of articulation in bilabial sounds

Upper right hook
:   n. Diacritic used to indicate that a sound

Upsilon [ʊ]
:   n. Near-close back rounded vowel

Uvula
:   n. The muscular protrusion projecting from the rear edge of the soft palate; used for uvular consonants

Uvular
:   adj. Adjective form of the point of articulation uvula

Uvular trill
:   n. Trill articulated at the uvula
    See Trill.

V [v]
:   n. Voiced labiodental fricative

Variable feature
:   n. One of the five features of the speech mechanism that are responsible for the movements which produce changes in sound: lips, tongue, velic, glottis, and air stream

Velar
:   adj. Adjective form of the point of articulation velic

Velarization
:   n. Secondary articulation involving a velar approximant; symbolized by a Superscript Gamma [ˠ] or Middle Tilde [~]
    See Secondary Articulation.

Velic
:   n. Flap that controls air flow to the nasal cavity; referred to as an articulator

Velum
:   n. Often referred to as soft palate, located directly behind the hard palate

Vertical Line [ˈ]
:   n. Diacritic used to indicate stress placement

Vocal cords
:   n. Mucous membranes stretched across the larynx which vibrate with the passing of the air stream

Voice onset time (VOT)
:   n. Describes the point in time when the vocal cords begin to vibrate in relation to the time of the release of the articulators forming the consonant

Voiced
:   adj. Sounds which involve vocal cord vibration of modal quality
    See Modal Voice.

Voiced release
:   n. Consonant released into a short voiced vowel such as Schwa [ə]

Voiceless
:   adj., n. The state of the glottis in which the vocal cords are spread apart and not vibrating

Voiceless nasal
:   n. Nasal phone produced without voicing

Voicing
:   n. Vibration of the vocal cords; modal state of the glottis

Vowel cluster
:   n. A series of adjacent vowels with no intervening consonants

Vowel glide

n. A non-syllabic movement of the tongue from one vowel position to another

Vowel position

n. The position of a vowel from the front of the mouth to the back
See Front, Central, and Back.

Vowel reduction

n. The tendency to change vowels to the central unrounded position on unstressed syllables

W [w]

n. Voiced labial-velar approximant

Weak stress

n. Least prominent level of stress

Whisper

n. State of the glottis in which the vocal cords are tensed too much for voicing and the air stream is greatly restricted; symbolized with a Dot Below [.] in speech pathology

Whispered

adj., n. Speech style which involves whispered voiced

Wide range style

n. Speech style in which a wide range of tone fluctuation exists

Yogh

n. A letter (ȝ or ȝ), used in Middle English to represent palatal and velar phones, which is sometimes confused with the phonetic symbol Ezh [ȝ]

X [x]

n. Voiceless back-velar fricative

Z [z]

n. Voiced tip-alveolar fricative

+ATR

n. Abbreviation for Advanced Tongue Root

−ATR

n. Abbreviation for Retracted Tongue Root (also abbreviated RTR)

Index of Tables and Illustrations

Index of Exercises

General Index

The International Phonetic Alphabet (2005)

Consonant (Pulmonic)

	Bilabial	Labiodental	Dental	Alveolar	Postalveolar	Retroflexed	Palatal	Velar	Uvular	Pharyngeal	Glottal
Plosive	p b			t d		ʈ ɖ	c ɟ	k g	q ɢ		ʔ
Nasal	m	ɱ		n		ɳ	ɲ	ŋ	N		
Trill	ʙ			r					R		
Tap or Flap		ⱱ		ɾ		ɽ					
Fricative	ɸ β	f v	θ ð	s z	ʃ ʒ	ʂ ʐ	ç ʝ	x ɣ	χ ʁ	ħ ʕ	h ɦ
Lateral Fricative				ɬ ɮ							
Approximant		ʋ		ɹ		ɻ	j	ɰ			
Lateral Approximant				l		ɭ	ʎ	L			

Where symbols appear in pairs, the one to the right represents a voiced consonant. Shaded areas denote articulations judged to be impossible.

Consonant (Non-Pulmonic)

Clicks		Voiced Implosives		Ejectives	
ʘ	Bilabial	ɓ	Bilabial	ʼ	Examples:
ǀ	Dental	ɗ	Dental/alveolar	pʼ	Bilabial
ǃ	(Post)alveolar	ʄ	Palatal	tʼ	Dental/alveolar
ǂ	Palatoalveolar	ɠ	Velar	kʼ	Velar
ǁ	Alveolar lateral	ʛ	Uvular	sʼ	Alveolar Fricative

Vowels

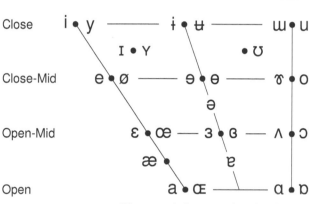

Where symbols appear in pairs, the one to the right represents a rounded vowel.

Other Symbols

ʍ	Voiceless labial-velar fricative	ɕ ʑ	Alveolo-palatal fricatives
w	Voiced labial-velar approximant	ɺ	Voiced alveolar lateral flap
ɥ	Voiced labial-palatal approximant	ɧ	Simultaneous ʃ and x
ʜ	Voiceless epiglottal fricative		
ʢ	Voiced epiglottal fricative		Affricates and double articulations can be represented by two symbols joined by a tie bar if necessary. k͡p t͡s
ʡ	Epiglottal plosive		

Suprasegmentals

ˈ	Primary Stress
ˌ	Secondary Stress

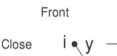 ˌfoʊnəˈtɪʃən

ː	Long	eː
ˈ	Half-long	eˈ
˘	Extra short	ĕ
ǀ	Minor (foot) group	
ǁ	Major (intonation) group	
.	Syllable break	ɹi.ækt
‿	Linking (absence of a break)	

Tones and Word Accents

Level			Contour		
é or	˥	Extra high	ě or	˅	Rising
é	˦	High	ê	˄	Falling
ē	˧	Mid	᷄	˧˥	High rising
è	˨	Low	᷅	˩˧	Low rising
ȅ	˩	Extra Low	᷈	˥˩˥	Rising-falling
↓	Downstep		↗	Global rise	
↑	Upstep		↘	Global fall	

Diacritics

Diacritics may be placed above a symbol with a descender, e.g. ŋ̊

̥	Voiceless	n̥ d̥	̤	Breathy voiced	b̤ a̤	̪	Dental	t̪ d̪
̬	Voiced	s̬ t̬	̰	Creaky voiced	b̰ a̰	̺	Apical	t̺ d̺
ʰ	Aspiration	tʰ dʰ	̼	Linguolabial	t̼ d̼	̻	Laminal	t̻ d̻
̹	More rounded	ɔ̹	ʷ	Labialized	tʷ dʷ	̃	Nasalized	ẽ
̜	Less Rounded	ɔ̜	ʲ	Palatalized	tʲ dʲ	ⁿ	Nasal release	dⁿ
̟	Advanced	u̟	ˠ	Velarized	tˠ dˠ	ˡ	Lateral release	dˡ
̠	Retracted	e̠	ˤ	Pharyngealized	tˤ dˤ	̚	No audible release	d̚
̈	Centralized	ë	~	Velarized or pharyngealized	ɫ			
̽	Mid-centralized	ě̽	̝	Raised	e̝ (ɹ̝ = voiced alveolar fricative)			
̩	Syllabic	n̩	̞	Lowered	e̞ (β̞ = voiced bilabial approximant)			
̯	Non-Syllabic	e̯	̘	Advanced Tongue Root	e̘			
˞	Rhoticity	ɚ a˞	̙	Retracted Tongue Root	e̙			

The International Phonetic Alphabet Expanded

Consonant (Pulmonic)

	Bilabial		Labiodental		(Inter)Dental		Alveolar		Alveopalatal		Retroflexed		Palatal		Velar		Uvular		Pharyngeal		Glottal	
Stop	p	b	p̪	b̪	t̪	d̪	t	d	t̠	d̠	ʈ	ɖ	c	ɟ	k	g	q	ɢ				ʔ
Nasal	m̥	m	ɱ̊	ɱ	n̪̥	n̪	n̥	n	ñ̥	ñ	ɳ̊	ɳ	ɲ̊	ɲ	ŋ̊	ŋ	ɴ̥	ɴ				
Trill	ʙ̥	ʙ					r̥	r									ʀ̥	ʀ				
Tap or Flap	ѵ̥̟	ѵ̟	ѵ̥	ѵ			ɾ̥	ɾ			ɽ̥	ɽ					ɢ̥̆	ɢ̆				
Fricative	ɸ	β	f	v	θ	ð	s	z	ʃ	ʒ	ʂ	ʐ	ç	ʝ	x	ɣ	χ	ʁ	ħ	ʕ	h	ɦ
Lateral Fricative							ɬ	ɮ			ꞎ	ɭ̝	ʎ̝̊	ʎ̝	ʟ̝̊	ʟ̝						
Approximant	ɸ̞	β̞	ʋ̥	ʋ			ɹ̥	ɹ			ɻ̥	ɻ	j̊	j	ɰ̊	ɰ						
Lateral Approximant			ɭ̪̊	ɭ̪	l̥	l	l̥	l			ɭ̥	ɭ	ʎ̥	ʎ	ʟ̥	ʟ						

Where symbols appear in pairs, the one to the right represents a voiced consonant. Shaded areas denote articulations judged to be impossible.

Consonant (Non-Pulmonic)

Clicks				Voiced Implosives			Ejectives	
ʘ	Bilabial	‖‖	Dental lateral	ɓ	Bilabial	ʼ	Examples:	
ǀ	Dental	‖	Alveolar lateral	ɗ	Alveolar	pʼ	Bilabial	
ǃ	Alveolar	ǂ	Palatal lateral	ʄ	Palatal	tʼ	Alveolar	
ʞ	Retroflexed	ǃǀ	Alveolar Flap	ɠ	Velar	kʼ	Velar	
ǂ	Palatoalveolar	ǃǃ	Retroflexed	ʛ	Uvular	sʼ	Alveolar	

Other Symbols

ʍ Voiceless labial-velar fricative
w Voiced labial-velar approximant
ɥ Voiced labial-palatal approximant
ʜ Voiceless epiglottal fricative
ʢ Voiced epiglottal fricative
ʡ Epiglottal plosive
ʡ̯ Epiglottal flap
 я Epiglottal trill

ɕ ʑ Alveolo-palatal fricatives
ɺ ɺ Voiced alveolar lateral flap
ꞎ ꞎ Retroflexed lateral flap
ɭ̆ ɭ̆ Velar Lateral Flap
ᴅ̥ ᴅ Alveolar Flap
ɧ Simultaneous ʃ and x

Affricates and double articulations can be represented by two symbols joined by a tie bar if necessary.

k͡p t͡s

Diacritics

Diacritics may be placed above a symbol with a descender, e.g. ŋ̊

̥	Voiceless/Slack	n̥	g̊	̈	Breathy voiced	b̤	a̤	̪ Dental t̪ d̪
̬	Voiced/Stiff	s̬	t̬	̰	Creaky voiced	b̰	a̰	̺ Apical (tip) t̺ g̺
ʰ ʱ	(Pre)Aspiration ʰt tʰ dʰ				Linguolabial	t̼	d̼	̻ Laminal (blade) t̻ g̻
̹	More rounded	ɔ̹	y̹	ʷ	Labialized	tʷ	dʷ	̃ Nasalized ẽ ɫ̃
̜	Less Rounded	ɔ̜	y̜	ʲ	Palatalized	tʲ	dʲ	ᵐⁿŋ Nasal release t̚ⁿ dⁿ
̟	Advanced	u̟	y̟	ˠ	Velarized	tˠ	dˠ	ˡ Lateral release t̚ˡ dˡ
̠	Retracted	e̠	ȳ	ˤ	Pharyngealized	tˤ	dˤ	̚ No audible release d̚
̈	Centralized	ë	ï	̴	Velarized/pharyngealized ɫ	ᶣ	Palatal-Velarized tᶣ dᶣ
̽	Mid-centralized	ĕ	ĭ	̝	Raised	e̝	ɹ̝	̪ Strident ɑ̪ g̪̃
̩	Syllabic	n̩	ɹ̩	̞	Lowered	e̞	β̞	. Whispery ɑ̣ ġ
̯	Non-Syllabic	e̯	ŷ		Advanced Tongue Root	e̘		Fortis t̂ ĝ
˞	Rhoticity	ɚ	ɝ		Retracted Tongue Root	e̙		Lenis t̬ g̬

Vowels

Front   Near-Front   Central   Near-Back   Back

Close
Near-Close
Close-Mid
Mid
Open-Mid
Near-Open
Open

Where symbols appear in pairs, the one to the right represents a rounded vowel.

Suprasegmentals

ˈ Primary Stress
ˌ Secondary Stress

ˌfoʊnəˈtɪʃən

ː Long eː
ˑ Half-long eˑ
̆ Extra short ĕː

| Minor (foot) group
‖ Major (intonation) group
. Syllable break ɹi.ækt
‿ Linking (absence of a break)

Tones and Word Accents

Level			Contour		
e̋ or ˥	Extra high		ě or ˦	Rising	
é ˦	High		ê ˥	Falling	
ē ˧	Mid		e᷄ ˦	High rising	
è ˨	Low		e᷅ ˩	Low rising	
ȅ ˩	Extra Low		e᷈ ˧	Rising-falling	
↓	Downstep		↗	Global rise	
↑	Upstep		↘	Global fall	

Made in the USA
Lexington, KY
03 April 2012